Windows® XP
Answers from the Experts

About the Authors

Jim Boyce has authored and co-authored over 50 books on computers and technology. Jim has written extensively about Windows, Office applications, CAD, hardware, and many other topics. In past lives Jim has been an engineering technician at a shipyard, a college instructor, Unix system administrator, CAD trainer, and owner/operator of an ISP and web development company. He writes frequently for techrepublic.com, Microsoft. com, and other online sites and publications. You can find more information about Jim and his books at www.boyce.us.

Debra Littlejohn Shinder (MCSE, MVP) is a technology consultant, trainer and writer who has authored a number of books on computer operating systems, networking, and security. These include Scene of the Cybercrime: Computer Forensics Handbook, published by Syngress, and Computer Networking Essentials, published by Cisco Press. She is co-author, with her husband, Dr. Thomas Shinder, of Troubleshooting Windows 2000 TCP/IP, the best-selling Configuring ISA Server 2000, and ISA Server and Beyond. She and her husband write whitepapers, product documentation and marketing material for Microsoft and other prominent software companies. Deb currently specializes in security issues and Microsoft products and was awarded the Microsoft Most Valuable Professional status in the field of server security. She lives and works in the Dallas-Ft Worth area and occasionally teaches computer networking and security courses at Eastfield College in Mesquite, TX.

About the Technical Editor

Will Kelly is is a long-time computer book technical editor having edited a number of popular books about Microsoft Office, Microsoft Outlook, HTML, Web development, and related topics over the past ten years. He currently works as freelance technical writer and requirements analyst working on projects for Federal government and commercial clients. He resides in the Washington, DC area where he gets away from work and computer book manuscripts by hitting the gym and going to spinning class.

Windows® XP
Answers from the Experts

Jim Boyce
Debra Littlejohn Shinder

McGraw-Hill/Osborne
New York Chicago San Francisco
Lisbon London Madrid Mexico City
Milan New Delhi San Juan
Seoul Singapore Sydney Toronto

McGraw-Hill/Osborne
2100 Powell Street, 10th Floor
Emeryville, California 94608
U.S.A.

To arrange bulk purchase discounts for sales promotions, premiums, or fund-raisers, please contact **McGraw-Hill**/Osborne at the above address. For information on translations or book distributors outside the U.S.A., please see the International Contact Information page immediately following the index of this book.

Windows® XP Answers from the Experts

Copyright © 2005 by The McGraw-Hill Companies. All rights reserved. Printed in the United States of America. Except as permitted under the Copyright Act of 1976, no part of this publication may be reproduced or distributed in any form or by any means, or stored in a database or retrieval system, without the prior written permission of the publisher, with the exception that the program listings may be entered, stored, and executed in a computer system, but they may not be reproduced for publication.

1234567890 CUS CUS 01987654

ISBN 0-07-225767-9

Vice President & Group Publisher Philip Ruppel	**Copy Editors** Lauren Kennedy, Bob Campbell
Vice President & Publisher Jeffrey Krames	**Proofreaders** Paul Medoff, Linda Medoff
Acquisitions Editor Megg Morin	**Indexer** Valerie Perry
Project Editor Julie M. Smith	**Composition and Illustration** Apollo Publishing Services
Acquisitions Coordinator Agatha Kim	**Series Design** Peter F. Hancik, Lyssa Wald
Technical Editor Will Kelly	**Cover Series Design** Jeff Weeks

This book was composed with Adobe® InDesign® CS.

Information has been obtained by **McGraw-Hill**/Osborne from sources believed to be reliable. However, because of the possibility of human or mechanical error by our sources, **McGraw-Hill**/Osborne, or others, **McGraw-Hill**/Osborne does not guarantee the accuracy, adequacy, or completeness of any information and is not responsible for any errors or omissions or the results obtained from use of such information.

To Julie, who has always been there for me

Contents at a Glance

Contents

Acknowledgments

Writing a book isn't a solitary process; several people contributed to this project in one way or another to make it what it is.

I would first like to thank Megg Morin, Acquisitions Editor at McGraw-Hill, for bringing me the project, David Fugate, my agent at Waterside Productions, for working out the details, Agatha Kim, Acquisitions Coordinator at McGraw-Hill, for taking care of all the process details and Julie Smith for the management of the book.

Thanks also go to my good friend Deb Shinder, who did an outstanding job of developing and writing a few of the chapters, and who offered some excellent advice on targeting the content. I also thank Rob Tidrow for contributing several excellent chapters and once again helping me meet deadlines.

I also appreciate Lauren Kennedy's light but deft touch on the copy editing, and Will Kelly's targeted tech comments. Both helped fine-tune the book in an important way. Thanks also to Tabi Cagan, Peter Hancik, Jan Benes, Paul and Linda Medoff, and Valerie Perry.

Introduction

One way to describe Windows XP Answers from the Experts is to explain what it isn't. This book isn't intended for network experts or system administrators. It's also not intended for novice computer users. Instead, Windows XP Answers from the Experts is intended to help average people who use Windows XP on a regular basis get more out of their computer and applications, be more productive, and work smarter. You'll also learn how to work more securely with your computer and with Windows XP in particular.

Windows XP Answers from the Experts explores those middle-of-the-road topics that most people who are comfortable using Windows find most challenging. We don't focus on basics like using the mouse or working with windowed applications, nor do we focus on running a Web site from your computer or any of the other topics that only a small percentage of people typically want to do. Instead, this book is all about the 80% of Windows XP that average people need to understand and control to get their jobs done. We also cover some of the upper-end topics that users occasionally run up against when trying to troubleshoot a problem with the computer or application where a network or computer expert just isn't available. And, we'll help you learn about some of the more important management tasks if you are that one person in your small company or department who everyone else looks to for answers to computer problems.

The book is divided into four main sections.

Part I. Upgrading, Controlling, and Troubleshooting

This section of the book will help you get up to speed on how to control the way Windows XP starts and runs, as well as troubleshoot common problems. Chapter 1, "Upgrading to Windows XP," explains the process for installing Windows XP to help you make the transition from Windows 9x, Me, or 2000.

Chapter 2, "Controlling Startup and Shutdown," will help you understand how your computer starts up, what happens when Windows XP starts, and how to control startup and shutdown. Why is that important? You'll learn how to make applications start automatically, clear out programs you don't want, and simplify tasks with startup, logon, logoff, and shutdown scripts. Chapter 2 also explains how to control Autoplay, which enables Windows XP to automatically start programs when you insert a CD.

Keeping Windows XP up to date is one of the best ways to avoid potential problems, and Chapter 3, "Keeping Your System Current," will help you keep your computer as up-to-date as possible. You'll learn about ways to automatically update your computer, install service packs and updates, and even remote updates if needed.

Chapter 4, "Windows XP Service Pack 2," explores Microsoft latest update release for Windows XP, including how to get it, what it does, and how to install it. Service Pack 2 fixes a handful of problems with Windows and adds several new features for improved security.

The final chapter in Part 1, "General Troubleshooting," will help you learn to identify and fix problems that crop up on your computer. Chapter 5 describes and explains general troubleshooting techniques and will help you learn how to manage devices and services. Chapter 5 also explores the Recovery Console and other ways to fix problems with Windows XP.

Part II. Customizing and Using Windows

Part II makes the transition from setting up and controlling Windows XP to using it and your applications. Chapter 6, "Customizing Windows XP," will help you fine-tune your desktop, Start menu, and taskbar. You'll also learn about screensavers and why they are important for security. Chapter 6 ends with a look at how group policy can help you configure Windows XP automatically.

Chapter 7, "Getting the Most from Windows XP Media," explores audio, video, and digital photos, and how you can integrate them all within Windows XP. You'll learn how to create an on-disk library of your favorite CDs, work with streaming audio, and even hook your computer to your stereo. The chapter will also help you work with your digital photo library, for example making sure it's backed up so you don't lose your favorite photos. You'll also learn about digital video and find tips on using Windows Messenger to share media with friends and family or just chat.

Chapter 8 brings digital media and TV together to explore Windows XP Media Center Edition (MCE). MCE integrates special hardware and extra software with Windows XP to create a complete media solution for TV, audio, and even digital video recording. Chapter 9 takes a close look at the other special edition of Windows XP, called Windows XP Tablet PC Edition. This version of Windows incorporates new features for the newest computer device on the block, the Tablet PC. If you have just purchased one or are thinking about new ways to take your work with you, Chapter 9 will help you understand the ups and downs of the Tablet PC.

If you think about how you use your computer, you'll quickly realize that your documents are the most important aspect of your system. Keeping they safe and secure is very important, so Chapter 10, "Simplifying Backups," will help you understand backup options and how to apply them to keep your data safe.

Chapter 11, "Scripting and Automating Windows XP," explores the many ways you can automate tasks in Windows XP and in your applications. In the chapter, I offer an overview of some of the third-party programs you can use to record step-by-step macros, to give you a taste for how simple it is to automate tasks. Chapter 11 also covers batch files and the Scheduled Tasks folder, two other automation tools available with Windows XP. The chapter finishes with a look at Windows Scripting Host. If you're interested in learning about programming, WSH is a good first step.

Security is increasingly important, and you'll find useful tips and suggestions in Chapter 12, "Windows XP Security," to help you secure your e-mail messages and documents. You'll also learn to secure your computer against viruses, hackers, and other potential threats.

Chapter 13 rounds out this part of the book with a look at the many administrative and management tools included with Windows XP. You'll also learn how to bring together the tools you use most often into your own custom management console.

Part III. Working with Applications

It's likely that two applications you use often are Internet Explorer and Outlook Express. Chapter 14, "Internet Explorer Tips and Tricks," will help you understand how to use Internet Explorer's features to simplify Web browsing and browse the Internet more securely. Chapter 15, "Outlook Express Tips and Tricks," will help you get the most out of Outlook Express while learning to keep spam and viruses at bay.

Part IV. Networking, Communications, and Remote Access

One of the tasks that many people face these days is setting up a small network, whether at home or in a small office. Chapter 16, "Networking Windows XP," will help you choose the right type of equipment and get it all set up. You'll also learn how to set up a wireless network and make it work with a wired one.

Chapter 17, "Remote Access," is all about using computers remotely. The chapter explains how to use Windows XP's Remote Assistance feature to get and give help. The section on Remote Desktop Connection will help you access your computer remotely, such as when you need to control your computer at home from your office computer, or vice-versa. The chapter rounds out the remote access discussion with a look at virtual private networking (VPN) connections and how you can use them to access remote resources securely and easily.

Chapter 18, "Hacking Windows XP," will likely take you into some uncharted territory. Here you'll learn how to recover lost passwords and use other tools to recover from system failures and overcome network problems

Upgrading, Controlling, and Troubleshooting

Upgrading to Windows XP

I n this chapter you'll find the answers to the following questions:

- How can I make sure my documents and applications aren't lost when I upgrade to Windows XP?
- Can I use Windows Backup in my current version of Windows in Windows XP?
- Is there an easy way to copy e-mail accounts and other program settings to Windows XP from my old system?
- I don't have a network. How do I move settings and documents between my old computer and my new one?
- How do I make sure my computer is compatible with Windows XP before installing it?
- How do I ensure that my hardware will work with Windows XP?
- Do I update my applications before or after I install Windows XP?
- What's the different between a "clean install" and an upgrade?
- What is Windows XP's Product Activation?

Installing Windows XP is generally an easy process. If you've purchased a new system it's likely that Windows XP is already installed and ready to run. This is particularly true if you purchased a Media Center PC, Tablet PC, or computer from a retail store.

Maybe you are building a new system for yourself, upgrading to Windows XP from a different version of Windows, or just wanting to reinstall Windows XP and start from scratch. Whatever the reason, I'll help you navigate the pitfalls you might face when installing Windows XP in different situations. Let's start with making sure your documents and customized application settings are safely backed up.

NOTE *Backing up your application settings and data is most important when performing a clean installation of Windows XP or reformatting your hard disk when reinstalling Windows XP. If you are performing an upgrade from a previous version of Windows, in most cases your application settings and documents will come through unscathed. Even so, it's a good idea to back up beforehand.*

Backing Up Application Settings and Data

Going through a system reinstall or an upgrade and coming out the other side to find that either your data or your application settings are gone is incredibly frustrating. Fortunately, avoiding the problem is easy provided you plan ahead and do a little work beforehand. In this section I'll explain how you can easily back up your data as well as application settings and make sure both are available after installing or upgrading to Windows XP.

Is Windows Backup an Option?

All versions of Windows include a Backup program that you can use to back up and restore files. You might be tempted to use Backup to back up your application files, documents, and other files prior to installing Windows XP. Unless you are reinstalling Windows XP over an existing Windows XP installation, I don't recommend using Windows Backup. The reason is that the Windows XP version of Backup can't read the backup sets created by Windows 9x and Windows Millennium Edition (Me). This means you won't be able to restore the files from these backup sets after you install Windows XP. So, copying the files to another local hard disk, CD-R/CD-RW, or network drive is often the best solution.

Backing Up and Restoring Office Settings with the Office Resource Kit

Microsoft Office is by far the most popular productivity application in use today, and it's a safe bet that you use at least one Microsoft Office application. All of the Office applications give you the capability to customize toolbars and menus and configure a host of settings that change the way the program looks and functions. Many of the applications store customized data in additional files in your user profile (the set of folders that store your user-specific data). For example, Microsoft Outlook stores nicknames in the file <profile> .nk2, where <profile> is the name of your Outlook profile. Nicknames are shortcut names for AutoComplete, which enables you to type a few characters and have an e-mail address filled in automatically in the To, Cc, or Bcc fields. Another example is Microsoft Word, which stores many of your customized Word settings in the template file Normal.dot. If you don't back up these additional Microsoft Office files, your customized settings can be lost when you install Windows XP.

The Microsoft Office Resource Kit, available for Office 2003 by download from http:// www.microsoft.com/office/ork/2003/default.htm, includes a tool called the Profile Wizard that enables you to easily back up your entire Microsoft Office configuration, complete with these additional folders and files. You'll find Resource Kits for other versions of Office at http://office.microsoft.com/officeupdate/default.aspx?CTT=98, and Microsoft Press offers print versions that include documentation and technical articles and the Resource Kit tools on CD.

TIP *The Profile Wizard is also useful for deploying the same Microsoft Office application settings to a group of users. Install Microsoft Office, customize the applications as needed, and then run the wizard to create a standard OPS file that you restore on each user's computer. Note that you can also use group policy to control Office application settings if the computers reside in a Windows 2000 Server or Windows Server 2003 domain. See my book,* Outlook 2003 Inside Out *(Microsoft Press, 2003) for details on how to deploy and manage Office with group policies.*

The Profile Wizard is easy to use thanks to a simple interface. Here's how to back up your settings:

1. After you install the Resource Kit, start the wizard by choosing Start, Programs (or All Programs on Windows XP), Microsoft Office, Microsoft Office Tools, Microsoft Office 2003 Resource Kit, Profile Wizard. Click Next in the introductory dialog box to view the Save or Restore Settings page shown in Figure 1-1.

2. Choose the Save the Settings from This Machine option.

3. Place a check beside each application whose settings you want to back up. All of the applications are selected by default.

4. If the path specified in the Settings File doesn't suit your needs, type a new path and filename or click Browse to choose a location. The OPS file is the file in which the Profile Wizard will store all of your settings.

5. Click Finish.

The result of the Profile Wizard at this point is an OPS file containing all of your Microsoft Office application settings. What should you do with this file? Back it up, of course! Copy the OPS file you created with the Wizard to a network server, other hard disk, or removable media such as a CD-R/CD-RW or DVD-RW disc, or ZIP disk. Choose a location that will be safe when you run Setup to install Windows XP.

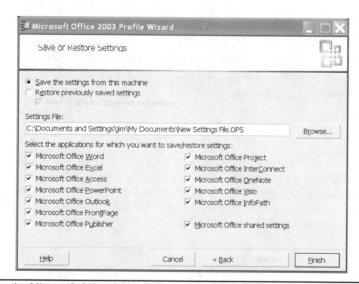

Figure 1-1 Use the Microsoft Office 2003 Profile Wizard to back up all of your Microsoft Office customized settings.

TIP *Be careful about where you put your backup files. My main system includes four disks, three that are part of a hardware-based small computer system interface (SCSI) Redundant Array of Independent Disks (RAID) array and a fourth Integrated Development Environment (IDE) drive, which I use for backups. During a reinstall of Windows XP some time ago, I didn't notice that the BIOS had changed the drive configuration when I ran Setup. I reformatted drive C without looking closely at the disk configuration, thinking that it was the drive where Windows XP was installed. It turned out to be the drive where my backups lived! It was an unhappy experience. Putting your backups on an external disk or network server is the best course of action to ensure that your files are safe if you need to reformat your computer's hard disk. Make sure you know exactly where your backups are located and which disk you are reformatting if you choose that route.*

In most cases, your application settings will come through an upgrade without any problems. If you choose to reinstall Windows XP or perform a clean installation rather than upgrade from a previous Windows version, however, your settings will not be transferred to your new user profile. Fortunately, you can use the Profile Wizard to restore your Microsoft Office settings from your backup OPS file:

1. After you install Windows XP, install Microsoft Office and the Microsoft Office Resource Kit.

2. Make sure no Microsoft Office applications are running.

3. Start the Profile Wizard and choose Restore Previously Saved Settings.

4. If you want the Profile Wizard to reset all Office application settings to their default values before applying your saved settings, choose the option Reset to Defaults Before Restoring Settings.

5. Choose the OPS file you created prior to installing Windows XP.

6. Place a check beside all of the applications whose settings you want the wizard to restore from your backup.

7. Click Finish.

TIP *In most cases you can use the Profile Wizard without changing the way it works. However, you can customize the wizard to add other folders or files in the backup, or exclude folders or files. See http://www.microsoft.com/office/ork/2003/ref/refA07.htm to learn how to customize the wizard and use startup switches to control the way it works. See the documentation for other Resource Kit versions for startup switches for other Office versions.*

Backing Up Other Application Settings

If you use applications other than those in the Microsoft Office suite, you should also consider backing up those applications' settings before installing Windows XP. Unfortunately, most applications don't offer a backup tool like the Profile Wizard so you'll likely have to back up files manually for these applications. Check with the application developer's web site or technical support staff to determine if there is a backup utility, and if not, how you can back up your application settings and custom files.

The same caution applies when backing up these applications as for Microsoft Office: make sure you place the backups in a backup location that is safe and will be accessible after you install Windows XP.

Backing Up Documents and Other Data

When your application settings are safely backed up, turn your attention to your documents and other data. Where your documents are stored now depends on a couple of factors, including which operating system you are using and whether you are using a nonstandard location for your documents. Windows 98 and later all provide a My Documents folder that you can use to store your documents. The benefit of using My Documents as your main document storage location is that the folder is tightly integrated with Windows. For example, the standard Open and Save dialog boxes use My Documents as the default file storage location. This makes your documents readily available when you need them.

There is little to prevent you from storing your documents in almost any location. The exception is NT File System (NTFS) permissions on a Windows 2000 or Windows XP system, which prevent you from storing files in a folder for which you do not have the necessary permissions. So, you should carefully examine your existing system to make sure you know where all of your documents and other data are stored so you can back them up.

TIP *See the section "Using the Files and Settings Transfer Wizard" to learn how to easily back up your Windows settings and data.*

Restoring from Windows 2000 Backup Sets

As I mentioned earlier in this chapter, the Windows Backup utility is often not the best choice for backing up your documents if you are upgrading from Windows 9x or Windows Me because the backup sets created by these versions of Windows Backup are not compatible with the Windows XP version. However, backups made with the Windows 2000 version of Backup are fully compatible with the Windows XP version. To open a Windows 2000 backup set in Windows XP backup (or a Windows XP backup made with another installation of Windows XP), follow these steps:

1. Open Windows Backup in Windows XP.
2. Click the Restore and Manage Media tab, then choose Tools, and go to Catalog a Backup File.
3. You Catalog a Backup File from the Tools menu.
4. In the Open Backup File dialog box, type or browse to the location where the BKF file is located, then click OK.
5. After cataloging the backup file, you can restore from it as you would from a backup file created with Windows XP Backup.

Using the Files and Settings Transfer Wizard

Windows XP includes a very handy tool called the Files and Settings Transfer Wizard that makes it easy to move common Window settings and your data from one computer to another. The wizard is useful whether you are moving from one computer to another, upgrading your existing computer from a previous version of Windows, or installing a clean copy of Windows XP on your existing system.

NOTE *See the section "Upgrade Versus Clean Install" later in this chapter for a discussion of the benefits of these two approaches—performing an upgrade or a clean install—when installing Windows XP.*

The Files and Settings Transfer Wizard copies a wide range of information from your old computer to your new one:

- **Windows settings**   The Wizard transfers a wide range of settings for Windows' appearance (desktop, sounds, taskbar, etc.); environment settings such as key repeat rate and mouse settings; Internet settings such as home page, favorites and bookmarks, cookies, Web security settings, dial-up connections, and proxy settings; and mail settings and data for Microsoft Outlook and Outlook Express including accounts, messages, contacts, rules, and so on.

- **Application settings**   The Wizard transfers settings for Microsoft Office applications, but I recommend that you also run the Profile Wizard from the Microsoft Office Resource Kit to ensure that everything gets transferred. The Wizard can also transfer settings for other applications. However, it doesn't transfer applications themselves, just their settings.

- **Files**   The Wizard transfers several types of common document files in its default configuration. You can direct it to copy other types of files, as well.

TIP *The Files and Settings Transfer Wizard is installed by default when you install Windows XP, making it readily accessible on your new computer. You can run the Wizard from the Windows XP CD on your existing computer, or use the Wizard to create a diskette for your existing computer.*

The Files and Settings Transfer Wizard offers four ways to copy information:

- **Direct Cable Connection (DCC)**   This option enables two computers to be networked through serial (COM), parallel (LPT), and infrared ports. The serial and parallel port options require special cables. The Files and Settings Transfer Wizard only supports DCC with serial connections, however.

- **Home or small office network**   This option transfers your files across a network to the new computer.

- **Floppy drive or other removable media**   With this option, a high-capacity removable disk such as a ZIP disk might work, but it's unlikely that floppy disks will serve your needs because of the amount of data to be transferred.

- **Other**   This option saves the data to a local folder, removable drive, or network share.

The Files and Settings Transfer Wizard copies a large number of files, particularly if you have Microsoft Office installed on the original computer. In almost every case, a network connection between the two computers, a network share on a file server, or a high-capacity removable drive (such as an external hard disk) works best. So, your first consideration is how you will transfer the data from the old system to the new one. The following sections explore the available options.

NOTE   *If you are upgrading an existing system to Windows XP, most (if not all) of your applications and settings will transfer, eliminating the need to use the Wizard. If you are performing a clean install of Windows XP on your existing computer, however, you can use the Wizard to transfer settings from the old computer to the new one. You can also use the Wizard if you are moving your settings and data from your old computer to a new one.*

There are a handful of different paths to take to use the Files and Settings Transfer Wizard. The next section explains how to start the wizard. Following sections take you through the remaining steps to complete the wizard.

Starting the Wizard

You can either run the Files and Settings Transfer Wizard from the Windows XP CD or from a diskette created with the wizard. Follow these steps to create a diskette:

1. On the computer where Windows XP is already installed, click Start, All Programs, Accessories, System Tools, Files and Settings Transfer Wizard, and then click Next.
2. Choose New Computer and click Next.
3. Place a blank, formatted diskette in your new computer's floppy disk drive.
4. Choose the option I Want to Ceate a Wizard Disk in the following drive (Figure 1-2), choose your floppy disk drive, and click Next, then click OK. The wizard creates the disk.
5. When the wizard has finished creating the disk, place it in your old computer and click Start, then Run, and enter **A:Fastwiz.exe** to start the Wizard.
6. See the following sections to complete the process depending on which transfer method you are using.

To run the wizard from the Windows XP CD on your old computer, follow these steps:

1. Boot your computer and insert the Windows XP CD in the CD-ROM drive. If the CD does not automatically run, open My Computer, double-click the CD-ROM drive, and double-click Setup.exe.
2. When the Welcome to Microsoft Windows XP screen appears, click Perform Additional Tasks.
3. Click Transfer Files and Settings, then click Next after the wizard starts. If you are running the wizard under an operating system other than Windows XP, the wizard does not prompt you to specify whether this is the old computer or the new one.

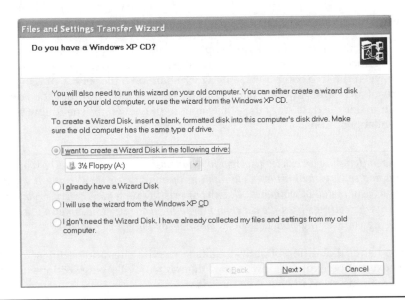

FIGURE 1-2   Choose the floppy drive in which the Wizard will create the disk.

Which method should you choose to start the Wizard? In reality, it doesn't matter. The main reason to run it from a diskette rather than the CD is if your old computer doesn't include a CD-ROM drive. Otherwise, running from the CD saves you the extra step of creating the diskette.

Now that you have the Wizard running, the following sections explore the different ways you can transfer data to your new Windows XP installation.

Direct Cable Connection

Direct Cable Connection (DCC) is a Windows feature that enables systems to be networked through their serial, parallel, or infrared ports. DCC requires a special cable for the serial or parallel port options. Check at your local computer retailer for the right cable according to which port option you will use. Using the parallel port should provide slightly better performance than the serial option, but null-modem cables for a serial connection are often more readily available.

DCC normally takes some configuration to set up, but the Files and Settings Transfer Wizard takes over those functions to configure the connection for you. Follow these steps to transfer your settings and data from one computer to another with the Files and Settings Transfer Wizard:

1. Start the Wizard on each computer using one of the methods described in the preceding section, "Starting the Wizard."

2. On the old computer, click Next until you see the Select a Transfer Method page (Figure 1-3).

3. Choose the option Direct Cable and click Next.

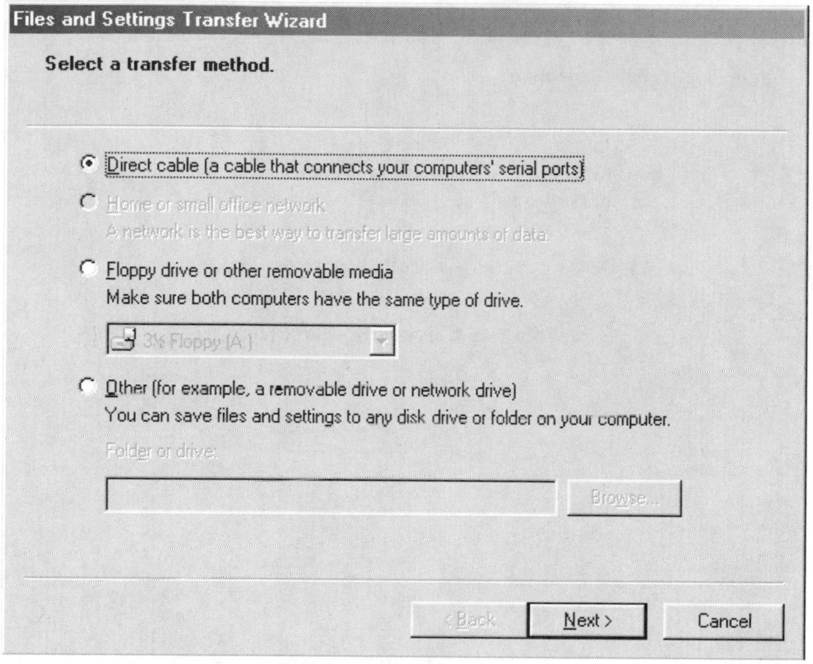

FIGURE 1-3   Select the Direct Cable option to transfer using DCC.

4. On the new computer, start the Files and Settings Transfer Wizard. Choose New Computer and click Next, choose I Don't Need the Wizard Disk and click Next, then choose Direct Cable and click Next.

5. Connect the two computers with the null-modem serial cable.

6. On the Set Up Your Serial Connection page (Figure 1-4) on both computers, click Autodetect.

7. After both computers show a green check mark on the page to indicate a successful connection, click Next on the old computer to display the What Do You Want to Transfer? page. See the section, "Choosing What to Transfer" to specify what the wizard will transfer. After you click Next, the wizard will establish a connection and begin transferring the data between the two. Restart the new computer after the transfer is complete.

Home or Small Office Network

If you are transferring between computers and both are on the same network, you can use the Wizard to transfer your files and settings across the network from the old computer to the new one. Here's how:

1. Start the Wizard on each computer using one of the methods described in the section "Starting the Wizard."

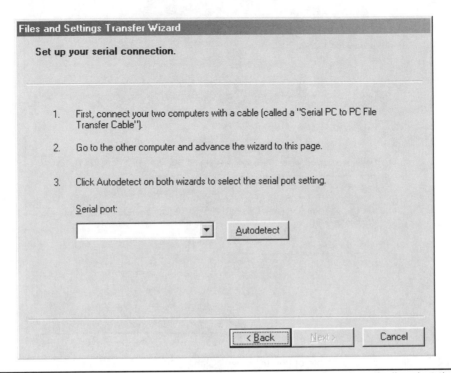

FIGURE 1-4   Use Autodetect on the Set up your serial connection page to automatically select the serial port for the DCC connection.

2. On the new computer, click Next, choose New Computer, and click Next. Choose I Already Have a Wizard Disk and click Next.

3. On the old computer, click Next until you see the Select a Transfer Method page (Figure 1-3).

4. Choose the option Home or small office network.

NOTE   *The Home or small office network option will be dimmed (unavailable) if you have not already started the Wizard on the new computer. In addition, both computers must have functioning connections to the network and be able to see one another on the network. See Chapter 16, "Networking Windows XP," to learn how to set up a network if you do not already have one.*

5. Click Next to display the What Do You Want to Transfer? page. After specifying your transfer options per the upcoming section, "Choosing What to Transfer," click Next. If there is more than one computer running the Files and Settings Transfer Wizard on the network, the Wizard on the old computer prompts you to choose the target computer (Figure 1-5). Click the target computer and click OK.

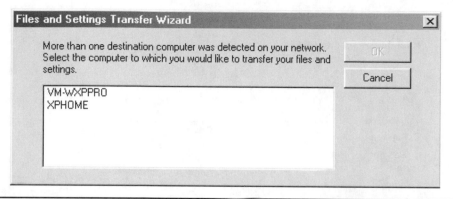

FIGURE 1-5   Choose the computer to which the data should be copied.

6. The Wizard on the new computer displays a dialog box containing a password. Enter that password in the dialog box that appears on the old computer, and then click OK. The Wizard then completes the transfer.

Floppy Drive or Other Removable Media

The main reason to use this option is that you are transferring the settings to a single computer after you have upgraded it to Windows XP or reinstalled Windows XP on it. A secondary reason is that your old computer doesn't include a network adapter and you don't want to use DCC to transfer the data. Whatever the case, follow these steps to transfer data using a floppy disk or other removable media:

1. Start the Wizard on the old computer (or existing Windows installation). If you are running the Wizard under Windows XP, choose the Old Computer option and click Next.

2. Choose the option Floppy Drive or Other Removable Media, then choose the Removable drive from the drop-down list.

3. Click Next to display the What Do You Want to Transfer? page. See the upcoming section, "Choosing What to Transfer," to configure the transfer options, then click Next.

4. The Wizard writes your data to disk, prompting for multiple disks if needed.

5. After the Wizard is finished on the old computer, take the removable disk to the new computer. If you're installing or reinstalling Windows XP on the same computer, perform the installation. After Windows XP is installed, run the Wizard from the StartAll ProgramsAccessoriesSystem Tools menu.

6. Click Next, choose New Computer, and click Next. Choose the option I Don't Need the Wizard Disk, and then click Next. Choose the option Floppy Drive or Other Removable Media, choose the appropriate drive from the drop-down list, and click Next. The Wizard will start the transfer and prompt for additional disks if there is more than one.

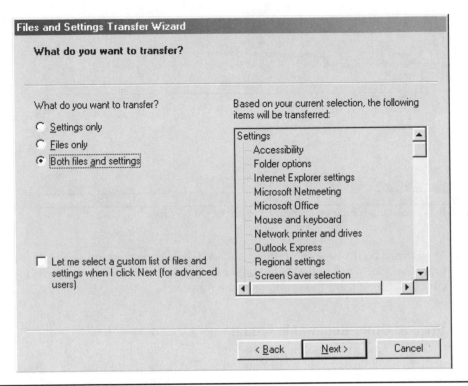

FIGURE 1-6   You can choose to transfer files, settings, or both.

Other

This last option is useful when you want to transfer the data to a network server or a different local hard disk on a system on which you will install Windows XP after running the wizard. Follow these steps to use this method:

1. If you will be transferring the data to a network share, connect to the remote computer where the share is hosted.

2. Start the Wizard on the old computer and click Next. If the computer is running Windows XP, choose Old Computer, and click Next.

3. Choose the Other option, then click Browse and browse for the location where the files will be temporarily stored.

4. Click Next, then see the following section, "Choosing What to Transfer." After you choose what will transfer, click Next. The Wizard writes the data to the specified location.

5. On the target computer after Windows XP is installed, start the Wizard and click Next.

6. Choose New Computer and click Next. Choose the option I Don't Need the Wizard Disk and click Next.

7. Choose the option Other, browse to the location where the data was stored in step 4, and click Next to start the transfer.

Choosing What to Transfer

The Files and Settings Transfer Wizard gives you the option of transferring settings, files, or both (Figure 1-6). If you don't have any files that you want transferred to the new Windows XP installation, choose the Settings option, which will result in a much smaller amount of data and shorter transfer time.

If you want to have more control over what the Wizard will transfer, select the option Let Me Select a Custom List of Files and Settings When I Click Next. When you do click Next, the Wizard displays the Select Custom Files and Settings page, shown in Figure 1-7. Here you can add and remove settings, add folders to be copied, add individual files, and add file types. To remove an item from the list, just click the item and then click Remove. After you are satisfied with the transfer selection, click Next to start the transfer process.

Checking Your System's Compatibility with Windows XP

Windows XP is compatible with a wide range of hardware. Some older hardware, however, might not be supported by Windows XP, or might be only partially supported. Whether your hardware is fully compatible with Windows XP also raises performance issues. In

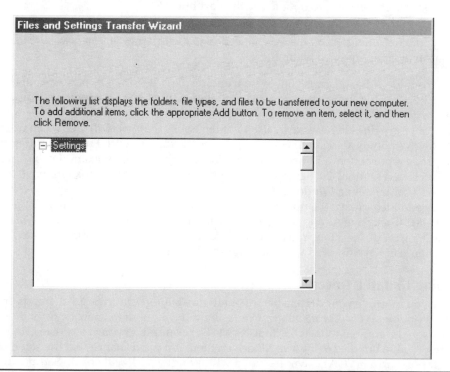

FIGURE 1-7   You can add other files, settings, and folders to the list of items to be transferred.

many cases, a generic Windows XP driver could enable a device to work under Windows XP, but a driver from a manufacturer is often required to take advantage of all of a device's features. What's more, an incompatible or poorly designed driver could cause Windows XP to hang or interfere with other hardware in the computer.

Therefore, it's important that you make sure all of the hardware in your computer is compatible with Windows XP's bundled drivers, or obtain updated Windows XP drivers prior to installing Windows XP. The following section, "Checking Compatibility Before Installing Windows XP," explains how.

Checking Compatibility Before Installing Windows XP

The Windows XP CD includes a tool called the Upgrade Advisor that scans your system to identify hardware that will require updated drivers that aren't included with Windows XP, and to identify software that is not compatible with Windows XP.

To run the Upgrade Advisor, insert the Windows XP CD in your computer. If the CD doesn't automatically start, run Setup from the CD. When Setup displays a menu of choices, click Check System Compatibility, and then click Check My System Automatically. The Upgrade Advisor offers two options:

- **Yes, Download the Updated Setup Files**   If your computer has a connection to the Internet, choose this option to allow Setup to download updated files. Setup will download the files from Microsoft over the Internet and then restart. After Setup restarts, choose the No option (see the next bullet).

- **No, Skip This Step and Continue Installing Windows**   Choose this option if your computer doesn't have a connection to the Internet or you have already downloaded updated Setup files.

The Upgrade Advisor scans your system and displays a summary of the results of its scan (Figure 1-8). The summary lists items with which the Advisor suspects a compatibility problem with Windows XP.

The summary doesn't necessarily list all of the issues that you will face when upgrading or installing Windows XP on your computer. To see the full list, click Full Details (Figure 1-9). This upgrade report offers additional information. In Figure 1-9, for example, the Upgrade Advisor detected Outlook 2000 on the computer and warns that Outlook will have to be reinstalled after installing Windows XP.

It's a good idea to save the upgrade report so you can review it before installing Windows XP. Click Save As and then click Save to save the file with its default filename, Upgrade.htm, on the desktop. You can also click Print to print the upgrade report. Click Finish when you have finished with the Upgrade Advisor.

Obtaining Updated Drivers

Whether you upgrade your drivers before or after installing Windows XP depends on whether Windows XP's drivers will work in a limited way with the hardware, and whether the hardware is required to install Windows XP. For example, if your video card isn't supported with a bundled Windows XP driver, there is a good chance that the standard video graphics array (VGA) driver included with Windows XP will enable Setup to install Windows and for Windows XP to run on your computer. You just won't get the most out

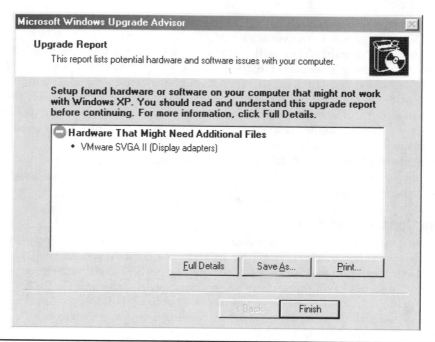

FIGURE 1-8   The Upgrade Advisor displays a summary of potential compatibility problems.

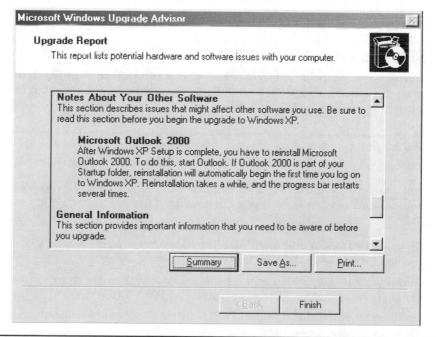

FIGURE 1-9   You can view additional upgrade information in the Upgrade Advisor.

of your video card until you install an XP-compatible driver. In this case, you can install Windows XP and upgrade the driver afterward.

If the hardware is required to install Windows XP and the existing or a bundled driver won't work, you'll have to upgrade the driver during Setup, which will prompt you for the driver. The best place to get updated drivers for your hardware is from the manufacturer. So, your first step to making your system compatible is to visit the manufacturer's web site to download updated drivers. If no Windows XP driver is available, you have two options: use a Windows 2000 driver for the hardware or replace the hardware with an alternative that is Windows XP-compatible.

After you obtain the updated driver, create a folder on your hard disk and place the driver it that folder, or if you will be reformatting your hard disk for a clean installation, burn the driver(s) to a CD.

When to Update Applications

The Upgrade Advisor checks software compatibility as well as hardware compatibility, and if it finds an application that won't run under Windows XP, it tells you so. The Upgrade Advisor also informs you of potential problems the application might experience if you do run it under Windows XP. In cases where an application will cause problems with Windows XP, the Upgrade Advisor will advise you of that and Setup will disable the application. It's a good idea to uninstall these applications before running Setup, and then install the updated version after Windows XP is installed.

If the application will run on your current version without any problems, you can certainly upgrade the application before installing Windows XP. If the upgrade offers special features that only work with Windows XP, however, it's best to install Windows XP first, then upgrade the application.

Installing Without a Bootable CD-ROM Drive

If your computer is older, the BIOS might not support booting from a CD-ROM drive. If that's the case, you can obtain a set of boot diskettes that will enable you to start the Setup process from a bootable floppy disk.

NOTE *You don't need the boot diskettes if your system already contains Windows 9x or later. Instead, you can run Setup and direct it to copy the installation files to your computer, if needed.*

The setup disk set you use depends on which version of Windows XP you are running. This list includes the links from which you can download the right version for your copy of Windows XP:

- **Windows XP Home Edition without SP1**   http://www.microsoft.com/downloads/release.asp?ReleaseID=33290

- **Windows XP Home Edition with SP1 integrated on the CD**.   http://www.microsoft.com/downloads/release.asp?ReleaseID=33291

- **Windows XP Professional without SP1**.   http://www.microsoft.com/downloads/release.asp?releaseid=42818

- **Windows XP Professional with SP1 integrated on the CD.**   http://www. microsoft.com/downloads/release.asp?releaseid=42819

After you download the file appropriate to your copy of Windows XP, run it. The resulting program will step you through the process of creating the diskettes.

Upgrade Versus Clean Install

You have two options for installing Windows XP: perform an upgrade or a clean install. This section of the chapter explores these two installation options.

Advantages and Disadvantages of Clean Installs

In a clean install, you install Windows XP in its own directory without upgrading the existing operating system. The result is a pristine installation of Windows XP without any of your existing applications, operating system settings, or documents. The main advantages to this approach to a Windows XP installation is that it leaves all of your old operating system "baggage" behind. You don't have to worry about incompatible applications or performance problems that might creep into Windows XP from registry problems or buggy applications.

The main disadvantage to a clean install is that you have to reinstall all of your applications after installing Windows XP. With that disadvantage, when is a clean install a good option?

If you have relatively few applications on your computer and reinstalling those applications won't be a major chore, I recommend a clean install. In fact, the best approach is to back up your documents, reformat your hard disk, and install Windows XP onto that newly formatted disk. You're likely to see a significant performance improvement in doing so.

If your computer contains several applications that you don't want to have to reinstall, an upgrade is the best way to go. After installation, run the Windows XP Disk Defragmenter from the Computer Management console to defragment the disk for better performance. Right-click My Computer and choose Manage to open the Computer Management console.

NOTE *You can defragment the disk prior to installing Windows XP if you prefer. The only real advantage this offers is a speedier installation.*

Advantages and Disadvantages of an Upgrade

An upgrade installs Windows XP on top of your existing operating system, replacing it. Most of your existing settings—such as desktop configuration, application settings, and other working environment options—are migrated to Windows XP. Unless your applications are incompatible with Windows XP, they are migrated as well, which eliminates the need for you to install new versions or reinstall applications after installing Windows XP. The fact that your applications will continue to run without requiring a reinstallation is the biggest advantage of an upgrade versus a clean installation.

There is a relatively small chance that some existing registry setting will cause problems for Windows XP after installation. More likely is the possibility that you'll see slightly decreased performance when compared to a clean install because of a bloated registry.

Although there are third-party applications you can obtain to clean out the registry prior to (or after) installing Windows XP, a clean installation will result in the smallest, most problem-free registry.

If you have lots of applications that you don't want to reinstall, perform an upgrade. Otherwise, perform a clean install and reinstall all of your applications afterward.

Dealing with Product Activation

Windows XP, unlike previous versions of Windows, requires that you activate the software after installation. Product activation is one of Microsoft's answers to the problem of software piracy.

In the activation process, Windows XP examines your computer's hardware configuration and comes up with a numeric hash value based on that hardware. After the hash value has been generated, there are then two ways that activation can proceed. First, Windows can send the product key and the hash value across the Internet to Microsoft's activation servers to obtain an activation key automatically. Or, you can call Microsoft, read the hash value and product key to a live person, and obtain and enter the activation code yourself. The first approach works best, particularly if you have a broadband Internet connection—activation generally takes only a few seconds.

TIP *You also have the option of registering your copy of Windows XP with Microsoft in addition to activating it. Registration is optional; activation is required within 30 days after installation.*

Contrary to what a few paranoids might think, Setup doesn't send any secret or confidential information about your computer to Microsoft when it activates the product. Microsoft doesn't know what applications you are running, how much money is in your bank account, or even what kind of hardware you are using.

Is product activation a hindrance? The short answer is, "Not really." Product activation takes only a few minutes at most and is not something you have to do repeatedly. You don't even have to reactivate Windows if you reinstall it on the same computer. The activation information is stored on the hard disk and remains there during reinstallation unless you format the hard disk during installation.

There is one scenario in which you might have to reactivate Windows XP after a reinstallation on the same computer, however. If the hardware has changed significantly from the original configuration, Setup will generate a different hash from the original installation. For example, installing a new video card, different network adapter, and a few other items could result in a different hash and the need to reactivate.

When you do need to reactivate, don't expect major problems. Although Microsoft hasn't publicly stated the number of times automatic product activation will work with different hashes before failing, my experience has been that you can install at least a couple of times before the problem occurs. If your activation fails, just call Microsoft's activation number (which Windows displays for you during product activation) and let the technician know that you're reinstalling on the same computer but that you have changed hardware. I've never had a problem obtaining an activation key in this situation.

Backing Up and Reusing Your Activation Information

Windows stores the product activation code in the file Windows\System32\wpa.dbl. If you do want to reformat your hard disk while reinstalling Windows XP, and don't want to go through a reactivation, you can simply back up and restore this file. Here's how:

1. Open My Computer, format a floppy disk in your system's boot floppy drive (typically, drive A), and choose the option Create an MS-DOS Startup Disk.
2. Copy the file Windows\System32\wpa.dbl to this floppy disk.
3. Reinstall Windows XP and allow Setup to reformat the hard disk. Use FAT as the file system rather than NTFS for now.
4. After installation has finished, boot the computer using the floppy disk.
5. Copy the file wpa.dbl to Windows\System32.
6. Remove the floppy disk and restart the computer.

This method assumes that the hardware is sufficiently similar to the original configuration that it would not require reactivation.

Moving Windows XP Between Computers

You can't simply install Windows XP on two computers and then copy the wpa.dbl file from one to the other to successfully move Windows XP to a different computer. If product activation fails on the second computer, call Microsoft and inform the technician that you are moving Windows XP to a different computer and removing it from the original. Unless you have done this several times, you should have no problem obtaining an activation code for the new computer.

Avoiding Product Activation Altogether

Copies of Windows XP obtained through a volume licensing program such as Open License or Select License do not require activation. The purpose of these licensing programs is to allow businesses to obtain a single copy of Windows XP and install it on multiple computers. You simply pay for a license for each of the computers on which you will install Windows XP. Windows does not run the activation process on these computers. Check with your computer reseller to obtain pricing and availability information for volume licensing options.

Dual-Boot Configurations

A dual-boot configuration is one in which the computer contains more than one operating system and can boot to whichever one you choose at system startup. For example, you might want to keep your existing operating system in place but install a clean copy of Windows XP on the same computer. Or, maybe you want Linux and Windows XP to coincide on your computer.

TIP *Systems that contain more than two operating systems are often called multiboot configurations. For simplicity I use the term dual-boot here for systems that can boot more than one operating system regardless of the number.*

Dual-boot is useful when you need to retain your existing operating system, applications, and data, but still want to use Windows XP. The key point to remember is that with a dual-boot configuration, you can use only one operating system at a time. If you want to switch from Windows XP to Windows 98, for example, you have to reboot the computer.

The following sections explore the requirements and process for creating a dual-boot configuration for various operating systems.

TIP *For what it's worth, I don't recommend using dual-boot. A virtual machine such as VMware or Virtual PC is a much better alternative in most cases. See the section, "Alternatives to Dual-Boot Systems" later in this chapter for more details.*

Configuring a Dual-Boot System for Other Microsoft Operating Systems

There are several issues to consider in setting up a dual-boot configuration with Windows XP and any of the other Microsoft operating systems:

- **One volume per operating system.**   Each operating system must be installed on its own volume, each represented by a different drive letter. You can install multiple physical disks in the computer to create these volumes, or partition a single large disk into multiple partitions with multiple volumes.

- **File system compatibility.**   Older Microsoft operating systems do not support file systems introduced in later versions. Since each operating system will reside on its own volume, file system compatibility only becomes an issue if you want to access one operating system's volume from another's. See Table 1-1 for file systems supported by each operating system.

- **NTFS version.**   You must install Service Pack 5 or later on Windows NT to enable it to coexist with Windows 2000 or later because of changes introduced in NTFS with Windows 2000.

- **Application installation and location.**   To use an application with more than one operating system, you must install the application in each one. In some cases you can install the application to the same shared volume, but it's best to install a separate copy of the application on each operating system's volume that will use it.

When you've decided which operating systems you will install and have worked out the compatibility issues I've already mentioned, you can start installing operating systems. The following sections offer tips for specific platforms.

TIP *Hard disks are fairly inexpensive these days, so I generally recommend adding another physical drive to your system if you want to dual-boot. If you already have a huge drive and want to re-use it, but all of the space has already been partitioned, you can simply resize the existing partition. Check out Partition Magic at http://www.powerquest.com/partitionmagic if you want to change partition size without reinstalling your current OS.*

Operating System	Supported File Systems
MS-DOS	FAT
Windows 3.x	FAT
Windows NT	FAT, NTFS
Windows 95	FAT
Windows 98	FAT, FAT32
Windows Me	FAT, FAT32
Windows 2000	FAT, FAT32, NTFS
Windows XP	FAT, FAT32, NTFS
Windows Server 2003	FAT, FAT32, NTFS

TABLE 1-1   File System Compatibility by Operating System

MS-DOS, Windows 3.x, Windows 9x, and Windows Me

The key to making Windows XP coexist with any of these operating systems is the installation order. Install the operating systems, each on its own volume, in the following order: MS-DOS, Windows 3.x, Windows 9x, and Windows Me. After these operating systems are installed, you can install Windows XP. If you install any of these other operating systems after installing Windows XP, you'll lose the capability to boot Windows XP because Setup will overwrite the Windows XP boot loader with its own. If you experience this problem, boot the Recovery Console from the Windows XP CD and use the FIXBOOT command to restore the boot loader.

Windows NT 4.0

There are two main keys to successfully creating a dual-boot system with Windows NT 4.0 and Windows XP. The first is to install Windows NT before you install Windows XP. The second is to install Windows NT Service Pack 5 or later before installing Windows XP.

If you reinstall Windows NT after installing Windows XP, you'll have to restore the Windows XP versions of Ntdetect.com and Ntldr. If the boot volume uses a FAT file system, you can simply copy these two files from the i386 folder on the Windows XP CD to your boot disk. Otherwise, boot the Windows XP Recovery Console from the Windows XP CD and use the FIXBOOT command to restore the files.

Windows 2000, Windows XP, and Windows Server 2003

There are no major considerations for multibooting these operating systems other than to ensure that each is installed to its own volume.

Windows XP and Linux Dual-Boot Configuration

Setting up a dual-boot system with Windows XP and Linux isn't very difficult. You don't need to worry about application compatibility because neither operating system will run the other's applications. You also can ignore file system compatibility unless you need one OS to be able to see the other's file system. If that's the case, use FAT for your Windows XP volume. Or, make sure your Linux distribution includes an NTFS driver that supports NTFS version 5 or later.

Here are the general steps for setting up a Windows XP/Linux system:

1. Make sure you have a large enough hard disk to accommodate Windows XP, Linux, and the Linux swap partition.

3. Create (or resize) a partition for Windows XP, leaving at least 5GB unpartitioned for Linux. Or, install a separate disk for Linux.

4. After installing Windows XP, install Linux, creating a partition for it in the unpartitioned space. Leave sufficient space for the swap partition according to the amount of RAM in the system. Generally, the swap partition should be about twice the size of the amount of RAM in the system.

4. During the Linux installation process, make the Linux partition the active partition.

5. After Linux is booted, you can optionally mount the Windows XP volume under Linux if you need access to it from Linux.

Alternatives to Dual-Boot Systems

Although dual-boot systems are certainly useful, they have one major drawback that leads to several lesser drawbacks: you can only run one operating system at a time. Running a different operating system requires shutting down the current OS and booting another.

There are two virtual machine products very much worth mentioning as alternatives to dual-boot. These applications create virtual machine environments that enable you to run another operating system in a window. One is a third-party application and the other a Microsoft application.

VMware

VMware (http://www.vmware.com) offers several virtualization solutions. Its user-targeted solution, VMware Workstation, is designed for end users and enables multiple operating systems to be run on a single computer. Two versions are available to allow either Windows or Linux systems to serve as the host operating system. For example, you could run Windows XP Professional as your host operating system, then run Linux in one window and Windows Server 2003 in another window. (Figure 1-10 shows Windows 98 and Windows Server 2003 virtual machines running on a Windows XP Professional host operating system.) Or, you might run Linux as your main operating system with Windows XP running in a window. Two other products, GSX Server and ESX Server, are targeted at businesses needing to consolidate servers.

TIP *If you need to convert a physical machine to a virtual machine, check out VMware's PV2 tool at http://www.vmware.com/products/vtools/p2v_faqs.html.*

You can easily switch between virtual machines without disturbing running applications. You can also cut and paste between virtual machines and even drag files from one virtual machine to another.

You can download an evaluation copy of VMware Workstation from VMware's web site.

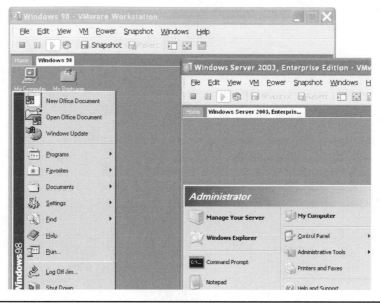

Figure 1-10   Here, VMware is running Windows 98 and Windows Server 2003.

Microsoft Virtual PC

Microsoft also offers a virtualization tool, which it purchased from Connectix and redeveloped. Like VMware, Virtual PC enables you to run multiple operating systems at one time on a single workstation. Unlike VMware, however, Microsoft does not support Linux as the host operating system. It does, however, offer a Mac version that enables Mac users to run PC operating systems. Microsoft also offers Virtual Server, which runs on Windows Server 2003 and is targeted at server consolidation and virtualization. See www .microsoft.com/virtualpc to learn about these Microsoft solutions.

Controlling Startup and Shutdown

I n this chapter you'll find the answers to the following questions:

- I remember Autoexec.bat and Config.sys from older versions Windows. Does Windows XP still use these files?
- Are there other startup files that Windows XP uses?
- What are environment variables and how do you set them in Windows XP?
- What can I do to make things happen automatically when I start or shut down Windows XP, or when I log on or off?
- How do you control when and how scripts execute?
- Why are all these programs starting automatically when I log on, and how can I control them?
- How can I have a program or document start automatically when I log on?
- Tell me how to turn off CD autoplay for a specific drive.

Windows XP, like other Windows operating systems, offers several ways to start applications automatically and control how the system starts in other ways. You can certainly use Windows XP without understanding the options you have for controlling Windows XP startup and shutdown, but understanding those features will help you gain complete control over Windows.

In this chapter I explore ways to control Windows XP's startup, shutdown, and CD autoplay, as well as application startups using a variety of methods.

NOTE *Some of the sections in this chapter explain how to control your computer with group policies. You must log on with an account that is a member of the administrators group to configure group policy on the local computer.*

What About Config.sys Autoexec.bat?

If you have been using Windows 9x or Me for some time, you're probably very familiar with its two main startup files: Config.sys and Autoexec.bat. Config.sys is used to load drivers and configure other environment settings for the operating system and Autoexec.bat is used to load drivers, run terminate-and-stay-resident (TSR) applications, and perform various configuration tasks.

These two files are not used by Windows XP at all, even if they are present in the root folder of the boot disk. If your computer is configured to dual-boot Windows Me or earlier, then that earlier operating system will use Autoexec.bat and Config.sys.

If you browse your system you'll find two files that look suspiciously like Autoexec.bat and Config.sys. The following section explains the roles these files play in Windows XP.

The DOS Environment, Config.nt, and Autoexec.nt

The \Windows\System32 folder contains two configuration files, Config.nt and Autoexec.nt, which are used to configure the MS-DOS environment for 16-bit applications and console sessions started with Command.com. Windows XP and consoles started with Cmd.exe do not take their configuration from these two files.

Autoexec.nt and Config.nt perform the same functions for 16-bit applications and Command.com sessions as they do in Windows Me and earlier. There are few reasons to run 16-bit applications these days, and even fewer reasons to use Command.com under Windows XP instead of Cmd.exe. However, in rare cases you might need to load drivers or configure settings for these environments. Simply edit the Autoexec.nt and Config.nt files in the \Windows\System32 folder according to the specific needs of the application.

Managing Environment Variables in Windows XP

An *environment variable* is a value stored in memory with a unique variable name. Windows XP uses a handful of environment variables to store information about the operating system. Most of today's applications store their settings in the registry. However, a few applications can make use of environment variables. What's more, all applications to some degree are affected by some of the global environment variables set by Windows.

In most cases you won't need to modify environment variables under Windows XP. However, if your application requires a certain variable or you need to modify one of the global variables, you can easily do so. Just right-click My Computer, choose Properties, click the Advanced tab, and click Environment Variables to display the Environment Variables dialog box (Figure 2-1).

There are two types of variables: user variables and system variables. User variables apply only to the current user. These appear in the upper list in the Environment Variables dialog box. System variables apply to all users. These appear in the lower list in the dialog box.

After a quick review of the existing variables you will discover that the only user variables by default are the TEMP and TMP variables, which define the location of the temp folder where Windows stores temporary files. By default, this folder is located in the user's profile in \Documents and Settings\<user>\Local Settings\Temp. Both of these variables point to the same location.

There are several system variables that set the default command console, specify the number of processors, set the temp folder, identify the folder in which Windows is installed, and configure other settings. In most cases there is no reason to change most of these settings. The two variables that deal with the system path, however, are a different story.

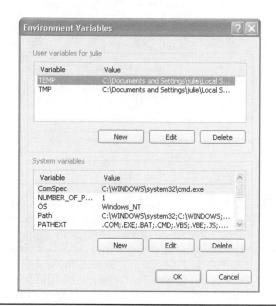

FIGURE 2-1   Use the Environment Variables dialog box to modify or add environment variables.

The PATH variable specifies the folders that Windows will search for applications when no path is specified. For example, open a command console, type an application name by itself, and the console will be able to locate and start the application only if the folder containing the application is part of the path.

The PATHEXT variable works in conjunction with the PATH variable. PATCHEXT specifies the file types that will be searched for along the path when no file extension is specified. For example, open a command console and type **SOMEAPP**, and the console will find Someapp.com, Someapp.exe, and a handful of other file types (assuming they exist) based on the extensions specified in the PATHEXT variable.

Adding and modifying environment variables is easy. To add a new one, click New in either the user area or system area, depending on the type of variable you want to create. Windows XP displays a dialog box similar to the one shown in Figure 2-2, in which you enter the variable name and value. To edit an existing variable, click the variable and then click Edit.

Startup, Logon, Logoff, and Shutdown Scripts

It's often useful to have a computer automatically perform actions at certain times, including when it starts or shuts down, or when a user logs on or off. For example, you might want a logon script to map a network drive, connect a printer, or even make a secure connection to a remote network. There are as many uses for scripts as there are for other computer programs. For that reason I won't focus on what you can accomplish with scripts, but instead on how to create and use them in Windows XP.

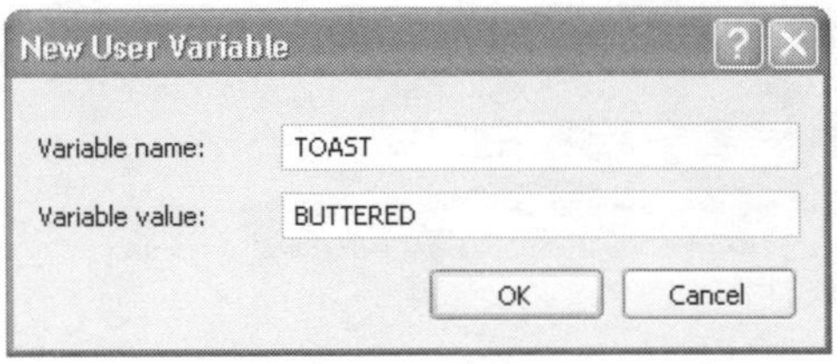

FIGURE 2-2 Use the New User Variable dialog box to add a user environment variable.

Writing a Script

In the good old days when DOS reigned, batch files were the only type of script you could execute on a DOS-based PC. Even so, you could, and still can, do some remarkably useful things with batch files. With the integration of Windows Scripting Host in Windows XP, you can accomplish even more complex actions with scripts and have additional choices for programming: Visual Basic Scripting Edition and JScript (Java). Let's start with batch files.

The simplest form of script is the batch file. These are simple text files that contain a series of console commands. Windows XP will run batch files with a BAT or CMD file extension. To create these scripts, open Notepad, add the commands one line at a time, and save the file with either a BAT or CMD extension. For a list of available commands, open a command console and type **HELP | MORE** at the command prompt. Type a command name followed by /? (such as **START /?**) to view additional information for that specific command.

You can also write a script in Visual Basic or Java and execute it through the Windows Scripting Host. The following is a Visual Basic script that displays a message in a dialog box:

```
msgbox "Hello world!"
```

You can accomplish the same thing with JScript, except it requires several more lines of code:

```
<package>
  <job id="helloworld">
    <script language="JScript">
      WScript.Echo("Hello World");
    </script>
  </job>
</package>
```

Try it out! Create a text-only file containing one of the preceding scripts. For Visual Basic Scripting Edition (VBS), give the file a VBS file extension. If you choose the JScript example, give it a WSF file extension. Save the file on the desktop. Then, simply double-click the file's icon. You should see a small dialog box appear on the display.

These simple scripts, while functional, are just barely so. No doubt your scripts will need to accomplish much more than display a simple message. For several sample scripts to accomplish a wide variety of tasks, point your Web browser to http://www.microsoft .com/technet/community/scriptcenter/default.mspx.

Assigning Startup and Shutdown Scripts with Group Policy

You can run scripts when Windows XP starts and when it shuts down to accomplish global tasks that are not associated with a specific user. You assign these startup and shutdown scripts through group policy.

NOTE *You must log on with an account that is a member of the administrators group to configure group policy on the local computer.*

You can apply group policy at the local level for all computers, including those that are not part of a domain but instead reside in a workgroup or are standalone computers. You can also apply group policy at the site, domain, or organizational unit (OU) levels. You must modify group policy objects in the Active Directory to assign group policy at the site, domain, or organizational unit (OU) level. This chapter focuses on how to assign local policy:

1. Click Start, Run, and enter GPEDIT.MSC in the Run dialog box.

2. In the Group Policy console, expand the Computer Configuration\Windows Settings\Scripts (Startup/Shutdown) branch (Figure 2-3).

3. Double-click the Startup policy.

4. In the Startup Properties dialog box (Figure 2-4), click Add.

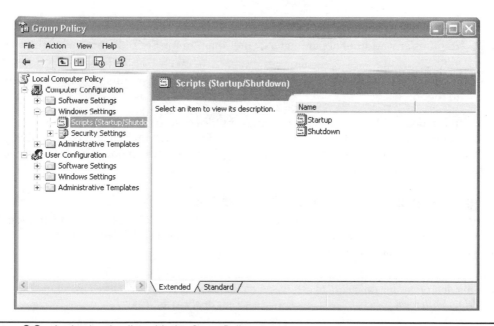

FIGURE 2-3   Assign local policy with the Group Policy console.

Figure 2-4 Use the Startup Properties dialog box to add startup scripts.

5. In the Add a Script dialog box, click Browse to select the script file. If the script requires any additional parameters, enter them in the Script Parameters field, then click OK.

6. Click OK. When you restart the computer, the specified script(s) will execute prior to logon.

You use a nearly identical process to assign shutdown scripts. Open the Computer Configuration\Windows Settings\Scripts (Startup/Shutdown) branch and then double-click the Shutdown policy. Assign scripts as you did for the Startup policy and close the Shutdown Properties dialog box.

Assigning Logon/Logoff Scripts with Group Policy

In addition to assigning startup and shutdown scripts, you can also assign logon and logoff scripts. Unlike startup and shutdown scripts, logon and logoff scripts apply at the user level when a user either logs on or logs off.

Tip You don't have the capability to assign specific scripts to specific users when assigning the scripts with local policy. Instead, all assigned scripts apply to all users.

Follow these steps to assign a logon or logoff script:

1. Click Start, Run, and enter **GPEDIT.MSC** in the Run dialog box.

2. In the Group Policy console, expand the User Configuration\Windows Settings\ Scripts (Logon/Logoff) branch.

3. Double-click either the Logon or Logoff policy, click Add, and browse to the script file you want to add.

4. Repeat step 3 to add any other scripts, then close the policy property dialog box.

Controlling When and How Scripts Execute

Windows XP offers a handful of policy settings that determine how and when policy-based scripts—like the ones I described in the previous two sections—execute. The first set of policies reside in Computer Configuration\Administrative Templates\System\Scripts:

- **Run logon scripts synchronously**   Enable this policy if you want all logon scripts to complete before Windows XP displays the Windows Explorer user interface. If the policy is disabled or not configured, logon scripts can execute after Windows Explorer starts.

- **Run startup scripts asynchronously**   By default, startup scripts run synchronously—one must complete before the next one starts. Enable this policy to allow startup scripts to run at the same time as others.

- **Run startup scripts visible**   Startup scripts are hidden by default—users do not see the scripts execute. Enable this policy if you want scripts to be displayed in a console window as they execute.

- **Run shutdown scripts visible**   Like startup scripts, shutdown scripts are not visible to the user by default. Enable this policy if you want shutdown scripts to be displayed in a console window as they execute.

- **Maximum wait time for group policy scripts**   Use this policy to specify the amount of time that policy-based scripts can run before the system stops script processing and records an error to the event logs. A value of 0 for this policy will allow scripts to run indefinitely.

Windows XP also offers four policies in the User Configuration container to control the way scripts execute:

- **Run logon scripts synchronously**   This policy is identical to the same policy in the Computer Configuration container, which also takes precedence over this policy if both are set.

- **Run legacy logon scripts hidden**   When enabled, this policy causes logon scripts written for Windows NT or earlier to execute in a hidden mode.

- **Run logon scripts visible**   Enable this policy to have logon scripts visible as they execute.

- **Run logoff scripts visible**   Enable this policy to have logoff scripts visible as they execute.

Controlling Automatic Program Startup

Windows XP can start program automatically using several methods. Understanding how all of these methods work will help you get a handle on your computer's startup. For example, it can help you bypass a program not listed in your computer's Startup folder that is hanging the system or causing other problems.

First, let's take a look at the ways programs can start automatically with Windows XP, beginning with the Startup folders.

The Startup Folders

The first place to begin looking for programs that start automatically is your Startup folder, located on the Start, All Programs menu. There are actually two Startup folders in play: yours, and the one for the Default User profile. Your Startup folder is located in \Documents and Settings*user*\Start Menu\Programs\Startup, where *user* is your logon account name. The Default User Startup folder is located in \Documents and Settings\Default User\Start Menu\Programs\Startup. The items in both of these folders launch automatically after you log on.

TIP *The Startup folder can contain shortcuts to documents as well as shortcuts to applications, enabling you to open documents automatically after you log on.*

Disabling items in the Start menu is easy—just delete the item's shortcut from the folder. Or, move it to the desktop if you only want the item disabled temporarily. You can later move it back to the Startup folder simply by dragging it.

TIPS *Even though the contents of the Startup folder comes from two physical folders as I've already explained, you don't need to worry about browsing those two folders separately. The contents of both folders appear in the Startup folder. Just drag items out as needed. However, keep in mind that when you drag an item back to the Startup folder, it goes into your own Startup folder, not the common folder that is part of the Default User profile. Also, keep in mind that your account must be a member of the Power Users or Administrators group to make changes to the Default User profile.*

If you want to bypass the items in the Startup folder only occasionally, you don't need to move or delete items in the Startup folder. Instead, when Windows XP prompts you to log on, choose your account and enter your password. But before you click OK, press and hold the SHIFT key. Click OK and continue to hold down the SHIFT key until the desktop appears. Windows XP will bypass the items in the Startup folder.

Registry Keys that Start Programs

There are also a handful of registry keys that can be used to start applications. These include the following:

- HKEY_LOCAL_MACHINE\SOFTWARE\Microsoft\Windows\CurrentVersion\Run

- HKEY_LOCAL_MACHINE\SOFTWARE\Microsoft\Windows\CurrentVersion\ RunOnce

- HKEY_CURRENT_USER\Software\Microsoft\Windows\CurrentVersion\Run

- HKEY_CURRENT_USER\Software\Microsoft\Windows\CurrentVersion\ RunOnce

The applications and documents listed in the Run keys execute each time you log on. The applications and documents in the two RunOnce keys run only a single time. Typically, the RunOnce keys are used after a program is installed to accomplish final setup steps. The RunOnce values are then set to empty so the specified applications don't run again the next time you log on.

To bypass applications that start from the Run registry keys, follow these steps:

1. Click Start, Run, and enter **regedit** in the Run dialog box.

2. In the Registry Editor (Figure 2-5), browse to the registry key that you want to modify and click the Run key.

3. Choose File, Export, and export the Run key to a REG file for backup.

4. Browse through the Run key and selectively delete the values for those items you do not want Windows XP to start.

5. Close the Registry Editor and restart the computer to test your changes.

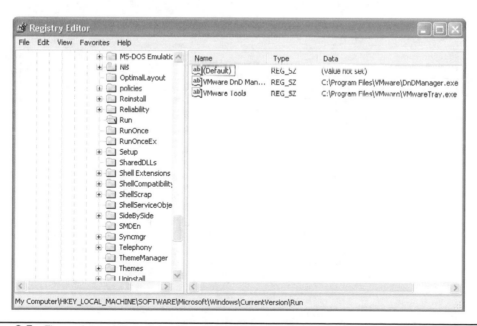

Figure 2-5   The registry also contains keys that launch programs automatically.

Services

Another place to look for applications that start automatically is the Services console (Figure 2-6). Most of the services you are likely to find in the Services console belong to Windows XP itself. However, some third-party applications are designed to run as services.

TIP *You'll find the Services console in the Administrative Tools folder. Or, right-click My Computer, choose Manage, and expand the Services and Applications branch to locate the Services console.*

You can't remove a service with the Services console, but you can change the way it starts (and also prevent it from starting). Services are assigned one of three startup modes:

- **Disabled**   The service will not start, even if another service is dependent on it.
- **Manual**   The service can be started by you or by a dependent service, but will not be started automatically when the system starts.
- **Automatic**   Windows XP will start the service automatically when the system starts.

NOTE *Make sure you understand the function the service performs and the possible consequences of disabling it before you reconfigure its startup mode. Also, you must be a member of the Administrators group to configure service behavior.*

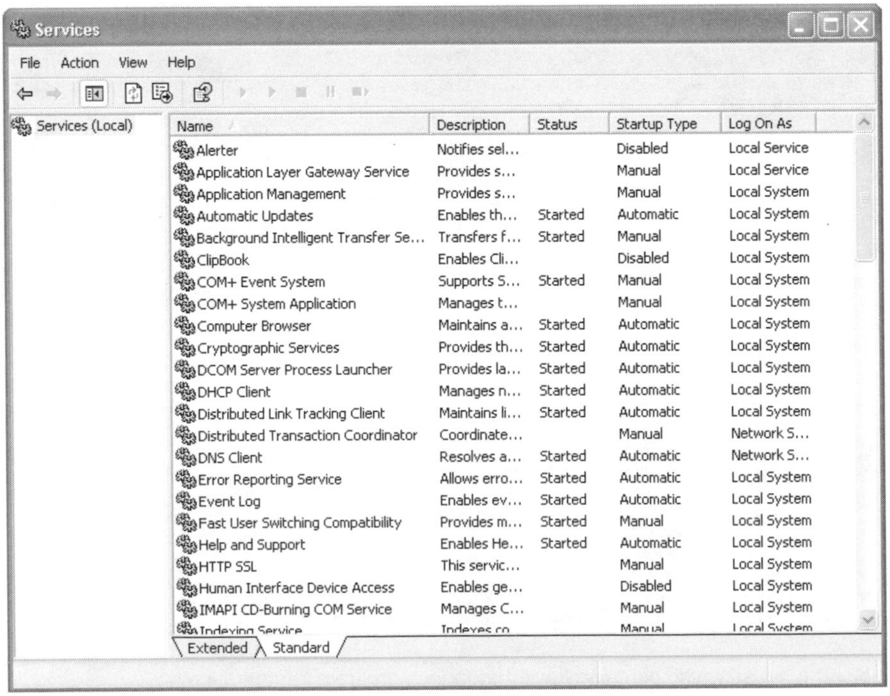

FIGURE 2-6   Use the Services console to enable and disable services.

To configure a service's startup mode, double-click the service in the Services console. In the properties for the service (Figure 2-6), choose from the Startup Type drop-down list the startup mode for the service, then click OK.

TIP   *See the section "Managing Services" in Chapter 5 for more information on configuring service behavior. See the section, "Managing Services with the Recovery Console," also in Chapter 5, for an alternative method for enabling and disabling services.*

Setting Up Your Own Automatic Programs

So far I've focused on preventing existing programs from starting automatically. You might want a few of your applications that currently don't start automatically to do so. The easiest method by far is to add a shortcut to your personal Startup folder to the application or document that you want Windows XP to start it for you. For example, if you always use Microsoft Outlook, why not add a shortcut to it in your Startup folder so it will start when you log on?

To create a shortcut in your Startup folder, open the folder where the document or application's executable file resides. Click on the object's icon and drag it to the Start menu, but don't release the mouse button yet. When the Start menu opens, drag and hold the pointer over the All Programs menu. When the All Programs menu opens, drag the item to the Startup folder and release it. Windows XP will create a shortcut to the item in your personal Startup folder.

If you want to create a shortcut that starts an application or opens a document for all users, open the folder \Documents and Settings\Default User\Start Menu\Programs\Startup. Then, in another window, open the folder where the application's executable or document is located. Right-drag the document to the Startup folder and choose Create Shortcut Here after you release the mouse button.

TIP   *If your system uses NTFS for its file system, you must have sufficient privileges to add shortcuts to the Default User profile. By default, members of the Administrators and Power Users groups can create and modify items in this folder. On a computer running Windows XP Home Edition, your account must be designated as a Computer Administrator rather than a Limited Account in order to modify the contents of the Default User profile. Use the User Account applet in the Control Panel to modify account properties.*

If you want to start programs for all users but don't want to use a shortcut in the Default User Startup folder, you can modify the registry:

1. Click Start, click Run, and enter **regedit** in the Run dialog box.
2. In the Registry Editor, open the HKEY_LOCAL_MACHINE\SOFTWARE\Microsoft\Windows\Currentversion\Run key.
3. Choose Edit, then New, and then String Value.
4. Type a name for the value and press ENTER.

5. Double-click the value you just created and in the resulting dialog box, set its value as the path to the document or executable you want Windows XP to start automatically.

Configuring Startup and Recovery Options

Windows XP offers a handful of other settings that control the way it starts and how it behaves when a critical error occurs. Let's start with startup and recovery options.

Setting Startup and Recovery Options

To configure these settings, right-click My Computer and choose Properties, click the Advanced tab, and click Settings under the Startup and Recovery group.

TIP You can also open the System Properties from the System applet in the Control Panel.

The Startup and Recovery dialog box contains the following options:

- **Default Operating System**   This drop-down list contains only one entry if your computer does not have another operating system installed and you have not added any other boot options. Otherwise, choose which boot option you want Windows XP to use by default.

- **Time to Display List of Operating Systems**   Specify the number of seconds that Windows XP will display boot options before automatically starting the default operating system.

- **Time to Display Recovery Options When Needed**   Specify the number of seconds that Windows XP will display recovery menu options during an automated recovery.

- **Edit**   Click this button to open the Boot.ini file in Notepad for editing. See the following section, "Understanding Boot.ini," for more details.

- **Write an Event to the System Log**   Choose this option to have Windows XP write an event to the System Event Log if the system experiences a critical error. You can later review the events with the Event Viewer to possibly determine the cause of the problem.

- **Send an Administrative Alert**   Choose this option to have Windows XP send a network pop-up alert to members of the administrators group if the computer experiences a critical error.

- **Automatically Restart**   Choose this option to have Windows XP automatically restart the computer when a critical error occurs. If this option is not selected, Windows XP displays an error screen, commonly called the Blue Screen of Death (BSOD), with information about what caused the error. In general, it's a good idea to leave this option unchecked because the BSOD often offers helpful information that will enable you to troubleshoot the problem. Only enable this option if you need to have the computer reboot automatically.

- **Write Debugging Information**   You can choose from three debugging options with this drop-down list. The Small Memory Dump option records only a limited amount of information but requires at least 2MB of free space on the disk. The Kernel Memory Dump option saves only kernel memory to disk, but requires from 50MB to 800MB of free disk space, depending on the amount of RAM in the system. The Complete Memory Dump option records all memory, but requires an amount of available disk space equal to the amount of RAM in the system plus one megabyte. In general, you won't need to set these options unless you are working with a Microsoft support technician, so set it to whichever option the technician recommends.

- **Small Dump Directory**   If you choose the Small Memory Dump option, use this field to specify the path in which the memory dumps will be stored. Windows XP does not overwrite the file each time, but instead creates a new file in the specified folder.

- **Dump File**   Use this option with the Kernel Memory Dump and Complete Memory Dump options to specify the path and filename for the memory dump file.

- **Overwrite Any Existing File**   Choose this option to have Windows XP overwrite the existing dump file, if any, in the specified folder.

Understanding Boot.ini

Windows XP uses a file named Boot.ini to store its boot configuration options. Figure 2-7 shows a Boot.ini file in Notepad. Boot.ini is located in the root of your computer's system drive (typically, drive C). By default, Boot.ini contains two sections:

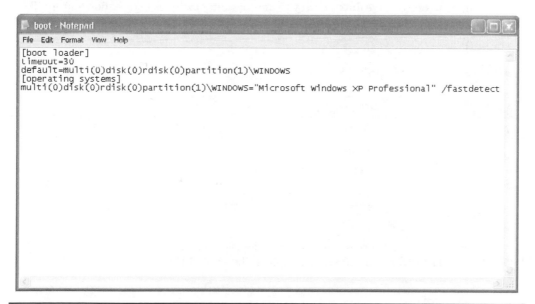

```
[boot loader]
timeout=30
default=multi(0)disk(0)rdisk(0)partition(1)\WINDOWS
[operating systems]
multi(0)disk(0)rdisk(0)partition(1)\WINDOWS="Microsoft Windows XP Professional" /fastdetect
```

FIGURE 2-7   Boot.ini defines the boot options and default operating system for the computer.

- **[boot loader]** This section includes settings that control Windows XP's boot process. The *timeout* value specifies the length of time that Windows XP waits for you to choose a boot option before starting the computer with the default option. The *default* value specifies the entry in the [operating systems] section that Windows XP will boot by default if you don't choose a different boot option from the boot menu.

- **[operating systems]** This section defines the bootable operating systems on the computer.

Most users never need to modify Boot.ini. In some situations, however, modifying Boot.ini gives you additional control over how your computer boots. You might want to create a second instance of your operating system that uses other settings to boot Windows XP. For example, you could use the /SOS switch to have Windows XP display device drivers as it loads them to help you identify a driver that is causing the system to hang.

An entry for Windows XP in the operating systems section consists of two main components. The first part to the left of the = sign specifies the location of the operating system. You'll find one of three syntaxes used in this portion of a boot string:

- **multi** This syntax is valid for IDE, ESDI, and SCSI drives, and relies on standard BIOS calls to locate and load the files necessary to start Windows XP. This is by far the most common boot syntax.

- **scsi** This syntax directs the Ntldr boot loader to load a SCSI device driver to access the boot partition and the files necessary to boot the operating system.

- **signature** This syntax is for Plug and Play systems with SCSI drives in which the SCSI adapter number can vary each time the system is booted.

In addition to one of these three keywords, the boot entry includes information that specifies the controller, disk, and other information. The structure for a multi-syntax boot line is

multi(W)disk(X)rdisk(Y)partition(Z)

Table 2-1 lists the description of the variable values.

Variable	Description
W	Number of the adapter, usually 0
X	Physical disk, always 0
Y	Logical disk number, value from 0 to 3
Z	Partition number

TABLE 2-1 Multi Syntax Variables

Following are two examples. The first specifies partition 1 on adapter 0, disk 0, and logical disk 0. The second specifies partition 3 on the same disk:

```
multi(0)disk(0)rdisk(0)partition(1)\WINDOWS="Microsoft Windows XP Profes-
sional" /fastdetect
multi(0)disk(0)rdisk(0)partition(3)\WINDOWS="Windows Server 2003,
Enterprise" /fastdetect
```

The syntax for scsi and signature boot entries are the same, with the exception of the W variable. Table 2-2 describes the variables.

Variable	Description
W	Host adapter number
X	Physical disk number
Y	Logical Unit Number (LUN), usually 0
Z	Partition number

TABLE 2-2   scsi Syntax Variables

For signature syntax, the W variable is the hexadecimal value written during Setup that identifies the disk. The signature value is stored in the Master Boot Record on the disk.

NOTE   *Windows XP uses signature syntax only if the system or boot BIOS doesn't support Extended INT13, and only if the target disk is larger than 7.8GB or the ending cylinder number is larger than 1,024.*

The data in quotes on the line to the right of the = sign in an [operating systems] boot entry specifies the text that the system displays in the boot menu. You can include additional switches after this text string. For example, a default Windows XP boot entry includes the /FASTDETECT switch, which disables serial mouse detection for all COM ports (this can speed up the boot process). Table 2-3 lists all of the switches you can use in a Boot.ini boot entry.

The easiest way to modify Boot.ini is to click Edit on the Startup and Recovery dialog box, which removes the read-only attribute from the file and opens the file in Notepad. The safest way to add boot entries is to copy and paste an existing entry.

TIP   *You can use the BOOTCFG command from a Windows XP command console to modify a Boot.ini file remotely. Open a console and execute the command BOOTCFG /? to learn more about Bootcfg.*

Configuring Error Reporting

The Advanced tab of the System Properties dialog box includes a button labeled Error Reporting that when clicked, displays the Error Reporting dialog box shown in Figure 2-8. You can use the options on this dialog box to configure how Windows XP handles error reporting to Microsoft.

By default, when a system error or Microsoft application error occurs, Windows XP will display a dialog box asking if you want it to report the error to Microsoft. Windows collects some useful information about the error and forwards it to Microsoft over the Internet automatically. No personal information is transmitted.

Switch	Purpose
/3GB	Increases user mode memory from 2GB to 3GB by moving kernel and executive components to the 3GB memory location.
/BASEVIDEO	Starts Windows XP with a standard VGA driver; useful when Windows XP fails to boot because of a faulty video driver.
/BAUDRATE=*nnnn*	Specifies the baud rate for debugging through the COM ports. Use in combination with the /DEBUG switch.
/BOOTLOG	Logs boot results to %systemroot%\ntbtlogl.txt.
/BURNMEMORY=*n*	Limits the amount of physical memory Windows XP can use.
/CRASHDEBUG	Loads debugger at boot but keeps it inactive until a kernel error occurs.
/DEBUG	Loads the debugger and allows it to be activated by any connected host debugger.
/DEBUGPORT=COM*n*	Specifies the COM port for debugging.
/EXECUTE	Starts Windows XP with Data Execution Prevention disabled. See Chapter 4 for a discussion of this setting.
/FASTDETECT	Disables serial mouse detection for all ports.
/FASTDETECT=COM*n*	Disables serial mouse detection for the specified port.
/MAXMEM:*n*	Specifies the maximum amount of RAM that Windows XP can use.
/NOEXECUTE	Enables Data Execution Prevention to prevent code from running in areas of memory not marked as executable.
/NOGUIBOOT	Hides the startup bitmap during boot.
/NODEBUG	Turns off debugging.
/NUMPROC=*n*	Forces a multiprocessor system to use a specified number of CPUs.
/PCILOCK	Prevents Windows XP from assigning IRQ and I/O resources dynamically to PCI devices (the BIOS assigns these resources).
/SAFEBOOT:*switch*	Force Windows XP to boot in safe mode using the specified *switch*. The value of *switch* can be *minimal*, *network*, or *minimal(alternateshell)*.
/SOS	Displays device drivers as they are loaded during the boot process.
/PAE	Enables Windows XP to support systems that use Physical Address Extension mode, which allows software to use more than 4GB of physical memory.

TABLE 2-3   Boot.ini Switches

Through the Error Reporting dialog box you can disable error reporting (if you don't want to be bothered with pop-up messages when errors occur), or specify which items are reported. For example, you can clear the Programs option if you only want to report operating system errors. Or, you can click Choose Programs to open a dialog box you can use to add other applications for reporting (Figure 2-9).

FIGURE 2-8   Use the Error Reporting dialog box to set error reporting options.

Group policy is a better alternative if you need to configure error reporting on a large number of computers. Use the Group Policy console to set policies in the Computer Configuration\Administrative Templates\System\Error Reporting branch. In addition to specifying the same settings as those I described previously, you can also change the

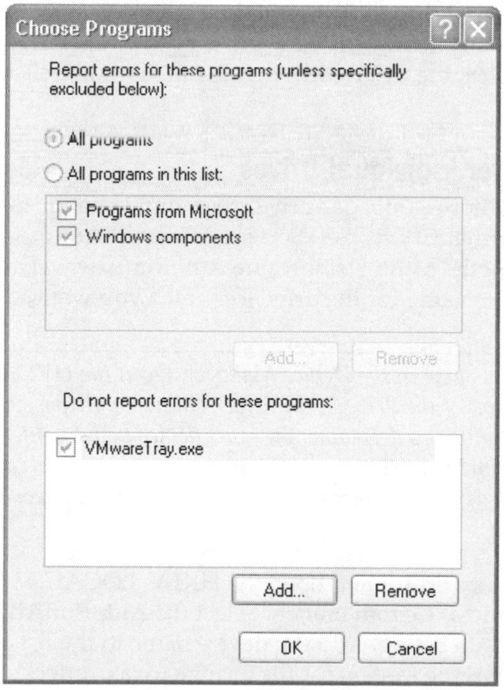

FIGURE 2-9   You can add to the list of programs for which Windows XP will report errors.

user's interaction with error reporting. For example, the Display Error Notification policy, if disabled, prevents the user from receiving notification when an error occurs. If the Report Errors policy is then enabled, the error reporting occurs essentially in the background without any interaction with the user.

TIP *Browse the policies in the Error Reporting branch to learn more about individual policies.*

Controlling CD Autoplay

When you insert a CD in a Windows XP computer, in most cases the CD will automatically play. Insert a music CD, for example, and Media Player begins playing the CD. In addition, many application CDs automatically launch a setup program when they autoplay.

Although you can bypass CD autoplay by holding down the SHIFT key on the keyboard while inserting the CD, you might prefer to turn off autoplay altogether. You can do so globally for all CD drives or control it on a drive-by-drive basis.

Managing Autoplay Globally

If you want to disable Autorun altogether for all CD-ROM drives, you'll have to edit the registry. Open Regedit and open the branch HKEY_LOCAL_MACHINE\System\ CurrentControlSet\Services\Cdrom. The Autorun value determines whether or not Windows XP automatically plays CDs. Set the value to 1 to enable autorun or 0 to disable autorun. Close the Registry Editor and restart the system. Now when you insert a CD, Windows XP won't take any action; instead, you'll need to open the CD yourself. Open My Computer and double-click the CD-ROM's drive icon. Or, right-click the icon and choose AutoPlay.

Managing Autoplay for Individual Drives

If you want to control Autorun on a per-drive basis, don't change the HKEY_LOCAL_ MACHINE\System\CurrentControlSet\Services\Cdrom\Autorun value. Instead, leave Autorun set to 1 and edit the Multi String value AutoRunAlwaysDisable from the same branch, adding the device name for the drive for which you want to disable Autorun.

TIP *You can find the drive name in the Device Manager. Open the DVD/CD-ROM drives branch, then note the listed name of the drive. If the drive contains multiple spaces or other characters that make it difficult for you to determine the exact device name, configure a text-only printer to print to a file. Then with the DVD/CD-ROM drives branch selected, choose Action, and then Print. Print the selected class to a text file, open the text file in Notepad, and copy the device string to the Clipboard.*

Next, open the Registry Editor and open the HKEY_LOCAL_MACHINE\System\ CurrentControlSet\Services\Cdrom branch. Select the AutoRunAlwaysDisable value and choose Edit, and then Multi String. Add the device name to the list and click OK. Close the Registry Editor and restart the system for the change to take effect.

Keeping Your System Current

I n this chapter you'll find the answers to the following questions:

- Where do I go to get updates for Windows XP? Do I really need them?
- Is Windows Update the only way to update a Windows XP computer?
- How can I download updates to install on more than one computer?
- What is a "hotfix"?
- What is a "service pack"?
- Can I install more than one update at the same time?
- I want to create a CD with Windows XP and all available updates. How do I do that?
- How do I configure Windows XP to update itself automatically?
- Is there a way to turn off automatic updates?

Now more than ever, it's important to keep your computer's operating system up to date. Hackers and similar ground-crawling, dirt-eating vermin delight in writing worms and viruses that take advantage of security flaws in Windows and applications such as Outlook and Outlook Express. Although most Linux proponents would rabidly disagree, it isn't that Windows is a significantly less secure operating system than, for example, Linux. Instead, Windows is a much more inviting target because it is more widely deployed.

When a new vulnerability is discovered, Microsoft rapidly issues a patch (software update) to fix the problem leading to the vulnerability. Several times in the last few years viruses or worms have attempted to exploit Windows system vulnerabilities after patches were released by Microsoft. Those systems that were left unpatched were typically infected, while those that were patched remained unaffected.

The amount of money individuals and companies spend trying to recover from these attacks is very real, and the risks and the costs associated with running unpatched systems will only continue to grow. Making sure your systems are up to date is and will continue to be one of the most important things you can do to ensure that your computers continue to work as they should. One of the easiest ways to make sure your systems are up to date is to use Windows Update, which is integrated with the Windows XP operating system. This chapter explains how to configure and use Windows Update and offers advice on other ways to keep your system updated and protected.

Windows Update

Windows Update is a Microsoft web site that provides an easy means for you to look for and install updates on your system. You'll find the site at http://windowsupdate.microsoft.com (Figure 3-1).

TIP *If you're looking for a way to simplify the installation process for Windows XP by incorporating all of the updates in the Setup process, see the section in this chapter "Creating a Slipstream Installation for Windows XP."*

When you visit the Windows Update site, an ActiveX control is installed automatically on your system. The ActiveX control (an Internet Explorer add-on) gathers information about your system including the following:

- Operating-system version number
- Internet Explorer version number
- Version numbers of other software for which Windows Update provides updates
- Plug and Play ID numbers of hardware devices
- Region and Language setting
- Product ID and Product Key

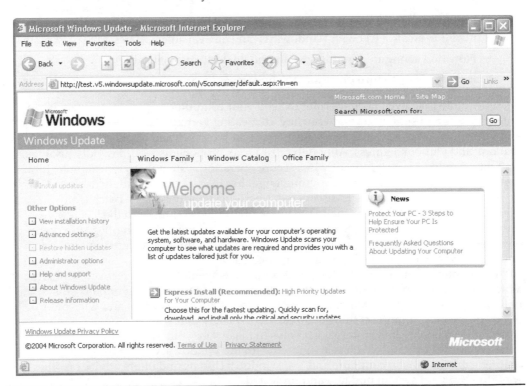

FIGURE 3-1   Use the Windows Update web site to keep your system updated.

Although Windows Update doesn't collect personal or identifying information such as your e-mail address, it does review your Windows XP Product ID and Product Key to determine if you are running a valid copy of Windows. This is one of the methods Microsoft uses to try to reduce software piracy. If your copy of Windows isn't valid, you can't download updates from the Windows Update site. Microsoft records the Product ID and Product Key only if it proves to be invalid. Otherwise, all gathered information persists only during the session.

TIP   Like most anti-piracy mechanisms, Windows Update isn't ironclad. There is nothing to prevent someone from downloading updates from the Windows Update Catalog (covered later in this section) from a system with a valid copy of Windows XP and installing those updates on other systems without valid copies.

Using Windows Update

It isn't difficult at all to update your system with Windows Update. Point Internet Explorer to http://windowsupdate.microsoft.com, which will redirect your browser to the current Windows Update site. If the ActiveX control hasn't been installed on your system, or a newer version is available, you'll be prompted to install the control (Figure 3-2).

After the ActiveX control is installed, you can choose between two installation methods:

- **Express Install**   Choose this option to have Windows Update scan only for critical and security updates. The resulting page lists the updates that Windows Update will install when you click the Install button on the page.

- **Custom Install**   Choose this option to scan for optional updates as well as critical and security updates (Figure 3-3).

NOTE   The Express Install option simply scans for updates and installs them on your computer.

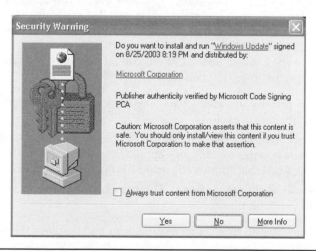

FIGURE 3-2   Windows Update will prompt you to install its ActiveX control.

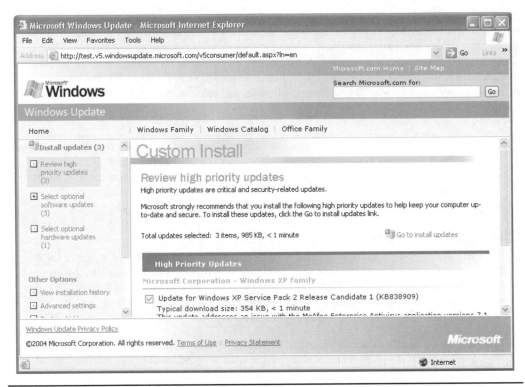

FIGURE 3-3   You can review updates before installing them.

Some updates require your computer to reboot, while others can be installed without a reboot. So, while Windows XP isn't quite as good as Windows Server 2003 when it comes to installing without rebooting, you can generally install a relatively large number of updates without a reboot in between. If an update must be installed separately, Windows Update lets you know that. You can deselect that one update, install the others, and then connect to Windows Update again to install the one you bypassed.

When you choose the Custom Install option, you'll find that Windows Update offers three categories of updates in the left pane:

- **Review high priority updates**   This category includes updates that address bugs and security, including exploits.

- **Selection optional software updates**   This category includes updates that are not critical, such as updates to accessory applications that come with Windows XP, Media Player, and other improvements to the operating system.

- **Select optional hardware updates**   This category contains updated drivers for hardware in your computer.

Windows Update scans all three of these categories and displays the results of the scan in the left pane as shown in Figure 3-3. Windows Update only selects the items in the first category, however. If you want to review and install the other items, click the category link to view the items identified by Windows Update. Review the list and place a check beside each item you want to install. Then, click the Go to Install Updates link to start the installation.

Obtaining Updates for Multiple Systems

Many users, particularly IT administrators, need an easy way to install updates for multiple computers without using Windows Update from each one. The Windows Update Catalog serves just that purpose. It gives you the capability to scan for updates for specific operating systems and download those updates without installing them. You can then use those downloaded files to deploy the updates to multiple computers or integrate the updates into slipstream installations, covered later in this chapter in the section "Creating a Slipstream Installation for Windows XP."

You access the Windows Update Catalog through the Windows Update web site. Click Administrator Options in the left pane, then click the URL under the Windows Update Catalog description to navigate to the Windows Update Catalog (Figure 3-4).

The Windows Update Catalog lets you search for operating system updates and driver updates. To download operating system updates, click the operating system updates link, choose your operating system version and language, and click Search. The Windows Update Catalog shows the results of the search (Figure 3-5) and you can selectively add them to your download basket.

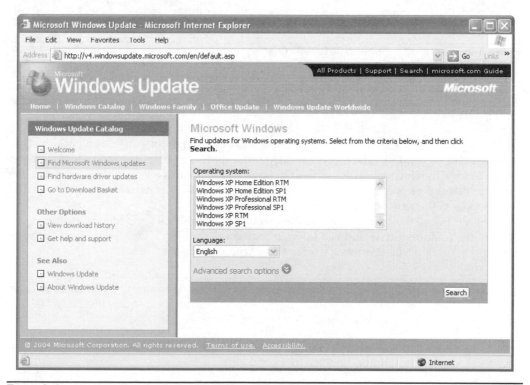

FIGURE 3-4   Use the Windows Update Catalog to download updates to install later or on other systems.

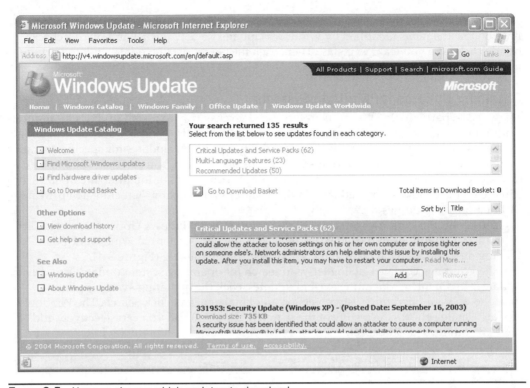

FIGURE 3-5   You can choose which updates to download.

TIP *As with Windows Update, the updates are categorized. Click on a category to view items in that category.*

After you have selected the updates you want from each of the categories, click the Go to Download Basket link. The right pane then prompts you to enter or browse to a folder in which to save the downloads. Windows Update Catalog creates a WU folder in the specified target folder and then creates subfolders within the WU folder as needed to accommodate the updates as they are downloaded.

You can install the updates individually simply by double-clicking an update file. Most of the updates also include an Internet shortcut that, when clicked, navigates to the technical article on Microsoft web site for that particular update.

TIP *See the next section, "Installing Service Packs and Hotfixes," for more information on methods for installing operating system updates, including how to create a slipstream installation of Windows XP that includes all updated files during Setup.*

Installing Service Packs and Hotfixes

The easiest way to install an update is either to let Windows Update install it for you, or to download the update file from the Windows Update Catalog and then double-click the downloaded file. There are other ways to install updates when multiple computers are involved, however, and that's the focus of this section. First, let's take a look at the difference between a service pack and an update.

What Are Service Packs and Hotfixes?

An operating system update, also called a *hotfix*, is one or more files that address a specific issue in Windows XP. For example, when Microsoft identifies a security exploit in Windows, the Windows development team creates one or more updated files that correct the problem. These files are then made available as an update on the Windows Update web site. These updates, therefore, address very specific issues.

A *service pack* is essentially a collection of all updates that have been issued prior to the release of the service pack. In addition, a service pack often incorporates new features developed specifically for the service pack's release, as well as features that have been developed since the operating system's release and that are ready for release when the service pack is ready. So, a service pack is essentially a compilation of all available updates and enhancements for the operating system.

Windows XP service packs are cumulative. For example, Windows XP Service Pack 2 includes all of the upgrades in Service Pack 1. For that reason, you don't need to install SP1 followed by SP2. Instead, you can simply install SP2 on a newly installed version of Windows XP to install all of the updates available at the time of the service pack's release. It's important to understand that installing the latest service pack doesn't necessarily mean your system is completely up to date. Additional updates will be published within a few weeks after a service pack's release, and the process continues. Look to a service pack as a means to install a broad range of updates and feature enhancements in a single operation, not as an alternative to using Windows Update to keep your system current.

Obtaining and Installing a Service Pack

As with individual updates, you have two ways to download a Windows XP service pack. To locate the service packs, navigate to http://www.microsoft.com/windows and click the Downloads link. Then, click the link for your version of Windows XP. The latest service pack should appear on the resulting page (Figure 3-6).

When you click the service pack link, the target page offers two installation methods:

- **Express Installation**   Choose this option if you want updates installed as needed on your computer. You are redirected to the Windows Update Web site, where you can scan for and install updates as I've already explained previously in this chapter in the section, "Windows Update."

- **Network Installation**   This option enables you to download a single file that contains the entire service pack. You can double-click the downloaded file to install the entire service pack on a computer. The advantage to this method is that you can place it on a CD or a network share to enable others to install it on their computers (or for you to install it on multiple computers).

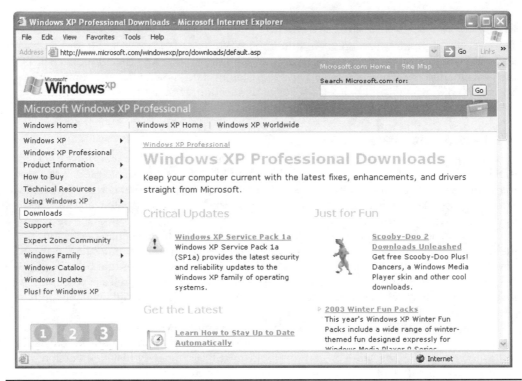

FIGURE 3-6   The main downloads page for your version of Windows XP includes a link to the latest service pack.

The primary reason to use the Express Installation option is if you have already installed several updates on your computer and only want to "top off" with the remaining updates. Use the Network Installation option if you have installed no or few updates on the computer. Also choose the Network Installation option if you want to create a slipstream installation, as explained later in the section "Creating a Slipstream Installation for Windows XP."

TIP   *When you install a service pack, Setup gives you the option of backing up your files so you can later remove the service pack if needed. If you have the available disk space, back up your configuration. Although it hasn't happened often, there have been a couple of instances where a service pack caused more problems for some users than it cured. The Windows NT SP6 is a good example. Microsoft replaced SP6 with SP6a, which addressed a handful of problems in the original service pack release. It's much better to back up the configuration and not need it than to install the service pack without a backup and then regret that you can't uninstall it.*

Identifying and Chaining Hotfixes

Microsoft has developed a couple of tools that will help you identify which updates are installed on a computer and help you deploy needed updates. The first of these tools is Qfecheck.exe, available from http://support.microsoft.com/default.aspx?scid=kb;EN-

US;282784. You can use Qfecheck to identify which updates have been installed on a computer. Qfecheck can also identify updates that are installed improperly, such as those whose binary file dates don't match the information for the update in the registry. See the aforementioned web site for more details on using Qfecheck.

The second update tool is called Qchain.exe. This tool was developed by Microsoft to simplify installation of multiple updates. Qchain enables you to chain multiple updates together in a single operation, reducing the time needed to update the system because the system needs to only be restarted once during the upgrade process. For complete details on downloading and using Qchain, see http://support.microsoft.com/default. aspx?scid=kb;EN-US;296861.

Creating a Slipstream Installation for Windows XP

A *slipstream* Windows XP installation is one where a service pack and/or multiple updates have been incorporated into the Windows installation files. The benefit to using a slipstream installation is that the updates are incorporated as you install Windows XP. You don't have to install Windows XP, and then install the service pack separately. Depending on your access to the service pack, a slipstream installation can save as much as an hour or more for each Windows XP installation.

You can use a slipstream installation in one of two ways: from a network share or from a bootable CD. In the former, you run Setup from the network share to install Windows XP. In the latter, you create a bootable CD from the slipstream files, and then boot the computer from the CD to install Windows XP.

Follow these steps to create your slipstream files for Windows XP:

1. Download the Network Installation version of the service pack to your hard disk and store the file in the folder XPSP (for XP Service Pack).

2. Open a command console and change to the XPSP folder, then execute the following command, replacing <filename> with the name of the downloaded service pack executable file:

   `<filename>.exe -x`

   Example: `xpsp1a_en_x86.exe -x`

3. When prompted for the folder in which to extract the service pack files, specify the XPSP folder and click OK.

4. Create a folder named XPSlip on your hard disk.

5. Copy the entire contents of your Windows XP CD to the XPSlip folder.

6. Open a command console, switch to the XPSP\Update folder, and execute the following command:

   `Update /s:c:\XPSlip`

7. Replace the path c:\XPSlip with the location of your Windows XP files if you used a different disk or folder name.

8. Update adds the service pack files to your Windows XP source files. Click OK when Setup indicates that it has completed the slipstream installation.

9. If you want to be able to install the slipstreamed version of Windows XP from a CD, create a bootable CD from the XPslip folder. Refer to your CD burning software to learn how to create a bootable CD.

Integrating Hotfixes in a Slipstream Installation

As I mentioned earlier in this chapter, the update publishing process doesn't stop when Microsoft releases a service pack. Microsoft continues to issue updates after the service pack is released, and while these updates will eventually be rolled up into the next service pack, there will generally be at least a year between service packs. For that reason, you might want to incorporate individual updates into your slipstream Windows XP installation in addition to a service pack if you will be installing Windows XP on several computers.

NOTE *Identifying and integrating hotfixes in a slipstream installation requires a lot of planning and work and is really useful only if you need to install Windows XP on many computers. If you only need to install Windows XP on one or a handful of computers, I recommend you create the slipstream installation as I described in the preceding section, "Creating a Slipstream Installation for Windows XP," install Windows XP, and then visit the Windows Update site to install any remaining updates.*

The first step in the process is to identify the updates you will include. Microsoft occasionally publishes update *rollups* that incorporate multiple updates into one package. For example, Microsoft published Update Rollup 1 for Microsoft Windows XP (KB826939) on May 07, 2004, which includes several updates published after Service Pack 1. Rather than install individual updates, you can install the rollup and then install any other applicable updates not included in the rollup.

NOTE *This section assumes you have not installed Service Pack 2, which will incorporate all updates published prior to the release of Service Pack 2.*

Start by visiting the Windows Update Catalog site to identify the updates that are available for your version of Windows XP. Make a list of the updates and then weed out the ones included in the rollup. If you are installing the Update Rollup 1 for Microsoft Windows XP (KB826939), you can omit the following updates from your slipstream installation because they are included in the rollup:

- **323255 MS02-05**   Unchecked Buffer in Windows Help Facility May Allow Attacker to Run Code
- **328310 MS02-07**   Flaw in Windows WM_TIMER Message Handling Can Enable Privilege Elevation
- **329048 MS02-054**   Unchecked Buffer in File Decompression Functions May Allow Attacker to Run Code
- **329115 MS02-050**   Certificate Validation Flaw Might Permit Identity Spoofing
- **329170 MS02-070**   Flaw in SMB Signing May Permit Group Policy to Be Modified

- **329390 MS02-072** Unchecked Buffer in Windows Shell Might Permit System Compromise
- **329441** You Cannot Create a Network Connection After You Restore Windows XP
- **329834 MS02-063** Unchecked Buffer in PPTP Implementation May Permit Denial-of-Service Attacks
- **331953 MS03-01** Flaw in RPC Endpoint Mapper Could Allow Denial of Service Attacks
- **810565** Hyperlinks Open in Internet Explorer Instead of in Default Browser or Help and Support Center
- **810577 MS03-005** Unchecked Buffer in Windows Redirector May Permit Privilege Elevation
- **810833 MS03-001** Unchecked Buffer in the Locator Service Might Permit Code to Run
- **811493 MS03-013** Buffer Overrun in Windows Kernel Message Handling Could Lead to Elevated Privileges
- **811630** HTML Help Update to Limit Functionality When It Is Invoked with the window.showHelp Method
- **814033** Cannot Install Driver Updates from the Windows Update Web Site
- **815021 MS03-007** Unchecked Buffer in Windows Component May Cause Web Server Compromise
- **817606 MS03-024** Buffer Overrun in Windows Could Lead to Data Corruption
- **817287** Windows Update 643 Error and the Catalog Database
- **821557 MS03-027** An Unchecked Buffer in the Windows Shell Could Permit Your System to Be Compromised
- **823559 MS03-023** Buffer Overrun in the HTML Converter Could Allow Code Execution
- **823980 MS03-026** Buffer Overrun in RPC May Allow Code Execution
- **824146 MS03-039** A Buffer Overrun in RPCSS May Allow Code Execution

After you have determined which updates you will install, you can integrate them with the slipstream file set. Visit http://www.microsoft.com/windowsxp/pro/downloads/servicepacks/sp1/hfdeploy.asp for specific instructions on how to incorporate the files.

Removing Service Packs and Updates

Whether you can remove a service pack or not depends on whether you allowed Setup to create a backup when you installed the service pack. If so, you can open the Add or Remove Programs applet in the Control Panel, locate the service pack in the list of installed applications, and click Remove to remove it. However, if you have installed Service Pack 2, you must select the Show Updates option at the top of the Add or Remove Program applets window (Figure 3-7) to view the service pack.

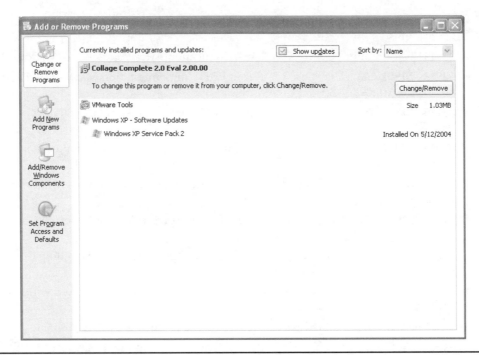

FIGURE 3-7   With Service Pack 2, the service pack and updates do not show unless you click the Show Updates option.

You can also remove updates that you have installed. Locate the update in the Add or Remove Programs applet, select it, and click Remove.

NOTE *In most cases there is no reason to remove a service pack or update. I recommend doing so only if you have been directed to do so by a support technician.*

Managing Automatic Updates

Windows XP offers another mechanism for installing updates, which works automatically. It's called, appropriately, Automatic Updates. The benefit to using Automatic Updates to keep your computer current is that the updates can be downloaded and installed to your computer automatically. This means your computer can stay up to date without any effort on your part.

You configure Automatic Updates from the Automatic Updates dialog box. Figure 3-8 shows the Automatic Updates page for Windows XP Service Pack 1 (SP1) or earlier. To open this tab, open the System applet in the Control Panel and click the Automatic Updates tab. To configure Automatic Updates in Windows XP Service Pack 2 (SP2) or later, open the Automatic Updates applet from the Control Panel. Figure 3-9 shows the resulting Automatic Updates dialog box.

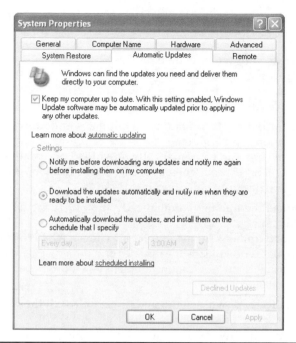

FIGURE 3-8   Use the Automatic Updates tab to configure dynamic updates for your computer.

FIGURE 3-9   Windows XP Service Pack 2 has slightly different Automatic Update options.

Automatic Updates offers four modes. The following list describes the options for the two versions of Automatic Updates (SP1/SP2):

- **SP1   Keep my computer up to date.**
  SP2: Turn off Automatic Updates.
  For SP1, choose this option to enable Automatic Updates. For SP2, choose this option to disable Automatic Updates.

- **SP1   Notify me before downloading any updates and notify me again before installing them on my computer.**
  SP2   Notify me but don't automatically download or install them.
  Windows XP will notify you when updates become available but will not download or install the updates until you direct it to do so.

- **SP1   Download the updates automatically and notify me when they are ready to be installed.**
  SP2   Download updates for me, but let me choose when to install them.
  Automatic Updates downloads the updates and then displays a prompt asking if you want to install them. You can install them when prompted or choose to delay installation until later

- **SP1   Automatically download the updates, and install them on the schedule that I specify.**
  SP2   Automatic. Specify the frequency at which you want Automatic Updates to download and install updates without prompting you. With this option, your computer stays up to date automatically.

Configuring Automatic Updates with Group Policy

Group policy provides a mechanism by which systems running Windows 2000 or later can be configured and managed automatically. You can apply group policy at the local computer level, and if the computer is a member of a Windows 2000 or Windows 2003 domain, you can also apply group policy at the site, domain, and organizational unit levels.

TIP *To learn more about group policy, visit http://www.microsoft.com/windowsserver2003/ technologies/management/grouppolicy/default.mspx.*

Windows Update is one of the many features you can configure with group policy. The policies configure Automatic Updates for two scenarios: using the Windows Update Web site, or using Windows Update Services (WUS). WUS is an add-on for Windows Server 2003 and Windows 2000 Server that enables administrators to make downloads available from an internal server. WUS also gives administrators better control over which updates are available and how they are deployed. Because this book focuses on Windows XP, I cover group policies for WUS but I don't cover Software Update Services (SUS) in detail. Visit http://www.microsoft.com/windowsserversystem/sus/default.mspx to learn more about WUS.

You must add a set of administrative templates to make the Windows Update policies available in the Group Policy console. The following steps assume you are configuring group policy at the local computer. The process is the same if you are using the Group Policy console to edit domain-based policy:

1. Click Start, Run, and enter **GPEDIT.MSC** in the Run dialog box.

2. In the Group Policy console, right-click Computer Configuration\Administrative Templates and choose Add/Remove Templates.

3. Click Add in the Add/Remove Templates dialog box and choose Wuau.adm from the templates listed in the \Windows\Inf folder, and then click Open.

4. Click Close to close the Add/Remove Templates dialog box.

5. Click the Computer Configuration\Administrative Templates\Windows Components\Windows Update branch.

The Windows Update template in Windows XP SP1 or earlier includes four group policies that control system updates:

- **Configure Automatic Updates**   Enable Automatic Updates and configure the option and schedule to be used to download and install updates.

- **Specify intranet Microsoft update service location**   Specify a local server on your intranet as the location from which clients will obtain updates and upload update statistics. See http://www.microsoft.com/windowsserversystem/sus/default.mspx to learn more about SUS and obtain the SUS server and client components. Note that the client component is included with Windows XP SP1.

- **Reschedule Automatic Updates scheduled installations**   Configure the amount of time for Windows XP to wait after a missed scheduled automatic installation.

- **No auto-restart for scheduled Automatic Updates installations**   When this policy is enabled, Automatic Updates will not automatically restart the computer after installing an update that requires a restart. Instead, it prompts the user to restart.

TIP   *To obtain the updated policy template file for Windows XP SP1 systems, visit http://www*
.microsoft.com/downloads/details.aspx?FamilyId=D26A0AEA-D274-42E6-8025-8C667B4C94E
9&displaylang=en.

If you are running Windows XP SP2 or have obtained the updated Automatic Updates template, you'll see some additional policies for Automatic Updates:

- **Enable client-side targeting**   Specify a group name for the computer that will be used by Software Update Services to determine which updates should be installed on the computer. The target SUS server must be configured to support client-side targeting.

- **Automatic Updates detection frequency**   Specify the frequency in hours at which Automatic Updates will check for new updates. The actual update period is this value minus up to 20 percent of the time specified (to randomize the time used by each client and reduce network and server load). The default value is 22 hours if this policy is disabled or not defined.

- **Allow Automatic Updates immediate installation**   If this policy is enabled, Automatic Updates will automatically install all updates that don't interrupt services or require a restart.

- **Delay Restart for scheduled installations**   Specify the wait time after updates are complete before Windows XP is restarted.

- **Re-prompt for restart with scheduled installations**   Specify a period of time after which Automatic Updates will prompt the user to allow a restart if a previous restart was postponed. The default value is ten minutes.

- **Allow non-administrators to receive update notifications**   Enable this policy to allow non-administrators to receive notice of available updates when they are logged on. If the policy is disabled or not configured, only logged-on administrators receive notification.

Other Centralized Update Management Options

In larger organizations, allowing users to update their operating systems on their own is generally not a good idea. First, such a situation places the burden of ensuring up-to-date systems on the users, rather than on administrators, where the burden belongs. Second, it's a good practice to test and evaluate updates before a wide-scale deployment.

Windows Update Services provides what I feel is the best solution for most organizations for rolling out updates to client systems. WUS works in conjunction with group policy to give administrators a good level of control over how and when updates are applied.

However, WUS is not the only tool available to administrators to aid in the deployment of operating system updates. For example, organizations can turn to Systems Management Server (SMS) to deploy operating systems, OS updates, applications, and application patches across the enterprise. SMS, therefore, provides a much broader range of capabilities than WUS, although WUS is still a better choice if OS updates are your main focus.

For more information about SMS, see http://www.microsoft.com/smserver/default.asp.

Windows XP Service Pack 2

In this chapter you'll find the answers to the following questions:

- What is Service Pack 2 (SP2)?
- Will SP2 make changes to any of my Windows XP applications?
- Is there anything new in SP2 for networking?
- How can I make it easier to set up a wireless network?
- If I install SP2, will any of my applications stop working?
- Where do I get SP2?
- I hear that SP2 includes a firewall. What is it?
- I use Windows Messenger a lot. What changes are there in SP2?
- Will SP2 do anything to improve security in Internet Explorer or Outlook Express?

A Windows service pack incorporates bug fixes, security improvements, and feature enhancements with the target operating system. Most of the bug fixes and security improvements in a service pack have typically been released as individual updates prior to the release of the service pack, and are available from the Windows Update web site at http://windowsupdate.microsoft.com. See Chapter 3 for a discussion of Windows Update and other methods for keeping your system current.

Microsoft recently released Windows XP Service Pack 2 (SP2), which includes several new feature changes and enhancements. This chapter explores the new features offered by SP2.

NOTE *This chapter offers an overview of SP2's features. These features are covered in more detail throughout the book where applicable. Look for the SP2 icon in the margin to identify discussion of SP2 features. The changes in SP2 for Tablet PC are fairly significant and are covered in Chapter 10.*

Network Protection

There are several changes and enhancements in SP2 to improve and add security for networking in Windows XP. This section of the chapter explores these new features.

Alerter and Messenger Services

Microsoft has changed the behavior of two networking-related services in SP2: the Alerter and Messenger services. Both of these services are designed to transmit simple messages between computers on a network. The Alerter service is intended for administrative alerts, while the Messenger service is used by applications and services to send messages.

Prior to SP2, the Alerter service is configured for Manual startup and the Messenger service is configured for Automatic startup. In SP2, both of these services are configured as Disabled. The reason for this change is that both of these services, if running, can increase the possibility of a successful attack from a virus or worm. Disabling them by default decreases the number of ports and services that are exposed to the network and subject to possible attack or compromise (also called the *attack surface* of the computer).

Unless you are a developer of an application or a service that requires one of these two services, or you use an application that requires them, this change has no negative consequence. Otherwise, simply configure the services to whatever startup configuration is required by the installed application.

NOTE *The Messenger service and Windows Messenger are two separate services that perform different functions.*

Bluetooth

Bluetooth is a wireless networking standard that targets what Bluetooth developers call Personal Area Networks (PAN). Unlike Wi-Fi and some other wireless technologies, Bluetooth is geared toward connecting devices rather than connection computers. For example, Bluetooth would be a good candidate for connecting your PDA or cell phone with your computer for synchronization, pulling songs from your computer to an MP3 player, transmitting songs from your MP3 player to your car stereo, and so on.

SP2 adds native Bluetooth device support to Windows XP. When Bluetooth support is enabled, you will find changes in the Network Connections folder to accommodate Bluetooth, a Bluetooth Devices applet in the Control Panel for configuring Bluetooth settings, an icon for Bluetooth tasks in the tray, and a Bluetooth File Transfer Wizard in the Accessories\Communications menu.

DCOM Security Enhancements

Distributed Component Object Model (DCOM) enables applications and application components to communicate with one another across a network. SP2 adds new launch and access restrictions to give administrators control over all call, activation, or launch requests on the computer. By default, only administrators have Local Launch, Local Activate, Remote Launch, and Remote Activate authorization on a Windows XP SP2 computer. The built-in Everyone group has only the Local Launch, Local Activate, Local Call, and Remote Call permissions. Anonymous users have only Local Call permission.

Support for local versus remote permissions enables administrators to give local users the necessary permissions with Component Object Model (COM) components and applications while restricting remote access. You can see these permission in the Component Services console. Open the properties for an item under the DCOM Config folder, click the Security tab, and click Edit under the Launch and Activate Permissions or the Access Permissions control groups. The Launch Permissions dialog box (Figure 4-1) shows these new permissions.

RPC Interface Restriction

Remote Procedure Call (RPC) enables a client computer to submit a request to execute a call (application procedure) on a remote server and have the server return the results to the client. The RPC service in Windows XP enables a Windows XP computer to function as an RPC server.

Windows XP SP2 incorporates a handful of changes to the RPC service to improve security and reduce the computer's attack from RPC-based exploits. In particular, the RPC service now provides some measure of control over how clients can initiate RPC requests. You can now add the registry value HKEY_LOCAL_MACHINE\ SOFTWARE\Policies\ Microsoft\Windows NT\RPC\RestrictRemoteClients setting and set it to one of the following three values:

- **0**   This is the default behavior in Windows XP SP1 and earlier. The system bypasses the new interface restrictions added by SP2.

- **1**   This is the default value for SP2. The computer rejects all anonymous RPC calls unless a particular RPC interface registers a security callback and provides the RPC_IF_ALLOW_CALLBACKS_WITH_NO_AUTH flag. The restriction then does not apply to that RPC interface.

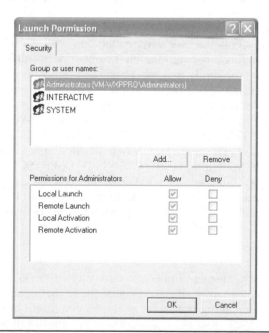

FIGURE 4-1   SP2 supports new permissions for COM components.

- **2**   This value rejects all remote anonymous RCP calls, regardless of the RPC_IF_ ALLOW_CALLBACKS_WITH_NO_AUTH flag. This setting effectively disables anonymous RPC.

NOTE *RPC calls that use the named pipe protocol sequence are exempt from the interface access restrictions.*

Another change in SP2 for RPC is the way remote clients initiate an RPC session. In Windows XP SP1 and earlier, the RPC Endpoint Mapper on the server computer is available through anonymous calls, enabling remote clients to anonymously request an endpoint to initiate a session. The registry setting HKEY_LOCAL_MACHINE\SOFTWARE\Policies\ Microsoft\Windows NT\RPC\EnableAuthEpResolution on the client computer causes the client to use NT LAN Manager (NTLM) authentication to request an endpoint from the RPC server. Set this value to 1 to enable authentication or to 0 to use anonymous calls to the Endpoint Mapper on the RPC server.

WebDAV Redirector

Web-based Distributed Authoring and Versioning (WebDAV) is a standard that defines extensions to HTTP, which enable users to remotely and collaboratively edit and manage files stored on a server that supports WebDAV. For example, Microsoft Windows SharePoint Services 2003 supports WebDAV. The WebDAV redirector in Windows XP is the operating system component that enables Windows XP systems to access WebDAV shares as if they were standard Server Message Block (SMB) remote shares, such as file shares hosted by a file server.

A potential security risk in Windows XP SP1 and earlier is that if the server is configured to support basic authentication, the user's credentials could be transmitted across the network in clear text, enabling any computer on the network to sniff those credentials. Windows XP SP2 adds the capability to disable basic authentication for the WebDAV redirector. If basic authentication is disabled, Windows XP SP2 either uses a different authentication method if it's supported by the server or fails the request.

If you need to enable basic authentication, add the registry DWORD setting HKEY_ LOCAL_MACHINE\SYSTEM\CurrentControlSet\Services \WebClient\Parameters\ UseBasicAuth and set it to 1. The default value of 0 disables basic authentication. You can also use the registry DWORD setting HKEY_CURRENT_USER\SOFTWARE\Microsoft\ Windows\CurrentVersion\Internet Settings\DisableBasicOverClearChannel, set to a value of 1, to disable basic authentication over nonsecure channels. With this option set to 1, basic authentication is supported only for Hypertext Transfer Protocol over Secure Socket Layer (HTTPS) and Secure Socket Layer (SSL).

Windows Firewall

You might be familiar with Internet Connection Firewall (ICF) in Windows XP SP1 and earlier. This simple firewall enables you to configure filters that control which ports are exposed and can receive incoming traffic. For example, you might block all ports except 80 (HTTP), 53 (DNS), 110 (POP3), and 443 (SSL) to allow a computer to browse the Web and retrieve e-mail from a Post Office Protocol3 (POP3) server but nothing else. ICF is disabled by default, which means it does not block any incoming traffic until you enable and configure it.

In Windows XP SP2, Windows Firewall replaces ICF (Figure 4-2). Unlike ICF, Windows Firewall is enabled by default on all interfaces when you install SP2. There are several other changes in Windows Firewall, described in the following sections.

TIP *To configure Windows Firewall on a network interface, open the Network Connections folder, right-click the interface, and choose Properties. Then, click the Advanced tab and click Settings. For details on configuring the firewall, see the section "Using a Firewall" in Chapter 12. Chapter 17 also offers tips on configuring a firewall to work with Remote Assistance and Remote Desktop Connection.*

Boot-Time Security

During the boot process, a computer can be open to attack even when a local firewall application is installed. This window of opportunity is open between the time the system loads and initializes its network drivers and when the firewall is started. SP2 addresses this potential problem by providing a boot-time firewall configuration that blocks all but the most basic network traffic (such as Domain Name System (DNS), Dynamic Host Configuration Protocol (DHCP), and application of group policy). These boot-time filters

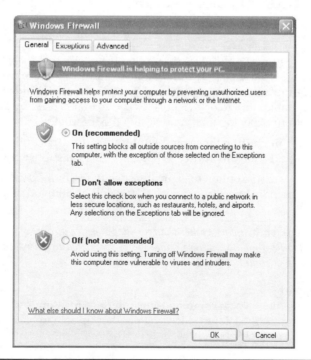

FIGURE 4-2   Windows Firewall replaced ICF in SP2.

are enabled when the Windows Firewall is enabled. If Windows Firewall is disabled, Windows XP provides no boot-time firewall filtering.

NOTE   *Boot-time firewall filtering cannot be modified. After the boot process is complete and the Windows Firewall service is started, the boot-time filters are unloaded and the regular filters, which can be modified, are loaded.*

Global Configuration

Prior to SP2, the ICF supported separate configurations per the type of network interface. For example, a wireless connection would have a separate firewall configuration from a LAN interface. Changes made to one interface did not affect the other, which potentially made it difficult for users, particularly novices, to configure a consistent and secure firewall setup.

SP2 provides global configuration for all network interfaces in Windows Firewall. When you add an interface, that interface takes on the configuration of the existing interface. A change to the global configuration affects all interfaces. However, you can still make changes on a per-interface basis if needed.

Local Subnet Restriction

A *subnet* is a segment of an IP network. An example of a range of addresses in a common private subnet is 192.168.0.1 through 192.168.0.254. If yours is a small network, you likely only have one subnet. Larger networks often have several subnets. All of the computers in a subnet form a logical group for routing network traffic.

SP2 adds the capability to restrict incoming traffic to one of three sources for any particular interface:

- **My network (subnet) only**   Use this option to specify that incoming traffic for a specified port is allowed only if the traffic comes from a computer on the same subnet as your own (such as in your workgroup or in your Active Directory domain). This option enables you to open a port for traffic that is used by computers on your network without exposing that same port to the Internet.

- **Any computer (including those on the Internet)**   Use this option to allow incoming traffic on the port from any source, whether it's a local subnet or the Internet.

- **Custom list**   Use this option to explicitly specify the individual computers, range of IP addresses, or subnets from which traffic will be allowed on the specified port.

TIP   *You configure scope for each port, rather than for the interface as a whole. This means that some ports can receive traffic from any address, some can be restricted to your local subnet, and some can be restricted to a custom list, as needed.*

Command-Line Support

Microsoft introduced a new Netsh command-line interface for Windows Firewall with the Advanced Networking Pack. SP2 introduces yet another update to Netsh to enable you to configure Windows Firewall for both IPv4 and IPv6 traffic.

On with No Exceptions Mode

This mode directs Windows Firewall to close any static holes (opened ports) and drop all connections through those ports. This mode has the effect of dropping all unsolicited incoming traffic and essentially locking down the interface without having to actually reconfigure ports. Changes made to the configuration in this mode are stored but not applied until the firewall is set back to the standard On state.

Windows Firewall Exception Lists

Many server applications must listen for incoming traffic from all remote hosts on a broad range of ports because the server application does not know the location of the client and, in some cases, does not know what port the client will use. It can be difficult to configure a firewall to support these situations and still maintain security.

SP2 addresses this problem by providing per-application exception lists. An application on the exception list can listen on the network for incoming traffic even if the target port is blocked for incoming traffic. Windows can then open ports as needed for the application, and do so regardless of the security context of the application (for example, the application need not run in the context of the administrator account). The benefit to this new structure is that Windows controls the ports rather than the application. If the application hangs, Windows can still close the ports.

Multiple Profiles

If you work with a portable computer, it's likely that you have different needs for firewall protection depending on your current connection to the network. For example, if your computer sits behind a corporate firewall when you are in the office, you probably don't need your own firewall. At the very least, you don't need as strict a configuration as you do when your computer is connected to a public network.

Support for multiple profiles in SP2's Windows Firewall enables you to specify different firewall configurations for different situations. However, your computer must be a domain member to use multiple profiles. Workgroup computers have a single profile.

RPC Support

ICF prior to SP2 does not allow RPC traffic, which is required for services such as file and print sharing, remote administration, and others. Windows Firewall with SP2 treats RPC differently. An RPC server application can request that Windows Firewall open the necessary ports as long as the application is running in the Local System, Network Service, or Local Service security contexts. In addition, you can configure the RPC application on the exceptions list to enable it to accept incoming traffic on dynamic ports.

Restore Defaults and Unattended Setup

Windows Firewall in SP2 gives you the capability to easily restore the firewall configuration to its default, out-of-the box configuration. This simplifies the task of resetting the firewall to its default settings. You can also modify the default settings.

In addition to allowing you to specify the default firewall configuration, Windows Firewall also allows you to specify the desired custom firewall configuration during an unattended installation. You can configure the operational mode, applications on the exception list, static ports on the exception list, Internet Control Message Protocol (ICMP) options, and logging.

Group Policy Support

An important consideration for enterprise users and administrators is the capability to control Windows Firewall with group policy. Previously, ICF was supported by only one group policy, which disabled the firewall for the client computer's DNS domain. Windows Firewall in SP2, however, can be fully configured by group policy, enabling administrators to control the firewall on a granular level (site, domain, organizational unit, or local).

TIP *See "Configuring Windows Firewall with Group Policy" in Chapter 12 for detailed information on controlling the firewall with group policy.*

Other Changes

Windows Firewall introduces a handful of other changes as well as those I've already described. For example, Windows Firewall will allow a unicast response for three seconds on the same port from which the multicast or broadcast traffic came. This change makes it possible for applications and services to alter firewall policy as necessary to accommodate client/server scenarios that use multicast and broadcast traffic without unnecessarily exposing ports.

In addition, Windows Firewall now supports IPv4 and IPv6 traffic through a single service, which simplifies firewall configuration—you don't have to configure two separate groups of settings. The user interface has also been simplified and enhanced to make it easier to configure the firewall settings.

Windows Media Player

SP2 automatically installs Windows Media Player version 9 (Figure 4-3), which incorporates several feature and security improvements. If you install SP2 on an existing Windows XP installation, Setup backs up the current version and enables you to remove version 9 after SP2 installation is complete. If you install SP2 as part of a new installation over an existing Windows XP installation, you will not be able to remove version 9 and restore the previous version.

TIP *See "Getting the Most from Media Player" in Chapter 7 for more details on using Windows Media Player and learning how to back up licenses prior to installing SP2.*

Windows Messenger

SP2 introduces a handful of changes to Windows Messenger, the online chat and desktop conferencing application included with Windows XP. First, Windows Messenger with SP2 blocks file transfers if the sender is not on your Contacts list and the file is on the unsafe file list maintained by Internet Explorer 6 (and also used by Outlook Express). If the sender is on your Contacts list, Windows Messenger prompts you to decide what action (open or save) to take with the file based on the file type.

TIP *See "Windows Messenger" in Chapter 7 to learn more about the new features in Windows Messenger and how to configure the unsafe file list.*

FIGURE 4-3 Windows Media Player supports streaming audio, video, and other multimedia playback.

Another change in Windows Messenger is that it requires a user display name that is different from the user's e-mail address. This change helps mitigate the possibility that a virus could extract the e-mail address from the text files that store your conversations (if you save them). In addition, because Windows Firewall is enabled by default, you must configure it to allow Windows Messenger traffic (although the default Windows Firewall configuration places Windows Messenger on the exceptions list).

Wireless Networking Improvements

Not too many years ago, wireless networks were few and far between. Now, you can hook your PDA or notebook into a wireless hot spot in the mall's food court, airports, coffee shops, hotel lobbies, and many other places. Windows XP greatly simplified wireless networking; SP2 adds even more refinements.

Wireless Provisioning Services

Wireless Provisioning Services in SP2 integrates with changes being introduced in Windows Server 2003 SP1 to simplify wireless client network setup and access. These changes not only simplify identification and signup for wireless hotspots, but they also provide better security by integrating authentication and encryption in the connection process. Wireless Provisioning Services also enables information about wireless networks and hotspots to be updated automatically, which makes it easy for you to connect to a newly added hotspot if you already have an account with a wireless provider.

Wireless Network Setup Wizard

SP2 adds a Wireless Network Setup wizard that helps users configure wireless devices. The wizard stores the information as XML data on a removable device such as a Universal Serial Bus (USB) flash drive, and you migrate the settings to the other computers on the network with that removable device. You can print the data for configuring those devices that don't support the automatic XML-based configuration from the wizard's data.

Memory Exploit Protection

Many viruses and worms use a common exploit to run malicious code on a computer: executing code in nonexecutable memory locations. Newer processors from Intel and AMD provide the capability to mark virtual memory pages as executable. When an application attempts to run code in a nonexecutable area of memory, a processor exception occurs.

Applications and drivers that generate code dynamically and do not mark code with execute permissions will generate an exception error and the process will fail. This means that it is possible that some applications will not work properly after SP2 is installed. To overcome that problem temporarily, you can use one of two switches to start Windows XP:

- **/NOEXECUTE**   This switch starts Windows XP with data execution prevention (DEP) enabled. Code attempting to run from pages not marked as executable will fail.

- **/EXECUTE**   This switch starts Windows XP with data execution prevention disabled (similar to Windows XP SP1 and earlier). Use this switch if you have several applications that fail to work properly with SP2.

You can also use compatibility settings to enable a single application to disable DEP, which enables Windows XP SP2 to run with DEP enabled for all other applications.

TIP   *You'll find additional information about the Application Compatibility Toolkit at http://www .microsoft.com/windows/appcompatibility/default.mspx.*

Outlook Express Improvements

Windows XP SP2 makes a few changes in Outlook Express to reduce spam, provide better handling of HTML messages, and provide improved attachment checking for applications that interact with Outlook Express.

To help reduce spam, Outlook Express includes a new feature that blocks external Hypertext Markup Language (HTML) content until you explicitly download it (Figure 4-4). Some spammers include links to remote content in messages so that when you view the message, that content is downloaded from the server and your e-mail address is verified as

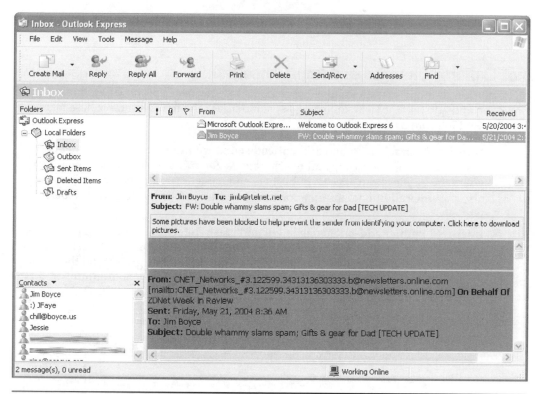

FIGURE 4-4   Outlook Express, like Outlook 2003, blocks web beacons (external HTML content).

valid. Blocking the external content prevents those spammers from validating your e-mail address. You can configure Outlook Express to allow external content downloads, if you prefer.

TIP   *Blocking external content can also reduce online time. When you are viewing a message offline with Outlook Express in SP2, it will not try to connect to the Internet to retrieve the HTML content.*

You can configure Outlook Express to render received messages using plain text, which helps eliminate the possibility of HTML script exploits. In SP2, Outlook Express makes it easier to view safe HTML messages when plain text mode is enabled. You can click on a message and choose View, Message in HTML to render the message using HTML.

Finally, Outlook Express includes an Attachment Execution Service Application Programming Interface (API) that supports attachment checking for Outlook Express as well as external applications. So, applications that need to check an attachment in your Outlook Express mail store can call the AES API rather than incorporate code within the application itself to accomplish the same task. The AES API is, therefore, targeted at developers rather than end users.

Tip   *See Chapter 15 to learn more about SP2 features in Outlook Express.*

Internet Explorer Changes and Improvements

SP2 incorporates many changes and enhancements for Internet Explorer (IE) to improve browsing and add security. The following list summarizes the new features. These features are explored in more detail in Chapter 14.

- **Download, attachment, and authenticode enhancements**   SP2 makes changes to IE to make downloading and file checking safer and more consistent, enabling you to block files from specific publishers and have IE prompt you for others. IE also provides additional information about add-on publishers to help you decide whether to install an add-on.

- **Internet Explorer add-on management and crash detection**   SP2 adds an interface for viewing and managing IE add-ons (Figure 4-5). IE also attempts to detect crashes caused by add-ons and displays that information if possible, giving you the chance to block the add-on. SP2 adds a handful of group policies to enable administrators to configure these settings.

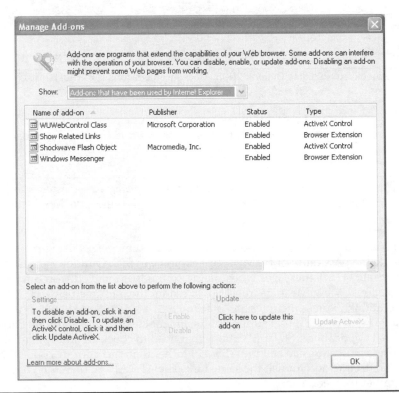

Figure 4-5   IE provides an interface for viewing and managing add-ons.

TIP *See http://www.boyce.us/gp for a searchable database of group policy settings.*

- **Internet Explorer binary behaviors security setting** Binary behaviors are a feature introduced in IE 5.x that enable site developers to build functions for the Web that can modify HTML tags and resulting behavior—without exposing the underlying code on the page as a script. By default, IE blocks binary behaviors in the Restricted Sites zone.

- **Internet Explorer BindToObject mitigation** SP2 applies the ActiveX security model to all cases where URL binding is used to create an instance of and to initialize an object. This change helps mitigate several IE exploits.

- **Internet Explorer Information Bar** This new IE interface element appears between the toolbars and web page area of the browser and displays information related to security, pop-up blocking, and similar warning and status information (Figure 4-6). The Information Bar becomes hidden again when you navigate away from the page that generated the error or warning.

- **Internet Explorer feature control security zone settings** SP2 adds a handful of additional settings to IE to help prevent certain exploits, These include mime sniffing, which enables IE to detect file type based on bit signature rather than file extension; changes to prevent privilege elevation; and the restriction of script-initiated pop-up windows. These settings can be configured on a zone-by-zone basis as well as through group policy.

- **Internet Explorer settings in group policy** Several new group policy settings are added to enable administrators to control security settings in IE across the enterprise.

Information bar

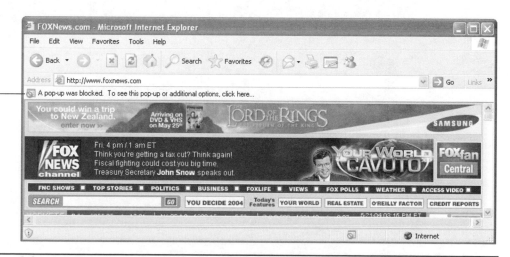

FIGURE 4-6 The Information Bar displays messages related to security, content blocking, and other information.

- **Internet Explorer local machine zone lockdown**   SP2 imposes additional security restrictions on the local machine zone to help mitigate exploits that attempt to elevate privileges and gain access to the local file system and other resources.

- **Internet Explorer MIME handling enforcement**   SP2 adds features to IE that help prevent Multipurpose Internet Mail Extension (MIME)–related exploits. For example, IE now performs additional checks before it will open a served file and will not elevate the privileges of the file if the MIME type's registered application is unable to load the file. IE can also now employ MIME sniffing to determine file type based on bit signature rather than file extension.

- **Internet Explorer object caching**   IE with SP2 no longer allows a page to access objects cached from another site. This change helps prevent the exposure of user data to malicious sites.

- **Internet Explorer pop-up blocker**   SP2 adds a pop-up blocker to IE that blocks background and automatic (scripted) pop-ups but allows pop-ups from clicked links (Figure 4-7). The pop-up blocker is on by default but can be disabled, user customized, and controlled by group policy. IE always blocks pop-ups that are larger than or outside of the viewable desktop.

- **Internet Explorer untrusted publishers mitigations**   IE with SP2 now offers users the capability to block all signed content from specific publishers. This feature blocks the content without repeated prompts and also blocks the installation of code without valid signatures.

Figure 4-7   IE now includes a built-in pop-up blocker.

- **Internet Explorer window restrictions**   IE with SP2 imposes restrictions on the capability to open windows outside of the viewable area of the desktop. These changes help protect against malicious sites that attempt to hide site content from the user. In addition, the status bar is always enabled for all windows.

- **Internet Explorer zone elevation blocks**   IE with SP2 prevents the security context for any link on a page from being higher than the overall security context of the root URL. This feature also blocks JavaScript navigation where the security context is absent.

Windows XP Configuration and Setup Changes

SP2 incorporates several changes that affect Windows XP setup, configuration, and updates. The following list provides an overview of these features, which are covered in more detail throughout this book where applicable:

- **Filter for Add or Remove Programs**   Windows XP with SP2 adds a check box to the Add or Remove Programs applet that enables the user to decide whether service packs and updates appear in the list of installed components. By default, service packs and updates are hidden. You can disable this feature with a registry value or group policy setting.

- **Microsoft Windows Update Services and Automatic Updates**   Microsoft has added support for deploying driver updates and updates to Office applications, SQL Server, and Exchange Server with the Windows XP Automatic Updates feature. This feature works in conjunction with Windows Update Services running on Windows Server 2003.

TIP See Chapter 3 for a complete discussion of Windows Update. See http://www.microsoft.com/ windowsserversystem/sus/wusbeta.mspx for information about Windows Update Services.

- **Resultant Set of Policy (RSoP)**   RSoP enables administrators to view the result of group policy settings that are applied to a user or group for a selected computer. The Group Policy Management Console (GPMC) can request RSoP information from a target computer to display the resultant policies. Because Windows Firewall is enabled by default on SP2, you must make a few changes to support RSoP data across the network. See "Management Changes for SP2" in Chapter 13 for details on resolving this issue.

- **Security Center**   The Security Center applet in the Control Panel provides a single location from which users can view security-related configuration information and access settings for Windows Firewall and Automatic Updates. Security Center can also detect if an antivirus application is installed and notify you of the antivirus application status. See "Using and Controlling the Security Center" in Chapter 12 for details.

- **Setup**   SP2 Setup incorporates several new switches for the Update.exe package installer. See Chapter 3 for a discussion of these switches.

- **Windows Installer 3.0**   SP2 includes version 3.0 of the Windows Installer service, which is a standard mechanism for installing applications. See Chapter 3 for a discussion of the changes in Windows Installer 3.0.

General Troubleshooting

In this chapter you'll find the answers to the following questions:

- I don't know anything about troubleshooting. Where do I start?
- How can I avoid problems before they occur?
- Windows XP won't boot! How do I get it to start again?
- I've heard there is a "safe mode" in Windows XP. How can I use it?
- I added a new device and now Windows XP won't work. How do I disable it?
- Can I restore Windows XP to the way it was a week or two ago?
- Is there anything I should do before I install a new piece of hardware or program?
- How can I tell what is wrong with my computer when it starts acting up?
- My system flashes a blue screen, then reboots. What is the blue screen and how can I view it?
- Is there any way to repair Windows XP or do I have to reinstall it if a major problem happens?

The best course to take with computers, as in life, is to stay out of trouble in the first place. But like life, computers don't come with a guarantee that nothing will ever go wrong. Frequently, things do go awry. That's when it pays to have a plan to get out of trouble.

Windows XP provides some very useful tools for recovering the system and working through problems when they occur. In some cases, just maintaining a current log of what changes you've made to the system can be invaluable in recovering from a system problem. In other cases, tools such as Restore Points and the Recovery Console can save the day.

In this chapter, we explain common troubleshooting methods and tools that will help you recover your own systems when problems inevitably crop up.

A Troubleshooting Primer

I confess I don't always follow my own advice when troubleshooting a problem. occasionally taking a shotgun approach because I don't seem to have the time for a more methodical approach. However, the methodical approach is generally the best and will often save you time chasing down the wrong path for a solution. In this section, let's look at the methods you can use for basic troubleshooting and to avoid problems before they occur.

Avoiding Problems in the First Place

There are certain things you can do to avoid potential problems with your computer. First and foremost, take the point of view that your system is just fine as it is and doesn't need any more cool tools or add-ons. Every time you install an application or a new device, you run the risk of upsetting the apple cart. Do you really need that new JPG viewer? Is that Internet Explorer add-on something you can't live without? If your computer is working fine and doing the job you need it to do, why mess with perfection? Keep plugging along and leave those interesting but noncritical applications off of your computer.

In a similar vein, don't visit web sites you don't really need to visit. In a recent search for hacking tools and tips for the last chapter of this book, we stumbled across at least one site that hosed our computer. We couldn't navigate anywhere with Internet Explorer except that particular site, and several other unwanted changes happened to our system. Fortunately, we could easily roll back to a previous configuration with Restore Points and recover from the problem. Had we stayed away from that site, the problem wouldn't have occurred in the first place.

TIP *See the "Using Restore Points" section in this chapter to learn how to create restore points and restore the system's configuration when a problem occurs.*

When you do need to add hardware or software, always back up your system's configuration by creating a restore point *before* you add the hardware or software. Also make sure the hardware and software is compatible with Windows XP. Ideally, hardware should have signed drivers to indicate they have passed Windows XP certification requirements.

Keeping and Reviewing Logs

Often, fixing a problem first requires that you understand what has changed. If the computer was working just fine yesterday, what is different today? Did you install some software? Did you plug in a new device? Did you delete some files, compress a folder or drive, or make some other change to your computer?

One of the best troubleshooting tools is a good activity log. You should get in the habit of logging any changes you make to your system. You don't need to note every time you change printer settings, but it certainly doesn't hurt to keep track of more major actions, such as installing applications, adding a new device, updating a device driver, deleting a nondocument folder, and so on. Windows XP doesn't provide a tool for logging those actions, but it's a simple matter to use Notepad to maintain a simple, text-based log file of recent actions. When a problem crops up, your first step should be to review your change log and see what changes you've made recently to the system. While there is no guarantee that the source of the problem will be some change you made to the system yourself, it's a great starting point.

Here is an example of a simple log file that you might create with Notepad:

```
Date              Event
6-12-04           Clean XP installation
6-12-04           Applied SP2
6-16-04           Installed Microsoft Office 2003
6-19-04           Added a new Epson printer and installed printer drivers
6-25-04           NIC card stopped working, replaced with new card
```

Where to Start?

We've been using personal computers since the early 80s, so we certainly have some experience in troubleshooting. Even so, we occasionally run across a problem that makes us ask, "Where do I start?"

The best place to start is to understand as fully as possible what is happening. Like a doctor who diagnoses a patient by the symptoms he exhibits, you need to identify your computer's symptoms so you can start tracking down the cause of those symptoms. Sometimes the symptoms will be obvious: the system no longer boots, an application no longer starts, documents are missing, or a device no longer works. At other times the symptoms will be less obvious. However, knowing in detail what is happening to your computer is the first step to tracking down *why* it's happening. Take notes as you go along to help you keep track of what you find.

Before you get too far along in troubleshooting the computer, try the simple things first. Is it plugged in? Is there a cable loose? Sometimes, a simple reboot just might fix the problem. If that doesn't do the trick, shut the computer down completely, leave it and all of the peripherals powered off while you recheck all of the cables, then power everything back up again.

Using Safe Mode Options and Startup Switches

Windows XP, like many previous versions, offers a special operating mode called Safe Mode that can help you overcome problems with your system. In particular, Safe Mode is great when a service or device driver is preventing the system from booting properly or preventing you from reconfiguring the system to overcome the problem.

In Safe Mode, Windows XP loads only a minimal set of drivers. For example, Safe Mode uses a standard video graphics array (VGA) driver to ensure that the system will start even if you've installed an incompatible video driver. You can boot in Safe Mode, replace the video driver, then reboot in normal mode.

To boot the computer in Safe Mode, restart the computer and press the F8 function key when the system starts to boot. Windows displays a boot menu similar to the one shown in Figure 5-1. The first three menu items boot the computer in Safe Mode, but with different capabilities:

- **Safe Mode**   This option boots the computer in Safe Mode with a Windows graphical user interface (GUI), but does not load network drivers. Windows uses the standard Vga.sys video driver.

- **Safe Mode with Networking**   This option boots the computer in Safe Mode with network drivers enabled, which is useful when you need to download a driver from the Internet, connect to a server to restore files, or perform other network-related tasks. Windows uses the standard Vga.sys video driver.

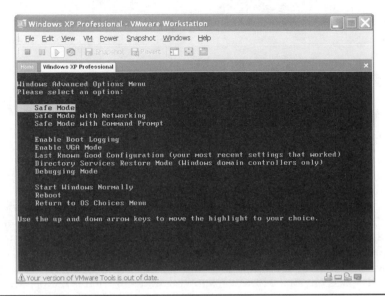

Figure 5-1   Use the boot menu to boot the system in Safe Mode.

- **Safe Mode with Command Prompt**   This option boots the system to a command prompt, which is handy when you want to boot the system quickly and can use console commands to troubleshoot the problem at hand. It can also enable you to access the computer when a problem with Windows Explorer is preventing the GUI from loading.

The boot menu offers several other options that you can use to help troubleshoot the system when problems occur that prevent the computer from booting:

- **Enable Boot Logging**   This option directs Windows to log startup to the file \%systemroot%\Ntbtlog.txt (such as C:\Windows\Ntbtlog.txt). After the system boots, you can open the file in Notepad to explore the boot results and possibly determine the source of the problem, such as a driver failing to load.

- **Enable VGA Mode**   This option boots the computer in 640x480 mode with the configured display driver rather than the standard Vga.sys driver. It is useful when you have configured the display for a resolution that your monitor won't support and need to set it to a different, supported resolution.

- **Last Known Good Configuration**   When you use this option, Windows XP boots the computer using the registry from the last successful boot attempt. It often enables you to boot the system if the registry has become corrupted.

- **Directory Services Restore Mode**   On Windows XP systems, this option has the same effect as the Safe Mode with Networking option. Windows XP computers can't host directory services (a Windows 2000 Server and Windows Server 2003 feature), so there is no advantage to booting with this option.

- **Debugging Mode**   This option enables debugging information to be sent through the computer's COM port to a debugger.

You can also use a handful of switches to start Windows XP to help overcome problems. To use these switches, boot the computer using the Safe Mode with Command Prompt option and use the Edit command to edit Boot.ini, or boot in Safe Mode and use Notepad to edit the file. Then, edit the existing entry for Windows XP in the operating systems section or copy the existing entry and paste it at the end of the section, then edit that entry. See the "Understanding Boot.ini" section in Chapter 2 to view a complete list of Windows XP startup switches and how to edit Boot.ini to include them.

Device Manager

The Device Manager in Windows XP provides the means to view hardware configurations, upgrade device drivers, disable devices, and manage devices in other ways. To view Device Manager, right-click My Computer and choose Manage, then click Device Manager in the left column.

If Device Manager detects a problem with a device, it displays an information icon beside the device (Figure 5-2) so you can easily identify problem devices. You can then update the driver if you feel that it is the problem or disable the device. Right-click the device and choose Update Driver to update the driver or choose Disable to disable the device. Then, restart the system to see if the problem goes away.

TIP   *See the "Troubleshooting with Hardware Profiles" section, later in this chapter, for additional tips on using Device Manager to troubleshoot Windows XP.*

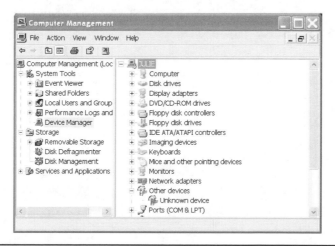

FIGURE 5-2   Use Device Manager to update device drivers and disable problem devices.

Clean Boot

A *clean boot* is another method for troubleshooting a Windows XP computer. A clean boot bypasses startup settings, drivers, and certain settings that might otherwise prevent the computer from booting. If a computer starts with a clean boot, it's likely a driver or application is at fault. If you can't perform a clean boot on a computer, there's a good chance that a corrupted registry or a failed hardware device is the culprit.

You can use the Msconfig tool to configure a computer for a clean boot. If you can't boot the computer normally, boot the computer in Safe Mode. Then, click Start | Run, and enter **msconfig** in the Run dialog box. On the General tab (Figure 5-3), choose the Selective Startup option and then clear the Process SYSTEM.INI File, Process WIN.INI File, and Load Startup Items check boxes.

Next, select the Services tab and click the Hide All Microsoft Services option. Clear the check boxes beside any remaining services. Then, close Msconfig and restart the computer to see if the problem goes away. If so, you have determined that an entry in the RUN.INI or WIN.INI files in the Windows directory or a third-party service is the problem. You can then selectively add items back to the boot process with Msconfig and reboot. When the problem reappears, you've found the source of the problem—whatever you added last is causing the problem.

TIP *Do not clear the Load System Services item on the General tab unless you are willing to lose all of your system's restore points. This option, if cleared, prevents Windows from loading any of the standard Microsoft services listed on the Services tab. Instead, under the Services tab, selectively disable services as needed for troubleshooting, but don't disable the System Restore Service.*

When you're ready to return the system to a normal configuration, run Msconfig again and choose Normal Startup on the General tab, then restart the computer.

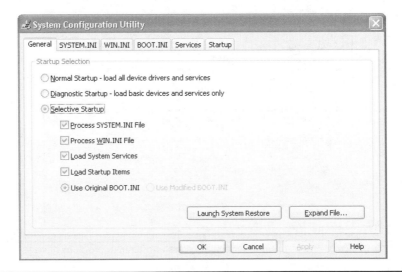

FIGURE 5-3 Use the System Configuration Utility to configure Windows XP for a clean boot.

Try a New User Account

When a problem occurs with Windows XP, it's possible that the problem is related to the user profile, such as a problem with registry settings in the user's portion of the registry. If you can, try creating a new user account and using that account. If the problem goes away when you use the new account, move the documents from the old user account to the new one and delete the old account.

Using Restore Points

I have five children still at home and it seems like they do something to their computer every other day. Fortunately, I've been able to recover from most problems simply by restoring the system from a *restore point*. This section of the chapter explains how to create and use restore points to recover from system problems.

Restore Points Explained

A restore point is a snapshot of the system's configuration. System Restore in Windows XP actively monitors the systems disks and automatically creates a restore point when certain actions occur, such as when you install an application that uses Windows Installer to install the application or when you install an unsigned driver. System Restore creates restore points for you in other situations, as well. You can also create your own restore points.

When you need to restore the computer to a certain state, you run System Restore and choose the restore point that will take your computer back to the desired configuration. For example, if the computer worked fine last Monday but has a problem today, you'd restore the system using Monday's restore point. The whole process takes a few minutes at most and can eliminate a whole host of problems, from corrupted registry files to viruses and spyware.

NOTE *System Restore does not manage document files or the files in your My Documents folder. It is designed to manage the system and application files instead.*

Automatically Created Restore Points

As I mentioned previously, Windows XP System Restore automatically creates restore points for several circumstances:

- **Initial system restore point**   System Restore creates this restore point the first time you start your computer.

- **System checkpoints**   These restore points are created every 24 hours, or if your computer has been off longer than 24 hours, as soon as the system is started again.

- **Program name installation restore points**   Installers such as Windows Installer that are designed to integrate with System Restore, create restore points when you install an application.

- **Automatic update restore points**   Windows Update creates a restore point prior to installing an update.

- **Restore operation restore points**   When you restore the system using System Restore, a restore point is created prior to the restoration so you can, in effect, undo the restore operation.

- **Unsigned driver restore points**   System Restore creates a restore point if you allow an unsigned driver to be installed. This enables you to restore the system to the state prior to installation of the driver.
- **Microsoft Backup restore points**   When you use the Microsoft Backup application to restore files to the system, System Restore creates a restore point before performing the restore operation.

Creating Your Own Restore Points

You can create your own restore points any time you feel it is necessary. For example, if you're about to install an application that doesn't use an installer compatible with System Restore, you should create a restore point so you can restore the system if the application's installation breaks the system.

To create a restore point, follow these steps:

1. Choose Start | All Programs | Accessories | System Tools | System Restore.
2. Choose the Create a Restore Point option (Figure 5-4) and click Next.
3. Enter a descriptive name for the restore point and click Create.

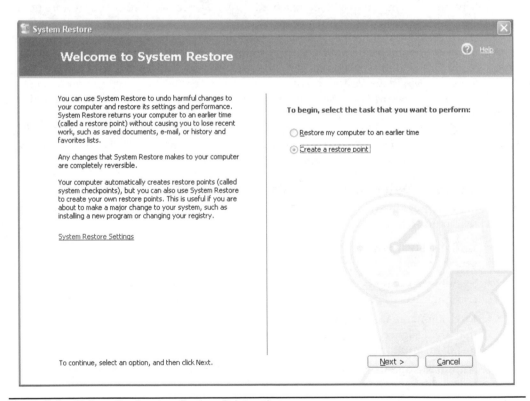

Figure 5-4   Choose the Create a Restore Point option.

If you later need to restore the system to this restore point, look for the description you specified in Step 3. The following section, "Restoring Windows XP with a Restore Point," explains how to restore the system.

Restoring Windows XP with a Restore Point

When you have a problem with your computer and need to restore it to a pre-problem state, or you want to restore it to a previous state for other reasons, it's easy to do so. Here's how to do so:

1. Choose Start | All Programs | Accessories | System Tools | System Restore.

2. Choose the option Restore My Computer to an Earlier Time and click Next.

3. System Restore presents you with a calendar (Figure 5-5) that shows all of the restore points. Dates where restore points exist are shown in bold. Click a date to see that date's restore points. Click the left or right arrow buttons on the calendar to move back and forth in the calendar to locate other restore points.

4. After you click a date, click the restore point in the list beside the calendar and then click Next. System Restore displays a warning message; click Next to start the restore. The restore will likely take a few minutes.

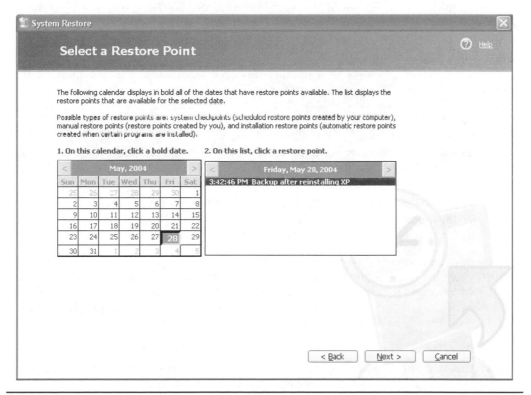

FIGURE 5-5   Choose a restore point from the calendar.

Starting a Restore from the Command Prompt

There are two command-line interfaces you can use to troubleshoot Windows XP. The first is the Recovery Console, discussed later in this chapter in the section, "Using the Recovery Console." The other is the Safe Mode with Command Prompt option in the boot menu, which I explained in the "Using Safe Mode Options and Startup Switches" section. Although you can't launch System Restore from the Recovery Console because there is no graphical interface available for it, you can launch it from a command console when you boot the system in Safe Mode. Here's how:

1. Press F8 at boot and choose the option Safe Mode with Command Prompt.

2. Choose an account (note that the Welcome screen does not show accounts that do not have administrative privileges).

3. When the command console opens, enter the command **%systemroot%\system32\ restore\rstrui.exe**. The System Restore wizard should then start.

Working with Events and the Event Viewer

Knowing what is going wrong with a system is the first step in fixing it. One of the main tools available to you for determining what is wrong with a system is its event logs. This section explores the event logs and how you can use them to troubleshoot problems.

Event Logs and Events Explained

As Figure 5-6 shows, Windows XP maintains three *event logs* that store information about certain types of events. These three event logs are

- **Application**   The application event log stores events generated by applications, whether an application is bundled with Windows XP or is a third-party application.

- **Security**   The Security event log stores security-related events such as log on, log off, and audit events. However, Windows XP, by default, does not log these events. Instead, you must configure security logging to have these events recorded.

- **System**   The System event log stores information about system-wide events such as those generated by Windows XP services. In a nutshell, any events not associated with a specific application or security event are stored in the System event log.

The Application event log is most useful for tracking down problems with applications; the Security event log is useful for identifying security breaches and problems with permissions; and the System event log is useful for troubleshooting global Windows problems.

An event has certain information associated with it. To view an event, simply double-click the event in the Event Viewer. An event's properties include

- **Date/Time**   These two properties store the date and time the event was generated.

- **Type**   This field identifies the type of event that occurred, whether it fall under Information, Error, Warning, Success Audit, or Failure Audit.

- **User**   This field displays the user context with which the event is associated.

- **Computer**   This field displays the computer on which the event occurred.
- **Source**   This field identifies the application or system component, such as a driver or service, which generated the event.
- **Category**   The source of an event can apply a category to the event, and that value appears here.
- **Event ID**   This field uniquely identifies the type of event.
- **Description**   This field describes the event.
- **Data**   Some events include additional data generated by the event, and that information appears here.

What good are the event logs and the events in them? The logs are often the most useful piece of information you can obtain when an error occurs. For example, an application might behave differently from what you're used to or a feature might not work, but, often, you don't have a concrete indication of what is wrong. Events in the event logs are often fairly specific. That specificity will help you not only identify what is going wrong but also the source of the problem.

Your first step when you start troubleshooting a problem is to browse through the event logs for events that seem related to the problem at hand. The newest events appear at the top of the log in the Event Viewer, so that's where you should start your search. If you're troubleshooting a problem with Windows XP itself, check the System log. For application problems, check the Application log. In either case, take the time to review both logs—you might find that what appears to be an application problem is actually a system problem, and vice versa.

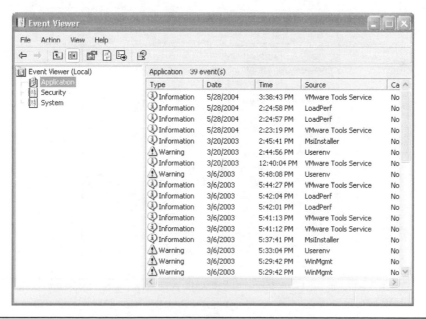

FIGURE 5-6   Use the Event Viewer to view the event logs.

Getting More Information about Specific Events

The Description field in the Event Properties form for an event includes a link to Microsoft's web site. When you click the link, Windows XP displays a dialog box with information about the event (Figure 5-7). Click Yes to send the information to Microsoft and retrieve a page with additional information about the event (Figure 5-8).

Sometimes you won't find any additional information about an event using the link in the Description field. Whether that is the case or not, you can also search Microsoft's servers for more information about the error. To do so, navigate to http://search.microsoft.com and click the Advanced Search link. Type the event ID in the All of these words field, type **Event ID** in the This Exact Phrase field, and click Go. You should get several hits that will offer more information about the event.

To narrow the search a bit you can navigate to http://support.microsoft.com and search the Knowledge Base for documents that reference the event ID and are associated with a specific product. Finally, don't hesitate to use your favorite non-Microsoft search site to look for more information. We frequently get hits on Google for pages on Microsoft's web site that get no hits with Microsoft search using the same keywords.

Trapping Blue Screen of Death Errors

When a critical stop error occurs, Windows XP does one of two things depending on how it is configured. The computer either reboots itself automatically or it displays a message on a blue background and hangs. This message is called the Blue Screen of Death, or BSoD.

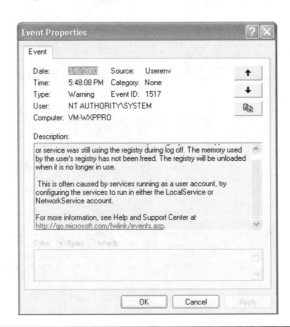

FIGURE 5-7   Click the link in the Event Properties dialog box to view more information about that specific event type.

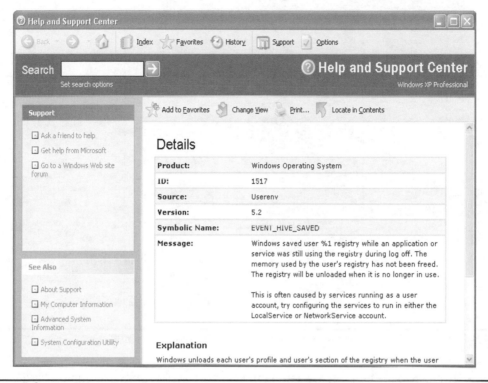

FIGURE 5-8   The Help and Support Center displays additional information about the event.

You won't see the BSoD if the computer is configured to automatically restart. To be able to view the BSoD, follow these steps:

1. Right-click My Computer and choose Properties, then click the Advance tab on the System Properties dialog box.

2. Click Settings in the Startup and Recovery group.

3. In the System Failure portion of the Startup and Recovery dialog box (Figure 5-9), clear the option Automatically Restart and click OK. Click OK to close the System Properties dialog box.

There are several common problems that can cause a stop error. The following list describes the most common:

- **PAGE_FAULT_IN_NONPAGED_AREA**   This error occurs when the system tries to read memory that isn't valid and can be caused by faulty hardware such as defective Random Access Memory (RAM) or a corrupted NT File System (NTFS) volume. It can also be caused by a faulty kernel-level driver or one that requires a later service pack than the one installed on the computer.

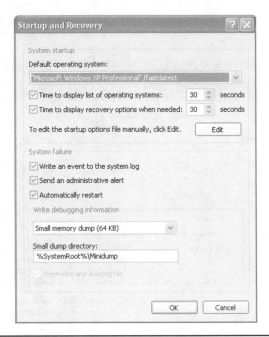

FIGURE 5-9   Use the Startup and Recovery dialog box to configure recovery options.

- **IRQL_NOT_LESS_THAN_OR_EQUAL**   This error is often caused by a hardware conflict or poorly written driver. If you have recently added a new device or updated the driver, remove the device and/or roll back the driver to the previous version.

- **KMODE_EXCEPTION_NOT_HANDLED**   This error is most often caused by an incorrectly configured device driver. Try rolling back the driver if you have recently updated it. In some cases, flashing the system's basic input/output system (BIOS) to a later version will also fix the problem.

- **UNEXPECTED_KERNEL_MODE_TRAP**   This error is most often caused by defective memory. Try reseating the memory first and if that fails, remove and test individual memory modules to see if the problem goes away.

- **KERNEL_DATA_INPAGE_ERROR**   This error indicates that Windows can't read from the virtual memory pagefile and is usually caused by a drive or drive cable problem.

- **INACCESSIBLE_BOOT_DEVICE**   This error indicates that Windows can't read from the boot drive and can be caused by a drive or drive cable problem, upgraded device driver, or device conflict. If you have added a new device, remove it and the drivers. If you have upgraded a driver, boot to Safe Mode and roll it back.

- **STATUS_CANNOT_LOAD_REGISTRY_FILE**   This error indicates Windows can't load the registry. The problem could be drive- or drive-cable-related, but is generally caused by a corrupted registry file. In most cases you'll have to restore the registry from a backup.

- **STATUS_IMAGE_CHECKSUM_MISMATCH**   This error indicates the checksum for a system file doesn't match the data in the file itself. You can often overcome the problem by booting to the Recovery Console and copying the file from the Windows XP CD. If you get this error with lots of different files, it's likely that there is something wrong in the hardware.

Managing Services

Windows XP includes numerous services that each perform a specific function. It's possible that your computer also includes third-party services. Often, troubleshooting a computer requires disabling services. This section explains how to manage services in Windows XP.

TIP   If you believe that a service is causing problems, identify the potential services and disable them one at a time, testing after you disable each one. Or, disable several and if the problem goes away, begin enabling them one at a time and testing after each until you find the culprit. Once you have identified the service, you can begin your search for information on how to overcome the problem. In the case of a third-party service, removing the application that installed the service is the most direct fix, but you should also check with the application vendor to see if an update or work-around is available.

Configuring Service Startup and Other Options

You use the Services console to manage services in Windows XP. To open the Services console, right-click My Computer, choose Manage, and then click the Services branch in the Computer Management console. You can also choose Start | Run, and enter **services.msc**. Figure 5-10 shows the Services console.

---

*TIP   You can also use Msconfig to selectively disable services. To run Msconfig, choose Start | Run, and enter **msconfig** in the Run dialog box. Use the Services tab to disable services.*

The Services console lists all services on the computer and, by default, shows the service name, a description, the service status, the startup type, and the security context (the account under which the service is operating).

TIP   When I need to determine at a glance if any services have stopped unexpectedly I click the Startup column to sort the services by startup type. I can then quickly scan the services that are configured for Automatic startup to identify any that are not running.

To see more information about a service or to configure its settings, double-click the service. Figure 5-11 shows a typical service property sheet.

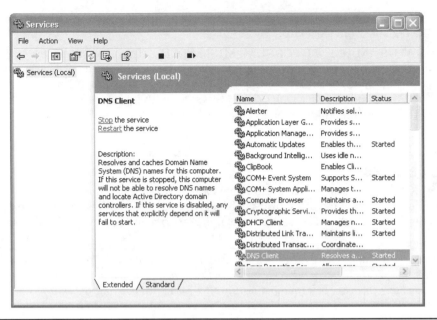

FIGURE 5-10   Use the Services console to manage service startup.

FIGURE 5-11   You can configure several properties for a service.

Although there are several properties you can set for a service, I'll focus here on only those that will help you with troubleshooting. On the General tab, you can set the service's startup type. A service can be one of these three types:

- **Disabled**   The service will not start, even if another service is dependent on it.
- **Manual**   The service can be started by you or by a dependent service, but will not be started automatically when the system starts.
- **Automatic**   Windows XP will start the service automatically when the system starts.

If you think a service is causing a problem, disable the service and restart the computer. If the problem goes away, you've identified the source of the problem. If not, re-enable the service and start it.

The Recovery tab (Figure 5-12) of a service's properties is another place to go when troubleshooting. On this tab you can specify what actions Windows should take when a service fails. By default, Windows takes no action, but you can configure the service to automatically restart, execute a program, or restart the computer. The second option— executing a program—gives you the capability to receive a notification that the service has failed. For example, you could write a script that e-mails you a notification along with

FIGURE 5-12   Use the Recovery tab to specify what should happen when a service fails.

the name of the service that failed. The following script sends a notification using a single parameter passed to the script (the service name):

```
set objArgs = Wscript.Arguments
Set objEmail = CreateObject("CDO.Message")
objEmail.From = "administrator<64>boyce.us"
objEmail.To = "jim<64>boyce.us"
objEmail.Subject = "Service down"
objEmail.Textbody = "The service " & objArgs(0) & " has failed."
objEmail.Send
set objArgs = nothing
set objEmail = nothing
```

Let's assume we save this script as SvcNotify.vbs. On the Recovery tab, select Run a Program from one of the three drop-down lists. Then, in the Program field, enter the path to SvcNotify.vbs. In the Command Line Parameters field, type a name for the service without any spaces, such as **BITS** or **TermSvc**. (It's a good idea to use the service name found at the top of the General tab to help keep things straight.) Set other properties for the service as needed and click OK. Now, when the service fails, Windows will execute the script and generate a message to the specified e-mail address that the service has failed.

Although this sample script sends an e-mail, you can write a script to do almost anything when the service fails. For example, you might want it to simply pop up a notification dialog box:

```
set objArgs = Wscript.Arguments
msgbox "The service " & objArgs(0) & " has failed."
set objArgs = nothing
```

Or, you might write a much more complex script that issues a notification, attempts to restart the service, and then notifies you of the results. Whatever the case, you can accomplish quite a bit with a script.

TIP *See Chapter 11 to learn more about writing scripts for the Windows XP environment.*

Another property you might find useful in your scripts is the number of times the service has failed. The option Append Fail Count to End of Command Line, if selected, causes Windows XP to append /fail=n to the command line, where *n* is the number of times the service has failed. Naturally, you will have to add code to your script to parse the argument from the command line and do something useful with it, such as include the fail count in the mail message. Or, you might have the script take a different action depending on the number of times the service has failed.

Whatever you decide to have the script do, consider writing the script in a generic way so it can be used for any service. You can include whatever service-specific parameters are needed in the Command Line Parameters field to tailor the script to each service.

TIP *See the "Controlling Services with the Recovery Console" section, later in this chapter, to learn how to list, disable, and enable services using the Recovery Console.*

Disabling and Bypassing Devices

Windows XP enables you to disable a device, which prevents its device driver(s) from loading. If you have installed a new device that seems to be causing a problem, or Windows is having problems correctly identifying an existing device, you can disable the device rather than remove it. This section explains two methods you can use for disabling devices.

Disabling Devices in Device Manager

Disabling a device is easy:

1. Right-click My Computer, and choose Manage to open the Computer Management console.

2. Click the Device Manager branch.

3. In the right pane, locate the device you want to disable (Figure 5-13).

4. Click on the device and then click Disable in the toolbar or choose Action | Disable.

After you disable a device, restart the computer to see if the problem goes away. If it docs, you can remove the device if you don't need it or take troubleshooting steps such as updating its drivers. To remove a device, run through the previous steps but click Uninstall in the toolbar instead of Disable. If you want to enable a disabled device, click the device and click Enable in the toolbar.

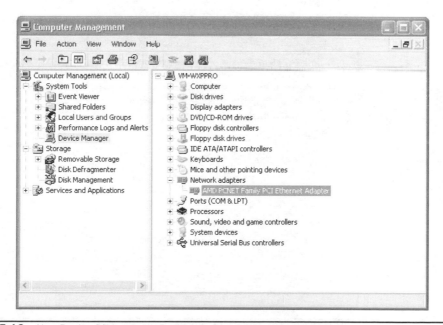

FIGURE 5-13   Use Device Manager to disable devices without removing them.

Troubleshooting with Hardware Profiles

A *hardware profile* in Windows XP is a collection of hardware settings. If multiple hardware profiles exist, Windows XP tries to determine which one should apply to your current network configuration. If the profiles are too similar, Windows XP asks you during the boot process which one you want to use. You select the profile from a menu and Windows then boots the computer using that profile.

Hardware profiles can be helpful for troubleshooting because when you disable a device, that device is disabled only for the current profile. If you think that a couple of hardware devices are conflicting with one another, you can create a hardware profile, disable one device in that profile, and then boot with each profile in sequence to see if the problem goes away.

Follow these steps to create a hardware profile and disable a device in one of the profiles:

1. Right-click My Computer and choose Properties, click the Hardware tab, and click Hardware Profiles to open the Hardware Profiles dialog box (Figure 5-14).

2. Click Copy and enter a name for the new hardware profile, then click OK.

3. Click the option Wait Until I Select a Hardware Profile and click OK.

4. Click OK to close the System Properties dialog box and restart the computer.

5. When prompted during boot, choose the hardware profile in which you want to disable the service.

FIGURE 5-14   Use the Hardware Profiles dialog box to manage hardware profiles.

6. After the system boots, open the Device Manager and disable devices as needed. When you disable a device, Device Manager disables it for the current hardware profile.

7. Restart the system with each of the hardware profiles to see if the problem goes away with the disabled services.

Repairing a Windows XP Installation

The best option for restoring a Windows XP computer is System Restore, but sometimes that option just won't work. For example, perhaps you have turned off System Restore and have no restore points on the system. In situations like these, you have a few other options for repairing the system. This section explains these options.

Before You Attempt a Repair

Before you try repairing the system, you should try a couple of other things first. For example, try booting the system using the Last Known Good Configuration option in the boot menu (press F8 at boot to see these options). Also, try booting in Safe Mode to check for a restore point, and if one is available, try restoring using that restore point. If you have a recent backup set in which you backed up the system state data, try restoring the system state data from the backup. Chapter 10 explains how to do that.

If none of these options works, you might be able to repair the system. If you can boot the system to Safe Mode, it's a good idea to back up your documents, if possible. Although a repair should not affect your documents, it's better to be safe than sorry.

When you're ready to try the repair, you have two options. The following sections, "Upgrading in Place" and "Using Repair Options in Setup," explain these two options.

TIP *In addition to these two methods, you can attempt to restore the registry from a backup. See the "Manually Backing Up and Restoring Registry Files" section at the end of this chapter to learn how to restore the registry using the Recovery Console. See the section "Backing Up and Restoring the Registry" in Chapter 10 to learn more about backing up and restoring the registry. I recommend you attempt a registry recovery before you try to repair Windows XP by either upgrading in place or using repair options in Setup.*

Upgrading in Place

The first of the two methods for repairing Windows XP is to perform an in-place upgrade. In other words, you reinstall Windows XP on top of your existing installation. Before you perform an in-place upgrade, you should understand some potential problems and requirements.

NOTE *An in-place upgrade should be a last resort if you are unable to boot in Safe Mode and use the other methods described in this chapter to recover the system.*

- *Restore points are deleted.*   When you perform an in-place upgrade, Setup deletes all existing restore points. Don't perform an in-place upgrade if you need to restore from one of those existing restore points.

- *Registry backups are deleted and replaced.*   Setup replaces the registry backup files in the %systemroot%\Repair folder when you perform an in-place upgrade. You should back up these files before running Setup in case you will need to use them later to restore the configuration. However, the backup registry will be useful only if you have recently backed up the system's registry. If you have never done so, there is no reason to back up the registry files before running Setup. See "Manually Backing Up and Restoring Registry Files," later in this chapter, for details.

- *Third-party storage drivers are needed.*   If your computer uses a third-party mass storage device driver, you'll need the driver files before running Setup because Setup will require those driver files in order to install Windows XP.

If you can boot the system in Safe Mode, you can start Setup for an in-place upgrade using the following steps:

1. Boot the system in Safe Mode.

2. Insert the Windows XP CD. If the CD does not autoplay, open the CD drive in My Computer and double-click Setup. Otherwise, on the Welcome page, click Install Windows XP.

3. When prompted to choose an installation type, choose Upgrade and click Next.

4. Follow the remaining steps to complete the installation.

TIP   *For additional information about in-place upgrades, go to Microsoft Knowledge Base article 315341 at http://support.microsoft.com/default.aspx?scid=kb;en-us;315341&Product=winxp.*

Using Repair Options in Setup

If you are unable to boot the computer in Safe Mode, you can start Setup from the Windows XP CD:

1. If your system is not configured to boot from CD, open the BIOS configuration program and configure it to boot from CD before booting from the hard drive.

2. Insert the Windows XP CD in the computer and restart the computer.

3. When Setup offers the option to set up or repair Windows XP, press ENTER to begin Setup.

4. Press F8 to accept the End User License Agreement (EULA), verify that your existing installation of Windows XP is selected in the menu, and press R to begin the repair.

5. Follow Setup's remaining prompts to complete the repair.

Using the Recovery Console

Another very useful troubleshooting and repair tool is the Recovery Console, a command-line environment that provides a limited set of commands for managing services and devices and working with the file system. This section of the chapter explains how to install and use the Recovery Console (RC). First, let's explore the two ways you can start the RC.

TIP *You must use the Administrator account to run the RC. However, you can configure the computer to automatically log on in the RC, eliminating the need to specify the administrator password when the RC starts. See the "Configuring Key RC Options" section, later in this chapter, for details.*

Running the RC from the CD

You don't have to install the RC on your computer to use it. Instead, you can run the RC from the Windows XP CD:

1. If your computer's BIOS is not configured to allow boot from CD, configure it to do so.
2. Insert the Windows XP CD and boot from the CD.
3. When given the option to repair Windows XP, press R.
4. Setup will load the RC, which will then prompt you to select the Windows XP installation you want to manage. Type the number of the installation (shown in the menu) and press ENTER.
5. If the RC is not configured for automatic administrative logon, the RC prompts you for the administrator password.

Installing the RC

If you will be using the RC frequently, it's a good idea to install it on the computer to save time during boot. Follow these steps to install the RC on a functioning Windows XP computer:

1. Boot Windows XP and insert the Windows XP CD.
2. Click Start I Run, and enter **D:\i386\winnt32.exe /cmdcons**. Replace D: with the drive letter of your CD drive if it's different.
3. Follow Setup's prompts to complete the installation of the RC.
4. Remove the Windows XP CD, restart the system, and choose the Recovery Console option from the boot menu.

Configuring Key RC Options

There are a couple of group policy settings you should consider configuring, either at the local level, or at a higher level if the computer is a member of a domain. To set these policies at the local level, click Start I Run, and enter **gpedit.msc** in the Run dialog box. Then, navigate to the Computer Configuration\Windows Settings\Security Settings\Local Policies\Security Options branch and set these two policies:

- **Recovery console: Allow automatic administrative logon**   Enable this policy if you don't want to have to specify the local administrator password when starting the RC. Enabling this option will help you avoid the potential problem of forgetting the administrator password. However, you should not enable this option if the primary user of the computer should not be allowed access to the RC.

- **Recovery console: Allow floppy copy and access to all drives and folders**   Enable this option to allow you to copy to and from the floppy disk and get access to all of the system's drives and folders. By default, the RC restricts access to a limited set of folders. If this option is enabled you will be able to back up and restore files from other folders or disks.

Troubleshooting the System with the RC

The RC provides a command-line interface much like the command console in Windows XP, although with a more limited set of commands. Rather than cover each available command here, I'll simply tell you how to view the help content for each command. After you enter the RC and specify the administrator password (if prompted), the RC displays a command prompt. Enter **HELP** at the command prompt to view the list of available commands. To view help for a specific command, enter **HELP** *command*, where *command* is the command for which you want to view syntax and examples.

Many of the commands in the RC are the same as those in a Cmd.exe command console. Table 5-1 describes those that are unique to the RC.

TIP   *To learn about the other commands in the RC that are similar or identical to those offered by Cmd.exe (the Windows XP command console), boot to the Recovery Console and type **HELP** at the command prompt. You can also type **HELP** at a command console prompt to learn about its commands. You can accomplish many different tasks in the RC, but two are the most common. The following sections explain how to accomplish these tasks with the RC.*

Controlling Services with the Recovery Console

If you can't boot the system in Safe Mode to disable or enable services or drivers, you can turn to the RC for that. After you start the RC, use the Listsvc command to view the list of services and device drivers on the system and their startup method. The Listsvc command displays the short name and long name for the service or driver. You'll use the short name with the Disable and Enable commands to control these services.

To disable a service, execute the following command, replacing *service* with the short service name derived from the Listsvc command:

```
Disable service
```

The Disable command displays the current service mode and then sets the startup type for the service to SERVICE_DISABLED. Make a note of the old service mode so you can restore it later with the Enable command.

Command	Description	When to Use
Batch	Execute the statements in a text file in batch fashion	When you're executing multiple commands, such as copying multiple files
Bootcfg	Modify the Boot.ini file	When you're re-creating Boot.ini or adding/changing boot options
Disable	Disable a service or device driver	When you suspect a service or device driver is the problem
Diskpart	Add or delete partitions	When you need to manage disks outside of the graphical interface
Enable	Enable a service or device driver	When you enable a service you have disabled
Expand	Extract a file from a compressed archive	When you restore files from the Windows XP CD
Fixboot	Create a new partition boot sector	When the boot sector is damaged and preventing boot
Fixmbr	Repair the master boot record (MBR)	When the MBR is damaged or has been overwritten by other operating system
Listsvc	List the services and drivers on the system	When you need to identify a service or driver to enable or disable
Logon	Log on to a Windows installation on the computer	When you choose which Windows XP installation to work with
Map	Display logical drive letters mapped to physical drives	When you identify physical drives for Fixboot and Fixmbr commands
Systemroot	Change to the Windows XP root directory (typically \Windows)	When you quickly change to the Windows root folder

TABLE 5-1   Commands Unique to the Recovery Console.

To enable a service or driver that you have disabled, execute the following command, replacing *service* with the short service name and *start_type* with one of the startup types described in Table 5-2:

```
Enable service start_type
```

Manually Backing Up and Restoring Registry Files

You can use the Microsoft Backup applet to back up system state data, which also backs up the registry to the %systemroot%\Repair folder. In some cases, you might want to back up the registry files manually. For example, if you are about to restore the system using the Repair option described previously, you should make a backup of the current registry files. Or, you might want to make a copy of the files in the %systemroot%\Repair folder before reinstalling Windows XP. Likewise, you might need to restore the registry files from a backup. You can accomplish these tasks with the RC.

Start Type	Meaning
SERVICE_DISABLED	The service is disabled and cannot be started by the system, manually, or by a dependent service.
SERVICE_BOOT_START	The service is started at boot.
SERVICE_SYSTEM_START	The system is started by the system during Windows initialization.
SERVICE_AUTO_START	The service is started automatically; this is the same as the Automatic setting in the Services console.
SERVICE_DEMAND_START	The service can be started manually, by the system, or by dependent services; this is the same as the Manual setting in the Services console.

TABLE 5-2   Service Startup Types

The registry files are located in %systemroot%\System32\Config. The backup registry files are located in %systemroot%\Repair. You can use the COPY command in the RC to copy files to or from these folders as needed. However, COPY will not accept wildcard characters, so you must copy the files one at a time. If you need to copy multiple files, create a text file containing multiple COPY commands. Then, use the BATCH command to execute the commands in the text file.

Customizing, Controlling, and Using Windows

Customizing Windows XP

I n this chapter you'll find the answers to the following questions:

- What is a Windows XP theme and how do I set it up?
- What can I do to make the display look better?
- Can I customize the Start menu?
- What is the area where the clock appears? Can I change it?
- Do I really need a screensaver?
- What can I do to make sure no one uses my computer while I'm away from my desk?
- Are there any settings I can use to control the way Windows XP looks depending on who is using the computer?

This chapter focuses on how to customize the desktop, Start menu, and taskbar. It also discusses screensavers and system security. Finally it provides a discussion of group policies to show you how to use policies to manage a local machine or a group of machines.

Customizing the Desktop

One of the first tasks users learn how to do in Windows XP is to customize their desktops. Usually this means changing wallpaper and screensavers to ones that most closely reflect their personalities. Let's look at the ways you customize the desktop in Windows XP, how customizations affect performance, and how to handle device driver issues when you change desktop settings.

Performance Versus Looks

Any time you change the desktop, there are a few things to consider, particularly how the change will affect the performance of Windows. The file size of high-resolution wallpaper, for example, may be too large for your system memory to display properly, especially when you run several memory-intensive applications simultaneously. You'll want to resize the wallpaper—usually by reducing its resolution in a graphics program—and then display it as your desktop wallpaper.

A few things to consider when making changes to your Windows desktop:

- Reduce the file size and resolution of wallpapers you use. The majority of the wallpaper files Windows includes are smaller than 100KB. However, the ubiquitous Windows XP Bliss.Bmp file (Figure 6-1) is 1.4MB.

- Keep the number of "active" items to a minimum, especially on systems that have a limited amount of RAM and graphics memory. Items that are considered "active" include programs or applets that are regularly or constantly updated from a remote server, such as an intranet or Internet site.

- Limit the number of menu, dialog box, mouse, and font effects you employ. You'll be shown later how to set up these effects, but it is not a good idea to configure all these settings at once without having a robust machine behind it.

Figure 6-1   The Windows XP Bliss bitmap

Changing Color Schemes and Screen Elements

Color schemes are used to change the appearance of common window elements, such as the active title bar or the default screen font. Windows XP includes three new schemes:

- Default (Blue)
- Olive Green
- Silver

Microsoft had planned on creating more, but apparently the development team creating the schemes ran out of time. Two schemes (called Ruby and Emerald) that were available during beta testing of XP never made it into the final production code.

If the three new schemes do not meet your needs, you can revert to schemes that were available in previous Windows editions. You use the Widows Classic style and then you have access to the following schemes:

Brick	Pumpkin
Desert	Rainy Day
Eggplant	Red, White, and Blue (VGA)
High Contrast #1	Rose
High Contrast #2	Slate
High Contrast Black	Spruce
High Contrast White	Storm (VGA)
Lilac	Teal (VGA)
Maple	Wheat
Marine (high color)	Windows Classic
Plum (high color)	Windows Standard

To change the color scheme, do the following:

1. Click Start, then Control Panel, and click or double-click the Appearance and Themes icon. Or right-click the desktop, choose Properties, and click the Appearance tab. (If you're running XP with the Classic Start Menu, choose Start, then Settings, and then Control Panel.) See Figure 6-2.

2. From the Widows and buttons drop-down list, select Windows XP Style or Windows Classic style.

3. From the Color scheme drop-down list, select a color scheme. If you want to pick a scheme available from previous Windows editions, you must select Windows Classic style in Step 2.

4. Click OK.

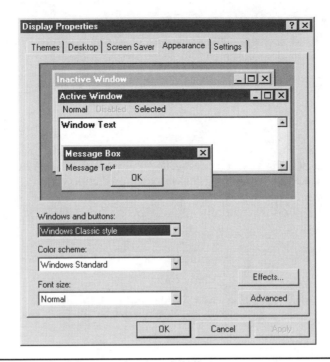

FIGURE 6-2   The Appearance tab lets you change color schemes.

Windows XP allows you to change just about any element of the screen environment. For instance, if you don't like the standard Windows XP color of the active window title bar, change it to a color you like better.

The following shows the screen elements you can change:

3D Objects	Inactive Title Bar
Active Title Bar	Inactive Window Border
Active Window Border	Menu
Application Background	Message Box
Caption Buttons	Palette Title
Desktop	Selected Items
Icon	ToolTip
Icon Spacing (Horizontal)	Window
Icon Spacing (Vertical)	

To change a desktop element, do the following:

1. Click Start, then Control Panel, and click or double-click the Appearance and Themes icon. Or right-click the desktop, choose Properties, and click the Appearance tab.

2. Click the Advanced button. The Advanced Appearance dialog box opens (Figure 6-3).

3. Click the Item drop-down list and select an item to change.

4. If available for the item you select, change the item's size by setting the Size option to a different setting. Some items, such as the Desktop item, do not allow you to change their size.

5. If available for the item you select, change the item's color by setting the Color 1 option to a different color. Some items, such as the Caption Buttons, do not allow you to change their colors. On the other hand, some items, such as the Active Title Bar, allow you to change two color settings.

6. If these options are available for the item you select, change the item's font size, color, and style. Some items, such as the Active Window Border, do not allow you to change their font settings.

7. After setting all the items you want to change, click the OK button. To save these settings to a Windows XP theme, see the section, "Using Themes" in this chapter.

8. When you're finished making changes to the display appearance, click OK again.

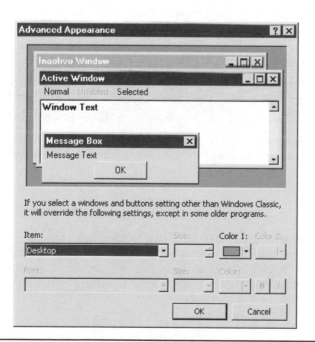

Figure 6-3   The Advanced Appearance dialog box gives you options for changing desktop elements.

As you make the preceding changes, keep a few things in mind. First, if you set the Window item to a different font color, the automatic font color in some programs you execute will also be affected. For example, if you use Microsoft Word and change the Window font color to red, your default font color will be red in any new documents you create.

Second, the Active Title Bar and Inactive Title Bar items use the same font color and font size settings. If you make a change to one, say the Active Title Bar, the same setting is reflected in the other item (the Inactive Title Bar item in this case).

Changing Screen Effects

Windows XP uses screen effects to add visual enhancements to menus, fonts, and icons. You can turn these effects on or off depending on your liking. The following is a list of the screen effects available:

- Fade or scroll menu items into view
- Fade or scroll ToolTips into view
- Smooth edges of screen fonts
- Smooth edges of screen fonts using Clear Type
- Use large icons
- Show shadows under menus
- Show window contents while dragging
- Hide underlined menu letters until you press ALT

To change these effects, use the following steps:

1. Click Start, then Control Panel, and click or double-click the Appearance and Themes icon. Or right-click the desktop, choose Properties, and click the Appearance tab.
2. Click the Effects button to display the Effects dialog box (Figure 6-4).
3. Check or uncheck the screen effect to your liking. The top two effects include drop-down lists that let you select alternative properties for the effect.
4. Click OK.

Using Themes

A *theme* is a set of desktop items that are related in some way, usually by a distinct color scheme, similar image collection, or sounds. Themes let you customize the appearance of your Windows environment, including fonts, mouse pointers, sounds, wallpaper, and screensaver, by quickly selecting the theme name. You don't have to spend time setting each of these elements individually.

To use a theme, follow these steps:

1. Click Start, then Control Panel, and click or double-click the Appearance and Themes icon. Or right-click the desktop, choose Properties, and click the Themes tab.

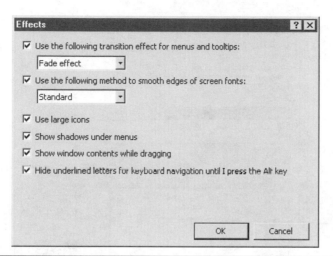

FIGURE 6-4   The Effects dialog box lets you control screen effects in Windows XP

2. From the Theme drop-down list, select a theme, such as Windows XP, Windows Classic, or other theme (Figure 6-5). If you have Windows XP Plus! installed, you will have other themes available as well, including the following:

   • Plus! Aquarium

   • Plus! daVinci

   • Plus! Nature

3. Click OK.

If a theme does not satisfy your customization needs, simply modify an existing one or create your own from scratch. When you modify a theme, you make changes to one or more of the desktop items and then save the settings. You can save the settings to a different theme name or to the original theme name. The problem with saving to the original theme name is that you copy over the original theme, losing the original theme. Of course you can always set the theme back to its original setup if you remember all the settings. The Microsoft recommended procedure is to save the revised theme to a different theme name so that you can always revert to the original theme later.

To modify a theme, perform the following steps:

1. Click Start, then Control Panel, and click or double-click the Appearance and Themes icon. Or right-click the desktop, choose Properties, and click the Themes tab.

2. From the Theme list, click the theme that you want to modify.

3. Using the options on the Desktop, Screen Saver, and Appearance tabs, make changes to the elements of the theme that you want to change. See the earlier discussion, "Changing Color Schemes and Screen Elements," on individual desktop elements that you can change. Table 6-1 shows desktop elements and the tab under which you can find that element.

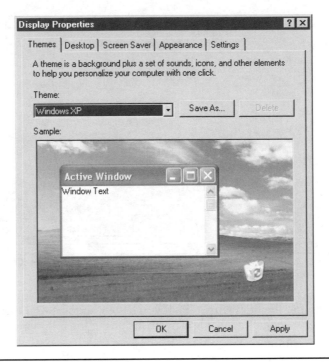

FIGURE 6-5 Setting up a Windows XP theme

Element	Tab Name	Option to Select
Desktop wallpaper	Desktop	Select a wallpaper item from the Background list
Other desktop wallpaper	Desktop	Click the Browse button and select a wallpaper filename. Click Open.
Size of wallpaper	Desktop	Select Center, Tile, or Stretch from the Position list.
Background color	Desktop	Select a color from the Color drop-down list.
Desktop icons	Desktop	Click the Customize Desktop button and select an option from the General tab of the Desktop Items dialog box.
Screen saver	Screen Saver	Select a screensaver from the Screen Saver drop-down list. Read more about screensavers in the "All About Screensavers" section later in this chapter.
Window and button styles	Appearance	Select a style from the Windows and buttons drop-down list. See "Changing Color Schemes and Screen Elements," earlier in this chapter.
Screen elements	Appearance	Click the Advanced button and then select a screen element and change its appearance. See "Changing Color Schemes and Screen Elements" earlier in this chapter for more information.

TABLE 6-1 Desktop Elements

1. Change your mouse pointer scheme or the appearance of individual pointers. To do so, open Control Panel and then open the Mouse applet. On the Pointers tab (Figure 6-6), specify different pointers for your theme, or select a predefined pointer scheme by choosing one from the Scheme drop-down list. Click the Apply button.

2. Click OK to close the Mouse Properties dialog box.

3. Change your sound scheme or modify program event sounds. To do so, open Control Panel and then open the Sounds and Audio Devices applet. On the Sounds tab (Figure 6-7), specify different sounds for system events, or select a scheme from the Sound scheme drop-down list. Click the Apply button.

4. Click OK to close the Sounds and Audio Devices dialog box.

5. Switch back to the Themes tab and click the Apply button.

6. Click the Save As button to open the Save As dialog box (Figure 6-8).

7. Type a name for the new theme and click Save. Notice that Windows provides a generic new name (My Favorite Theme) for the theme so you do not accidentally type over the original theme name. Also, new themes are saved with a THEME file name extension and are saved in your my Document folder by default.

8. Click the Save button.

9. Click OK to close the Display Properties dialog box.

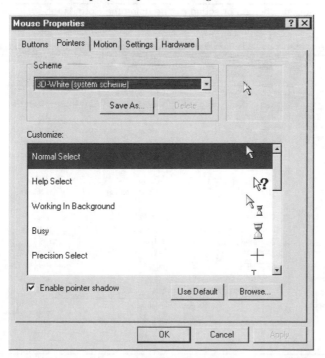

FIGURE 6-6   Change mouse pointers for your modified theme using the Pointers tab.

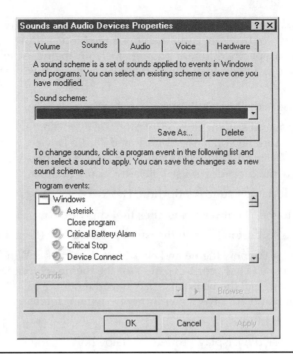

FIGURE 6-7   Change sound schemes or sound events using the Sounds tab.

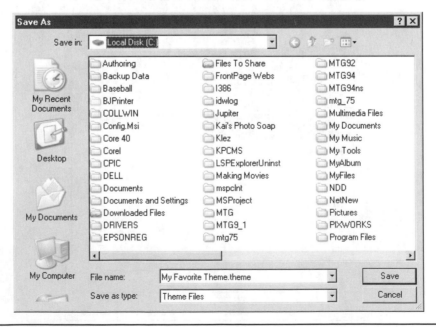

FIGURE 6-8   Name your theme using the Save As dialog box.

Using Active Desktop Content

Active Desktop content is web content that you can display on your Windows desktop. To use this feature, you must have a connection to the Internet. If you plan to display graphics-intensive Active Desktop content, you may want to have a high-speed connection to the Internet.

To set up Active Desktop content, follows these steps:

1. Right-click the desktop and click Properties.

2. Click the Desktop tab and click Customize Desktop.

3. Click the Web tab (Figure 6-9).

4. Click the New button.

5. In the Location box of the New Desktop Item dialog box, type the complete Internet address (URL) of the web page you want to display.

6. Click OK.

7. To modify the content and to specify a password for the content, click the Customize button on the Add Item to Active Desktop dialog box that appears (Figure 6-10). If you don't need to customize the content, skip to Step 15.

8. Click Next to display the Offline Favorite Wizard dialog box (Figure 6-11).

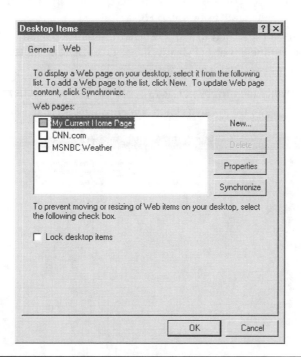

FIGURE 6-9   Use the Web tab to set up Active Desktop content.

FIGURE 6-10   The Add Item to Active Desktop dialog box.

9. Specify the synchronization schedule using one of the following options:

   - **Only when I choose Synchronize from the Tools menu**   Use this option when you want your active content to be updated only when you choose Synchronize from the Internet Explorer Tools menu. The best time to use this option is if you have a dial-up connection to the Internet. This way you control when the content is updated when you are online.

   - **I would like to create a new schedule**   Use this option when you want Windows to automatically update the active content based on a schedule. This is best used when you have a continuous connection to the Internet, such as a broadband connection at home or work.

10. Click Next. If you specified to set up a schedule in the preceding step, the schedule screen of the Offline Favorite Wizard dialog box appears (Figure 6-12).

11. Specify the following scheduling options:

   - **Every**   Specify the number of days between synchronizations.

   - **Days at**   Specify the time of day to synchronize.

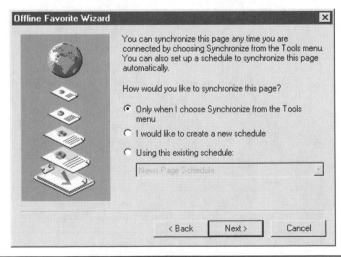

FIGURE 6-11   The Offline Favorite Wizard dialog box offers you choices on when you want to synchronize active content.

FIGURE 6-12   Set up a synchronization schedule for your active content.

- **Name** Specify a name for the schedule.
- **Connection option** Specify if you want Windows to connect to the Internet to synchronize the active content if the computer is not connected when the scheduled time starts.

12. Click Next.

13. If a password is required, select Yes, My User Name and Password Are (Figure 6-13). Type your username and password for the web site into their respective boxes. Retype the password in the Confirm Password box.

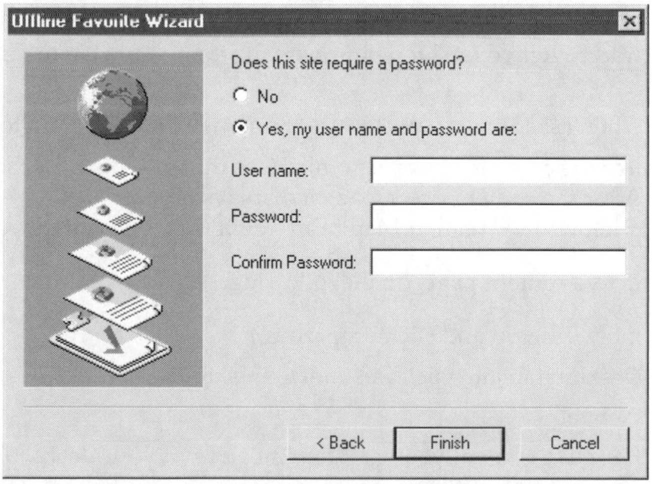

FIGURE 6-13   Specify the username and password for the active content page in the Online Favorite Wizard dialog box.

14. Click Finish.

15. Click OK. Windows XP will download the web page and then display the web tab with the name of the active content listed in the web pages list.

16. Click OK.

The web page displays on your desktop in a small window. If you want to resize it, open the Web tab again (see the preceding Steps 1–3) and uncheck the Lock Desktop Items option and click OK twice. You can now move and resize the active content window on the desktop. Also, sizing controls appear on the top right of the window after you select it. Here you can maximize, minimize, or close the window. Figure 6-15 shows an example of active content on a desktop.

NOTE *You can add more than one page of active content to your desktop. Simply set up additional pages on the Web tab as you did in the preceding steps. This is a good way to keep track of web sites that offer continuously updated information, such as news sites or financial pages.*

Microsoft offers a gallery of web sites specifically designed for active content. To visit the Microsoft Desktop Gallery web site, do the following:

1. Connect to the Internet.

2. Right-click the desktop and click Properties.

3. Click the Desktop tab and click Customize Desktop.

4. Click the Web tab.

5. Click the New button.

6. Click the Visit Gallery button on the New Desktop Item dialog box. This opens Internet Explorer (IE) and connects to the Internet Explorer 4.0 Desktop Gallery web page as shown in Figure 6-14.

7. Click the Add to Active Desktop button on the item you wish to display on your desktop.

8. Click Yes when asked if you want to add an Active Desktop item to your desktop.

9. To customize the content, click Customize (see the preceding Steps 9–16). Otherwise click OK. After the content downloads it displays on your desktop as active content. Figure 6-15 shows the Weather Map from MSNBC active content page.

To turn off an active content page, do the following:

1. Right-click the desktop and click Properties.

2. Click the Desktop tab and click Customize Desktop.

3. Click the Web tab.

4. Deselect the active content you want to remove from your desktop. This turns off the Web page, but keeps it listed for future reactivation. To completely delete its listing, select it and click the Delete button, and then click Yes.

5. Click OK.

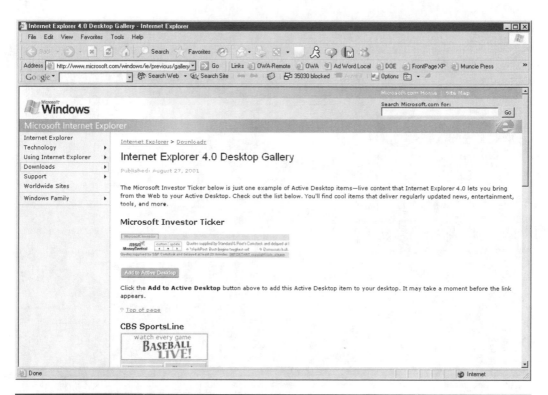

FIGURE 6-14   Visit the Microsoft Desktop Gallery web site to download active content items from Microsoft.

Active Desktop content is displayed according to the security settings established for IE. Certain content may not display correctly if your security settings are too restrictive. The advantage to setting high security, however, is that potentially harmful web content can be excluded. You can configure security settings in Internet Explorer by choosing Tools, Options, and clicking Custom Level on the Security tab. Windows XP with SP2 offers four security levels. When you choose a security level, Internet Explorer sets a variety of security related options. Each of the four levels causes Internet Explorer to prompt you before certain types of actions are taken, such as downloading an ActiveX control, Each security level disables more options than the next, with the High level disabling most features that can pose a security risk.

TIP   *See Chapter 14, "Internet Explorer Tips and Tricks," for more information about IE security.*

NOTE   *As an alternative to Windows Active Desktop, many users and organizations have installed Rich Site Summary (RSS) readers. RSS uses an XML-formatted definition to reference web content that RSS readers can use to retrieve news and other information to users' desktops. To handle the RSS information, users must have an RSS reader installed. To find out more about RSS and RSS readers, visit http://www.webreference.com/authoring/languages/xml/rss/.*

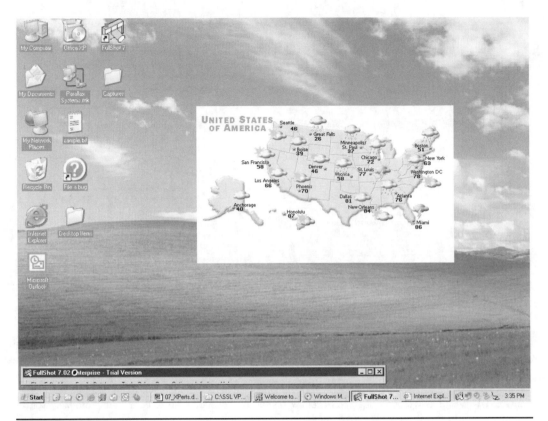

FIGURE 6-15   The Weather Map from MSNBC is available from the Microsoft Desktop Gallery.

Customizing the Start Menu and Taskbar

The Start menu and taskbar have been part of the Windows environment since Windows 95. Windows XP lets you customize these elements more to your liking than previous versions of Windows let you. For instance, you can keep the new Windows XP Start menu look (Figure 6-16) or return to the classic Windows look, which resembles and behaves like the Start menu (Figure 6-17) first available in Windows 98.

The new style of the Windows XP Start menu provides several enhancements over the previous versions. One of the key enhancements is its placement of shortcuts to frequently used programs and recently used programs. These shortcuts allow users to return quickly to favorite programs or ones that were recently launched and exited, thereby eliminating some of the problems of users not knowing where to find shortcuts to these programs.

The Start menu has left and right parts. The left part is divided into three main areas, separated by divider lines. The top part is called the Pinned list. It allows users to place shortcuts to programs or documents that they want to frequently access. By default Windows

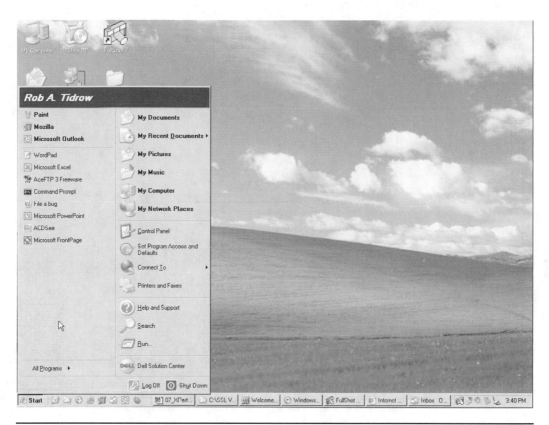

FIGURE 6-16   The Windows XP Start menu

places the user's default web browser and e-mail program in this area. You can add to it, which we describe later in the "Customizing the Start Menu" section.

The middle part of the Start menu is called the Most Frequently Used list. This list shows programs that have been recently used. Of the most frequently used programs, those used most show up at the top of the list, and those used least show up on the bottom of the list.

The bottom part has a link called All Programs that displays submenus of all the programs installed under Windows.

Another key feature is the Start menu's shortcuts to other Windows configuration areas, such as the Control Panel, network connections, and printers. These are shown on the right side of the Start menu. With Windows XP SP2, users now have a new link called Set Program Access and Defaults that displays the Add or Remove Programs dialog box's Set Program Access and Defaults settings. These settings, as shown in Figure 6-18, let you customize configuration settings for Microsoft and other manufacturer programs on your system. For instance, to change the default web browser for your system, select a browser under the Choose a Default Web Browser heading.

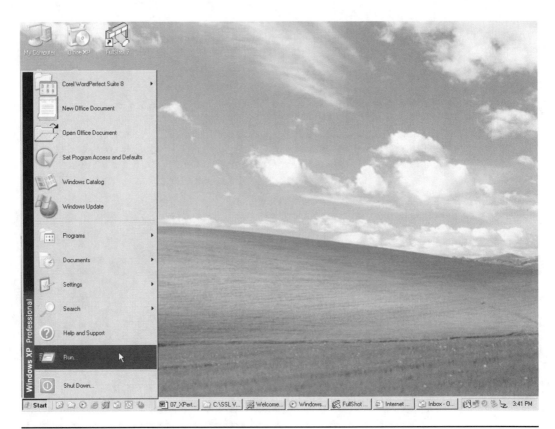

FIGURE 6-17 The Classic Start menu in Windows XP

The right side of the Start menu includes the following links:

My Documents	Set Program Access and Defaults
My Recent Documents	Connect To
My Pictures	Printers and Faxes
My Music	Help and Support
My Computer	Search
My Network Places	Run
Control Panel	

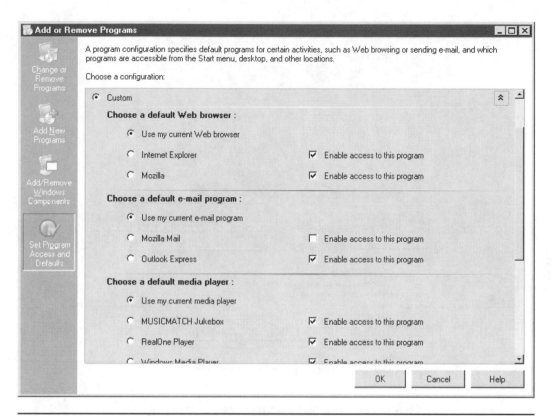

FIGURE 6-18   Set program defaults using the Add or Remove Programs dialog box.

Customizing the Start Menu

You can configure several features of the Start menu, including its menu style (XP or Classic), icon size, number of recently used programs to display, and other items. The following steps show how to configure the Start menu:

1. Right-click an open area of the taskbar and choose Properties.

2. Click the Start menu tab, as shown in Figure 6-19.

3. To change to the Windows Classic look, select Classic Start menu. Click the Customize button to change the programs that display on the Classic menu. Click OK twice to save your settings.

4. To keep the Windows XP menu style but customize it, click Start menu and then click Customize. This displays the Customize Start Menu dialog box (Figure 6-20).

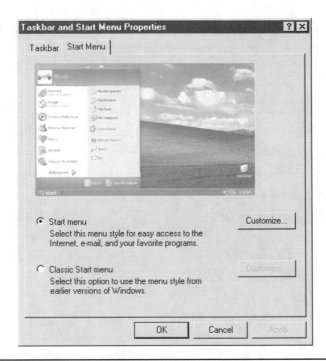

FIGURE 6-19   Use the Start Menu tab to change Start menu options.

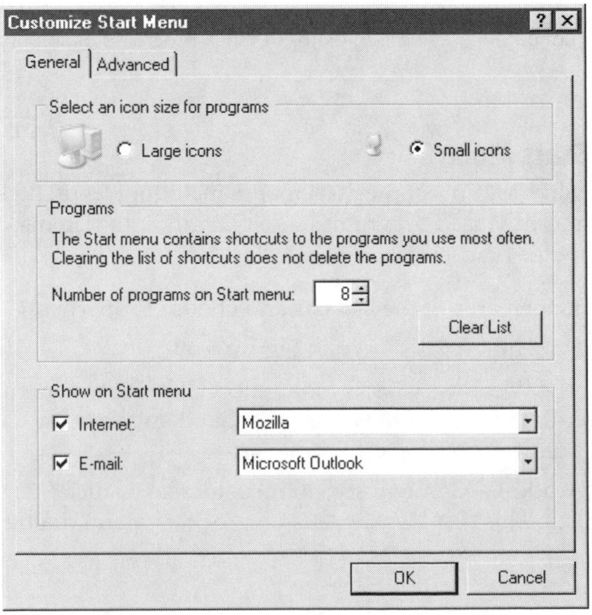

FIGURE 6-20   The Customize Start Menu for the XP menu style

5. On the General tab, set the following options to fit your user style:

- **Large icons**   Sets program icons on the Start menu to a large size.

- **Small icons**   Sets program icons on the Start menu to a small size.

- **Number of programs on Start menu**   Sets the number of most frequently used programs to display on the Start menu. The maximum number is 30, but you may want to keep this to a much smaller number, such as 6–10. Also, if you want to clear the list of programs currently showing on the Start menu, click the Clear List button. From this point forward, as you use programs their icons will display on the Start menu.

- **Show on Start menu**   Determines the browser and e-mail applications to show at the top of the Start menu. If you don't want either one to show, clear its box.

6. Click the Advanced tab (Figure 6-21).

7. Set the following options to fit your user style:

- **Start menu settings**   Set to have the Start menu display submenus when you hover the mouse pointer over them. Uncheck this if you want the submenus to open only after you click them. Also, you can have Windows XP highlight recently installed programs. This makes it much easier to find that new program you installed.

- **Start menu items**   Set a number of Start menu items here. To see the entire list, refer to Table 6-2.

- **Recent documents**

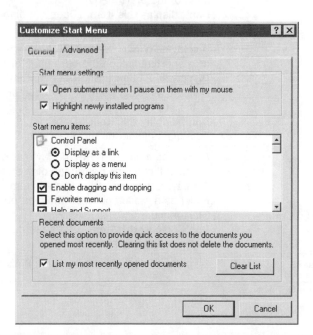

FIGURE 6-21   The Advanced tab

8. Click OK.

9. Click OK again.

Item	Description
Control Panel	**Display as a link** Shows Control Panel as a shortcut link on the right pane of the Start menu. **Display as a menu** Each item in Control Panel is shown as a menu option on the right pane of the Start menu **Don't display this item** Does not display the Control Panel on the Start menu.
Enable dragging and dropping	Allows you to drag and drop items to and from the Start menu.
Favorites menu	Displays the Favorites folder on the right pane of the Start menu.
Help and Support	Displays a link to the Help and Support web page.
Manufacturer Link	Displays a link to the computer manufacturer's web site (if it's been preconfigured by the manufacturer).
My Computer	**Display as a link** Shows My Computer folder as a shortcut link on the right pane of the Start menu. **Display as a menu** Shows each item in the My Computer folder as a menu option on the right pane of the Start menu. **Don't display this item** Does not display the My Computer folder on the Start menu.
My Documents	**Display as a link** Shows the My Documents folder as a shortcut link on the right pane of the Start menu. **Display as a menu** Shows each item in the My Documents folder as a menu option on the right pane of the Start menu. **Don't display this item** Does not display the My Documents folder on the Start menu.
My Music	**Display as a link** Shows the My Music folder as a shortcut link on the right pane of the Start menu. **Display as a menu** Shows each item in the My Music folder as a menu option on the right pane of the Start menu. **Don't display this item** Does not display the My Music folder on the Start menu.
My Network Places	Displays a link to the My Network Places folder.

TABLE 6-2   Start Menu Options

Item	Description
My Pictures	**Display as a link** Shows the My Pictures folder as a shortcut link on the right pane of the Start menu. **Display as a menu** Shows each item in the My Pictures folder as a menu option on the right pane of the Start menu. **Don't display this item** Does not display the My Pictures folder on the Start menu.
Network Connections	**Display as a link** Shows the Network Connections folder as a shortcut link. **Display as a menu** Shows the Network Connections folder as a menu. Each connection is shown on a submenu on the right pane of the Start menu. **Don't display this item** Does not show the Network Connections folder at all.
Printers and Faxes	Displays the Printers and Faxes folder on the right pane of the Start menu.
Run command	Displays the Run command shortcut on the right pane of the Start menu.
Scroll Programs	Displays icons on the Programs menu as a scrollable page.
Search	Displays the Search shortcut on the right pane of the Start menu.
Set Program Access and Defaults	Displays the Printers and Faxes folder on the right pane of the Start menu.
System Administration Tools	**Display on the All Programs menu** Shows the System Administration tools shortcut on just the All Programs submenu. **Display on the All Programs menu and the Start menu** Show the System Administration tools shortcut on the All Programs submenu and the right pane of the Start menu. **Don't display this item** Does not show the System Administration tools shortcut at all.

TABLE 6-2   Start Menu Options (continued)

Controlling the Taskbar and Tray

The taskbar is used to help you switch between open applications, choose an item from the Start menu, or use an item from the task tray. It is the thin bar of icons positioned at the bottom of the Windows desktop, and includes the Start menu button, toolbars, application icons, and the task tray. The task tray is the small section on the far right of the taskbar. It includes icons for items that load during startup, network connection icons, and the clock.

By default, Windows XP places the taskbar along the bottom of the desktop, but you can reposition on the top or sides of the screen. To reposition the taskbar, do the following:

1. By holding down the left mouse button, grab an open spot on the taskbar.

2. Drag and drop the taskbar to a different location on the desktop (Figure 6-22).

Taskbar Grouping

Windows XP includes a feature that enables you to group similar documents and program items together. Taskbar grouping has two features. First, all documents opened by the same program are displayed in the same area of the taskbar. This enables you to find these documents a little more easily.

Second, when you have multiple documents open from the same application, Windows can combine all of the document icons under the same icon, thereby eliminating a lot of the

Figure 6-22   An example of displaying the taskbar on the right side of the desktop

clutter of the taskbar. To switch to a document grouped under a single icon, click the icon, navigate the list, and then select the document of your choice.

To set up Windows XP's taskbar grouping feature, do the following:

1. Right-click a blank area of the taskbar and choose Properties.

2. On the Taskbar tab, select Group Similar Taskbar Buttons (Figure 6-23).

3. Click OK.

Taskbar Appearance Settings

The taskbar has several appearance settings you can configure. One of them allows you to lock the taskbar so it cannot be moved or resized. If you're a systems administrator or help desk person, this feature is handy so that you can lock the taskbar on novice users' machines. Many times inexperienced users will accidentally move the taskbar and not know how to return it to its original location. By locking the taskbar on these users' machines, you can eliminate this problem.

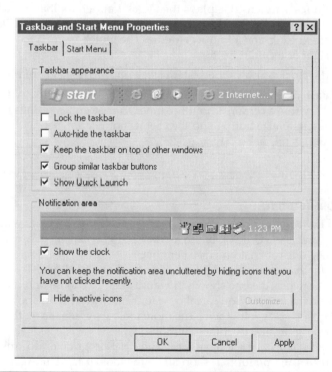

FIGURE 6-23   Set the Group Similar Taskbar Buttons options using the Taskbar tab.

To change the taskbar appearance settings, do the following:

1. Right-click a blank area of the taskbar and choose Properties.

2. On the Taskbar tab, set the following options as desired:

   - **Lock the taskbar**   Locks the taskbar so it cannot be moved or resized. This option also locks the toolbars on the taskbar so that they cannot be moved or resized.

   - **Auto-hide the taskbar**   Hides the taskbar when a window appears onscreen. The benefit of this option is you get a little more screen area to display a window when the taskbar is hidden. To make the taskbar reappear, move the mouse pointer to the area where the taskbar is hidden.

   - **Keep the taskbar on top of other windows**   Displays the taskbar at all times, even when a window is maximized or resized to fill the screen.

   - **Group similar taskbar buttons**   Keeps all like programs and documents together. See the preceding section, "Taskbar Grouping," for more details.

   - **Show Quick Launch**   Displays the Quick Launch toolbar, which includes shortcuts to various Windows components, such as the Show Desktop icon, Internet Explorer, and Windows Media. The Quick Launch toolbar appears just to the right of the Start button.

   - **Show the clock**   Shows the system clock on the right side of the task tray.

   - **Hide inactive icons**   Enables you to hide icons on the task tray that you have not used within a certain amount of time. To customize settings for each icon, click the Customize button and then set its notification behavior in the Customize Notifications dialog box (Figure 6-24).

3. Click OK.

Creating Custom Toolbars

As we mentioned in the preceding section, the taskbar includes toolbars you can display. The most common one is the Quick Launch toolbar, but you can choose from other toolbars, as well as create new ones or customize current ones.

To see a list of toolbars available, right-click the taskbar and choose Toolbars. A submenu of toolbars displays, such as the one shown in Figure 6-25. To choose one, simply select it and it will display on the taskbar. You can choose to display more than one at a time on the taskbar, but don't go too crazy with them. The more toolbars you have on the taskbar, the less room you have for program and document buttons.

If you want to add items to the toolbar, drag and drop program or document shortcuts to the toolbar. This creates an icon for that shortcut on the toolbar taskbar. Again, for best results, limit the number of icons you place on your toolbars so you don't get so many icons on the taskbar that you don't have room for icons for your running programs or open documents.

To close a toolbar, repeat the procedure to display the toolbar, but this time deselect the toolbar name.

Custom toolbars are created by choosing or making a folder that includes the shortcuts you want displayed on the taskbar toolbar. For instance, if you want a custom toolbar to be all the items shown in your My Documents folder, you can do so (although this folder

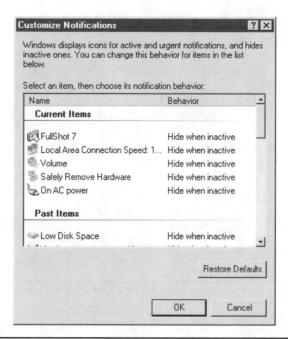

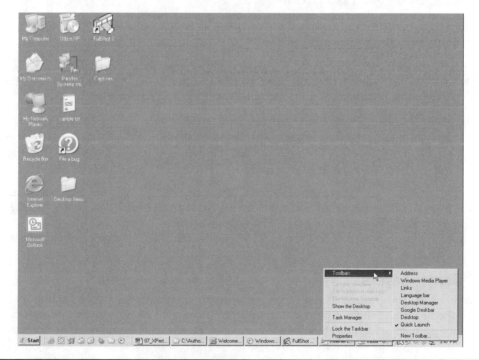

FIGURE 6-24   Set inactive icon notification behaviors using the Customize Notifications dialog box.

FIGURE 6-25   The taskbar's list of toolbars

FIGURE 6-26   Create a new taskbar toolbar using the New Toolbar dialog box.

usually has a plethora of items in it so it isn't always a good idea to use it as a taskbar toolbar). Or you can create a new folder using Windows Explorer, drag and drop items to the folder, and then display the folder as a taskbar toolbar.

To create a new custom toolbar, do the following:

1. Right-click the taskbar and choose Toolbars.

2. Choose New Toolbar to display the New Toolbar dialog box (Figure 6-26).

3. Select a folder, or select a folder in which to create a new folder and click the Make New Folder button. Type the new folder name and press ENTER.

4. Click OK. The selected folder appears on the taskbar.

5. If the folder already contained items, they will display as toolbar buttons. However, if the folder was empty or you just created it in Step 1, you will need to drag and drop items to the toolbar to populate it.

TIP   *You also can add or remove icons from a toolbar by opening the toolbar's folder in Windows Explorer or My Computer and managing the items from there.*

All About Screensavers

Screensavers are programs that run when your computer sits idle for a specific amount of time. In the beginning days of personal computers, when a PC sat idle, monitors would experience burn-in, which is when the static image on the screen would actually leave a burned in image on the monitor screen. Screensavers were introduced to eliminate burn-in.

To set up a screensaver, do the following:

1. Right-click the Desktop tab and choose Properties.
2. Click the Screen Saver tab.
3. From the Screen Saver drop-down list, select a screensaver name.
4. Click the Settings button to see if there are any settings you can change for the selected screensaver. For some, such as the Windows XP screensaver, there are no settings to change. However, if you select the Marquee screensaver, you can set up the marquee text and its properties using this button.
5. Click Preview to turn on the screensaver for a sample view of it.
6. Set the Wait increment to the amount of time you want Windows to wait before the screensaver activates when your PC is idle.
7. Click the On Resume, Password Protect option to password-protect the screensaver.
8. Click OK.

When the screensaver comes on your screen, move the mouse a little to deactivate the screensaver. Systems using the option, On Resume, Password Protect, will display the Computer Locked screen (press CTRL-ALT-DELETE and type in your user password) if they are set up to connect to a network domain. On a system that is part of a workgroup (or standalone computer) the option, On Resume, display Welcome screen, causes the system to display the Windows XP Welcome screen, which enables you to choose the account to log on. On both types of systems, clearing the password protection option causes Windows XP to simply resume displaying the desktop without prompting for a password.

What Good Are They?

Nowadays screensavers are not needed for burn-in. Our state-of-the-art monitors no longer experience burn-in. However, we still like to have screensavers on our computers for purely aesthetic reasons or because of the security they offer.

Screensavers and System Security

In some businesses, schools, large corporations, and government agencies, screensavers are encouraged or even required when systems store confidential or private data. In these cases, users are required to apply a password to shut off the screensaver when they return to the Windows XP desktop. This limits the users on that machine to those who have the screensaver password. For organizations that require users to log onto a Windows NT, 2000, or 2003 domain, the screensaver password is the same password as the currently logged in user.

Create a Custom Screensaver

Windows XP includes a screensaver option that enables you to place your own digital pictures as screensaver images. To set this feature up, do the following:

1. Open Windows Explorer or My Computer and set up a folder that includes the images you want to display on your screensaver. By default, Windows uses the My Pictures subfolder inside your My Documents folder for this feature. However, you can create a new folder and copy images to it.

PART II

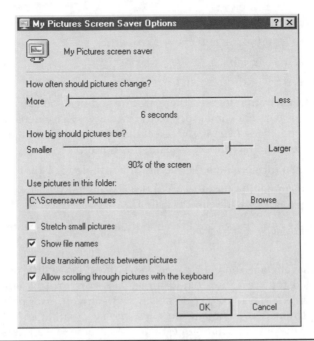

FIGURE 6-27   The My Pictures Screen Saver Options dialog box

2. Display the Screen Saver properties tab.

3. Select My Pictures Slideshow from the Screen Saver drop-down list.

4. Click the Settings button to display the My Pictures Screen Saver Options (Figure 6-27).

5. Move the top slider bar to the time you want to display each picture. Six seconds is the default and the minimum.

6. Move the second slider bar to the size you want Windows to show each picture. Ninety percent is the default.

7. Click the Browse button under the Use pictures in this folder option and select the folder containing your pictures.

8. To stretch images that are small, select Stretch Small Pictures. This may distort some pictures, but it will make smaller pictures easier to see.

9. If you want to view filenames for each image, select Show File Names. This places the path and filename at the top of the screen.

10. To display a transition effect after a picture, select Use Transition Effects Between Pictures.

11. To move through the list of pictures using your keyboard, select Allow Scrolling Through Pictures with the Keyboard.

12. Click OK twice.

Using Local and Group Policy to Control Windows XP

Windows uses policies to help you manage system settings on multiple computers. Policies let you customize system settings on one computer and then copy those settings to other computers in your organization. The amount of time to set up individual computers is reduced several-fold when you use policies.

Group Policy Explained

Policies can be stored locally on individual computers or set up to download to computers when the computer logs onto a network. Policies stored on a computer are commonly called *local policies. Group policies* are those policies that are managed by the system administrator on a network domain. If you have a simple workgroup of machines—that is, without a domain—you must store the policy locally.

To create these policies, you use the Group Policy snap-in for the Microsoft Management Console (MMC), or *Group Policy editor* for short. Changes you make in the Group Policy editor directly customize settings in the Registry. The items you customize are called Group Policy objects.

To use the Group Policy editor, do the following:

1. Make a complete back up of your system and Registry files.

2. Choose Start and then click the Run command.

3. Type **gpedit.msc** and press ENTER. This displays the Group Policy editor, as shown in Figure 6-28.

4. Select an item in the left pane to expand it, such as Administrative Templates. You may need to expand items several layers to see all the settings you can manage.

5. Select an object in the right pane to modify it. For instance you can set the policy Disable showing the splash screen for Internet Explorer.

6. Double-click the object to modify to open the object's properties sheet (Figure 6-29).

7. Select Enabled. If available, continue setting properties for the item you select.

8. Click OK.

Managing Local Policies

To manage a local policy, simply perform the edits necessary for the objects you want to modify. Each time you start Windows under this user, Windows uses the policy you just created. The policy file is stored in the \Windows\System32\GroupPolicy folder.

Managing Group Policies

Group policies are stored on a domain server so that when a computer connects to the domain, the policy is downloaded locally and policies are established on that local computer. The group policy files are stored on the Active Directory Controller in your domain until they are downloaded. The group policies you download take precedence over any locally modified policies.

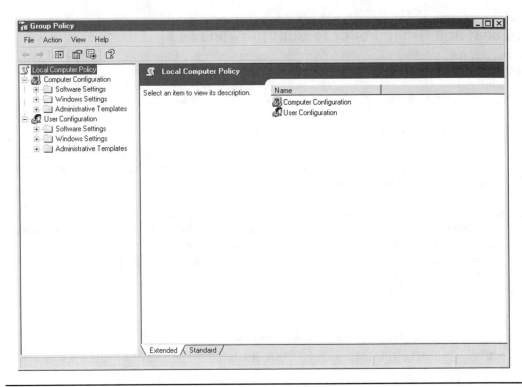

FIGURE 6-28   The Group Policy editor

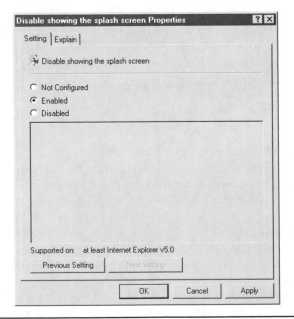

FIGURE 6-29   A properties sheet for the Internet Explorer policy Disable showing the splash screen

Getting the Most from Windows XP Media

I n this chapter you'll find the answers to the following questions:

- How do I copy my music CDs to my computer?
- Can I listen to the radio on my computer?
- How do I copy pictures from my digital camera to my computer?
- I need help modifying and printing digital pictures. What's available in Windows XP?
- How do I back up my digital photos so they aren't lost?
- Can I copy video to my computer to make my own movies?
- How do I put a video I made on my computer onto a CD?

Audio

What a difference a few years makes. The little application that once simply played back your favorite Yanni or Metallica CDs while you worked is now a major multimedia application. With Media Player 9, you can play CDs, copy music to CDs, tune in radio stations, and watch high-quality video. Some Media Player features include

- Playing music CDs
- Playing digital audio files
- Copying audio tracks from CDs
- Creating a customized playlist of your music
- Playing video files
- Copying audio files to a CD-R (Compact Disc-Recordable) or CD-RW (Compact Disk-Rewritable) disc
- Playing a radio station on the Internet
- Playing DVD (Digital Video Disc) and VCD (Video Compact Disc) discs
- Applying skins to let you "visualize" your music

- Viewing online information about an artist or album you're playing
- Adding lyrics to a file
- Transferring music and videos to portable players, such as Pocket PCs and MP3 players

Getting the Most from Media Player

On the surface, Windows Media Player is fairly easy to use. If you want to simply play back audio CDs, insert the CD and, if prompted, select the option to play an audio disc. To play back a music file stored on your hard disk, double-click the file. With either of these cases, your copy of Media Player will automatically launch and start playing the music.

NOTE *Computers with other media playing programs (such as MusicMatch Jukebox) may be configured to automatically handle audio files on your system. If this is the case and you want Media Player to be your default player, use the Tools | Options | File Types tab in Media Player to change file-type associations. Just assign all audio and video file types to Media Player.*

Windows Media Player supports the following file types:

- Windows Media (.asf, .asx, .drv-ms, .wpl, .wm, .wmx, .wmd, .wmz)
- Windows Media Audio (.wma, .wax)
- Windows Media Video (.wmv, .wvx)
- DVD Video
- Music CD (.cda)
- Windows Video (.avi)
- Windows Audio (.wav)
- Movie file (.mpeg, .mpg, .mpe, .m1v, .mp2, .mpv2, .mp2v, .mpa)
- MP3 audio (.mp3, .m3u)
- MIDI (.midi, .mid, .rmi)
- AIFF audio (.aiff, .aif, .aifc, .aiff)
- AU audio (.au, .snd)

Backing Up and Restoring Licensed and Protected Files

Licensed and *protected files* are digital media files used to protect copyrighted material, namely audio and video files used by Media Player. These files authorize you to use the files legally on your computer for a period of time or indefinitely. Without a license for a file, Windows Media Player cannot play the file. Licenses are granted by the owner of the art and can be downloaded from the Internet or purchased via other means (such as retail outlets).

Before you upgrade to Windows XP SP2, you will want to back up your music licenses and the restore them after SP2 is installed. Actually, any time you upgrade or reinstall the operating system on your system, plan on backing up your licenses. Also, Media Player is set up to remind you periodically to back up the licenses.

To back up licenses, do the following:

1. Start Windows Media Player.

2. Choose Tools and then License Management. The License Management dialog box appears (Figure 7-1).

3. Click the Change button to set the Location path to a backup location. By default the licenses will be backed up to the ...\My Documents\My Music\License Backup folder. Select a different folder if desired and click OK.

4. Click the Back Up Now button to back up the licenses.

5. Click the OK button when the Transfer Complete dialog box appears.

You may need to restore your licenses if you perform a system upgrade, move files to a different computer, or have to reinstall Windows after a system crash. To restore your licenses, do the following:

1. Connect to the Internet, if you are not already connected.

2. Start Windows Media Player.

3. Choose Tools and then License Management.

4. Click the Restore Now button. The License Management dialog box shown in Figure 7-2 appears. It explains that you will need access to the Internet to restore your licenses.

5. Click OK. Media Player sends a request out over the Internet to ensure the licenses you are restoring are valid for your system. Depending on your system speed, number of licenses, and connection speed to the Internet, this process can take several minutes to complete.

6. Click OK when the Transfer Complete dialog box appears.

***

NOTE *To learn more about licenses and protected files, visit the Windows Media Player 9 Series Privacy Statement at http://www.microsoft.com/windows/windowsmedia/privacy/9splayer.aspx.*

Moving Your CDs to Your Hard Disk

Media Player lets you move your CD audio collection to your hard disk and build a *digital jukebox* of music. A digital jukebox provides several benefits and features over simply

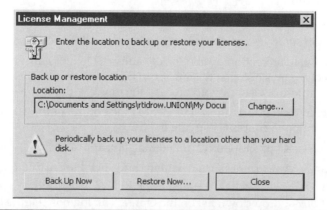

FIGURE 7-1   Use the License Management dialog box to back up and restore your licenses.

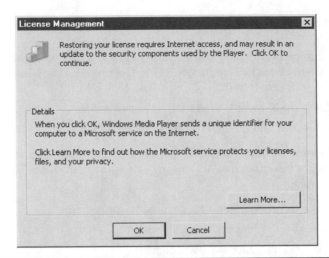

FIGURE 7-2   Restore your Media Player licenses using the License Management dialog box.

playing back CDs on a regular CD player. Some of these benefits and features include the following:

- Enables you to search for music more easily and quickly
- Helps you organize your music
- Enables you to burn CDs of your music
- Lets you create custom "mixes" of your music
- Provides a way to create playlists of your music
- Allows you to rate songs
- Enables you to add lyrics to your music

To move audio CD content to your hard drive, do the following:

1. Insert the audio CD.
2. From the dialog box that appears (Figure 7-3), choose Copy Music from CD.
3. Click OK. On some systems, the Copy Options (1 of 2) dialog box appears.
4. Select the music protection option for the audio CD you've inserted. You can copy protect the music so that the music can be played only on this computer or a compatible secure device. Or you can copy the music without copy protection added.
5. Click the copyright information statement at the bottom of the dialog box. You must select this option to continue copying the CD.
6. Click Next. The Copy Options (2 of 2) dialog box appears.
7. Select Change My Current Format Settings and click Finish. (Note that you can keep your settings by clicking the Keep My Current Format Settings and clicking Finish.)
8. From the Format drop-down list on the Options dialog box (Figure 7-4), select the audio format bit rate. If you choose Windows Media Audio variable bit rate, you

FIGURE 7-3   By default, this dialog box appears when you insert a CD.

save on disk space, but you also can lose some of the audio quality. The Windows Media Audio Lossless setting, however, provides the best audio setting but it also can greatly increase the file size. (It can use more than 400MB per CD.)

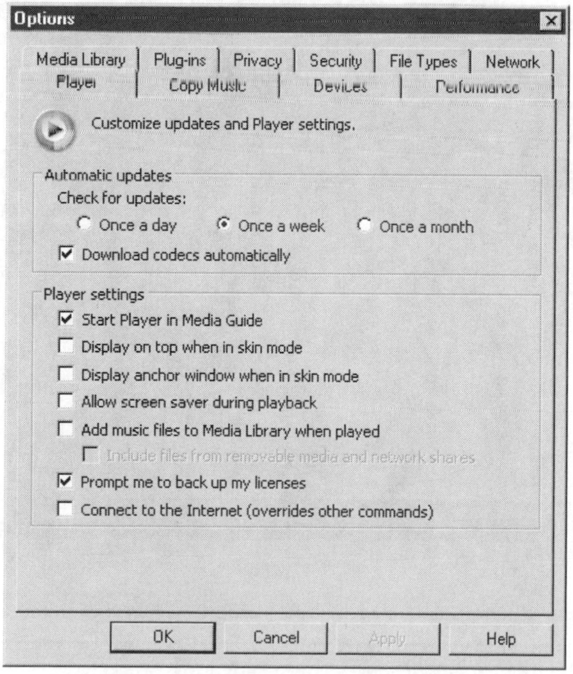

FIGURE 7-4   The Options dialog box lets you change audio copy settings.

9. If you select Windows Media Audio and want to adjust the audio quality setting, move the Audio Quality slider up or down to modify the file size setting.

10. Click OK. Windows Media Player starts copying the CD, as shown in Figure 7-5.

As Media Player finishes copying a track, the Copy Status column displays the label Copied to Library. To stop the copying process, click the Stop Copy button at the top of the Media Player window.

Click the Media Library button on the left pane of the Media Player to display the All Music pane, which lists all of the media items set up to play back in Media Player (Figure 7-6). If this is the first time you have used the Media Library, you can have Media Player search for media files on your computer and list them in the All Music pane. You also can click F3 or choose Tools | Search for Media Files to run the search. Click Search from the Add To Media Library By Searching Computer dialog box (Figure 7-7). Click the Advanced Options to additional searching options (Figure 7-8).

From the All Music pane, expand the All Music and Albums categories to see the listing of the audio CD you just copied. To play back a track, double-click it in the Title column.

FIGURE 7-5 Windows Media Player copying a CD

FIGURE 7-6   View media items with the Media Library option.

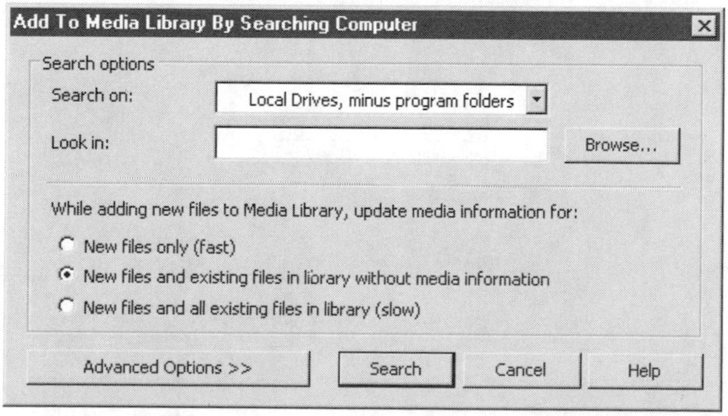

FIGURE 7-7   Search for media items using the Add To Media Library By Searching Computer dialog box.

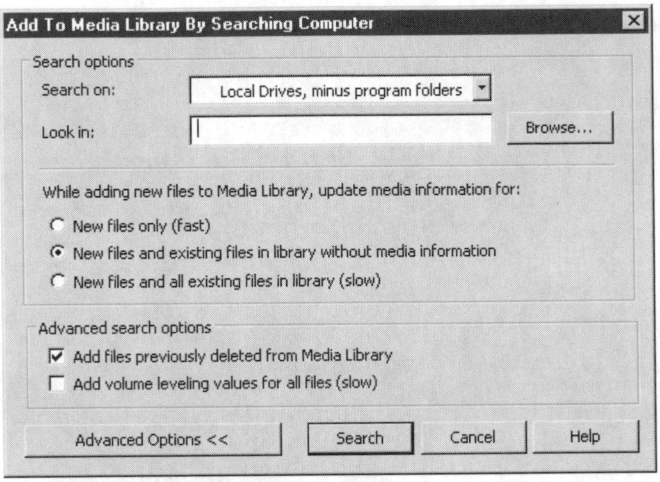

FIGURE 7-8 Pick additional search options for your search.

To add information about a track, right-click on the track and choose Advanced Tag Editor. On the Advanced Tag Editor dialog box (Figure 7-9), fill out the Track Info, Artist Info, Lyrics, Pictures, and Comments tabs as desired. Some of the fields are automatically filled in by the information that Media Player collects from the CD or from online sources. Click OK when finished.

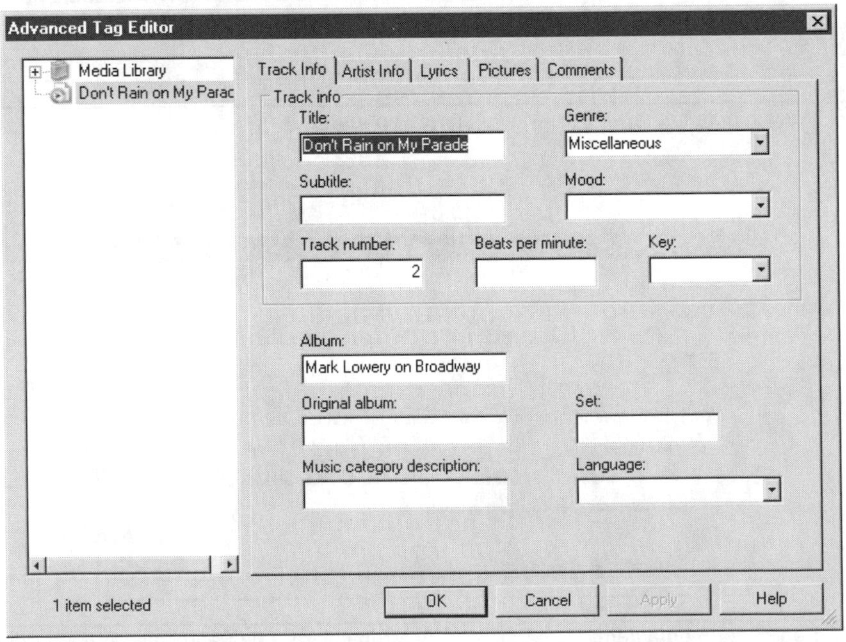

FIGURE 7-9 Fill out track information using the Advanced Tag Editor dialog box.

Streaming Internet Radio

Another feature of Windows Media Player 9 Series is streaming Internet radio. With streaming Internet radio you can listen to radio stations that broadcast over the Internet. Connect to the Internet and then click the Radio Tuner icon on the left pane of the Media Player. Icons for radio stations on the Internet will appear. Click these icons to find out more about the stations and to learn how you can access the streaming radio content.

Some Internet radio stations do not offer their content for free. You sometimes have to pay a monthly or annual fee to receive a username and password to access the station's content. Some stations, however, do offer free content—usually archived stories or news reports—so you can sample the station before deciding to purchase time on the station.

To add a station to your Media Player library, do the following:

1. Start Media Player and click the Radio Tuner.

2. Find the station you want to add to your library.

3. Choose File and then click the Add to Media Library command.

4. Click Add Currently Playing Track. A link to the radio station is added to the Radio category when you click the Media Library icon on the left pane of Media Player.

NOTE *Internet radio content is streamed to Media Player for playback. If you are behind a firewall or proxy server, you may need to ask your network administrator how to set up Media Player to handle this type of data. In some cases, in fact, you may not be allowed to stream content to Media Player if your administrator has barred this type of data to your computer. To see the settings for your version of Media Player, choose Tools | Options and click the Network tab. To set a specific port in which streaming content is accessed by your Media Player, select Use Ports and specify a range of ports. To set up proxy settings, click the Configure button and fill out the Configure Protocol dialog box settings.*

Broadcasting Music from Your PC to Your Stereo

Most standard PC speakers are good enough to listen to standard computer audio files. However, if you plan to listen to high-quality audio CDs or want to watch your DVDs with high-quality audio, consider broadcasting over your stand-alone stereo. There are a couple of different options to choose from when deciding to do this.

The basic way is to hook up the stereo receiver to your PCs audio jack. This is the same jack you use to hook up external PC speakers. On your stereo, change the input control to auxiliary and play the audio file on your PC. One problem with this approach is that you must hook up your PC and receiver physically, meaning you must run long enough cable between the two devices, or simply position your PC close to your stereo.

Another option for broadcasting music from the PC to the stereo is to use a wireless solution. One type of device for this is the Linksys Wireless-B Music System. This device uses a wireless connection based on the Wireless-B (802.11b) network specification to allow your PC and stereo to communicate. You do not need to make physical connections to make this option work.

To learn more about wireless solutions for broadcasting music from your PC to stereo, visit http://www.linksys.com/products/product.asp?grid=33&scid=38&prid=631 on the Internet.

Windows Messenger

Windows Messenger is a chat program. With Windows Messenger you can communicate with other users who have a .NET Passport ID. This can include colleagues, family, friends, clients, and coworkers. You can send and receive real-time messages from other users, much like communicating with a telephone call but you use text instead.

NOTE *You can obtain a .NET Passport ID the first time you use Windows Messenger. Or you can visit http://www.passport.net and click the Register for your free .NET Passport button. Fill out the web pages with the requested information.*

Windows Messenger also allows desktop conferencing. You can send and receive data files, pictures, videos, and sound files with other users. With the Remote Assistance feature, you can allow remote users to log onto your computer and help you with a system problem or view a program on your computer.

Using Windows Messenger

Windows XP SP2 includes an enhanced security feature that locks down some of the holes in Windows Messenger. When you first launch Messenger after installing SP2, you are presented with a firewall screen asking if you if you want to keep certain areas of Windows locked down because of security reasons, or want to go ahead and unlock the features.

To start using Windows Messenger, do the following:

1. Click the Windows Messenger icon on the task tray.
2. Click the Click Here to Sign In link.
3. Walk through the .NET Passport Wizard depending on your status. For example, you can sign in with an existing Passport or create a new one.
4. Sign in using your .NET Passport ID and password.

To communicate with other users, you must set them up as contacts in your Contacts list. To do this, follow these steps:

1. In Windows Messenger, click the Add a Contact link (Figure 7-10).
2. In the Add a Contact dialog box, select By E-mail Address or Sign-in Name if you know your contact's address or sign-in name. Or select Search for a Contact if you need to search for a contact's address or sign-in name. Here we'll show you how to add a contact with the first choice.
3. Click Next.
4. Type the full e-mail address of the contact you want to add. The user must have a .NET Passport to become a contact in your Contacts list.

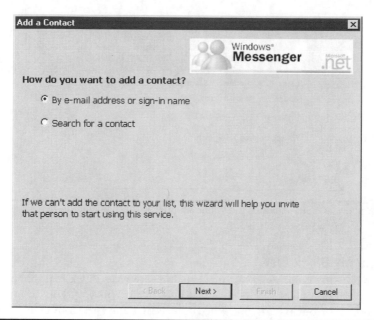

FIGURE 7-10   Add a new contact to Windows Messenger.

5. Click Next. Windows Messenger adds the contact to your list.

6. Click Next to continue adding users, or click Finish when done. New contacts are listed in the main window under the All Contacts heading.

To communicate with someone via Windows Messenger, open Windows Messenger and do the following:

1. Click the Send an Instant Message link to display the Send an Instant Message dialog box.

2. From the My Contacts tab, select the name of the user you want to send a message to.

3. Click OK.

4. If your Windows XP SP2 Firewall is enabled, you'll see a Windows Firewall dialog box like the one shown in Figure 7-11 warning you that this program (Messenger) can receive unsolicited and possibly harmful information from the Internet.

5. Select Unblock This Program to continue.

6. Click OK to continue to the Conversation window (Figure 7-12).

6. In the bottom part of the window, type your message. If desired, change the message font and add Emoticons (smiley faces, etc.) to your message.

7. Click Send. The user you selected will receive the message. When the user replies to it, the message appears in the upper part of the Conversation window.

8. Continue your conversation as necessary.

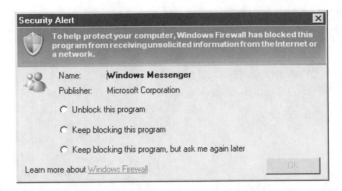

FIGURE 7-11 Windows XP SP2 includes the Windows Firewall that, by default, stops Windows Messenger from receiving data.

Changing the My Block List

With Windows XP SP2, Windows Messenger includes the My Block List that allows you to specify users you don't want to receive messages from. This way you do not receive unsolicited messages from just anyone who has a .NET Passport. Conversely, Messenger also includes the My Allow List that lets you list all those users who can send you messages and see your name in the online status window.

By default, all users you add to your Contacts List are added to your My Allow List. However, you can block any contact so they cannot send you messages unsolicited.

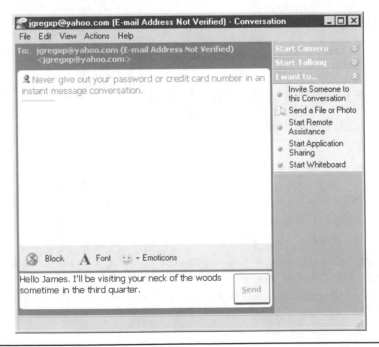

FIGURE 7-12 The Conversation window

To set up your My Allow List and My Block List, do the following:

1. Start Windows Messenger and click Tools.

2. Click Options and select the Privacy tab (Figure 7-13).

3. If you want to make sure only those that are included in your contacts list are allowed to send you messages and see you in the online status window, keep the Other .NET Messenger listing in the My Block List field.

4. To block a contact from the My Allow List, select the contact's name and click Block. This moves the contact to the My Block List.

5. Click OK.

Other SP2 stuff

SP2 introduces a handful of changes to Windows Messenger. First, Windows Messenger with SP2 blocks file transfers if the sender is not on your Contacts list and the file is on the unsafe file list maintained by Internet Explorer 6 (and also used by Outlook Express). If the sender is on your Contacts list, Windows Messenger prompts you to decide what action to take with the file (open or save) based on the file type.

Another change in Windows Messenger is that it requires a user display name that is different from the user's e-mail address. This change helps mitigate the possibility that a virus could extract the e-mail address from the text files that store your conversations (if you save them). In addition, because Windows Firewall is enabled by default, you must configure it to allow Windows Messenger traffic (although the default Windows Firewall configuration places Windows Messenger on the exceptions list).

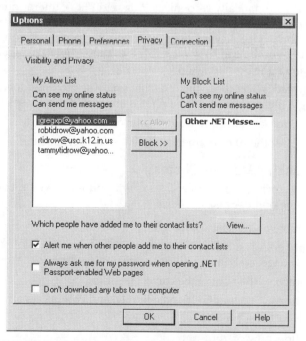

FIGURE 7-13   The Privacy tab lets you block or allow users.

Digital Photography

Digital cameras are now one of the most popular devices users hook up to their computers. Digital cameras allow users to snap photographs and instantly view, edit, and print out pictures. Windows XP includes several features that help you manage, edit, and work with digital photos.

Working with Digital Photos

If you have a computer that has a USB (Universal Serial Bus) port—most computers sold today do—you can use a digital camera to view and manage your photos. Some cameras include ports that allow you to directly connect your camera to the USB port to download pictures (this is called *tethering*). Others include a removable memory card that you can read using a built-in or attached memory card reader.

Whichever method your camera requires, Windows XP has the built-in software that allows you to view and transfer your pictures from camera to computer.

NOTE *Some digital cameras may require that you use their own propriety software to read some of the file formats that the camera uses. If this is the case, consult the digital camera documentation for help installing and using that software.*

To transfer pictures from your camera to the computer, do the following steps:

1. Connect your camera to the computer using the required cable (usually a Universal Serial Bus, or USB, cable). Or insert the memory card in an attached memory card reader.
2. Windows XP automatically recognizes Plug and Play cameras and the Scanner and Camera Wizard starts. Walk through the wizard to set up your camera. If prompted for it, insert the device driver CD for your specific camera. If your camera is not Plug and Play, you'll need to use the Printers and Other Hardware Control Panel applet to launch the Scanners and Cameras tool.
3. When prompted, select those pictures that you want to download to your computer. When using a memory card, all the photos are automatically selected for transfer.
4. Click Next. Choose a location to store your photos.
5. Click Next. After the photos are transferred, select Next or Finish.

Managing and Backing Up Your Photos

With Windows XP, you can perform several tasks with photos saved on your computer. The following are just some of those tasks:

- Saving, deleting, and backing up digital photos.
- Using a photo editor, such as Adobe PhotoShop, to modify a photo. This includes cropping an image, resizing a photo, and removing "red eye" from a picture.
- Rotating photos so they are in the correct position.
- Sending pictures via e-mail to friends, family, and coworkers.
- Printing photos in multiple sizes, including 5×7s, 8×10s, and wallets.
- Creating a slideshow of your photos.
- Using Windows XP to order prints of your photos online.

NOTE *You can download Photo Story 2 LE to get an introduction to Microsoft's digital photography story editor. Visit http://www.microsoft.com/windows/plus/dme/try.asp for more information.*

To back up your photos to a CD-R or CD-RW, do the following:

1. Insert a CD-R or CD-RW disc.
2. Open Windows Explorer or My Computer.
3. Navigate to the folder holding your photos.
4. Select all the photos you want to archive. Press CTRL-A to select all of them. Or, select the entire folder.
5. Right-click and choose Send To.
6. From the Send To menu, select the option to save files to your CD-R or CD-RW.
7. Click the CD-R or CD-RW icon in Windows Explorer or My Computer.
8. Click Write These Files to CD, as shown in Figure 7-14.
9. Click Next and let Windows burn the images to your CD.

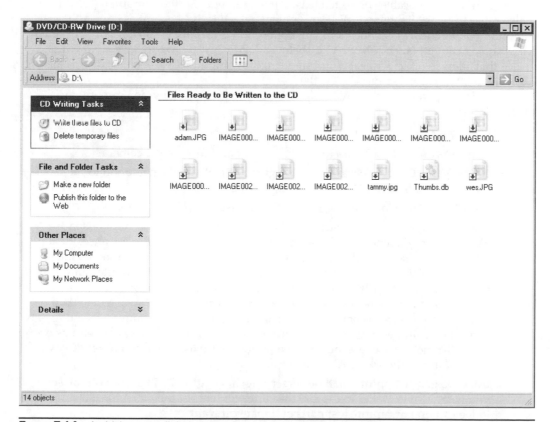

FIGURE 7-14   Archiving your digital photos is easy with a CD-R or CD-RW.

Digital Video

Windows XP is a nice platform for creating digital video files and editing them. In fact, Windows XP includes free movie editing software called Windows Movie Maker 2. With Movie Maker you can capture video from an external video device, such as a VCR, digital video camera, analog video camera, or Webcam. As you copy video to Movie Maker, Movie Maker creates segments of the video so you can manipulate those segments into your own custom movie.

NOTE *Movie Maker 2 is available with Windows XP SP2. However, you can download a copy of it from http://www.microsoft.com/windowsxp/using/moviemaker/default.mspx.*

There are additional transitions and visual effects available for Movie Maker included with the Microsoft Plus! Digital Media Edition software. To learn more about that package, visit http://www.microsoft.com/windows/plus/PlusHome.asp.

Moving Video Tapes to Your PC

In order to copy video content from a video device, you must have a way to download the video to your computer. With a digital video (DV) camera, this is usually accomplished by using an IEEE 1394 cable connected between the camera and the computer. (IEEE 1394 is also referred to as "Firewire.") Webcam content, which is live content, is copied to your computer via the Webcam connection. This connection is usually via a USB port. For older video analog content (such as your VHS, Beta, and 8MM), you have to have a hardware device that allows you to connect your camera to the computer. One such product is the AVerMedia DVD EZMaker Pro USB2.0 device.

The following steps show how to capture video from a digital video camera into Movie Maker:

1. Start Windows Movie Maker.

2. Connect your video camera to your computer and turn on the camera.

3. On the Video Capture Wizard screen (Figure 7-15), fill out the name and location fields for the video. By default, Windows places your video files in the My Videos folder.

4. Click Next. The Video Setting wizard screen displays (Figure 7-16).

5. Select the capture quality and format for your video file. The amount of space a file consumes depends on the quality of its playback setting. For instance, the top setting on this screen will consume 3MB of disk space for each minute of video you save. As you can see from this, a short video that's only 20 minutes long will consume almost 600MB of storage space, the amount you can save to a standard CD-R. However, the next setting (DV-AVI, which stands for Digital Video-Audio Video Interleave) will consume 178MB of disk space for each minute, meaning only about four minutes of video can be burned to a CD-R later. The Other settings drop-down list includes several other video settings, such as Video for Pocket PCs, Video for local area networks (LAN), and so on.

6. Click Next. The Capture Method screen appears (Figure 7-17). Here you can set if you want Movie Maker to capture the entire contents of the video from the digital video camera, or capture just parts of it that you want.

7. Click Next. If you selected to capture the entire tape, Movie Maker rewinds the tape to the beginning and then you can start capturing the contents. If you select the

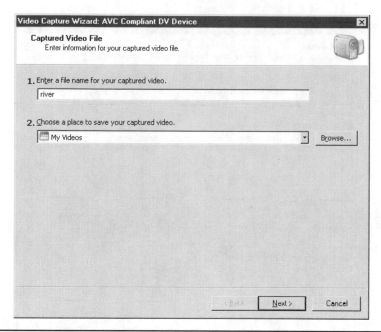

FIGURE 7-15 Windows displays a wizard to help you capture video to your computer.

option of capturing just parts of the tape, a Capture Video screen like the one shown in Figure 7-18 appears.

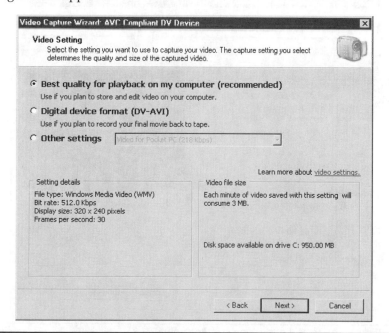

FIGURE 7-16 Set up your video capture settings here.

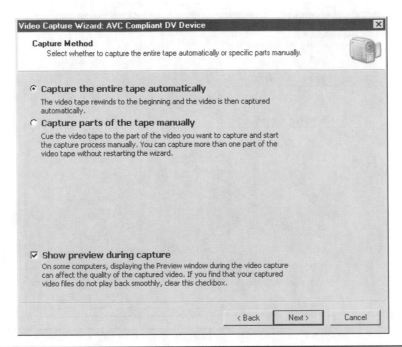

FIGURE 7-17   Set if you want Movie Maker to capture all or parts of your video.

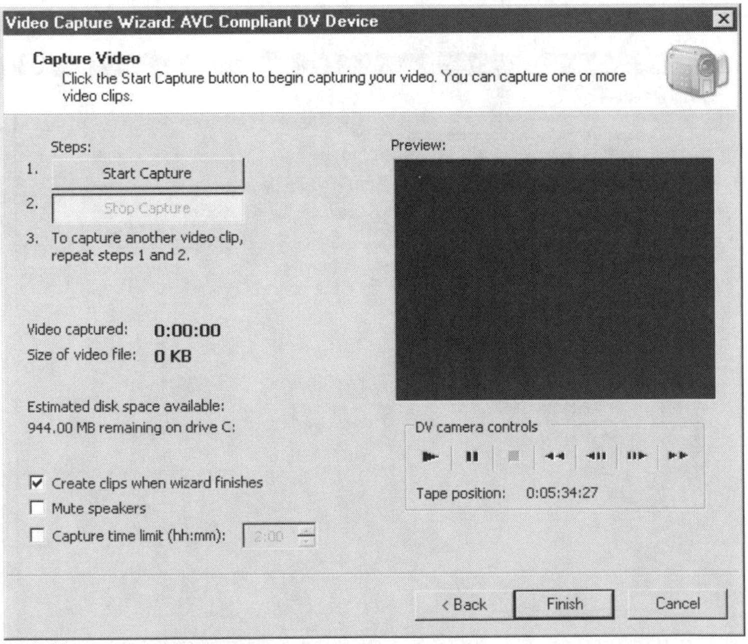

FIGURE 7-18   Pick the parts of the tape you want to capture.

8. Use the DV camera controls to move through your tape. When you find something to capture, stop and then click the Start Capture button. Click Stop Capture when you've captured the part you want to capture. Use the DV camera controls again to move through your tape as before. Repeat this process until all the parts you want to capture are saved to your computer. Then click Finish.

Movie Maker displays your video capture clips in the Collection pane. You can drag and drop these clips to the storyboard pane at the bottom of the window to create your own movie. See Figure 7-19 to see Movie Maker's window. To edit your movie, click the 2. Edit Movie step on the Movie Tasks pane to reveal the editing items available, including video effects, transitions, credits, and titles. Select an item and drag and drop it to the storyboard to add it to your movie.

NOTE *To learn more about creating movies with Movie Maker, visit the Movie Maker web pages beginning with http://www.microsoft.com/windowsxp/using/moviemaker/default.mspx.*

FIGURE 7-19 You can use Movie Maker to create your own movies to play back on your computer or other video devices, such as your home DVD player.

Putting Video on CD or DVD

After you create your own movies using Movie Maker or other video software, you can save them to CD-R/RW or DVD-R for storage and playback to standard DVD players. With Movie Maker you can save the movie to CD using Save to CD item in the 3. Finish Movie step in the Movie Tasks pane. To burn to a DVD, you must have a DVD recorder and DVD recording software. An example of this software is the Gear Pro Professional Edition (visit http://www.mp3towav.org/GEAR-PRO-Professional-Edition/ for more information).

The following steps show how to burn a CD using Movie Maker:

1. Create a movie using Movie Maker. Save your movie.

2. Insert a CD-R or CD-RW disc into your CD recorder. Click Cancel if prompted by Windows on what you want to do with the inserted CD.

3. Click the Save to CD link under the 3. Finish Movie step in the Movie Tasks pane.

4. Enter a filename and name of the movie for the CD on the Saved Movie File wizard screen (Figure 7-20).

5. Click Next.

6. Select a Movie Setting (Figure 7-21).

7. Click Next. Movie Maker saves your movie to disc.

8. Click Finish.

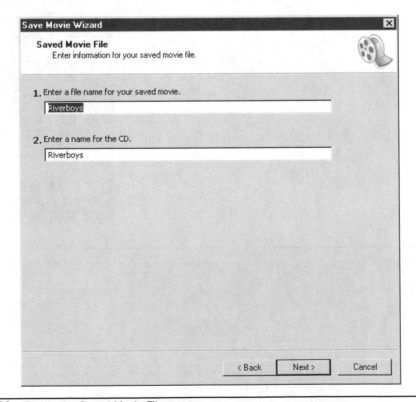

FIGURE 7-20   Fill out the Saved Movie File screen.

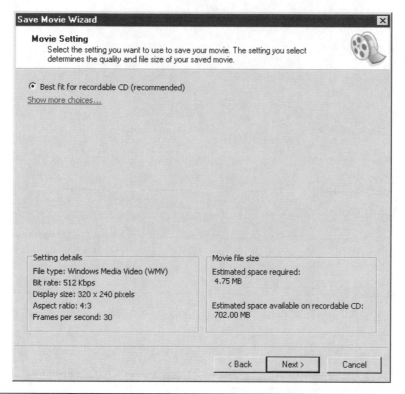

FIGURE 7-21   Select a movie setting, if offered, for saving your movie to CD.

Using Windows XP Media Center Edition (MCE)

In this chapter you'll find the answers to the following questions:

- What is the difference between Windows XP Media Center Edition and other versions of Windows XP?

- Can you install Media Center Edition on your existing computer or do you have to buy a new one with MCE preinstalled?

- What are the most important criteria for selecting a Media Center PC?

- In connecting my Media Center PC to my TV, which connection type will provide the best picture quality?

- What video sources can be used with the Media Center PC?

- What new features were added to Windows XP Media Center Edition 2004?

- What are the advantages of a Media Center PC over TiVO and other PVR services?

- How do I use the Media Center PC to watch and pause live TV?

- How do I use the Media Center PC to schedule TV programs to be recorded?

- How do I use the Media Center PC to organize and display my digital photos and videos?

- How do I use the Media Center PC to organize and listen to my digital music files?

- Can I watch TV programs recorded by the Media Center application on non-MCE computers?

- Can I use the Media Center PC to watch commercial DVD movies?

- How can I use the Media Center PC to listen to radio?

- Can I save my recorded TV programs on a CD or DVD?

PCs began as productivity tools, used primarily by businesses to produce and later to share documents, do research, and process information. Over the years, the personal computer has become much more personal. Today, PCs are used at home for many different purposes. One purpose that is growing in popularity is home entertainment.

Multimedia PCs are built on powerful hardware that is capable of handling processor- and memory-intensive audio and video applications. Users can now use their computers to play music, watch movies and TV, and display photos they take with their digital cameras.

Microsoft originally developed a software add-on for Windows XP code-named Freestyle. This was designed as an interface for centrally managing digital media. Prior to being released to the public in 2002, the concept grew into a whole new "flavor" of Windows XP, called Media Center Edition. MCE is a superset of XP Professional; in addition to all the features and functionality of Pro, it includes everything in XP Service Pack 1, along with the Media Center application that is the heart of the edition.

Media Center provides a user-friendly way to organize and view pictures, organize and edit digital home movies, organize and play music files and DVDs, listen to Internet radio, and—perhaps most significantly—record and play back TV programs. This last feature allows a Media Center computer to function as a personal video recorder (PVR) without some of the drawbacks and limitations of competing PVR devices. The Media Center connects to the Internet to download programming information for the Guide, which is then used to schedule recordings.

You can also use the Media Center PC for anything for which you would use a desktop XP computer: word processing, web surfing, e-mail, etc. It runs any program that will run on Windows XP Pro. In the next section, we'll look at the components of a Media Center PC—both the hardware and the software—and what's new in the latest edition, Media Center 2004.

Introducing MCE and MCE 2004

As a separate edition of Windows XP, Media Center Edition is not available to consumers as an upgrade or full operating system package. It is available only to original equipment manufacturers (OEMs) to preinstall on systems they sell. This ensures that MCE will be installed only on systems that meet the rather extensive hardware requirements. Microsoft anticipated that if they released the new flavor of XP to the public as software, it would result in overwhelming support issues as people tried to install the OS on unsupported hardware.

Thus, to get XP Media Center Edition, you must buy a computer that comes with it preinstalled. Hewlett-Packard shipped the first Media Center PCs in the United States, and other vendors soon followed. Media Center PCs are now available from HP, Sony, Gateway, Toshiba, ViewSonic, Dell, and a number of other Microsoft partner vendors who make custom systems.

NOTE   *There is an exception to the "only available preinstalled" rule. XP Media Center Edition software, like other Microsoft operating system software, is available to Windows developers through the Microsoft Developers Network (MSDN).*

The concept of PC as an entertainment device has been around for a long time. In fact, computer games were some of the most popular applications on the earliest home PCs. Photo editing and graphics manipulation weren't far behind. Fast processors and large amounts of memory, together with more sophisticated sound cards, video cards, and computer speakers, made it possible to listen to music and play CD or DVD video on the computer. Then high-speed Internet connections made it easy to download large multimedia files. Finally, large high-quality monitors and TV tuner cards made it practical to use the computer as an entertainment hub. This doesn't mean that the evolution of personal computer to home entertainment center has been an entirely smooth one. Lack of standardization—both on the hardware and software sides—has created a rocky and somewhat confusing road for consumers who want to tie their personal computers into their home entertainment systems. A number of software vendors provide home entertainment solutions, but many of these address only one part of the issue (for instance, DVR functionality). Hardware compatibility is another problem. The Media Center PC concept was designed to address these problems.

A Media Center PC can stand alone as an entertainment device, or it can be integrated into a home audio or home theater system for even greater flexibility. The consolidation of PC and TV was first marketed by Gateway with its Destination systems in the late 1990s that combined a 333 MHz Celeron processor, 32MB of RAM, and a huge (at the time) 3.2GB hard disk with a 27-inch television monitor and a remote control keyboard and mouse.

Since then, a number of video card vendors have included TV out, on-board tuners, and more recently, PVR software and remote controls with their cards, and technically savvy computer enthusiasts have been building their own media PCs for years. However, one thing was lacking: standardization. That's what Microsoft provides with XP Media Center Edition.

The Hardware: Choosing or Building an MCE PC

To work properly, a Media Center PC requires the following minimum specifications:

- A high-end processor (over 1 GHz)
- At least 256MB of memory (512MB to 1GB is better)
- A high-capacity hard disk for storing large video files, as the file for a half-hour TV program can be over 1.5GB (a minimum of 80GB; many MPCs come with a 250GB disk)
- A high-end video card and TV tuner (either on board the video card or as a separate card) that captures signal from cable, satellite, or antenna
- A CD-ROM and/or DVD drive (many come with DVD burners)
- A remote control with special controls designed to work with the Media Center application

These items comprise the minimum specifications required to run the Media Center PC OS. Of course, many vendors offer higher-end machines.

If the Media Center PC will be used with a television set rather than a computer monitor, you'll also want a wireless keyboard and mouse so that you can use the computer from a comfortable viewing distance.

A sound card is also necessary. Although not required, many MCPCs include high-end sound cards that provide multichannel output for surround sound speakers or connection to a home audio or home theater receiver/amplifier.

You can output video to a regular computer monitor (CRT or LCD), a regular TV, or a high-resolution TV (projection or plasma). A regular picture tube TV doesn't generally provide high enough resolution for computing tasks such as word processing or reading e-mail; in this case you might want to connect dual video devices: a computer monitor for computing tasks and a TV for using the entertainment features (watching DVD movies, recorded TV, and home videos).

Some Media Center PCs come as integrated one-piece devices with a monitor built in. Most are sold separately so that you can select a monitor of your choice. The Media Center application includes a TV Setup and Calibration Wizard that allows you to properly configure the software for your type of TV signal, type of display, and display settings (brightness, contrast, color hue, etc.).

Selecting a Media Center PC

Media Center PCs (MCPCs) from major vendors and custom PC makers come in a number of different hardware configurations and form factors. Most support at least 512MB of RAM and include IEEE 1394 (FireWire) and USB 2.0 interfaces, which are handy for connecting additional large external hard disks to store big video files. Many include built-in flash memory readers so that you can move a CF or SD card directly from your digital camera to the MCPC to download or view your photos.

Most vendors' Media Center PCs come in regular minitower or tower cases, while others, including Gateway, NeveusMedia, and ZT Group, offer a compact "flat box" or rack format that makes the PC look like an audio or home theater component to integrate better into your entertainment center, as shown in Figure 8-1.

Figure 8-1 MCPCs that look like home theater components integrate into your entertainment center.

Touch Systems markets a Media Center PC in a cube or "toaster" form factor. Another option is the all-in-one form factor offered by Gateway, with monitor, speakers, and CPU built into a single package. One vendor, Toshiba, even offers Media Center Edition on high-end notebook computers, allowing you to take your entertainment system on the road.

Selecting the right MCPC depends on your taste, where you want to locate the PC, and how you want to use it. Important considerations include these:

- Will the MCPC be used for everyday computing tasks (word processing, accounting, e-mail, etc.) as well as entertainment? If so, you might choose a regular tower PC that can sit on a desk and output to both a computer monitor and a TV.

- Is your space limited? If so, you might consider an all-in-one solution or a Media Center laptop, either of which is perfect for dorm rooms or small apartments.

- Will the MCPC be primarily a home entertainment device that needs to visually coordinate with your home audio and home theater components? If so, consider the "flat box" or AV "rack" style.

Building Your Own Media Center PC

Although the MCE software is not commercially available to consumers, many hobbyists have built their own Media Center PCs using the MSDN versions of the software or the operating system software that comes with an OEM Media Center PC. Building a Media Center PC is much like building any PC, but you need to ensure that you have sufficient processing power and RAM (more is better) and a hard disk that's big enough to store all those large media files. You also need to pay special attention to the video card, wireless keyboard and pointing device, and MCE-compatible remote control. You'll probably want a flash memory reader to easily transfer files from other devices. Finally, you'll want to consider case style if your MCPC will be "on display" in your living room or family room.

The MCE Video Card   Possibly the most crucial hardware component for the Media Center PC is the video card. Special drivers are required for a video card to work with the Media Center application, and only a few vendors provide such drivers. Luckily, two of the most popular video card vendors, ATI and nVidia, do provide drivers that support Media Center.

Wireless Keyboard and Pointing Device   Wireless input devices aren't mandatory, but if you intend to watch movies and recorded TV on a large-screen television set at a distance, you'll want them. A number of different vendors make wireless keyboard/mouse combinations. The most flexible type of pointing device is the wireless mouse that can be used in the air, like a presentation tool, as well as on a surface. Gyration makes one of the most popular, which can be purchased alone or along with a wireless keyboard.

There are different technologies used for wireless components. Infrared (IR) is often used for keyboards that work with Palm or handheld PCs. For your Media Center PC, you'll want the radio frequency (RF) type. Unlike IR, it doesn't require a direct line of sight and thus gives you more flexibility of positioning.

The MCE Remote Control   For full functionality and the real "Media Center experience," you'll need a remote control designed for MCE. Most MCE vendors will sell extra remotes, and you can buy XP Media Center remotes separately from vendors such as Gyration (http://www.gyration.com/mcr.htm).

Remotes differ slightly from one vendor to another, but all feature a "big green button"—the Media Center Start button that launches the Media Center application, along with transport buttons (stop, play, fast forward, reverse, and pause) for controlling TV, CD, and DVD playback. Shortcut buttons take you to different Media Center features (My TV, My Music, My Pictures, etc.), and a keypad lets you enter channel numbers or text characters. You'll also find volume and channel up/down controls and a quick record button. A typical MCPC remote control is shown in Figure 8-2.

Flash Memory Reader   Although not required, a flash memory reader will make it easy for you to transfer photo, video, and music files between your Media Center PC and other devices, such as digital cameras and MP3 players. Popular flash memory formats include the following:

- CompactFlash (CF) card
- SmartMedia (SM) card
- SecureDigital (SD) card
- MultiMedia Card (MMC)
- Memory Stick and Memory Stick Pro

Vendors often build flash memory slots into their MCPC computers. You can also buy inexpensive USB flash memory readers that accept multiple card types.

The MCPC Case   You can build a Media Center PC in any style of case that will fit the motherboard you've selected: tower, minitower, desktop, or various Small Form Factor (SFF) options. A popular choice is the Shuttle cube or "toaster" SFF platform that comes as a "barebones" unit with the motherboard already installed and a choice of chipsets and CPU sockets (for both AMD and Intel processors). See http://us.shuttle.com/index.asp for more information.

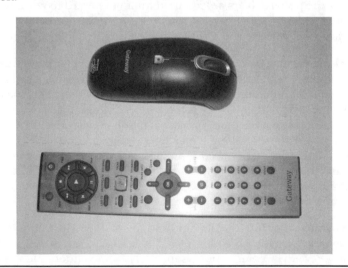

FIGURE 8-2   You can use the remote control or wireless mouse to access MCE features.

Integrating Your Media Center PC with Your Home Audio/Theater System

For the ultimate entertainment experience, you can connect your Media Center PC to your television set, home audio system, and/or home theater system.

Connecting the Media Center PC to Your Television Set or Display Device   For a bigger picture than your computer monitor provides, you can connect the Media Center PC's video output to a television set or large-screen display device such as a plasma or LCD monitor. There are a number of different ways to do this, depending on the MCPC model and display device model you have. In order, from worst to best picture quality, they include the following types of input/output jacks:

- **Composite video**   A single connector for the video signal; looks like a round RCA-type jack).

- **S-video**   A single connector that separates the video into two signals, one for black and white and one for color information; looks similar to a PS/2 mouse/keyboard jack with seven pins.

- **Component video**   Three separate connectors that separate the signal into its three components: black and white and two color difference signals; looks like three round RCA-type jacks, usually color coded or labeled Y, Cb, and Cr.

- **DVI (digital visual interface)**   A single connector that supports high-speed, high-resolution digital displays; looks somewhat like a serial port connector with 24 pins in three rows of eight. Generally only found on high-end HDTV sets.

The display on a regular tube TV has only a 640 × 480 resolution and an interlaced display with a 60 Hz refresh rate. This is not sufficient to display a computer desktop sharply. However, the Media Center application's user interface is designed to display well on this type of TV.

NOTE   *If you want to use a TV to run regular XP applications as well as the Media Center functions, you should connect the Media Center PC to a high-resolution projection or plasma television with component or DVI connectors.*

Connecting the Media Center PC to Your Video Source   To use the TV and PVR functions, you must connect your MCPC to a video signal source. This can be any of the following:

- An antenna

- A direct cable connection

- A digital cable box or satellite receiver ("set-top box")

Coaxial cable is used to connect an antenna or direct cable connection. Composite or S-video cables are used to connect a set-top box. If you have a digital cable box or satellite receiver, you'll also need to connect the MCPC's infrared control to the box's infrared sensor window or "eye." This allows the MCPC's remote control to change channels on the set-top box.

Connecting the Media Center PC to Your Audio or Home Theater System   The exact procedure for connecting your Media Center PC to a stereo sound system or home theater system depends on two things:

- The type of connectors on your MCPC's sound card
- The type of connectors on your audio or home theater system's receiver/amplifier.

Low-end sound cards usually have 1/8" miniphone jacks (round jacks similar to RCA jacks but smaller) and a single stereo jack that carries signals for both left and right speakers. High-end sound cards have separate RCA jacks for the left and right signals, and/or digital input/output jacks (coaxial S/PDIF or digital optical). Digital signals provide the best sound quality and use fiber optic cables. You can buy converters to connect one type of connector on the sound card to a different type on the stereo or home theater system.

To connect your MCPC to a DVD player or VCR, you can use coaxial, composite, S-video, or component cables, depending on the connectors available on the devices. See the manuals for your home sound/theater system and your MCPC for more specific instructions and diagrams.

NOTE *If you don't have a sound system or speakers for the MCPC, you can play the audio on the TV's speakers by connecting the PC's audio OUT jacks to your TV's audio IN jacks.*

Connecting the Media Center PC to the Internet

Internet connectivity is essential to the Media Center application's Personal Video Recorder (PVR) functionality. Most Media Center PCs come with a modem and/or Network Interface Card (NIC). You can connect your MCPC to the Internet in one of the following ways:

- Connect the modem to a phone line and use a dial-up Internet account.
- Connect the NIC's Ethernet jack to a cable or DSL modem or router to use a broadband connection.
- Connect the NIC's Ethernet jack to a hub or switch on a local area network to use the LAN's shared Internet connection.

The Software: Understanding the Media Center Edition OS

The Media Center Edition desktop and Start menu look exactly like those of Windows XP Pro, with the exception of the Media Center application, as shown in Figure 8-3. It's identified by its "green button" icon.

The first time you open the Media Center application, you'll be greeted by a Setup Wizard that guides you through the process of configuring the application to work with your particular TV input source (cable, satellite, or antenna) and your display type. The MCPC must be connected to the Internet to complete the Setup process.

After you've set up the software, you can open the Media Center application from the Start menu or by pressing the (big green) Start button on the remote control.

What's New in MCE 2004?

The first version of XP MCE was geared more toward the "dorm room" entertainment center model, based on the use of a computer monitor. MCE 2004 adds new features and

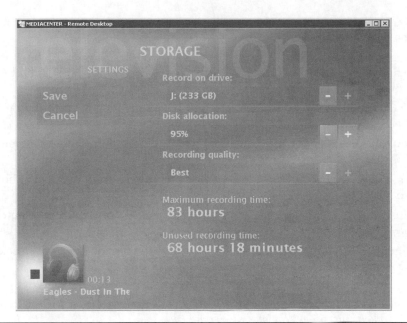

FIGURE 8-3 The Media Center PC Edition of XP includes the Media Center application.

functionality that make it integrate better with the home theater and big screen, including a Display Calibration Wizard that makes it easy to optimize the picture on regular TVs, rear and front projection, and plasma displays, as well as traditional CRT and LCD computer monitors. The new version of MCE also includes better support for the 16:9 widescreen aspect ratio and lets you switch between three video modes: normal, zoom, and stretch video.

Other features new to MCE 2004 include the following:

- Media Center supports accessibility options such as the screen magnifier and screen readers.

- The Remote Learning Wizard makes it easier to set up the Media Center remote control with set-top boxes for digital cable or satellite TV.

- If you're using the Media Center PC's analog modem and you have Caller ID service on the connected phone line, information about incoming phone calls can be displayed on the screen.

- The Media Center application automatically discovers and synchronizes your Windows Media Library files.

- If you use a dial-up connection, you can set Media Center to automatically connect to the Internet, download Guide content, and then disconnect.

- When TV programs that are set to be recorded don't broadcast at the expected time, Media Center will check within a window of time in case the program starts late. Media Center also checks the Guide and records the program if its schedule has been changed.

- You can set priorities on TV programs so that in case of conflicts, the most important one will be recorded.

- Filters have been added to the Guide to allow you to sort through the programming to find specific types of programs, such as news, movies, sports, or children's shows.

- Media Center will now "wake up" when in Standby mode to record programs that have been scheduled.

- You can rewind or fast forward through recorded TV programs at different speeds (3×, 40×, 250× normal speed).

- You can pause live Internet radio, rewind and skip forward within a radio broadcast.

- Music functionality has been enhanced to let you edit or create preset automatic playlists.

- Digital photo functionality has been improved so that you can print selected photos via a simple menu selection.

NOTE *If you have a Media Center computer running the original version of MCE, you can upgrade to MCE 2004 by installing Windows XP Service Pack 2.*

The Media Center Application

When you start the Media Center application, you'll see the interface shown in Figure 8-4. You can select from the following options:

- Online Spotlight
- My Videos
- My Pictures
- My TV
- My Music
- Radio

Online Spotlight, shown in Figure 8-5, is a new feature in Media Center 2004, and it allows you to download multimedia content from various sites, such as Napster, MovieLink, and CinemaNow. You can also get News and access Media Center tips over the Internet.

In the next section, we'll discuss in detail how to use each of the Media Center functions.

Using Media Center Functions

Microsoft's intent in designing the Media Center Edition of Windows XP was to give consumers a way to seamlessly integrate multimedia entertainment with personal computing. While the Media Center application provides ease of use in organizing your home videos, digital photos, and music files, and gives you easy access to Internet radio, the shining star of the Media Center computer is its ability to completely change the experience of watching television.

FIGURE 8-4 The user-friendly Media Center interface allows you to select from a variety of functions.

FIGURE 8-5 Online Spotlight is new in Media Center 2004.

My TV: Using Your PC as a Personal Video Recorder (PVR)

The My TV function within the Media Center application turns your MCE computer into a personal video recorder (PVR) device. Similar devices, such as TiVO and the recording devices provided by satellite companies, have grown tremendously in popularity. An MCE computer has all the same functionality as the standalone PVRs (or DVRs, for Digital Video Recorders, as some vendors call them), with the following advantages:

- There are no monthly fees to pay for programming (Guide content is free).
- There are no real limits on storage space, since you can simply upgrade or add hard disks as you would with any PC.

Of course, the initial cost of a Media Center computer is significantly higher than that of a dedicated PVR device, but not significantly higher than a typical personal computer plus PVR, which is what you get with the MCPC.

To use your MCPC as a PVR, you need to download the Guide. Then you can watch (and pause) live TV, record TV programs you're watching, schedule programs to be recorded automatically, search for specific programs, play back recorded programs, and (if your MCPC has the proper hardware) burn recorded programs to disc to save them. First, you may want to view and adjust the TV settings.

Viewing and Adjusting TV Settings

When you press the My TV button on the remote or select My TV from the Media Center main menu, you'll see four options in the My TV menu (shown in Figure 8-6):

- Guide
- Recorded TV
- Search
- Settings

From the Settings submenu, you can make the following adjustments:

- **Recorder option**   You can view the log showing the history of shows you've recorded, view statistics for the amounts of recording time that have been used and are available, change the recording quality (which will change the amount of disk space required for a program), and change settings for drive storage space.
- **Guide option**   You can update the Guide, edit listings, reset the lineup, and add missing channels.
- **Set up TV Signal option**   Choose or change the type of signal source (cable, satellite, or antenna).
- **Adjust display settings option**   Customize the video display settings such as brightness, hue, etc.
- **Audio option**   Select captioning and audio options.
- **My TV option**   Select whether live TV will start playing when you go to the My TV function (rather than requiring that you select the Live TV option in the menu in order to play it).

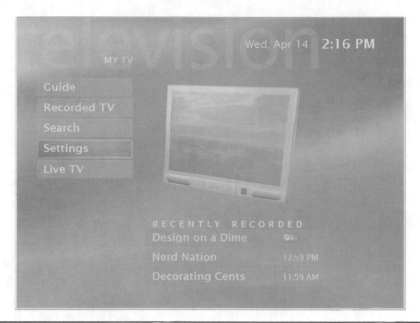

FIGURE 8-6   To view and adjust TV settings, choose Settings from the My TV menu.

Downloading and Using the Guide

When you open the Media Center application for the first time and run the Media Center Setup Wizard, you must enter information for setting up the Guide to download programming. You'll be asked to enter your ZIP code and select the name of your satellite or CATV provider. You can change these settings later (for example, if you switch to a different satellite or cable service) by selecting Settings from the Media Center's My TV menu, and then selecting Guide | Change Guide lineup.

Selecting and Scheduling a Program from the Guide   The Guide contains all the program listings for your TV channels. To use the Guide, select it from the My TV menu. Some Media Center remote controls have a button to take you immediately to the Guide.

You can scroll through the list of current and future programs. You cannot display programs that were delivered earlier than the current time. The Guide shows the channel and network, program name, and start time, as shown in Figure 8-7. If you select a program by highlighting it with the mouse, the up and down arrows on the keyboard, or the up and down controls on the remote and then pressing the OK button, Media Center will display a description of the program at the bottom of the screen.

NOTE   *By default, tips on using the Guide appear at the bottom of the screen. You can turn this feature off by selecting Settings from the Media Center main menu, selecting General, then Notifications, and checking or clearing the TV Tips check box.*

A program information page appears when you select a program (unless the program is currently playing). On this page, shown in Figure 8-8, you can schedule the program to be recorded.

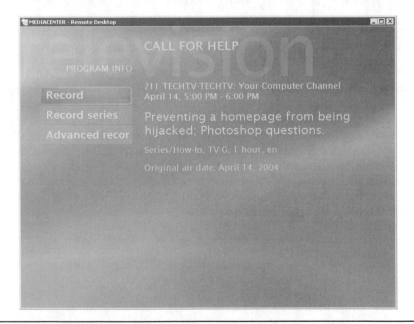

FIGURE 8-7   The Guide shows program information for current and future shows.

You can schedule a single program to be recorded by simply selecting it in the Guide and pressing the Record button on the remote or clicking it with the mouse. If you want to

FIGURE 8-8   You can schedule a recording using the program information page.

record a series (that is, record the show every time it comes on), highlight the show and press Record twice. For more detailed settings—such as whether all episodes should be recorded, or only new ones, and whether to record the series only when it comes on at the selected time and on the selected channel, or every time it comes on regardless of time or channel—use the program information page.

Filtering the Guide Content   You can use the built-in filters to sort Guide content into the following categories:

- Sports
- Movies
- News
- Kids
- Special

To filter, click the Guide button or select Guide on the My TV menu, and then click the Guide button again to display the filter categories. Select one using the mouse or the navigation buttons on the remote. Only the shows that fit into that category will be shown in the Guide.

Searching the Guide Content   You can search for a particular program in the Guide. This is useful if you want to schedule it to be recorded but you don't know when it comes on. Select Search from the My TV menu. The search page allows you to search by title, category, or keyword, as shown in Figure 8-9.

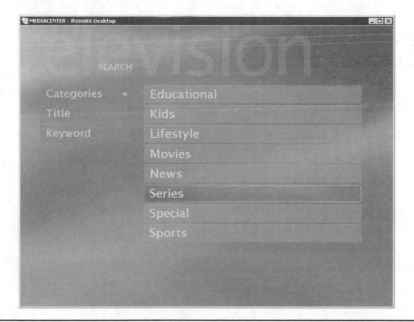

FIGURE 8-9   Use the Search function to find programs by title, category, or keyword.

You can use the keyword option if you know the name of an actor in the program, or a word that appears in the description of the program.

NOTE   You can schedule the Guide to automatically record all programs that feature a particular actor or keyword in the description by selecting My TV | Recorded TV | Add Recording and selecting Keyword.

Updating Guide Content   You can update Guide listings manually or automatically. When you update the Guide, it downloads 14 days of programming. Because scheduling sometimes changes at the last minute, it's recommended that you schedule the Guide to automatically update once or twice per day.

NOTE   You can find out when the Guide was most recently updated by selecting Settings from the Media Center main menu, then selecting TV, and then Guide. Select About Guide data to display information that includes the provider of the listings, the name of the cable or satellite provider and its ID number, the network type, the language, and the start and end dates of the current Guide information. The start date indicates when the information was downloaded.

To update the Guide manually, do the following:

1. In the Media Center main menu, select Settings, then TV, and then Guide.
2. Select Get Guide Data.
3. You will be prompted to begin downloading the Guide listings. Select OK.
4. When the download is finished, a dialog box will appear.

NOTE   You can use the Guide while the listings are being updated.

Recording TV Programs

You can record programs by scheduling them to be recorded in the Guide, as discussed in the previous section, or you can record a show that is currently playing by pressing the Record button on the remote. To stop recording, press the Stop button.

Scheduling Recordings by Channel and Time   If you don't have Guide information available (for example, if your Internet connection is down, so you can't download the Guide), you can still schedule recordings the way you do with a traditional VCR—by channel and time. This is referred to as *scheduling a manual recording*. Here's how:

1. Select My TV from the Media Center main menu.
2. Select Recorded TV from the My TV menu, and then select Add Recording.
3. Under Create a Custom Recording with, select Channel and Time.
4. Enter the channel number using the numeric keypad on the remote or the keyboard.
5. Under Frequency, select whether to record once, record daily, or record weekly.

6. For a one-time recording, select the date using the arrow buttons.

7. Enter a start time and a stop time using the numeric keypad on the remote or the keyboard.

8. Under Keep Up To, select how many programs (from one to ten) will be stored in the Recorded TV folder at a time.

9. Under Keep, select whether to keep the recorded program until space on the disk is needed, until you delete it, until you watch it, or for one week.

10. Select the picture quality for the recording: Fair, Good, Better, or Best. The better the picture quality, the larger the file will be, and thus, the more hard disk space will be used.

11. You can name the recording by selecting Add Title and typing in a name on the keyboard or with the keypad on the remote.

12. To schedule the recording, select Record.

Using Advanced Recording Features   You can select options for scheduled recordings by selecting **Advanced Record** from the left menu after you've selected to record the program, and you'll see a number of options as shown in Figure 8-10.

Table 8-1 shows the use of each advanced recording option. Some of the options are available only when you select to record a series rather than a single show.

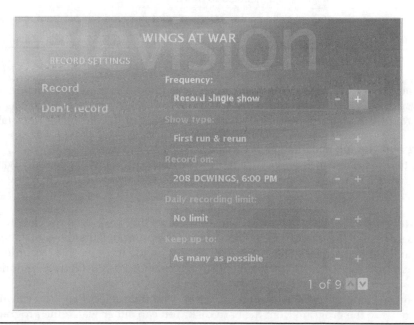

FIGURE 8-10   Selecting Advanced Record displays the Record Settings screen with a number of options.

Option	What It Does
Frequency	Allows you to select whether to record a single program or an entire series.
Show type (when recording a series)	Allows you to determine whether to record only first-run shows or also record reruns. You can also select to record live programs.
Record on (when recording a series)	Allows you to choose whether to record the show only on a specified channel, or on any channel where it is broadcast.
Daily recoding limit (when recording a series)	Allows you to specify that the show should be recorded only once per day, or can be set to unlimited.
Keep up to (when recording a series)	Allows you to set a number (from one to ten) of episodes that can be kept in the Recorded TV folder at one time.
Keep	Allows you to choose how long to keep the program on disk. You can keep it until the space is needed, until you delete it, until you watch it, or (for series only) you can keep the latest episodes and delete older ones.
Quality	Allows you to control file size by selecting Fair, Good, Better, or Best picture quality.
Start	Allows you to begin recording five, ten, or fifteen minutes before the program is scheduled to start.
Stop	Allows you to continue recording at the time the program is scheduled to end or from five minutes to three hours after that time.

TABLE 8-1   Advanced Recording Options

You can change the settings for a previously scheduled recording by selecting Recorded TV from the My TV menu, then selecting Scheduled and selecting Record Settings. The settings you can change are the ones shown in the Advanced Recording Options table.

Managing and Viewing Recorded TV Programs

There are two ways to watch previously recorded programs. You will generally watch them within the Media Center application interface, but you can also watch them using Windows Media Player.

Watching Recorded TV in Media Center   To view programs that have been previously recorded, select Recorded TV from the My TV menu. A list of the programs that have been recorded will appear. By default, they will be sorted by date, with the most recently recorded shown first. You can sort by name (listed alphabetically) or category by clicking those options at the left of the screen, as shown in Figure 8-11.

To play a recorded program, select the program and then select Play. You can also select Delete to remove the program from the hard disk. You can either watch the program in a window on the XP desktop, as shown in Figure 8-12, or you can maximize it to full screen. When you're watching a program in full screen mode, moving the mouse will cause the controls to appear at the top and bottom of the picture as they do when watching in a window.

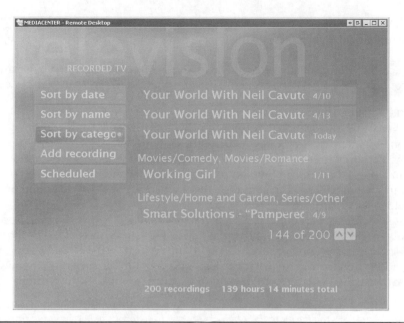

FIGURE 8-11   You can sort recorded programs by date, name, or category.

Watching Recorded TV in Windows Media Player   Media Center Edition 2004 comes with Windows Media Player version 9. You can watch a recorded program using WMP by navigating to the

FIGURE 8-12   You can watch recorded TV in a window on the XP desktop.

Recorded TV folder (located by default on the C: drive in Documents and Settings\All Users\Documents). Double-click the file for the program you want to see; this will open it in WMP.

Each recorded program is saved as a file in .dvr-ms format, as shown in Figure 8-13. The filename contains the name of the program, channel name, date, and time (in 24-hour format).

Viewing and Pausing Live TV

As with other PVRs, in addition to recording programs to watch later, you can use the Live TV function to watch a program that is currently showing. As you watch the program, Media Center records it to a buffer area on the hard disk. If you need to pause or stop the program, just press the Pause or Stop button on the remote and the recording continues for half an hour. That means you can start the program back up where you left off and finish watching it.

You can also replay part of the program you just watched by pressing the Replay button on the remote. This will "rewind" and replay the last seven seconds of the program. You can press it twice to go back another seven seconds, and so forth. Alternatively, you can use the Rew (rewind) button instead to go back to a specific point in the program. If you go too far back, you can use the Fwd (forward) button to advance through the recording.

NOTE   *If you pause or stop for more than half an hour, you won't be able to resume from the point where you stopped the program. If you need to stop watching for more than half an hour, you should use the* **Record** *button instead to start recording the program, and then play it from the Recorded TV menu.*

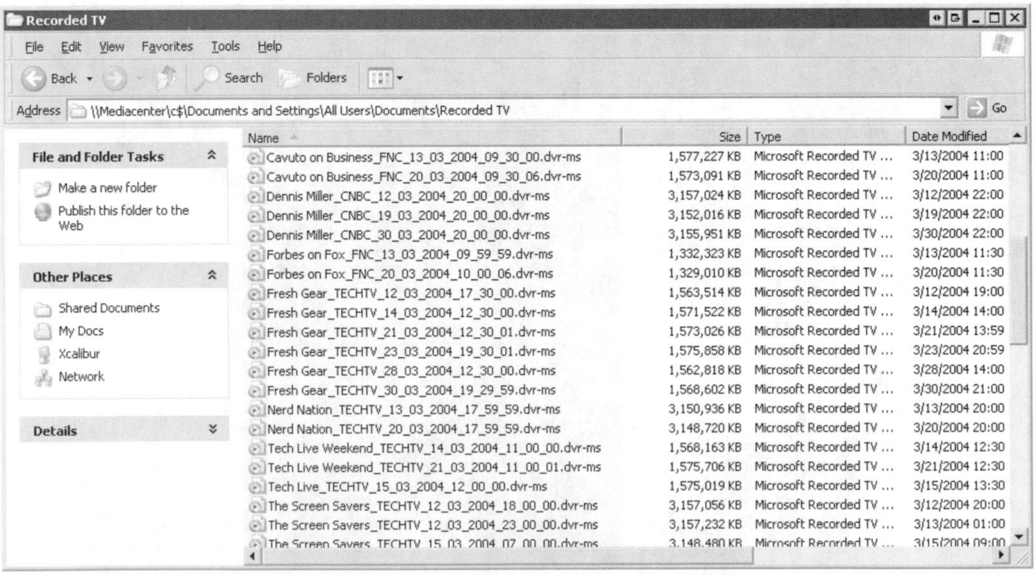

FIGURE 8-13   Recorded programs are saved in individual files in .dvr-ms format.

Media Center Video and Photo Functionality

Media Center's My Pictures and My Videos functions help you to organize your digital photographs and digital home movies. Instead of dragging out heavy picture albums (or worse, boxes of loose photos), you can display your photo collection for yourself or a group on your Media Center TV. Create slideshows without the hassle and expense of slide projectors, carousels, and mounted slides. Find your favorite family videos and show them without digging through boxes of cassettes or reels of film. You can also play prerecorded DVDs (if your Media Center PC has a DVD-ROM drive or DVD player/recorder installed).

My Videos: Organizing DVDs, Downloaded Movies, and Home Video

You can use the My Videos functionality of Media Center to organize and view your digital movies. Media Center can play videos in any of the following formats:

- .wm and .asf (Windows Media files)
- .wmv (Windows Media A/V)
- .avi (video files)
- .mpeg, .mpg, .mpe, .m1v, .mp2, and .mpv2 (movie files)
- .wmf (Windows Metafile)

Media displays your videos in thumbnail format, showing the first frame of the video, as in Figure 8-14.

FIGURE 8-14   Media Center displays a thumbnail of each video.

Media Center will recognize only video files that are stored in one of the following locations:

- The My Videos folder, located in Documents and Settings\<account/profile name>\ My Documents
- The Shared Video folder, located in Documents and Settings\All Users\Shared Documents
- Removable media such as a Compact Flash card or Memory Stick

---

NOTE *Media Center may not recognize videos that are in subfolders on removable media. Place the video files in the root directory of the card or stick, or copy them to the My Videos or Shared Video folder.*

If you want to view videos in other folders on your hard disk through the Media Center application, you can create shortcuts to them in the My Videos and Shared Video folder.

When you save videos directly from your camera, they are stored by default in your My Videos folder.

Organizing Video Files   The contents of the My Videos folder is available through the Media Center application only when the user to whom it belongs is logged on. The contents of the Shared Video folder is available to any user who logs on. You can create subfolders within the My Videos or Shared Video folder to organize the video files.

You can see details about a video, such as its time duration and when the file was created or modified, by pressing the MORE INFO button on your remote while the video is selected or playing, as shown in Figure 8-15.

FIGURE 8-15   Use the MORE INFO button to display details about a video.

Viewing Videos   To play a video, use the arrow buttons on the remote, the keyboard arrow keys, or the mouse to select the video, and then double-click it or press the OK/ENTER button on the remote. This starts the video playing in full screen mode. You can then use the controls on the remote to pause the video, fast forward or rewind, or skip ahead.

If you want to use other applications on the computer while watching the video, you can play the video in a window by clicking the Maximize button in the upper-right corner with the mouse (the buttons appear when you move the mouse) or by pressing the Media Center Start button on the remote.

My Pictures: Using the Digital Photo Album and Slideshow Features

Media Center's My Pictures function makes it easy to organize and display your digital still photos, in much the same way that you use My Videos for your movie files. You can share photos with other users of the computer by placing them in the Shared Pictures folder (Documents and Settings\All Users\Shared Documents) or make them available only when you're logged on by placing them in the My Pictures folder (Documents and Settings\ <account/profile name>\My Documents).

You can sort pictures within each folder by date or title, and you can view pictures on removable media. You can even view the photos as a slideshow. These options are available in the left menu when you click My Pictures, as shown in Figure 8-16.

Managing Your Pictures   You can download photos directly from your digital camera, download photos from the Internet, or transfer pictures from removable media or across a local network. You can import pictures from another computer on the network into the My Pictures folder so that Media Center will have access to them. You can create subfolders to organize your pictures.

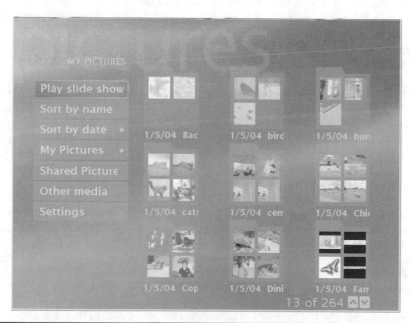

FIGURE 8-16   You can sort and view your digital photos from the My Pictures interface.

Media Center supports the following photo formats:

- .jpg and .jpeg (Joint Photographic Experts Group)
- .tif (Tagged Image File)
- .gif (Graphics Interchange Format)
- .bmp (Bitmap)
- .wmf (Windows Metafile)
- .png (Portable Network Graphics)

NOTE *Media Center does not support animated .gif files.*

To view details about a picture, press the MORE INFO button on the remote. This will show you the filename, title, file creation/modification date, size of the picture (in pixels), and location where the picture is stored.

Viewing Your Pictures   Select a picture using the mouse, keyboard arrow keys, or arrow keys on the remote. If you have created subfolders to organize your pictures, navigate through the folder levels until you find it. When you select a picture, it will be displayed in full screen mode by default.

If a picture displays sideways (because you held the camera sideways to take a vertical picture), you can rotate it 90 degrees in either a clockwise or counterclockwise direction by pressing the MORE INFO button on the remote and choosing Rotate.

You can magnify a picture to "zoom in" on a specific part of the picture. While reviewing the picture, press OK on the remote to magnify the picture by 150%. Pressing OK a second time will change the magnification to 225%. Pressing OK a third time will restore the picture to its original magnification.

You can view pictures in a slideshow by selecting Play Slide Show in the left menu or by pressing Play on the remote. Select a folder to play only the pictures in that folder as a slideshow. The slides will play in a continuous loop until you stop the show, using the Stop button on the remote or the Stop control in the control bar that appears at the bottom of the screen when you move the mouse.

You can play audio from your My Music collection or from a My TV recording during a slideshow. To do this, start the music or TV program playing as you normally would, and then open My Pictures and start the slideshow. The audio will keep playing and information about the song or program will appear in a small window within the slideshow.

In the next section, we'll discuss how to adjust the slideshow settings.

Changing Settings   By default, a caption is displayed with each picture that tells the filename and creation/modification dates. You can turn off this feature by selecting Settings from the left menu and unchecking the box labeled Show Caption.

You can also control many aspects of your slideshows using the settings interface, as shown in Figure 8-17.

With the Settings options, you can specify the following:

- Whether to show the pictures in random order (by default, they are shown in the order in which they're arranged in the folder)

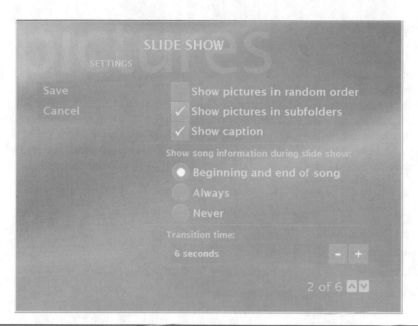

FIGURE 8-17   You can control how your slideshow plays using the Settings options.

- Whether to include pictures that are in subfolders
- Whether and when to show song information during a slideshow
- Transition time (how long each slide stays on the screen) in seconds
- Background color (border around pictures that don't fill the entire screen)

Fixing Pictures   You can use Media Center to do some very basic photo manipulation tasks, such as adjusting the contrast or removing "red eye" from portraits.

Select the picture and press the MORE INFO button on the remote. Select Fix Picture. Select Red eye or Contrast to specify the type of change you want to make. After the change is made, select Save if you want to keep the change. Note that the original picture will be replaced when you save the file, so if you don't want to lose it, you need to back it up first.

For more sophisticated photo touchups, use a photo editing program.

Printing Pictures   If you have a printer attached to your Media Center PC or you have XP configured to use a network printer, you can print photos by selecting them (or waiting for them to appear in a slideshow) and then pressing the MORE INFO button on the remote and selecting Print.

NOTE   *Local and network printers are installed and configured through the Printers applet in Control Panel.*

Playing Prerecorded DVDs

You can play DVD movies you've purchased or DVDs you've recorded. When you insert a DVD, Media Center asks if you want to play it. Selecting Yes starts the DVD. If you select No, you can play it later without removing and reinserting it, by selecting Play DVD on the Media Center main menu.

You can use the remote or the controls at the bottom of the screen to play, pause, stop, fast forward, rewind, or skip forward or back through the DVD. To get information about the DVD that is currently playing, you can press MORE INFO on the remote. This will tell you the title, chapter title currently playing, running time, current time, genre, and rating.

You can configure Media Center to block movies with particular ratings. Here's how:

1. Select Settings from the Media Center main menu and then select General.

2. Select Parental Controls. Enter your four-digit code.

3. Select Movie/DVD Ratings.

4. Select the check box labeled Turn On Movie Blocking.

5. Choose a movie rating to block, using the buttons on the screen.

6. Select Save to apply the settings.

NOTE *You can also block movies that have no rating by selecting the check box labeled Block Unrated Movies.*

Media Center Music and Radio Functionality

Media Center gives you a way to organize your digital music files and listen to music or talk radio over the FM band or over the Internet. For best audio playback, you'll need good-quality speakers connected to your Media Center PC. To play FM radio, you must have a tuner card that includes FM support.

My Music: Creating and Organizing Your Digital Song Collection

There are several ways you can add songs to Media Center's media library. You can import songs from another computer across your local network, download music from the Internet, or copy an audio CD. You can also create your own music.

Importing Songs from Another Computer   To import songs from another computer, copy the song files into your My Music folder (located in Documents and Settings\<account/profile name>\My Documents) or the shared My Music folder (located in Documents and Settings\All Users\Shared Documents).

Downloading Music from the Internet   You can download music from a variety of online sites. Many artists make their songs available free on their own web sites or sites such as MP3.com. You can also buy music online from services such as Napster. You'll also find downloads on the Windows Media web site at http://windowsmedia.com/MediaGuide/Home.

Copying Audio CDs   If your Media Center PC has a CD burner, you can copy your audio CDs to your music library. Here's how:

1. Press the Start button on the remote or open Media Center with the mouse or keyboard.

2. Put the CD into the CD-ROM drive. It should start playing automatically.

3. Select Copy CD from the menu. Media Center will copy the entire CD, starting with Track 1.

4. A dialog box will inform you when the copy is complete.

You can stop the copy operation before it is finished by pressing the Stop button on the remote or on the control bar.

Understanding Music Licensing   If a music file is protected by digital rights management (DRM) technology, you may need to obtain a license to play it. By default, Media Center will attempt to obtain a license when you try to play a protected music file. This may take you to the content provider's web site, where you might be asked to register, enter an ID for your media player software, or pay a licensing fee. You can turn off this feature by unchecking the box labeled Acquire License Automatically for Protected Content in the Media Center privacy settings.

NOTE   *Protected content will not play if you do not have the proper license.*

Adding, Deleting, Renaming, and Moving Library Files   The files in the media library are available to the Media Center application, but if you want to add, delete, rename, or move them, you must use Windows Media Player. Open WMP from the Start | All Programs | Accessories | Entertainment menu in XP. Select Media Library in the left menu as shown in Figure 8-18. Right-click the file you want to delete, rename, or move, and make the appropriate selection.

FIGURE 8-18   To edit the media library, you must use Windows Media Player.

Playing Music   You can find the music you want to play in one of several ways. You can browse My Music by album, artist, playlist, song, or genre. Media Center also keeps a list of recent music that you can browse. Finally, you can search for a song by title or keyword. These options are all available in the left menu in My Music, as shown in Figure 8-19.

To search, enter text using the keyboard or the keypad on the remote. You'll see a list of items that match your search criteria. Highlight the one you want and press OK on the remote to select it. You can use the controls on the remote or at the bottom of the screen to fast forward, pause, skip, or replay a track during a song.

You can create playlists in Windows Media Player and use them to play your selected songs in Media Center. Select Playlists in the left column of options in My Music. You'll also notice a selection called Auto Playlists. These are lists that are created automatically by Windows Media Player.

Internet Radio: Enjoying FM and Internet Radio

You can use Media Center to listen to your favorite radio programs, via an FM tuner or over the Internet.

Listening to FM Radio   On the Media Center main menu, select Radio, and then select Start FM. If you haven't used the radio feature before, use the Seek or Tune controls to find a station. If you've listened to radio previously, Media Center will return to the last station to which you listened. You can pause, stop, or skip forward or back while playing FM radio in the same way as when playing live TV.

You can preset your favorite FM stations so that you can quickly switch to them, as with the preset buttons on a car radio. To set a station as a preset, select Radio from the Media Center main menu and enter the frequency in the radio frequency field, using the numeric

FIGURE 8-19   You can browse or search for specific songs in My Music.

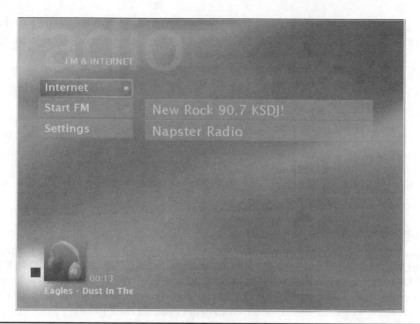

FIGURE 8-20   You can listen to Internet radio stations for which Web links have been installed.

keypad on the remote or the keyboard. Choose Save and the station will be assigned to a preset number. Preset numbers are assigned in order, so that if the last station you saved was 2, this one will be 3, and so forth. You can remove a preset station by selecting it and pressing the CLEAR button on the remote.

NOTE *Media Center 2004 supports only one tuner card. This means you cannot record or listen to live FM radio while you're recording a TV program. If you try to start an FM station while a TV program is recording, you will be asked if you want to stop the recording.*

Listening to Internet Radio   You can play Internet radio stations for which web links have been installed. In the Media Center main menu, select Radio, and then select Internet as shown in Figure 8-20.

You can install web links for additional stations from the Online Spotlight page.

Unlike with FM radio, you can play an Internet radio station at the same time you're recording a TV program without interfering with the recording.

Media Center Edition Tips and Tricks

After you've mastered the basics of using Media Center to listen to music files, view pictures and videos, play DVDs, watch and record TV, and listen to radio, there are a number of ways to enhance its functionality by using advanced features or additional programs.

You can save your recorded TV shows to a CD or DVD, improve the picture quality on your TV or computer monitor, and edit your home videos to make them more professional. With MCE 2004, you can even run the Media Center application via Remote Desktop, and you can add media file storage locations to get the benefit of external hard disks. Finally, Microsoft has released a set of "power toys" that add even more functionality to MCE 2004.

Saving TV Programs to CD or DVD

After you've recorded a TV program in Media Center, you can save it on a CD or DVD; however, this functionality is not included in the Media Center application. You'll need to use a third-party "burner" application. Often such software comes with a CD or DVD recorder when you purchase it. Sonic PrimeTime, included on some vendors' MCPCs, works within the Media Center environment. You can also purchase a program such as Nero to burn your CDs or DVDs.

Because high-quality program files are very large, they won't fit on a CD. Use a DVD or record the program at lower quality (Fair).

Improving Picture Quality

MCE 2004 includes a Display Calibration option that helps you to improve the quality of your monitor's or TV's picture. On the Media Center main menu, select Settings, then General, then Appearance, and finally Adjust Display Settings. Select Next to make adjustments to the contrast, brightness, color balance, and other picture quality settings. If you'd like, you can choose Watch Video to see a video that instructs you in how to best adjust your display settings.

Editing Home Video

To edit your home videos, you'll need a video editing program such as Microsoft's Windows Movie Maker. With a video editing program, you can create a storyboard, edit clips from your movie, add music, put in transitions between scenes, and apply other professional production techniques to enhance your videos.

You can download Movie Maker 2 for Windows XP from Microsoft's web site at http://www.microsoft.com/windowsXP/moviemaker/downloads/moviemaker2.asp.

Using Remote Desktop to Connect to Media Center

The first version of XP Media Center Edition did not allow you to connect via Remote Desktop. MCE 2004 does—but some of the Media Center application's functions cannot be accessed through the remote desktop connection.

First, ensure that the Remote Desktop service is enabled. See Chapter 19 for more information on how to enable Remote Desktop. When you connect to the MCPC via Remote Desktop, you will be able to open the Media Center application, change settings, schedule programs to be recorded, view pictures (including slideshows), view videos, and play music and radio. However, you will not be able to watch live TV or watch recorded TV programs. If you attempt to do so, you will get an error message as shown in Figure 8-21.

Adding Media File Storage Locations

With good-quality half-hour TV programs using as much as 1.5GB of disk space, even a large hard disk fills up fast. It's easy to add additional disks to your Media Center PC. You can add internal disks or external USB 2.0 or IEEE 1394 (FireWire) disks.

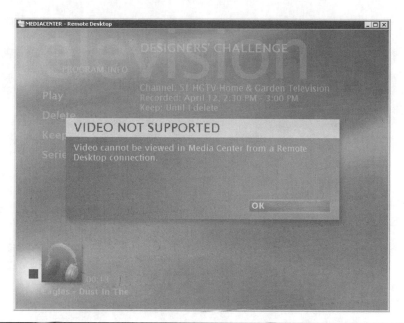

FIGURE 8-21   Video cannot be viewed in Media Center over a Remote Desktop connection.

To tell the Media Center to record programs on the new disk, select My TV from the Media Center main menu, select Settings, then Recorder, and then Recorder Storage. Here you can specify which drive to use for recording, as well as the percentage of the disk that should be used for recorded TV programs and the recording quality (Fair, Good, Better, or Best).

At the bottom of the screen, you'll see the maximum recording time for the amount of disk space you've allocated, as well as the amount of time still unused, as shown in Figure 8-22.

Media Center will create a Recorded TV folder on the new disk and start saving subsequently recorded programs there.

Using Media Center 2004 PowerToys

Microsoft has made available several "powertoys" (add-on programs for more functionality) for XP Media Center Edition 2004. These include

- An alarm clock that will play music or other programming at a set time and includes a "sleep" function to turn itself off after a preset amount of time.

- A playlist editor that lets you use the remote to create and edit playlists.

- A special edition of Solitaire that can be played using the Media Center remote control.

You can download the powertoys free from the Microsoft web site at http://www.microsoft.com/windowsxp/mediacenter/downloads/powertoys.asp.

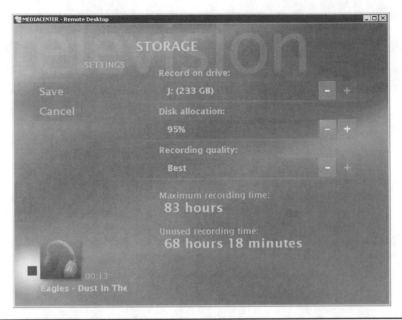

FIGURE 8-22   You can configure Media Center to record on any disk or partition you specify.

Troubleshooting Media Center Edition

Media Center is a complex application, and occasionally it may act in unexpected ways. In this section, we'll discuss how to troubleshoot some of the most commonly encountered problems involving TV recording and playback, music and radio, and video and pictures.

Troubleshooting TV Recording and Playback

Occasionally problems occur with recording and playing TV programs in Media Center. We discuss some of the most common problems, and what to do about them, in the next sections.

Watching One Program While Recording Another

The current version of Media Center Edition supports only one TV tuner card. This means you can't record two programs on two different channels at the same time, nor can you watch live TV on one channel while recording a program on another.

However, you can run separate signals from your cable or satellite box, one to the Media Center PC and another directly to your TV, if the TV has multiple signal inputs. (These are usually labeled as Video 1, Video 2, and so forth. Some input jacks may be component, others composite, and others S-video; new HDTVs also have DVI connections.) This will allow you to switch between video sources (the Media Center PC and the direct line in) so that you can watch TV on one channel on the direct input while the Media Center PC records a different channel.

NOTE *We've noticed that if you change the channel on your TV with your TV's remote control while watching through the direct input, your Media Center PC's infrared eye may pick up the signal and change the channel being recorded. You can work around this by changing the TV channel with the TV's channel up/down control on the front of the TV when the MCPC is recording on another channel, instead of using the remote.*

How to Add Missing Channels or Change Incorrect Information in the Guide

Sometimes the Guide information that is downloaded is not all correct, or some channels may be missing from the Guide lineup. You can edit the Guide to correct these problems. To add missing channels, do the following:

1. Select My TV from the Media Center main menu or press the My TV button on the remote.

2. Select Settings from the My TV menu.

3. Select Guide from the Settings menu.

4. Select Add Missing Channels.

5. Select Add Channel.

6. Enter the channel name and number in the next pages of the wizard.

You can also remove channels by selecting the X button by the channel.

To change the Guide listings, select Edit Guide Listings after step 3. You can add or remove channels, or edit the channel number.

Setting or Changing the Signal Speed for the Remote Control

If you have problems with channel changing on your set-top box (for example, the wrong channel is recorded for a prescheduled recording because the channel attempted to change but did not pick up all of the digits in the channel number), you might have the signal speed set incorrectly. Try changing the speed to the next slowest setting. Here's how:

1. Start the Media Center application or go back to the main menu if it's already started, and select Settings.

2. Select TV from the Settings menu, then select Set Up TV Signal. This starts the Signal Setup Wizard.

3. Follow the steps as the wizard walks you through the process of setting the correct signal speed.

Troubleshooting Music and Radio

Occasionally problems occur with playing music and radio in Media Center. We discuss some of the most common problems, and what to do about them, in the next sections.

The Media Library Appears to Be Empty

Media Center recognizes only the music that is stored in the media library. You might have music files on your hard disk, but if they have not been added to the library (in Windows Media Player), they won't appear in the Media Center interface. Add the files to the library using WMP.

You can configure WMP to automatically add songs you play to the library, to automatically add music you purchase, and to monitor selected folders to automatically add files. Open WMP and select Options from the Tools menu, and then select the Media Library tab.

You Can't Play a Music File

If a particular music file won't play, but others will, the file might be corrupted or in the wrong format. If it is a protected file, you might not have the proper license to play it. If this is the case, you should be prompted by Media Center to obtain a license.

Album Information Is Missing

You need to be connected to the Internet for Media Center to download album information. Check your Internet connectivity.

Another possibility is that Media Center is not configured to automatically download album information. To do so, perform these steps:

1. In the Media Center main menu, select Settings.

2. Select the General icon, and then select Privacy.

3. Select Settings again.

4. Scroll down if necessary, and select Retrieve Media Information for CDs and DVDs from the Internet.

5. Select Save to make the changes.

Troubleshooting Home Video and Pictures

Occasionally problems occur with playing videos and pictures in Media Center. We discuss some of the most common problems, and what to do about them, in the next sections.

Videos Don't Play

There are two common reason videos won't play in Media Center:

- The file format is not one supported by Media Center.

- You don't have the correct codec installed.

If the file format is not supported, you may be able to work around it by opening the file in a video editing program and saving it in one of the formats that Media Center supports.

A *codec* is compression/decompression software that's used to make digital media files smaller for storage on disk, and then decompress them when you play them. If you try to open the file in Windows Media Player instead of the Media Center application, WMP will often automatically download the codec that's needed, or give you an error message telling you the name of the missing codec. You can then do a Web search for the codec file and download it.

You Can't Fast Forward or Rewind Videos

If your video will play but the fast forward and rewind buttons don't work on a particular video (but do work on other video files or with the My TV function), the video format may not support these navigation features. If you need them, you might try opening the video in a video editing program and resaving the file in a different format.

You Can't Rotate or Fix a Picture

The rotation and touchup functions in Media Center may not work if the file is read-only or it's saved in a format that doesn't support manipulation. In this case, open the picture in a photo editing program and rotate it there, or resave it in a different format or without the read-only attribute.

Using Windows XP Tablet PC Edition

In this chapter you'll find the answers to the following questions:

- What is a Tablet PC?
- What's the difference between a slate model and a convertible, and which is better?
- Can a Tablet PC be upgraded?
- What are the advantages and disadvantages to using a Tablet PC?
- My handwriting is terrible. Will Windows XP be able to read my writing?
- Does a Tablet PC come with a keyboard?
- How do I use the pen to write in an application?
- Aren't there some shortcuts I can use with the pen?
- Can I use speech to control my Tablet PC?
- Are there any programs specifically for Tablet PC?
- What are Windows Journal and Microsoft OneNote?

Personal computing devices come in many shapes and sizes these days. Some are very specialized in their function and others offer almost all the power of a conventional desktop PC.

One of the latest form factors for personal computers is the Tablet PC. These highly portable personal computers are light in weight and enable you to simplify input, without sacrificing a lot in terms of power and capability.

In this chapter I explore Tablet PCs and the operating system that powers them: Windows XP Tablet PC Edition. If you have a Tablet PC, you'll find tips in this chapter to help you get more out of your PC. If you don't have one, you'll come away from the chapter with a good idea of the Tablet PC's strengths and weaknesses and an appreciation for what one could do for you. I'll start with the Tablet PC hardware.

Introducing Tablet PCs

Personal computing devices are getting smaller, and personal computers are no exception. The latest trend in personal computing form factor is the Tablet PC (an example of one is shown in Figure 9-1).

There are two general form factors for the Tablet PC. The NEC VERSA LitePad (Figure 9-1) is an example of a Tablet PC that uses what many call the true Tablet PC form factor—slate. These Tablet PCs do not have an integrated hardware keyboard but instead rely primarily on a stylus for input. The LitePad includes a compact, detachable Universal Serial Bus (USB) keyboard for those times when stylus input just won't cut it, as do most other Tablet PCs that use the slate form factor.

TIP *The stylus acts like a mouse. As you move the tip of the stylus across the Tablet PC's screen, the mouse cursor follows it. To click, simply tap the stylus lightly on the screen. To double-click, lightly tap the stylus twice. To right-click, tap and hold the stylus on the screen until a small mouse icon appears, then lift the stylus. Windows then displays the context menu for the selected object.*

The other Tablet PC form factor is the *convertible*. The Toshiba Portégé (Figure 9-2) is an example of a one. These Tablet PCs are much like typical notebook PCs in that they have an integrated keyboard and a mouse or a trackball. The difference is that the screen spins 180 degrees to convert the computer for stylus input (Figure 9-3).

The unique form factor for convertibles requires some changes in operating system capabilities and Tablet PC features. The operating system that comes bundled with a Tablet PC is Windows XP Tablet PC Edition. Before we get into the features and capabilities in Windows XP Tablet PC Edition that make it different from the other Windows XP editions, let's first take a look at Tablet PC hardware.

FIGURE 9-1   The NEC VERSA LitePad uses the true Tablet PC form factor.

FIGURE 9-2   This convertible Toshiba Tablet PC functions much like a typical notebook PC.

The Hardware: Choosing a Tablet PC

Although there are common threads that run through the Tablet PC market in terms of hardware, you still have a wonderful variety and range of choices. When choosing a Tablet PC, you need to take a much closer look at how you will use the computer than you would when buying a typical notebook or desktop computer.

Enough Horsepower?

For example, you won't find Tablet PCs with the fastest available processor. Today that means you shouldn't look for a Tablet PC with a 3.3Ghz processor because you won't find one. However, you will find a nice selection of Tablet PCs with processors at about half that speed. Even those with processors below 1Ghz could suit your needs. It really boils down

FIGURE 9-3   You can easily convert the screen for stylus input.

to how you intend to use the computer. For many business users, that level of hardware performance will be perfectly fine for word processing, e-mail, web browsing, and other typical productivity applications. It's only when you move beyond the typical applications to engineering or other processor-intensive applications that the Tablet PC might fall short.

Memory and disk space are other areas where you'll find a bit less flexibility in the Tablet PC form factor. The NEC VERSA LitePad I (Jim) used in developing the Tablet PC content for this book is a slate model. It included 256MB of RAM and a 933Mhz Mobile Intel Pentium III processor with a 133Mhz front-side bus. This particular model is expandable to 512MB of RAM. By contrast, the workstation I use as my day-to-day system has a 3.0Ghz P4 processor, an 800Mhz front-side-bus, 2Ghz of RAM, a 160GB primary hard disk, and an 80GB secondary hard disk.

Would this particular Tablet PC do everything I needed it to do as my primary computer? Although I would have to make a couple of concessions in the way I typically work, it would, provided I maxed out the computer's memory. However, my requirements are higher than the average user's, so it's a safe bet that almost any Tablet PC would fulfill the requirements of a large majority of PC users.

Peripherals

You'll also find that most manufacturers have taken a "less is more" approach to peripherals when it comes to the Tablet PC. Convertible designs often have built-in removable media drives, such as CD-ROM or DVD drives. Slate models, however, generally forego these peripherals as internal devices and instead opt for external devices. With USB 2.0 support, these external devices provide every bit the same performance as their internal counterparts. Being able to shed the weight of all of these devices when you don't need them helps make the slate format very attractive for users who don't want the bulk or weight of a notebook or convertible design.

One hardware feature you will find built into almost all Tablet PCs is network connectivity. The more versatile devices include built-in Ethernet as well as built-in wireless networking. Ethernet gives you the advantage of speed where wired connections are available, and wireless gives you the flexibility to connect in the mall, airport, office, or any other location where wireless access is available.

Choosing Your Tablet PC

Choosing the right Tablet PC is not really much different from choosing a typical notebook or desktop PC, because it all situations, you should consider how you will use the computer to best determine what you need. Because of its different input features, however, a Tablet PC does require some additional thought. Less flexibility in hardware configuration is also a factor.

Here are some key points to consider when choosing a Tablet PC:

- **What you want to accomplish with it**   Decide which applications other than general e-mail, web browsing, and productivity applications you need to run on your Tablet PC. Consider the minimum hardware requirements for these applications to make sure they will run adequately on your Tablet PC.

- **Hardware upgrades and accessories**   Look at what upgrades and accessories are available for your Tablet PC. Will the system accommodate enough RAM for your needs? Will the hard disk have sufficient capacity? Are optional battery packs available and easily changeable? Keep in mind that even if the model you really want doesn't offer exactly the peripherals you need, you still might be able to add those peripherals to your Tablet PC with external USB devices from other manufacturers.

- **Networking**   Almost all Tablet PCs incorporate built-in Ethernet, wireless networking, or both. If the model you like doesn't have wireless, for example, make sure it has a PC Card slot so you can add your own wireless card.

- **Slate or convertible**   My preference is slate, but my whole rationale for the Tablet PC is the slim form factor and light weight. If the slate models don't give you the features or performance you need, consider a convertible model. You gain more hardware features at the expense of weight. If you think you will still need the built-in keyboard and capabilities of a traditional notebook PC but like the simplified input offered by a Tablet PC, a convertible model is your best bet.

- **Portability**   One final consideration in your decision between slate and convertible models relates to portability. While both form factors are very portable, carrying a slate model with all of the external peripherals complicates things, if only slightly. If you want everything in one unit that you can grab and go, consider a convertible. If weight and portability are your main considerations, go with a slate model.

- **Battery life**   This is an important consideration for any portable computing device. A long battery life, the capability to quickly swap batteries without powering down, and a quick charging time all make for a more useful device.

- **Extensibility**   How well will the Tablet PC of your choice integrate with the other devices you use on a regular basis? For example, can the model you like be easily connected to your network? Is there a docking station available for it? Will you even need a docking station as long as you can easily connect an external monitor along with the USB mouse and keyboard? Decide how important these features are for you and choose a model accordingly.

Before you rush out and buy a Tablet PC, read through the rest of this chapter so you will understand the additional features Windows XP Tablet PC Edition offers. When you understand these features, you'll have a much better feel for how you will use a Tablet PC and what benefits it will offer you over other form factors, such as a traditional notebook PC.

Interacting with Windows XP Tablet PC Edition

The Tablet PC format introduces some new challenges because of its small form-factor and the shift from a focus on keyboard input to stylus input. Given it's a standard personal computer in a slightly different form factor, a standard operating system with a few new twists and turns is all it takes to get the most out of the it. That operating system is Windows XP Tablet PC Edition.

Windows XP Tablet PC Edition (TPC) is a superset of Windows XP Professional. In other words, TPC contains all of the features found in Windows XP Professional, but also includes some additional features and applications to suit the needs of the Tablet PC format. The remaining sections explore these additional features.

Using the Tablet PC Input Panel

The first thing you'll notice when you start up a Tablet PC is the onscreen keyboard that Windows presents to help you log on (Figure 9-4). You simply tap the onscreen keys with the tip of the stylus and then tap the onscreen ENTER key.

After logon is completed, you'll use the Tablet PC Input Panel to interact with the PC when you're not using an external mouse, a hardware keyboard, or other input device. To display the Input Panel, tap the Tablet PC Input Panel button on the taskbar just beside the Start button.

The Input Panel's Keyboard pane (Figure 9-5) serves as a simple, onscreen keyboard complete with Windows key, context menu key, cursor keys, and even a dedicated @ key to save you the time of tapping SHIFT when entering an e-mail address. Just tap on a key with the stylus to type that key. Tap SHIFT to choose an uppercase character or symbol on the numeric keys. The shift mode turns off as soon as you tap another key. Use the CAPS key if you need to type with all capital characters.

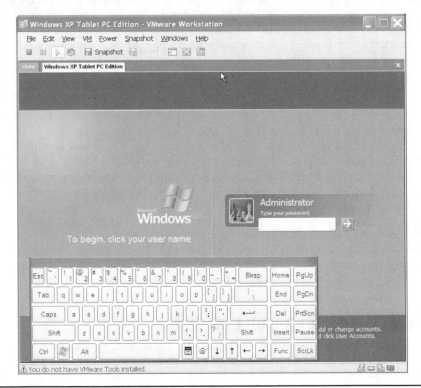

FIGURE 9-4   Use the onscreen keyboard to log on to your Tablet PC.

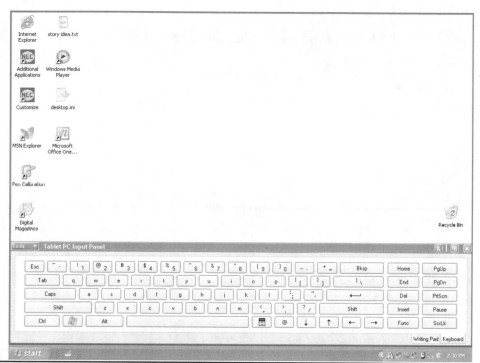

FIGURE 9-5   Use the Input Panel's Keyboard pane as an onscreen keyboard.

TIP *If you don't like the stylus that came with your Tablet PC, you might be able to obtain a different one from another manufacturer. For example, check out http://www.wacom.com for Tablet PC hardware accessory pens.*

The other input option offered by the Input Panel is the Writing Pad (Figure 9-6). In this mode you write on the pad with the stylus and Windows, after a short delay, converts what you type to text. For example, you can open a new message form in Outlook or Outlook Express, write an e-mail message in the Writing Pad, and Writing Pad will enter that text as typed text in the message form.

NOTE *The handwriting recognition built into TPC is remarkably good, capable of converting what I write with a very high degree of success, even when I write in cursive. You wouldn't realize how remarkable this is until you see my cursive, which is generally illegible, even by me! The next version of Windows XP Tablet PC Edition, due out in the latter half of 2004, should have even better handwriting recognition capability.*

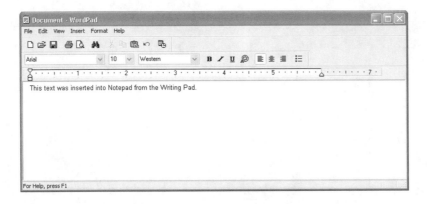

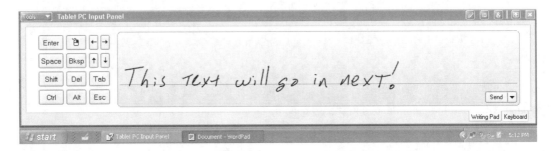

FIGURE 9-6   Use the Writing Pad to convert handwritten text to input.

The Writing Pad shows one or two horizontal lines, depending on how you have configured it. It uses these lines to determine how to convert written characters to text. For example, if you write a J above a line, the Input Panel converts it to an uppercase J. If you write the J character half above and half below, Input Panel interprets it as a comma (subject to how you write it). Get in the habit of using the line as the baseline for your characters for best results, just as you would when writing on lined paper.

When you use the Writing Pad, you might also want to turn on the Text Preview pane (Figure 9-7), which serves as a place to preview the converted text before sending it to the application. To turn on the Text Preview Pane, click Tools | Text Preview in the upper left of the Writing Pad's window. The text will appear in the Text Preview pane after a short delay. You can then click Send Text to copy the text to the current application window.

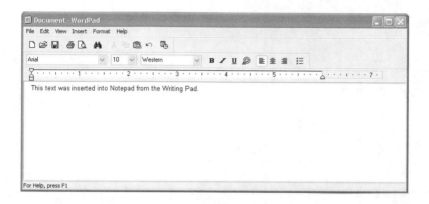

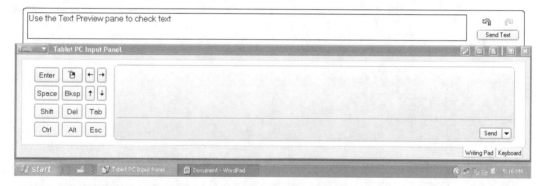

FIGURE 9-7   Use the Text Preview pane to view text before sending it to the current application window.

The symbols that are available on a standard keyboard on the upper row numeric keys are available by tapping the SHIFT button in the Keyboard panel. You can also click the Symbols Pad (&) button in the Input Panel to open the Symbol Pad (Figure 9-8) to access symbols when using either the Keyboard panel or the Writing Pad. The Symbols Pad disappears automatically after you tap a symbol.

TIP   *The Input Panel is docked by default at the top edge of the taskbar. You can float the Input Panel if you prefer. Just click Tools | Dock to dock or undock the Input Panel from the taskbar. Click and drag on the Input Panel's title bar to move it.*

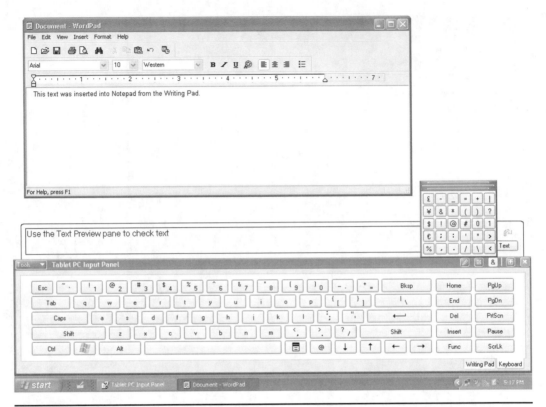

FIGURE 9-8   Use the Symbols Pad to enter symbols.

Correcting Text

If you make a mistake in your writing or the Input Panel misinterprets what you have typed, you can correct it before it goes to the active application. Before the Input Panel sends the text to either the Text Preview pane or the active window, just scratch through the text in the Writing Pad. Drawing a single line isn't enough; draw through it a few times until the text disappears from the Writing Pad.

If you have the Text Preview pane open, you can correct text there, as well. Just tap a word to enable a smart tag beside it (Figure 9-9). Tap the smart tag to view a menu of alternative words, delete the word, or highlight and rewrite (or dictate again) the word.

TIP   *You can also make corrections by highlighting the character or word in the application window and then typing the correct characters with the Keyboard panel or hardware keyboard, if attached.*

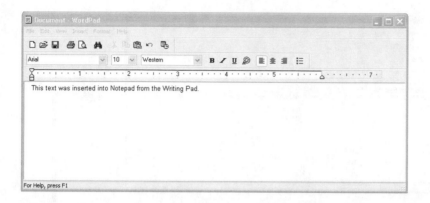

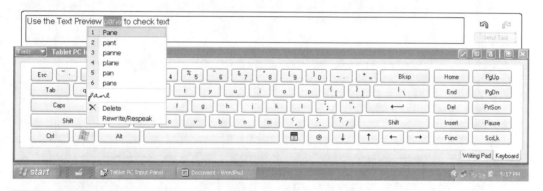

FIGURE 9-9   Tap the smart tag beside the selected word to make changes.

Using Write Anywhere

The Input Panel is certainly handy on its own for entering text and other characters, but wouldn't it be easier to just write in the application window? Windows XP Tablet PC Edition gives you the capability to do just that with its Write Anywhere feature (Figure 9-10). When Write Anywhere is turned on, a box appears on the display to indicate the outline of the Write Anywhere area. This box behaves much like the Writing Pad. After a short pause, what you have written in the Write Anywhere box is converted to text and sent to the active application window.

TIP   *If the Text Preview pane is open, you preview the text there before it's sent to the active application window.*

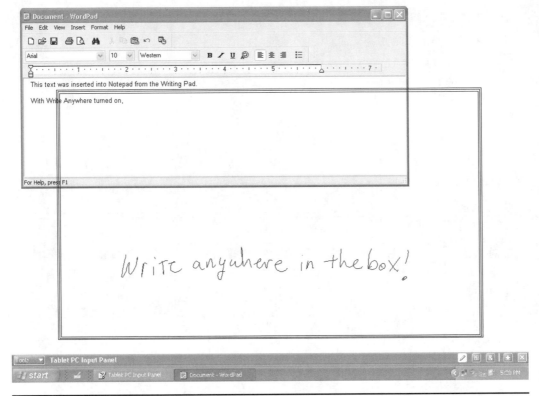

FIGURE 9-10   Use Write Anywhere to expand your writing area beyond the confines of the Writing Pad.

To turn on Write Anywhere, tap the Turn On Write Anywhere button in the upper right corner of the Input Panel. Tap the button again to turn it off. See the following section to learn how to configure the Input Panel to display this button.

Using the Character Recognizer

The Input Panel does a good job of recognizing most characters, but it doesn't always translate special characters very well. If you're having problems getting the Input Panel to recognize certain characters or symbols, trying turning on the Character Recognizer (Figure 9-11).

Input Panel offers three variations of the Character Recognizer. The first two show three areas: one for uppercase characters, one for lowercase characters, and one for symbols. The third option is similar to the Character Recognizer on the Palm operating system. To choose between these, tap Tools | Options and tap the Writing Tools tab. Choose Show Character Recognizer On Writing Pad and choose the desired option.

TIP   *The option Use Pocket PC Letter Recognizer, Including Accented Characters enables you to write accented characters such as á, ë, and others.*

FIGURE 9-11 The Character Recognizer will help you enter special characters and symbols.

Using Gestures

The Input Panel recognizes a small number of *gestures*, which are special handwritten symbols that it translates into specific keys or actions. Table 9-1 shows these gestures and their corresponding characters or actions.

You can use the Backspace, Space, Enter, Tab, and Scratch-Out gestures in the Input Panel or Write Anywhere pane. The Scratch-Out gesture is the only one you can use when there is other ink in the Input Panel or Write Anywhere pane. You can use the Start Input Panel gesture anywhere on the display.

TIP *If you can't get the Start Input Panel gesture to open the Input Panel, use longer strokes in the gesture. If Input Panel misinterprets your other gestures, trying making the strokes longer for those gestures, as well. See the "Configuring General Tablet and Pen Settings" section to learn how to adjust the Start Input Panel gesture.*

Using Speech Recognition

In addition to using the stylus to enter text and interact with your Tablet PC, you can also use speech thanks to the speech recognition built into Windows XP Tablet PC Edition.

Character or Function	Gesture
Backspace	
Space	
Enter	
Tab	
Scratch-Out (delete character or word)	
Start Input Panel	

TABLE 9-1 Tablet PC Gestures

Naturally, using speech input requires that you use the microphone built into your Tablet PC or an external microphone. To turn on speech input, open the Input Panel and tap Tools, then choose Speech. Additional controls appear at the top of the Input Panel (Figure 9-12). These controls are dimmed (unavailable) until you run the Microphone and Voice Training Wizards.

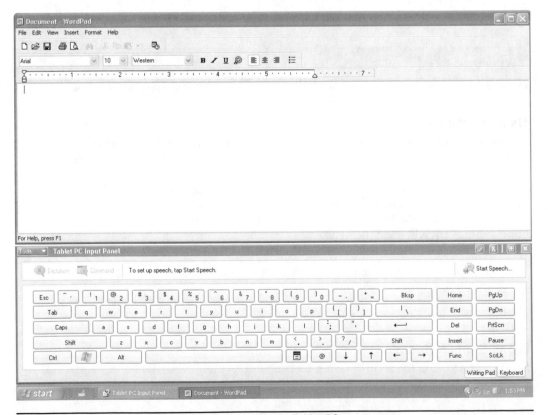

FIGURE 9-12 You can use speech to interact with your Tablet PC.

Input Panel offers two speech input modes: Dictation and Command. In Dictation mode, Input Panel translates you speech into text for insertion into the active window. (If configured to do so, Dictation mode automatically opens the Text Preview pane when you begin speaking.) Command mode treats the words you speak as commands. For example, say "File" to open the File menu, then say "Open" to display the Open dialog box to open a file.

TIP *To choose a speech input mode, just tap either the Dictation or Command buttons at the top of the Input Panel. Tap again to turn off speech recognition.*

Training Voice Recognition for Better Accuracy

The initial session through the Wizard will enable Windows to recognize a large percentage of your speech, but it will be far from perfect. To perform addition voice training, open the Input Panel, tap Speech Tools, and choose Voice Training to start the Voice Training Wizard. Choose the passage you want to read and click Next, and then read through the passage through to the end. The more passages you read in the Voice Training Wizard, the better Windows will be able to accurately recognize your speech.

Add Pronunciation for Specific Words

No matter how much time you spend with the Voice Training Wizard, you still might have problems with Windows recognizing specific words because of the way you pronounce them or because they are uncommon words. You can build a custom dictionary of words and pronunciations to overcome this problem. With the Input Panel displayed, tap Speech Tools and choose Add Pronunciation for a Word. In the Add Pronunciation dialog box (Figure 9-13), type the word, tap Record Pronunciation, and then speak the word. Windows adds it to the dictionary.

TIP *To change pronunciation of a word, tap the word and then tap Delete. Then, enter the word again in the dictionary.*

FIGURE 9-13   You can add pronunciation for troublesome or uncommon words.

Configuring Spoken Command Sets

The Input Panel's speech recognition offers several sets of verbal commands that you can enable or disable as desired. To configure which commands are available, tap Speech Tools and choose Voice Command Configuration to open the Voice Command Configuration dialog box (Figure 9-14). Place a check beside the sets of commands you want available through speech recognition.

If you select the Working with Text set, you can tap Details to specify other options (Figure 9-15). These options specify the commands that will be recognized when you are working with text. Choose the option Enable during dictation if you want commands to be recognized during dictation. Doing so can slow down or make voice recognition less accurate, however.

Setting Input Panel Options

The Input Panel offers several options you can configure to control the way the Input Panel works. To configure these options, click the Tools button and choose Options to display the Options dialog box (Figure 9-16).

The Writing Pad tab includes the following options:

- **One Line/Two Lines**   Choose the number of input lines you want displayed in the Writing Pad. This option changes the appearance of the Writing Pad but not its function. You can write two lines of text on the pad even when the One Line option is selected. The first line is sent to the application shortly after you start writing on the second line.

FIGURE 9-14   Use the Voice Command Configuration dialog box to specify the voice commands Windows will listen for.

FIGURE 9-15 You can configure additional speech recognition options.

- **Automatically insert text into the active program after a pause** When this option is enabled, the text is automatically sent to the active application window or the Text Preview pane (if open) after the specified delay. Use the slider to change the delay.

- **Ink thickness** Use this option to change line thickness for the Writing Pad.

The Writing Tools tab turns on or off the Character Recognizer and Quick Keys, as well as sets the location for the Quick Keys at either the right or left of the Input Panel. The Quick Keys panel includes BACKSPACE, SPACE, DELETE, and other common keyboard keys.

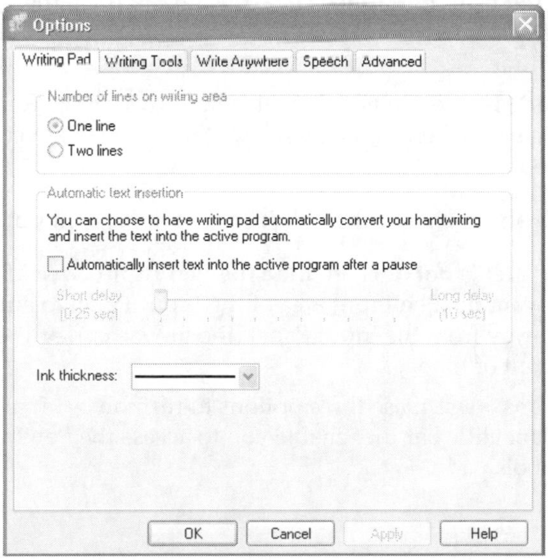

FIGURE 9-16 Use the Options dialog box to configure the Input Panel.

The Write Anywhere tab determines the properties for the Write Anywhere feature. The available options include

- **Show the Turn On Write Anywhere Button on the title bar** Choose this option to add the Turn On Write Anywhere button on the Input Panel title bar, enabling you to easily toggle the Write Anywhere area on and off.

- **Handwriting** Set the pen width and color for Write Anywhere with these options and specify the conversion/insertion delay.

- **Writing area** Specify whether the Write Anywhere area will be outlined on the display and set the outline color.

- **Recognize handwriting as text using** Choose which handwriting recognition option you want Input Panel to use.

Use the Speech tab to configure the following speech recognition options:

- **Show the Text Preview pane automatically when starting to dictate** Enable this option to have the Input Panel show the Text Preview pane automatically when you begin dictation.

- **Do not automatically show the Text Preview pane** Choose this option if you don't want the Preview Pane displayed while dictating.

- **Play sounds when the microphone turns on or off** Choose this option to have Input Panel play a sound when the microphone is turned on or off.

- **Play sounds when speech is recognized or cannot be recognized** Choose this option to have Input Panel play a sound when it can't recognize a word or command.

- **Voice Command Configuration** Click this link to open the Voice Command Configuration dialog box and specify which commands will be available through speech recognition.

- **Keyboard Mode Key settings** Click this link to open the Keyboard Mode Key Settings dialog box, where you assign keys that switch between Dictation and Command modes.

The Advanced tab offers a handful of additional options, including

- **When Input Panel is not docked, hide the Pen Input area after** Choose this option if you want the Pen Input area of the Input Panel to automatically hide when your focus is away from the Input Panel (the mouse cursor is elsewhere) for the specified amount of time.

- **Title Bar buttons** Use these three options to turn on or off the display of buttons in the Input Panel title bar that enable you to access the Pen Input area, Quick Keys pad, and Symbols pad.

Configuring General Tablet and Pen Settings

In addition to the settings for the Input Panel discussed in the previous section, "Setting Input Panel Options," Windows XP Tablet PC Edition also offers a selection of global options to enable you to control the way Tablet PC Edition looks and functions. To access these options, open the Tablet and Pen Settings applet from the Control Panel. Figure 9-17 shows the Settings tab, which contains the following options:

- **Handedness**   Choose between right- and left-handed use for your Tablet PC. Your selection affects handwriting recognition accuracy.

- **Menu location**   Use this group to specify whether menus should appear on the left or right.

- **Calibration**   Use this group to calibrate tablet input for portrait and landscape modes. Choose a mode from the drop-down list and then tap Calibrate. Windows will prompt you to tap the four corners of the display and then click OK.

Use the Display tab to configure screen orientation and brightness settings. The available options include

- **Orientation**   Choose the portrait or landscape orientation you want Windows to use for the display.

- **Change**   Tap this button to change the sequence in which Windows will cycle through screen orientation.

- **Screen Brightness**   Use these settings to adjust screen brightness settings for A/C and battery power.

Figure 9-17   Use the Settings tab to configure left- or right-handed operations and calibrate the stylus for portrait or landscape operations.

The Pen Options tab lets you configure the input stylus behavior. The Pen Actions group lets you configure options that determine the behavior for double-tap, press and hold, and other actions. Tap an action in the list and then tap the Settings button to open a dialog box in which you configure action-specific options.

The Pen Buttons group of options lets you specify whether the button on the stylus is recognized as a right-click when you press the button, and lets you use the top of the pen to erase (available only if the stylus supports this capability).

TIP *Your Tablet PC might offer additional tabs to configure other settings, such as how hardware buttons on the Tablet PC function.*

Windows Journal Versus Microsoft OneNote

One of the main benefits of using a Tablet PC, other than its relatively small form factor and light weight, is its capability to take notes much like you would with pen and paper. Currently there are two applications you can use for taking notes on a Tablet PC: Windows Journal and Microsoft OneNote. In this section I'll explore each and give you an overview of the main differences between the two.

NOTE *I won't go into detail here on how to use Windows Journal or Microsoft OneNote because they are relatively easy to learn and use. Instead, I'll focus on the main differences between them to help you understand which is best for you.*

Overview of the Windows Journal

Windows XP Tablet PC Edition adds an application called the Windows Journal to the long list of applications bundled with the operating system. The Windows Journal—not to be confused with the Journal folder in Microsoft Outlook—gives you the capability to take notes with your Tablet PC much like you would when working with paper and pen. Windows Journal lets you write, draw, highlight, and insert pictures in the note. Figure 9-18 shows a typical note created with Windows Journal.

A note in Windows Journal can have multiple pages, each with its own title and content. The number of pages in the note appears in the bottom right of the note window and you can use the Previous and Next buttons (which show a page with left or right arrow) to move through the pages.

You can convert written text in a note to text within the note or copy the text to the Clipboard, where it is available for use in other applications. You can also convert selected text to a new e-mail message. When you do so, Windows Journal starts a new e-mail message with your default e-mail editor, copies the selected text to the body of the message, and attaches the graphic version to the message as an attachment. When you need to use the note in a graphical form in another application, you can select the parts you need and copy them to the Clipboard.

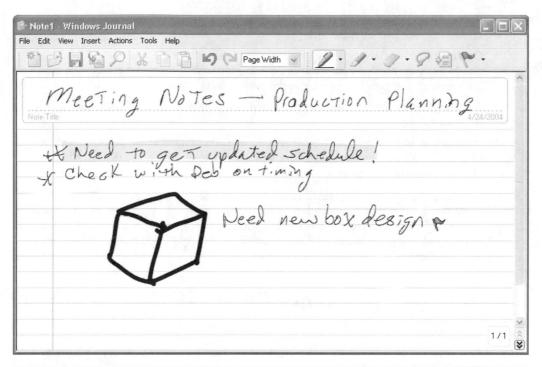

FIGURE 9-18   Take notes with your Tablet PC using Windows Journal.

Overview of Microsoft OneNote

Microsoft OneNote (Figure 19-19), a member of the Microsoft Office application suite, offers all of the features offered by Windows Journal. However, the two applications are as similar as a bicycle and a sports car. Microsoft OneNote goes well beyond Windows Journal to give you several additional features, including

- **Better organization**   You can create multiple notebooks with Microsoft OneNote, each with different sections. Each section can have multiple pages. The section tabs appear across the top of the window and page tabs appear at the right edge of the window, making it easy to navigate among sections and pages. Although the default folder for Microsoft OneNote is My Documents\My Notebook, you can easily create additional folders to further organize your notebooks.

- **More drawing tools and colors**   Microsoft OneNote offers more pens, colors, and drawing tools for adding content to a page than Windows Journal does.

- **Note flags**   Microsoft OneNote offers a selection of flags you can add to a page as visual indicators. These include To Do (checkbox), Important (star), Question, Remember for Later, and Definition flags. You can also create up to four additional flags and modify the existing flags to suit your needs.

- **Better formatting**   You have several additional features in Microsoft OneNote for formatting the text in your notes.

- **Outlining**   It's relatively easy to create structured, indented outlines with Microsoft OneNote. You can easily increase or decrease the indent level of a paragraph, add body text, and expand and collapse the outline as needed.

- **Audio**   You can record audio for inclusion on a page and easily play back the recording.

- **Integration with other Office features**   You can perform spell checking, create Outlook tasks, and accomplish other tasks with OneNote that make use of other Office application features.

TIP   *The OneNote Service Pack 1, available from http://www.microsoft.com/office/onenote/prodinfo/ sp1/default.mspx, offers several improvements, including the capability to import additional rich media types into notes, better integration with other Microsoft Office applications, better security, and many usability improvements.*

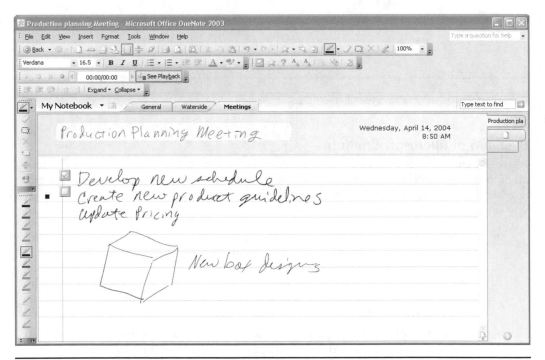

FIGURE 9-19   Microsoft OneNote offers many features beyond those Windows Journal offers.

Which Is Right for You?

Both Windows Journal and Microsoft OneNote are useful applications for taking notes. In terms of features, the comparison between these two applications is similar to a comparison between WordPad and Microsoft Word. The former is a basic application with basic functionality, and the latter offers a much broader range of features and capabilities.

If you take notes only occasionally with your Tablet PC and don't need to organize your notes into sections or integrate with Microsoft Office, the Windows Journal will likely serve most of your needs. If you do a lot of note-taking with your Tablet PC, Microsoft OneNote will be a good investment. This is particularly true if you use other Microsoft Office applications on your Tablet PC.

Ink Integration in Microsoft Office

In an effort to promote the Tablet PC platform, Microsoft has integrated features in Microsoft Office to support Tablet PC users. The Microsoft Office XP Pack for Tablet PC add-on, available from http://www.microsoft.com/downloads/details.aspx?FamilyID=33790048-269B-4838-AB9E-74B64626A494&displaylang=en, offers several feature add-ons for Office XP that support the Tablet PC platform. These features include:

- Writing e-mail messages using the stylus with Word as your e-mail editor
- Adding handwritten comments on slides in PowerPoint
- Adding handwritten comments in Excel spreadsheets and Word documents
- Drawing, diagramming, and adding notes in any Office application document
- Reusing Windows Journal items as Outlook items
- Importing Outlook meetings into Windows Journal

Microsoft Office 2003 integrates these features into the application suite itself without the need for an add-on, and also adds more features. For example, you can turn annotation on or off in Word, Excel, and PowerPoint to show or hide ink comments. In Excel, ink comments move with columns as new columns are inserted into the document; and in Word, they're are associated with the paragraph where they were inserted. These features enable ink comments to remain anchored to the items they were inserted in. Office 2003 adds other ink features, including additional ink toolbars, a new mode in Word that treats ink much like pictures or text boxes, and interface improvements.

TIP *For more information on ink integration in Office 2003, see http://www.microsoft.com/windowsxp/tabletpc/evaluation/office2003.mspx.*

Simplifying Backups

In this chapter you'll find the answers to the following questions:

- Do I really need to back up my computer?
- How often should I back it up?
- What should I back up?
- Windows Backup offers different backup types. Which is best and how to I use it?
- How can I make sure my backups are good?
- What is the best kind of backup device to use?
- I never remember to back up. Can I make it happen automatically?
- Is there anything I should back up separately?
- Is there anything in Windows XP to help back up and restore a computer when something goes wrong?

Frequent backups are an important tool for ensuring your data survives a catastrophic event such as a hard drive meltdown or a virus attack. But just backing up your system isn't enough. You also need to verify the backups and perform test restores to ensure you can restore the data. After all, what good is a backup if you can't restore it back onto your computer?

In this chapter we explore backup methods and offer tips on how to optimize the backup process and how to create good backups so you can successfully restore your system. We offer tips on choosing the right backup media and storing your backups, as well as explain how you can back up specific information such as the system state data.

TIP *After a problem occurs with your system is the wrong time to worry about backups. You should take a proactive stance regarding backups and make sure you implement a backup and restore process that will enable you to recover your system and data should the need arise.*

Why and When Should You Back Up Your System?

A haphazard scheme for backing up your data is a bad scheme. It's ideal to employ a completely automated process that backs up your files in the background without any intervention and notifies you when any errors occur. However, that approach isn't always possible. Often, a combination of methods is the best approach.

In the following sections we explain different backup methods and other general topics that will help you decide what backup scheme is best for your situation.

Backup Options Explained

There are several items you should back up on your computer. The sections to follow explore them one by one.

The Entire System

When you back up the entire system, you back up Windows XP, programs, documents, and settings, and all other data on the system—in short, every file on the computer's hard disk.

This type of complete backup is useful when you need to recover the system from a catastrophic problem such as a hard disk failure. Assuming you use a Windows-based backup application such as Microsoft Backup to create the backup, you must have a functioning copy of Windows XP installed on the computer in order to run the backup program and restore the files. This often means you'll need to reinstall Windows XP on the computer, then restore the system from the backup.

An alternative is a partition-cloning application such as Norton Ghost (http://www .symantec.com/sabu/ghost/ghost_personal) or its corporate counterpart, Symantec Ghost Corporate Edition (http://sea.symantec.com/content/product.cfm?productid=9). Ghost creates a complete copy of a disk partition, enabling you to restore the entire partition in a single operation. Naturally, successfully restoring the system in this way requires that you have a recent disk image with the application. In addition, any changes that have been made to the system since you created that disk image will be lost.

In most other cases there are better options for restoring a system, such as recovering from a restore point or restoring the registry. Restoring from a disk image or complete backup is a good solution when you can't boot the system at all and other recovery methods won't work. This type of recovery naturally works best when you have a recent backup.

Programs

Generally, programs install in the \Program Files folder. However, most programs also store settings in the registry and some add other files in other directories. So, backing up programs isn't as simple as backing up the \Program Files folder. Generally, backing up programs means performing a full backup complete with system state data.

The Registry

The Windows XP registry comprises several files that store the system's configuration and certain parts of the user's profile. A corrupted registry can prevent the system from booting or cause other problems. You can often cure a faulty system by restoring a recent copy of the registry.

You can back up the registry in one of two ways: by performing a system state backup in Microsoft Backup or by copying the files manually with the Recovery Console. See the "Backing Up and Restoring the Registry" section for more details. The next section, "System State Data," explains the system state data.

System State Data

System state data in Windows XP comprises several items. The following list describes these items (some items are specific to Windows Server):

- Registry

- System files that are under Windows File Protection
- COM+ Class Registration database
- Boot files, including the system files
- Certificate Services database
- Active Directory directory service
- SYSVOL directory
- Cluster service information
- IIS Metadirectory

In many situations you can recover a faulty system by restoring the system state data from a recent backup. Even though changes made to the system after the backup are lost, fully restoring the system in this way generally takes less time than reinstalling Windows XP and all applications.

Documents

My Documents is the default location for documents in Windows XP. Each user profile includes a My Documents folder. Subfolders under My Documents store music files, pictures, and other data. You should include My Documents in your backup scheme, along with any other folders where you store documents.

User Profile Data

The user profile stores information about the user's work environment and personal data, such as Internet Explorer favorites. Each user profile is stored by default in \Documents and Settings*user*, where *user* is the user's logon account name. Many applications also store data in the user profile. For example, the \Documents and Settings*user*\Local Settings\Application Data\Microsoft\Outlook folder is the default location for personal folder files, offline files, and other data. You should make sure to include your user profile(s) in your regular backups.

Understanding Backup Types

Now that you understand what you can back up, let's take a look at *how* you can back it up. Windows Backup, like many backup applications, supports the following backup methods:

- **Copy backup**   This backup type copies all selected files but does not clear the archive attribute (it does not mark each file as having been backed up). Use this backup type when you want to back up files between normal and incremental backups without affecting these other backup operations.

- **Daily backup**   This backup type copies all selected files that have been modified the day the daily backup is performed. The archive attribute is not cleared, so this backup type will not affect normal and incremental backups.

- **Differential backup**   This backup type copies files that have been created or changed since the last normal or incremental backup. The archive attribute is not cleared. To restore a system from a differential backup, first restore the last normal backup, and then restore the differential backup. A restore therefore only requires two backup sets with this type.

- **Incremental backup**   This backup type backs up only those files created or changed since the last normal or incremental backup and clears the archive attribute, marking the files as having been backed up. To restore a system using incremental backups, you must first restore the last normal backup and then restore all incremental backups performed since that normal backup.

- **Normal backup**   This backup type copies all selected files and clears the archive attribute. Restoring a system from a normal backup requires only the normal backup set, unless files have been created or modified since the backup.

So, which backup type or combination of types should you use? The answer to that question depends in large part on what you're backing up and how quickly you want to be able to restore it. A normal backup is the easiest because it requires that you restore a single backup set. However, unless you perform the backup yesterday, you'll likely lose at least some data.

A recent normal backup with daily incremental backups is a good solution when you don't want to perform a lengthy normal backup on a regular basis. For example, on servers that we manage, we typically perform a normal backup once a week on Friday or Saturday, with incremental backups every other day. This limits the lengthy backups to once a week, with quicker, incremental backups the rest of the week, for a full backup set that is as current as yesterday.

The Copy backup method is useful when you just want to back up a selected set of files without affecting the archive bit, which would affect incremental backups. The Daily and Differential backups are useful when you need to back up files that have been created or changed the day of the backup or since the last normal or incremental backup but don't want to affect the archive bit, which affects which files the next incremental backup copies. For example, assume you're going to install some new software and want to back up the system before doing so. Your last incremental backup was yesterday, and a new incremental backup is scheduled for later in the day. You could perform a daily backup to make sure you can restore changes since made yesterday's backup.

To decide which types of backups will work best for you and when you should use each type, think about how you use your computer, what information you need to back up, and how you would go about restoring the system in the event of a catastrophic failure or when you simply need to restore a file you accidentally deleted. Pick backup types and times that fit your work schedule and backup needs.

Where Should Backups Be Stored?

Ideally, backups should be stored either in a fireproof safe or off-site. If your office burns down or is destroyed by some other catastrophe, your backups will be destroyed along with them unless you take steps to protect them. Even a fireproof safe is not the best solution because tapes and CDs can be irreparably damaged by the heat inside the safe during a fire, even if the fire itself doesn't damage the media.

Ensuring Usable Backups

One final bit of advice about backups: Make sure you can actually restore them. Any number of things can happen to a backup set, depending on the type of media used, to render the backup set unrecoverable. It's a good idea to check each backup by copying at least one file from it back to your computer to make sure the set is usable. Also, make sure to store backup media in an appropriate location. For example, keep tapes away from magnetic sources such as speakers, motors, and of course, magnets!

Choosing the Right Backup Media

A backup can take a lot of time, particularly if you need to back up an entire system and multiple hard disks to a relatively slow medium such as tape. The media we prefer for personal backups is an external Universal Serial Bus (USB) hard disk, which can be moved between computers easily if needed and taken off-site when it's not being used for backup. Best of all, this option makes for quick backups, and more important, quick restores.

The most common media choices for backups are

- **Floppy disks**   These are good for backing up a few documents, but their low capacity makes them poor backup choices for most situations.

- **ZIP or other removable disks**   Even though this technology is getting long in the tooth, these types of drives are still good choices for backing up documents and other data because of their relatively high capacity.

- **External hard disks**   These are an ideal choice for backup media because of their relatively low cost per gigabyte, speed, and capacity. This is the option we prefer.

- **Tape**   Tape has long been the backup media of choice, but given the relatively low cost per gigabyte for hard disk storage, it no longer offers any advantage in terms of cost when you factor in the cost of the drive and media. We recommend tape only in situations where you need to create multiple backup sets of a lot of data, and the cost to accomplish the same results with removable hard disks or storage area network (SAN) solutions are not cost effective.

- **Network server**   This is a good option for backing up disk partition images and backup sets. However, you should employ some means on the server to back up the data as well, and move those backups off-site.

- **CD-R or CD-RW**   These writable media are a good option for backing up your documents and for creating an emergency partition image.

Backing Up and Restoring the Registry

The registry is, in a way, the brains of Windows XP. It stores operating system and application configuration data, device data, and lots of other information critical to the computer's operation. This section explains briefly how the registry works and details a couple of methods you can use to back it up.

The Registry Explained

The Windows XP registry comprises several files, which include the files in the \%systemroot%\System32\Config folder and Ntuser.dat file from the user's profile folder (\Documents and Settings*user*\Ntuser.dat). Windows XP combines these files to create the registry during boot and logon.

The registry contains the settings that define the system's hardware, operating system configuration, applications, and many other key items. Without the registry, the system won't boot. A corrupted registry file or even one or two wrong settings in the registry can also cause problems, including the inability to start the computer normally.

If you have a recent backup of the registry, you can often recover from problems like this by simply restoring the registry. The following sections explain how to back up the registry and how to restore it, if needed.

Backing Up System State Data

In the earlier "System State Data" section, we explained what data makes up the system state data. One of the items included in the system state data is the registry. You can create a backup of the registry by backing up the system state data with the Backup applet.

TIP *When you back up the system state data, you back up all of the system state data, not just the registry. Backup also creates a backup copy of the registry files in the %systemroot%\Repair folder.*

Follow these steps to back up the system state data with Backup:

NOTE *The following steps assume that Backup is not running in Wizard mode. The process to back up the system state data in the Wizard is similar.*

1. Click Start | All Programs | Accessories | System Tools | Backup.
2. Click the Backup tab (Figure 10-1).
3. Expand My Computer and locate System State in the list, then click Browse and choose a location and filename for the backup.

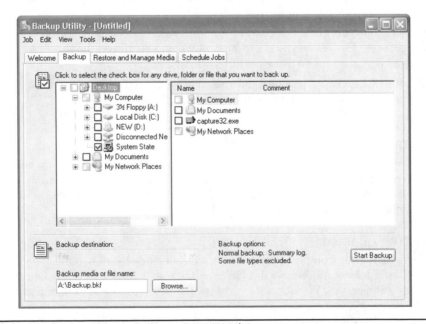

FIGURE 10-1 Use Backup to back up the system state data.

4. Click Start Backup, modify the backup description if desired, then click Start Backup to begin the backup process.

The %systemroot%\Repair folder should now contain a current copy of the registry. The following section, "Restoring the Registry from a Backup," explains how to recover the registry from a backup.

Restoring the Registry from a Backup

If the registry becomes corrupted, preventing a normal boot, you might be able to restore the system by restoring the system state data, which includes the registry. To restore the system state data from a backup of the system state data, follow these steps:

1. If the computer will not boot normally, boot the system in Safe Mode.
2. Start Backup and click the Restore tab.
3. Expand the backup sets in the left pane to locate the one containing the computer's most recent system state data.
4. Place a check beside System State in the left pane (Figure 10-2).
5. Click Start Restore to begin the restore operation.

NOTE *Restoring the system state data restores more than just the registry. See the following section, "Manual Registry Backup and Restore," to learn how to restore only the registry, if needed.*

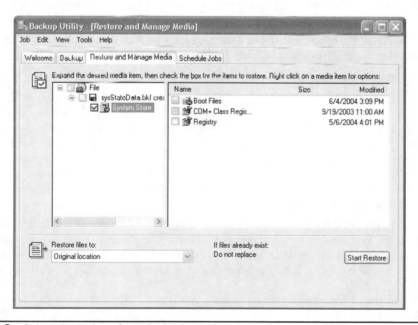

FIGURE 10-2   Select the registry from the backup set.

Manual Registry Backup and Restore

If you prefer to work from a command line, you can back up the registry and restore it manually. This is also a good option when you can boot the system using the Recovery Console but can't boot it otherwise.

TIP *See "Using the Recovery Console" in Chapter 5 to learn how to install and use the Recovery Console.*

Follow these steps to back up the registry manually through the Recovery Console:

1. Boot the computer to the Recovery Console.

2. Use the CD command to change to the %systemroot%\System32\Config folder.

3. Use the COPY command to copy the files in the Config folder to a backup location. See Chapter 5 to learn how to access other drives and folders from the Recovery Console.

Restoring the system registry from the Recovery Console is much the same. If you have performed a recent backup of the system state data, the copy of the registry in the %systemroot%\Repair folder will be current as of that backup. Or, you can restore any other registry backup you have created manually. Follow these steps to restore the registry files from a backup set in the Recovery Console:

1. Boot the computer to the Recovery Console.

2. Use the COPY command to copy the existing registry files to a new location. You can later use these to restore the existing registry files, if needed.

3. Use the COPY command to copy the registry files from the backup location to the %systemroot%\System32\Config folder.

4. Restart the computer.

TIP *The Recovery Console's COPY command does not support wildcards, which means you can copy only one file at a time. You can create a text file containing multiple COPY commands, one for each registry file, and then execute that file from the Recovery Console using the BATCH command. See Chapter 5 for more details.*

Automated System Recovery

Windows XP includes a feature called Automated System Recovery (ASR) that can simplify recovering a system. ASR creates a diskette with the system's drive configuration and a backup of the hard disk where Windows XP is installed. If your documents are stored on the same disk, ASR backs up your documents and application settings as well as your system files.

ASR backup and recovery are two separate processes. Follow these steps to create an ASR backup set:

1. Start Windows XP and open the Backup applet.

2. Click the Welcome tab and then click Automated System Recovery Wizard.

3. In the wizard, specify the path to be used to create the backup set (Figure 10-3). Make sure this is a backup location that will be accessible from the text portion of Setup. For example, you should create the backup on the local hard disk or on a CD.

4. Click Next, then click Finish to start the backup. After the backup is complete you'll need to insert a blank, formatted diskette for ASR to use to store the disk configuration and other data.

TIP *An extra internal hard disk or a removable hard disk is a great option for storing the ASR backup set because it holds the entire set and can be accessed by Windows Setup.*

You use Windows Setup to restore a system from an ASR backup set. Follow these steps to restore the system:

1. Boot the system using the Windows XP CD.

2. When Setup starts, press F2.

3. When prompted, insert the ASR backup diskette and follow the remaining instructions to restore the system.

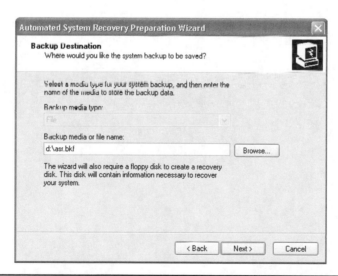

FIGURE 10-3   Specify the path to the backup set for Automated System Recovery (ASR).

Automating and Scripting Windows XP

I n this chapter you'll find the answers to the following questions:

- How can I automate tasks in XP?
- Can I schedule a program to run at a specific time?
- What are some programs I can use to automate tasks?
- Is it possible to write programs that automate tasks in Windows?

Back in the old days of Windows 3.x, the Windows Recorder, an application included with Windows, enabled you to record and play back keystrokes to automate tasks in Windows and in applications. This rather limited applet went the way of the dinosaur in subsequent Windows versions, taking away one very easy method for automating Windows and applications. However, Windows XP offers several methods for automation.

In this chapter, you'll learn about different tools you can use to automate Windows XP, including third-party tools, scripts, batch files, and more.

Automate Windows XP the Easy Way

You can perform some powerful actions with scripts in Windows XP, but writing a script requires an understanding of Windows Script Host (WSH), Visual Basic or Jscript, and general programming techniques. Even many administrators shy away from writing their own scripts because in the time it would take them to write and debug the script, they could accomplish the task manually. So, the best solution for most people is a point-and-click program that automates tasks without requiring any programming background. This section of the chapter explores just such solutions.

A better solution for many people is a *macro*, or a set of recorded steps that, when played back, automate a specific task. Macros can perform simple tasks, such as opening a dialog box and printing a document using specific settings, or very complex tasks, such as laying out a document complete with boilerplate text and images. It's all in how you design the macro.

There are several automation programs for Windows XP that make it very easy to automate specific tasks. Let's take a look at a few to give you a feel for how easy it can be to automate Windows XP.

Macro Express

I tested several macro programs for Windows XP when I developed this chapter, and one that struck me as very easy to use is Macro Express, from Insight Software Solutions (http://www.macros.com). Figure 11-1 shows the Macro Express window.

Let's take a very simple example. Here's the background: Microsoft Word, like most Windows applications, lets you press CTRL-V to paste the contents of the Clipboard into a document. However, like us, you might often want to paste text into Word without any formatting. To do so, you have to choose Edit | Paste Special, then select Unformatted Text, and click OK to paste the Clipboard contents without formatting. Wouldn't it be nice to simply press a keyboard shortcut like CTRL-L to paste the contents without formatting automatically? We'll show you how to build a macro with Macro Express to do just that.

1. Start by opening Word and maximizing the Word window.

2. Type some text and cut the text to the Clipboard.

3. Start Macro Express, choose Macros, and then choose Add Macro. Macro Express displays the Add Macro dialog box (Figure 11-2). With the Hot Key selected (the default), press CTRL+L to assign the CTRL+L keystroke to the macro.

4. Click Capture Macro to open the Macro Express Capture window (Figure 11-3).

5. In the Nickname box, type **Paste Special Unformatted**.

6. From the Program to start capturing in drop-down box, choose the Microsoft Word window.

7. Choose Quadruple Speed.

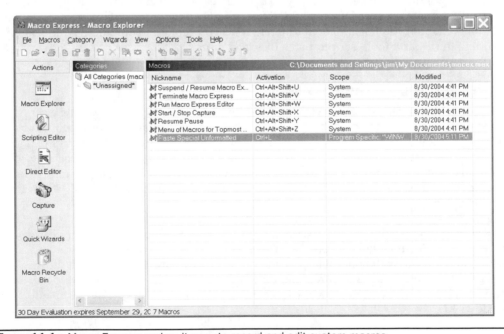

FIGURE 11-1   Macro Express makes it easy to record and edit custom macros.

FIGURE 11-2   Assign a shortcut keystroke to the macro in the Add Macro dialog box.

8. Click Start Capture.

9. In Word, choose Edit | Paste Special, select Unformatted Text, and click OK.

10. Right-click the Macro Express icon in the tray to stop recording.

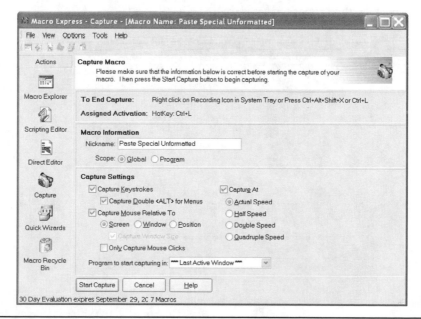

FIGURE 11-3   Set recording options in the Macro Express – Capture window.

Now, Macro Express should show a macro named Paste Special Unformatted in its Macro Explorer view. To test the macro, switch to Microsoft Word and press CTRL-L. The text you copied to the Clipboard should now appear in your document as unformatted text.

Now, what happens if you press CTRL-L with another program running? When you recorded the macro you didn't specify which window the macro should run in, so it will run in any window. With this example, this means your macro could perform some unexpected tasks if you try to run it with something other than Word. Why? Although the Edit menu is available in most Windows applications, the Paste Special command is not. In addition, the Unformatted Text option in the Paste Special dialog box is also specific to Word. This macro makes no distinction about what menu, menu item, or dialog box it is manipulating. Instead, it simply "knows" it needs to click the mouse at certain places on the display. Bottom line: the macro will work fine if you run it from within a maximized Word window, but it will give you unexpected and probably unwanted results in any other situation.

Macro Express, like many macro editors, lets you specify the scope for a macro. In this case, we want the macro to run only for Microsoft Word. So, let's tweak its properties accordingly:

1. With Macro Express open, double-click the Paste Special Unformatted macro in the Macro Explorer window.

2. Click the Scope tab (Figure 11-4).

3. Choose Program Specific and then click Select.

4. Scroll through the list of running programs in the Select Programs dialog box, click WINWORD.EXE, and click Add. Then, click OK.

5. Choose File, then choose Save.

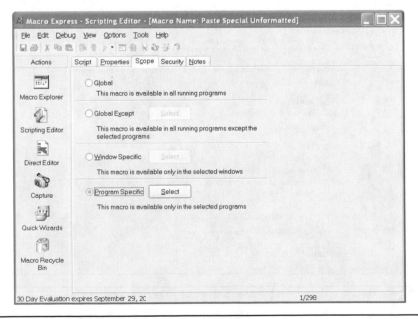

FIGURE 11-4   Use the Scope tab to set the macro's scope.

6. Minimize the Macro Express window and open a program other than Word; for example, open Notepad.

7. Press CTRL-L to test your macro's scope. Because Word is not running as the foreground application, the macro will not execute.

Though this example is fairly simply, it shows how relatively easy it is to create a macro that will automate a task in a program. Macro Express also offers more sophisticated macro capabilities. For example, you can use its Scripting Editor to quickly add actions to a macro (Figure 11-5) and to build a macro one action at a time rather than record it.

Macro Express also provides a wizard that helps you create macros to automate specific, common tasks. These include launching programs, selecting a printer, setting the display resolution, opening the Control Panel, connecting to a network folder, and many more.

If you want to try out Macro Express, visit http://www.macros.com and download the free evaluation copy.

AutoMate

Another popular Windows automation program is AutoMate, from Network Automation (http://www.networkautomation.com). Figure 11-6 shows the program's initial window.

The Available Actions appear in AutoMate in the left pane, categorized by function. Clicking the plus sign preceding a category opens the category and displays the actions available within that category. You can add an action to your macro simply by dragging the action from the left pane to the right pane. When you drag an action, AutoMate displays a dialog box prompt for additional information specific to the task. For example, if you drag the Send E-mail task from the Internet action category, AutoMate displays the Send E-mail dialog box (Figure 11-7).

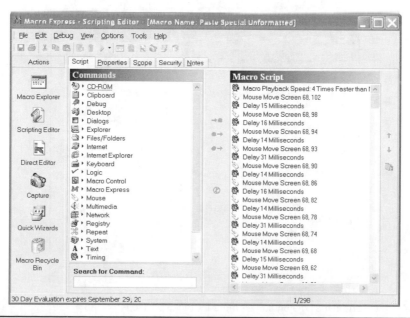

FIGURE 11-5 Use the Scripting Editor to build a script one action at a time.

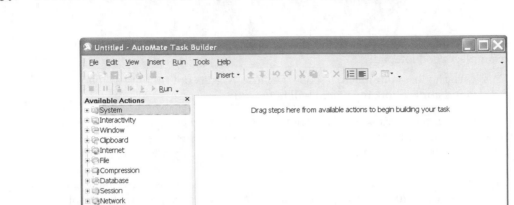

FIGURE 11-6   AutoMate makes it easy to create macros and automate tasks.

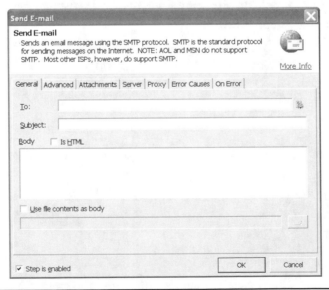

FIGURE 11-7   The Send E-mail dialog box prompts for task-specific information.

Like Macro Express, AutoMate also lets you record keyboard and/or mouse events. You can combine these recorded events with others that you add manually. AutoMate also provides a wizard that will help you build a macro. The wizard prompts for a macro name, triggers (events that cause the macro to execute), the steps to perform in the macro, and other properties.

Other Macro Tools

Macro Express and AutoMate are just two of the many macro tools for Windows XP. You'll find many others if you search the Internet. A good place to start is a shareware site such as http://www.download.com, http://www.wugnet.com, and http://www.tucows.com, among others. For most people, the key point to keep in mind when searching for a macro tool is ease-of-use. After all, you want to make it easier to user your computer through automation, not spend countless hours trying to write and fine-tune a complex script.

Using the Scheduled Tasks Folder

The Scheduled Tasks folder (Figure 11-8) provides the means for you to schedule a program to run at a specified time. You can schedule multiple programs as needed, and can schedule them to run daily, weekly, monthly, one time only, when the computer starts, or when you log on. You can schedule almost any kind of program. However, keep in mind that the Scheduled Tasks folder won't automate the program—it simply starts it at the specified time. The program itself must then take over and perform its task automatically.

To schedule a program to run, open the Scheduled Tasks folder from the Start\All Programs\Accessories\System Tools menu. When the Schedule Tasks folder opens, double-click the Add Scheduled Task icon to start the Scheduled Task Wizard. Then, click Next and choose the application you want to launch (Figure 11-9).

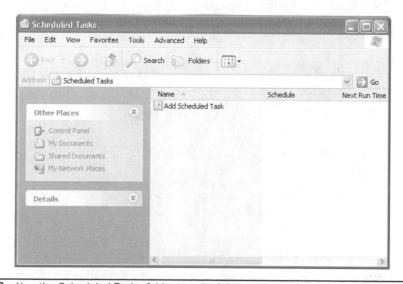

FIGURE 11-8   Use the Scheduled Tasks folder to schedule a program to run at a certain time.

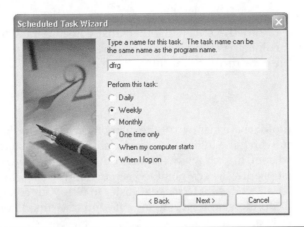

FIGURE 11-9 Choose the application to be launched.

After you choose the application and click Next, the wizard prompts you to choose when the program will run (Figure 11-10). Then, click Next and specify the account credentials under which the program will run (Figure 11-11). Click Next, then click Finish.

Configuring Advanced Settings

After you schedule a program, you can configure a handful of advanced settings for it. For example, the wizard does not offer the option of running the program when the system has been idle for a period of time, but the advanced options do offer that option. To set advanced options, open the Scheduled Tasks folder and double-click the item to open its property sheet.

The Task tab lets you choose the program, specify the startup folder for the application, enter optional comments, choose the account under which the program runs, and enable or disable the item.

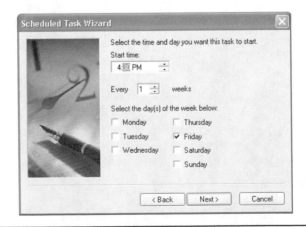

FIGURE 11-10 Specify when the program will run.

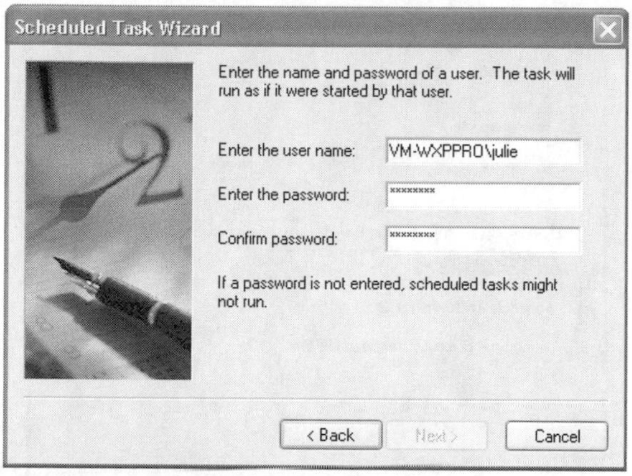

Figure 11-11   Enter the user account credentials for the program.

Use the Schedule tab (Figure 11-12) to specify when the program will run. Here you can choose from the same options offered by the wizard and also choose When Idle from the drop-down list to have the application run when the system has been idle for the specified length of time.

You can also configure multiple schedules for a single program. For example, perhaps you want a disk defragmenter to run once a week and also when the system has been idled for more than two hours. Whatever your situation, you can enable the Show Multiple Schedules check box on the Schedule tab to enable additional options on the tab. To add a

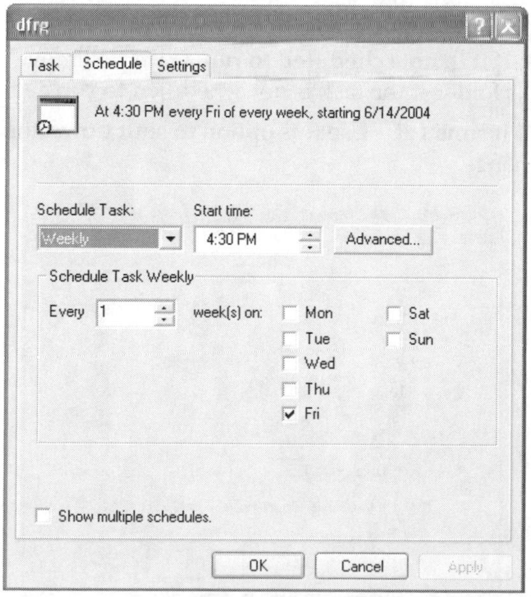

Figure 11-12   Use the Schedule tab to set advanced scheduling options.

FIGURE 11-13 Set up an additional schedule instance.

new instance to the schedule, click New, then specify the time (Figure 11-13). Click Advanced if you want to specify that the item should reoccur (Figure 11-14).

Use the Settings tab (Figure 11-15) to configure several other advanced settings for the task. These options include the following:

- **Delete the task if it is not scheduled to run again**   Remove the task from the Scheduled Tasks folder if the task is not scheduled to run again.

- **Stop the task if it runs for**   Use this option to shut down the task if it runs excessively or hangs.

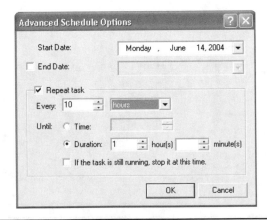

FIGURE 11-14   You can configure a reoccurring task.

- **Only start the task if the computer has been idle for at least**   Start the scheduled task only if the computer has been idle for the specified period of time.

- **Stop the task if the computer ceases to be idle**   Shut down the task if any activity occurs on the computer while the application is running.

- **Don't start the task if the computer is running on batteries**   Use this option on notebooks to prevent tasks from running when the computer is running on batteries.

- **Stop the task if battery mode begins**   Stop a running task if the computer switches from alternating current (AC) to batteries.

- **Wake the computer to run this task**   If the computer is suspended, resume it to run the task.

The AT Command

The AT command is a console command included with Windows XP that enables you to schedule tasks on the local computer or on a remote computer. In most situations, the Scheduled Tasks folder is easier to use because it provides a graphical interface. However, the AT command is a great option for scheduling tasks from batch files (covered in the next section, "Blast from the Past: Batch Files") and scheduling tasks on other computers.

You can schedule a task as a one-time occurrence or schedule recurring tasks with AT. The general syntax to schedule a task with AT is

```
AT <time> <command>
```

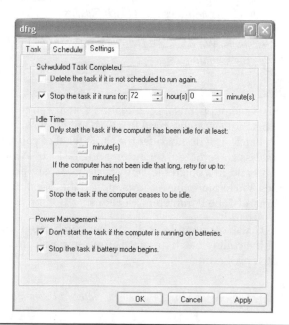

FIGURE 11-15   Configure additional properties on the Settings tab.

For example, if you wanted to run the script Cleanup.vbs at 7 P.M., you would use this command:

```
AT 19:00 Cleanup.vbs
```

The /interactive switch enables the scheduled application to interact with the Desktop, giving the user the capability to interact with the program. For example, you could use this syntax to schedule the Disk Defragmenter to open at 4:30 P.M. so the user could schedule a defragmentation:

```
AT 16:30 /interactive drfg.msc
```

The Scheduled Tasks folder is much easier to use to schedule tasks than the AT command, so I won't cover AT in any more detail. For more information on additional syntax and options, use the command **AT /?** at a command prompt to view the command's Help content.

Blast from the Past: Batch Files

If you have become familiar with the command console and want to automate tasks without writing scripts, batch files could be a good solution for your task automation needs. This section of the chapter offers an overview of batch files and some tips on writing and using them. Batch files are much easier to write than scripts in most cases, because the structure of a batch file is generally simpler and less "program-like" than a script.

> **NOTE** *I could devote a couple of chapters to batch programming. However, because scripts offer much more flexibility, I only offer an overview of batch files here to give you an alternative to Windows Scripting Host (WSH) (discussed later in this chapter in "Automating Windows with Scripts") and macro tools. Windows XP Help and Support Center includes a thorough explanation of batch file programming.*

Batch Files Explained

Essentially, a batch file is a string of console commands that are stored in a text file and executed one at a time. Batch files can have BAT or CMD file extensions, and are executed by CMD.EXE. Although batch files do not offer the same level of capability or flexibility as scripts, they are nevertheless a useful tool for automating tasks in Windows XP.

You can use any command in a batch file, but Windows XP supports several special commands for batch files. We explore these commands in the "Creating and Using Batch Files" and "Using Command-Line Parameters" sections.

- **CALL**   Use the CALL command to call another batch program without stopping the execution of the calling batch program. You can pass command-line parameters to the called batch program.

> **TIP** *See the section, "Using Command-Line Parameters," later in this chapter, for details on using parameters.*

- **ECHO**   Turn command ECHO on or off or display a message on the command line. When used by itself, ECHO displays the current ECHO setting. When ECHO is on, commands executed by the batch file are echoed to the command prompt as they are executed. Turn ECHO off if you do not want the commands to echo on the command line. Use ECHO ON or ECHO OFF to turn ECHO on or off. You can also use the ECHO command to display text. Type ECHO followed by the text you want displayed, such as

```
ECHO Preparing to reformat the hard drive...
```

TIP *Use the ECHO command followed immediately by a period to echo a blank line.*

- **ENDLOCAL**   End localization of environment variables to the batch file. When environment variables are localized, changes apply only to the batch file itself and not to the rest of the computing environment. Use in conjunction with the SETLOCAL command.

- **FOR**   Perform a specific command for each file in a set of files. For example, you might use this command to rename a set of files.

- **GOTO**   Move execution in the batch file to the line specified by the GOTO statement.

- **IF**   Perform conditional execution or branching within the batch file.

- **PAUSE**   Pause execution of the batch file and display a prompt for the user to press a key to continue.

- **REM**   Use at the beginning of a line in a batch file to indicate a commented line (add remarks to a batch file).

- **SETLOCAL**   Use SETLOCAL to localize environment variables changes made within the batch file so they affect the batch file only and not the rest of the computing environment. End localization with the ENDLOCAL command.

- **SHIFT**   Use this command to shift batch file parameters to the left. For example, after SHIFT, the value in the third parameter shifts to the second and the second shifts to the first. Use SHIFT to work with more than nine command parameters.

The Windows XP Help and Support Center includes a good explanation of each of these commands and examples of how to use them. To view the content, click Start | Help and Support, then enter **Batch Files** in the Search box and click Go. Click the Back Files link in the Suggested Topics results to view information about these commands.

Creating and Using Batch Files

You can use any text editor to create a batch file as long as the program writes the file as a plain text file. Notepad is a good tool for creating batch files. To create a batch file, simply open Notepad and enter the commands in the file, one per line, in the sequence you want them to be executed. Then, save the file with a BAT or CMD file extension. To run a batch file, open a command console, type the name of the batch file with any required parameters (see the following section, "Using Command-Line Parameters"), and press ENTER to start execution.

> **TIP** *If the batch file resides in a folder that is not in the path, use CD (Change Directory command) to change to the batch file's directory.*

Using Command-Line Parameters

You can use command-line parameters to pass additional information to a batch file. These parameters are represented by %1 through %9 in the batch file. The batch file name is stored in %0. In the following example, the batch file takes the two parameters typed with the command, adds them, and displays the name of the batch file along with the parameters and the result:

```
echo off
setlocal
set /a result=%1+%2
echo According to the batch file %0, %1 + %2 equals %result%
endlocal
echo on
```

Here is the result of the command:

```
C:\>add.cmd 2 4
According to the batch file add, 2 + 4 equals 6
```

Use command-line parameters any time you need to pass information to a batch file. As with script arguments, batch file parameters enable you to create a somewhat generic batch file and pass variable information to it as needed. You can also use parameters to pass information from one batch file to another with the CALL command.

> **TIP** *See the explanation of the SHIFT command in the "Batch Files Explained" section, earlier in this chapter, and the Help and Support Center information on batch files to learn how to shift the command-line parameters and use more than nine parameters.*

Automating Windows with Scripts

Windows XP includes a feature called Windows Scripting Host (WSH) that enables you to create and run scripts to perform a very broad range of tasks. WSH in Windows XP supports two programming languages: VBScript and Jscript. VBScript is very similar to Visual Basic for Applications (VBA), a programming language based on Visual Basic and included with many Microsoft applications (such as Microsoft Office). Jscript is loosely based on the Java programming language. I'll focus on VBScript in this chapter for simplicity.

Writing a Script

Writing a script for WSH requires some understanding of programming methods and techniques, so it isn't for everyone. In fact, many administrators never create or use scripts because the other methods available to them for accomplishing tasks serve their needs. Still, scripts can be a very powerful, flexible way to automate Windows. So, if you're the adventurous type and either have a programming background or the innate ability to understand program flow, you'll enjoy learning about scripting Windows XP. Before we get to a few examples, however, let's take a look at the mechanics of writing a script.

First, a WSH script is just a text file that contains script commands. You can write a script using any text editor, such as Notepad, that will save a file in text-only format. Second, when you create a VBScript file, give it a VBS file extension. This will allow WSH to recognize and execute the script.

Now, let's get to a few examples!

When you learn a new programming language, one of the most common beginner tasks is to learn how to display some text in a dialog box or popup window—in other words, output some information. Programming instructors and people who write about programming invariably use a variation of the "Hello, World!" program—a simple program that displays the text "Hello, World!" in a window, on the command console, or in a dialog box. Here's an easy introduction to VBScript with my own version of Hello, World:

1. Open Notepad.

2. Type the following text:
   msgbox "Hello, World!"

3. Choose File, and choose Save.

4. From the Save As Type drop-down list, choose All Files.

5. In the File Name box, type **Hello.vbs** and click Save.

6. Minimize all programs and look on the Desktop for the file Hello.vbs. Double-click its icon. You should see a small dialog box with the message displayed (Figure 11-16).

Now, let's extend this example just a bit to read some additional information from Windows and display it in the message box. We'll look up the user's logon account name and computer name using the WScript.Network object:

```
' Declare some variables
Dim user, computer, sh
' Create an instance of the WScript.Network object
Set sh = WScript.CreateObject("WScript.Network")
' Store the UserName property to the user variable
user = sh.UserName
' Store the ComputerName property to the computer variable
computer = sh.ComputerName
' Combine all of the message parts and display the message
msgbox "Hello, World!" & vbCrLf & "User: " & user & vbCrLf &
"Computer: " & computer
```

Figure 11-17 shows the results of this script.

FIGURE 11-16   A simple "Hello, World!" message displayed by a script

FIGURE 11-17   This dialog box includes additional information about the user and computer.

Note that this example includes several lines that start with a ' character. These are comment lines, or lines that contain information but are not executed by WSH. You can use comments to explain parts of your script, leave reminders for yourself within the code, and so on.

Also, note the use of the & character in the last line. This character concatenates or combines the text into one message. vbCrLf represents a Visual Basic carriage return/line feed, which starts a new line in the message box.

With this example we've shown you that it is possible to extract information from Windows. In this case, we've used the UserName and ComputerName properties of the WScript.Network object, which exposes many network-related properties to WSH. There are many other objects, each with their own properties, which expose other information.

Learning More About WSH

As we wrote at the beginning of this section, writing scripts to automate Windows isn't for everyone. The two simple examples we've included here are intended to show you that in terms of mechanics, it's relatively easy to create a script for Windows. However, writing scripts to perform complex actions not only requires at least some understanding of programming methods and techniques, but also an understanding of how Windows and applications work.

However, if you have some programming background or would like to use WSH as a springboard for learning about programming, you'll find many resources available to help. We suggest you start at http://msdn.microsoft.com/scripting. There you'll find a complete reference on WSH, VBScript, and script examples to help you get your feet wet.

Windows XP Security

In this chapter you'll find the answers to the following questions:

- How can I prevent someone from printing or changing a document I send them?
- Is there a way to prevent someone from forwarding an e-mail message I send to them?
- I've heard about Digital Rights Management (DRM). What is it and how does it work?
- I don't have Outlook but need to view a message or document that someone has protected with DRM. What do I do?
- What good is a user account?
- What are groups?
- How do I create or change user accounts or groups?
- What are the Guest and Administrator accounts?
- How do I configure Windows XP's new firewall?
- How do I make a particular program work through Windows Firewall?
- Is it possible to have an exception for one program in Windows Firewall?
- Would a different type of firewall than Windows Firewall be better for me?

Computer security has always been an important issue, but security has become even more important as identity theft, viruses, and other cyber-age threats have increased in prevalence. Today, an unprotected system connected directly to the Internet could easily be compromised in a matter of minutes after being connected. Today more than ever, your privacy and your data—both business and personal—are at risk if you don't take steps to protect them.

Windows XP provides several security-related features that will help you protect your data and your system as a whole. This chapter explains these features and offers tips on how you can get the most from them to improve security.

Securing Documents and Messages with Digital Rights Management

Digital Rights Management (DRM) is a group of technologies geared toward securing data to prevent it from being transmitted, copied, or printed by unauthorized persons. Microsoft has implemented its version of DRM with server- and client-side components, as well as features in Office 2003 and Internet Explorer (IE) 6.x. This section of the chapter explores Microsoft's implementations of DRM.

Information Rights Management Explained

Microsoft's client-side implementation of DRM is called Information Rights Management, or IRM. The goal of IRM is to provide a means by which users can prevent certain documents from being printed or copied. In the case of e-mail, IRM gives you the capability to prevent messages from being forwarded, copied, or printed. For example, assume you need to send an e-mail containing confidential information to a business partner outside of your organization. However, you don't want that person to be able to forward the message to anyone else, print it, or copy it to the Clipboard to include in another document (or print from that other application). IRM gives you that capability.

Microsoft's DRM components fall into two categories: a server-side component and client-side add-ons and features. These include the following:

- **Rights Management Services (RMS) for Windows Server 2003**   This add-on for Windows Server 2003 handles the certification of trusted entities, licensing of rights-protected data, enrollment of servers and users, and administrative functions for managing RMS. The service enables organizations to host their own rights-protected data and create templates and policies that define the level of access users have to protected data. Without RMS, organizations must rely on a free Microsoft Passport-based service from Microsoft that does not offer the capability to customize data access. In addition, Microsoft has indicated that this free service will not be available indefinitely, so organizations will likely be required to move to RMS at some point.

- **Rights-Management Add-on for Internet Explorer**   This add-on for IE enables users to view rights-protected documents while maintaining the restrictions imposed by IRM. For example, a user of Outlook 2003, which has IRM capabilities built in, sends an IRM-protected message to another user who does not have Outlook 2003. The recipient can then view the message in IE if the Rights Management Add-On is installed on his computer. The add-on enables users to view IRM-protected documents from other sources, as well.

- **IRM technologies in Office 2003**   Office 2003 applications have IRM capabilities built in, enabling users to protect documents as well as view IRM-protected documents, subject to their permissions.

In a nutshell, IRM encrypts a document and disables the controls and features in an application that would otherwise enable the user to save this document, copy it to the Clipboard, print it, or (in the case of e-mail messages) forward it on. IRM provides a mechanism by which users can be authenticated for access and view the content if they have been granted that right by the document publisher.

Adding IRM Capabilities to Windows XP and IE

The Rights Management Add-on for Internet Explorer enables Windows XP users to view rights-protected content if they have been designated by the publisher as having that right. The add-on is available as a free download from http://www.microsoft.com/windows/ie/downloads/addon/default.mspx.

To add IRM capabilities to IE, navigate to the download page, download RMUSetulp. exe, and double-click the file after downloading to start the installation process. If you need to uninstall the add-on, open the Add or Remove Programs applet in the Control Panel and remove the item titled Rights Management Add-on for Internet Explorer.

Securing Documents

If you are using Office 2003, you can begin protecting your documents and e-mail now with IRM. This chapter assumes you do not have an internal RMS server, but will be using the free Microsoft Passport-based service and Microsoft Passport.

Follow these steps to protect a document in an Office 2003 (Word, Excel, or PowerPoint) application:

1. Open the document you want to protect and choose File | Permission | Do Not Distribute.

2. If you don't have the Windows Rights Management Client installed on the computer, Office prompts you to download and install it, and offers a link to the Microsoft web site where you can download the client package. After downloading the package, simply double-click on it to start the client installation.

TIP *You'll find a link to the Windows Rights Management Client software at http://www.microsoft. com/windowsserver2003/technologies/rightsmgmt/default.mspx.*

---

3. If you don't have an IRM certificate on your computer yet, Office launches a wizard that prompts you for your Microsoft Passport and e-mail address to associate with the certificate. You can choose between using a standard certificate that can be re-used and renewed when it expires, or downloading a temporary certificate for a single use. Use the latter when you need to view content from a public computer.

4. The Permission dialog box now appears (Figure 12-1). Choose the Restrict permission to this document option.

5. To grant the right for someone to read the document but not print, copy, or edit it, click the Read icon to open your address book and choose the person. To grant permission to read, edit, and save changes to the document, click the Change icon and choose one or more people from the address book.

TIP *You can click Read in the Select Names dialog box to assign Read permission or click Change to assign Change permission.*

---

6. Click More Options if you want to specify additional options for the document. The Permission dialog box changes as shown in Figure 12-2.

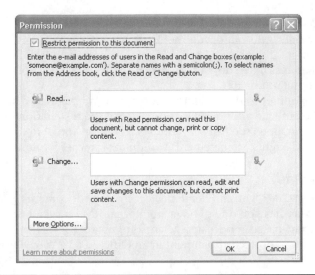

FIGURE **12-1** Configure IRM permissions in the Permission dialog box.

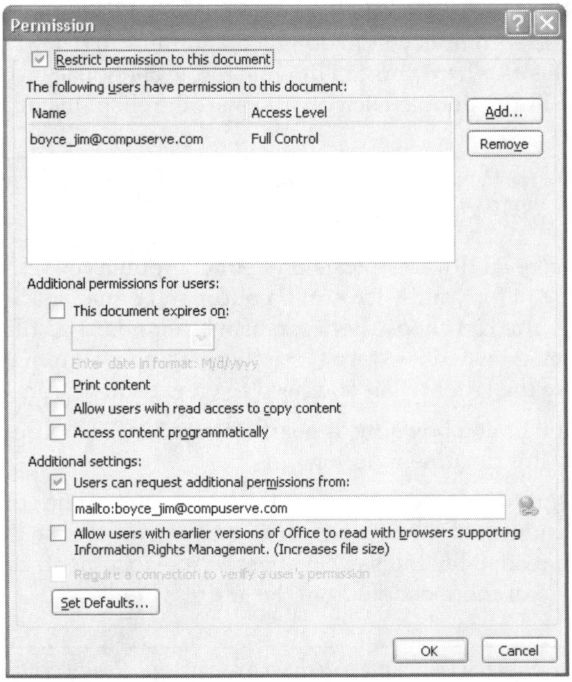

FIGURE **12-2** You can set additional properties for the document.

Configure options according to the following list:

- **Restrict permission to this document**   Choose this option to protect the document.
- **This document expires on**   Choose this option and specify an expiration date for the document. When the document expires it can no longer be viewed except by those with Full Control.
- **Print content**   Allow the user to print the document.
- **Allow users with read access to copy content**   If users have read access to the document, they can also copy the content to the Clipboard for inclusion in other documents.
- **Access content programmatically**   Allow programs to access the content.
- **Users can request additional permissions from**   Specify the e-mail address or URL from which the user can request additional permissions for the document.
- **Allow users with previous versions of Office to read with browsers supporting Information Rights Management**.   Choose this option to allow users without Office 2003 to view the document in IE with the Rights Management Add-on installed.
- **Require a connection to verify a user's permission**.   Force the user to connect to the Windows Rights Management server every time the content is opened. Use this option with RMS when the document permissions are likely to change periodically and you want to make sure the appropriate permissions are applied each time.

TIP *You might have multiple identities on the computer and can choose which one you want to use to create or view IRM-protected content. To do so, choose File | Permission | Restrict Permission As to open a dialog box in which you choose which identity to use.*

Securing E-Mail Messages

With Outlook 2003 you can set the Do Not Forward permission on a message to prevent recipients from forwarding, printing, or copying the message. To set this permission, start the new message and choose File | Permission | Do Not Forward.

Managing User Accounts and Groups

User accounts in Windows XP provide the means for securing resources. For example, each user has his own profile complete with a My Documents folder and other data folders. When the system uses NT File System (NTFS) as the file system, permissions are set such that one user can't access another's documents. You also use accounts to protect folders shared on the network.

This section of the chapter explores user accounts and groups and offers tips on using them to secure your data and other resources.

NOTE It's relatively easy to create and modify user accounts, so this chapter doesn't focus on those tasks; instead, it offers tips on special accounts and using groups. If you need to manage accounts, use the User Accounts applet in the Control Panel or the Local Users and Groups branch of the Computer Management console (Professional only).

The Guest Account

Windows XP Professional and Home Editions both include a Guest account. By default, this Guest account is disabled as a security measure. The only reason to enable the Guest account is if you intend to use Simple File Sharing (SFS) to share folders on the network. SFS is the default sharing method for Windows XP Professional and the only method available for Windows XP Home Edition for sharing folders on the network.

If you will be using SFS, you can enable the Guest account from the Local Users and Groups branch of the Computer Management console on a Windows XP Professional computer:

1. Right-click My Computer and choose Manage.

2. Click the Local Users and Groups\Users branch.

3. Right-click the Guest account and choose Properties.

4. Clear the Account Is Disabled option (Figure 12-3) and click OK.

For the Home Edition, follow these steps to enable the Guest account:

1. Log on with an account that has Computer Administrator rights and open the Control Panel.

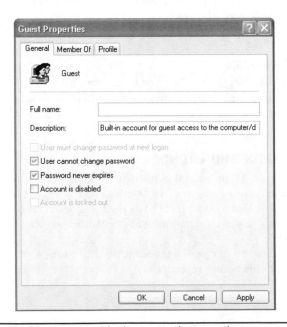

FIGURE 12-3   Enable or disable an account in the account's properties.

2. Open the User Accounts applet and click the Guest account.

3. Click Turn On the Guest Account (Figure 12-4) and then close the User Accounts applet.

Securing the Guest Account

The Guest account poses a security risk in anything other than home or small office networks because it offers the potential for unauthenticated access to resources on the network. There are a couple of group policies you can use to secure the Guest account. These include:

- **Computer Configuration\Windows Settings\Security Settings\Local Policies\ Security Options\Accounts: Guest account status** Set this policy to Disabled to disable the Guest account.

- **Computer Configuration\Windows Settings\Security Settings\Local Policies\ Security Options\Accounts: Rename guest account** Set this policy to change the name of the Guest account. Renaming the Guest account will help reduce the security risk when the Guest account is enabled.

___

TIP Run gpedit.msc to set local policy.

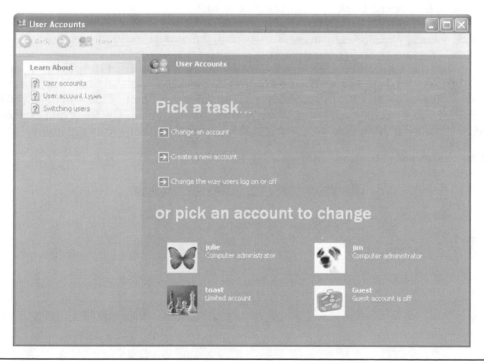

FIGURE 12-4   Use the User Accounts applet in the Control Panel to enable/disable accounts in Home Edition.

The Administrator Account (Professional Edition)

On Windows XP Home Edition computers, there is no Administrator account by default, although at least one account will have Computer Administrator rights. On Windows XP Professional, however, the Administrator account is a separate account.

The local Administrator account has full control over the computer, including the capability to access all files and folders, install hardware and update device drivers, and make many other changes that are not available to standard users or even members of the Power Users group.

It's generally a bad idea to work with the computer for extended periods with the Administrator account or with an account that is a member of the local Administrators group. Doing so exposes the system to potential compromise by viruses, worms, and other malicious applications that can gain access to the system while you are logged on (through an e-mail attachment or web site, for example). For this reason, you should create a regular user account for yourself as your main working account even if you are the only person using the computer.

Running Programs in the Administrator Context

The only inconvenience in using a regular account instead of the Administrator account is the inability to make certain changes to your computer. On way to get around it is to simply log off, log on as the Administrator, make the change, and then log off to log back on with your regular account. In many cases, however, you can simply run the application in question in the context of the Administrator account.

There are two ways to start the application in the Administrator context. First, you can right-click the application and choose Run As from the context menu to open the Run As dialog box (Figure 12-5). To use a different account, choose the option The Following User; then choose the Administrator account from the User Name list. Enter the password and click OK to start the program in the Administrator context.

You can also use the RUNAS command from a console prompt or the Run dialog box (click Start | Run) to start a program in the Administrator context. The following example starts the Microsoft Management Console (MMC) using the Administrator account:

```
RUNAS /user:administrator mmc.exe
```

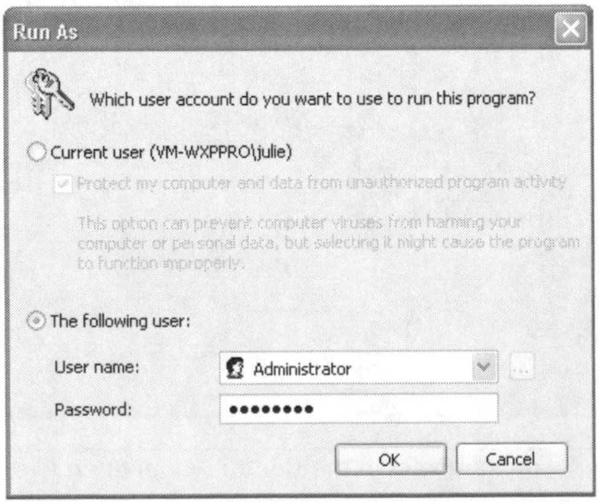

FIGURE 12-5   Use the Run As dialog box to run a program in a different user context.

By default, RUNAS loads the specified user's profile. You can speed up program load by adding the /noprofile switch to the RUNAS command, which prevents the user profile from being loaded. However, some applications require that the user profile be loaded to run properly. For example, if you run Microsoft Outlook with RUNAS in a user context other than your own and specify the /noprofile switch, Outlook will be unable to access the configuration data (or mail store) stored in the user profile and will not be able to open.

*TIP   For additional syntax for the RUNAS command, type **RUNAS /?** at the command prompt.*

Securing the Administrator Account

As with the Guest account, the existence of the Administrator account poses some security risks. However, the Administrator account is also a necessity. You can add some measure of security with two group policies:

- **Computer Configuration\Windows Settings\Security Settings\Local Policies\ Security Options\Accounts: Administrator account status**   Use this policy to disable the local Administrator account. The account is always enabled for Safe Mode.

- **Computer Configuration\Windows Settings\Security Settings\Local Policies\ Security Options\Accounts: Rename Administrator account**   Use this policy to rename the Administrator account. Doing so can reduce the chance that someone can guess the local Administrator account name and password.

When and How to Use Groups

Groups, which are available in Windows XP Professional but not Windows XP Home Edition, enable you to assign permissions to a group of accounts. There are a handful of existing groups by default, including Users, Power Users, Administrators, Guests, and several others.

When should you use groups? Any time you need to assign a certain set of rights to multiple users, assigning rights by group is the best approach to the problem. Create the group, assign rights to it as needed, and then add the individual accounts of users who need those rights to the group.

Follow these steps to create a group and add accounts to it:

1. Open the Computer Management console, right-click the Local Users and Groups\ Groups branch, and choose New Group.

2. Enter a name for the group and an optional description (Figure 12-6).

3. Click Add to open the Select Users dialog box, click Advanced, and click Find Now to list all existing local groups and accounts.

4. Select the accounts and/or groups you want to add and click OK.

5. Click OK to close the Select Users dialog box; then click Create to create the group.

TIP   To add accounts to an existing group, simply double-click the group and click Add to start adding accounts to it.

How do you protect resources such as shared folders or printers with groups? You assign permissions to the resource and grant the specified group the required permissions.

Using a Firewall

As we explained in the introduction to this chapter, an unprotected computer connected to the Internet can become infected by worms and viruses literally within minutes of being connected to the Internet. Most people aren't willing to give up Internet access for the security of their data and system, so some means of protection is needed. One of the best forms of protection is a firewall. This section explains how to configure Windows Firewall and explores other firewall options including hardware-based firewalls.

Windows Firewall

Windows XP includes its own firewall called Internet Connection Firewall in Service Pack 1 and earlier. The firewall is renamed Windows Firewall and given several enhancements in Service Pack 2 (SP2). This section of the chapter focuses on the changes to Windows Firewall in SP2.

Configuring Windows Firewall

Configuring Windows Firewall isn't difficult, but it does require some understanding of ports and services. This section explains these concepts in the context of configuring the firewall.

To begin configuring Windows Firewall, click Start, right-click My Network Places, and choose Properties. If your Start menu doesn't include My Network Places, open the Network Connections object in the Control Panel. After the Network Connections folder opens, right-click your network connection and choose Properties; then click Advanced (Figure 12-7).

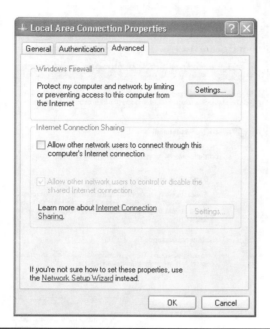

FIGURE 12-7   Use the Advanced tab to access Windows Firewall settings.

TIP *The property sheet for the network connection contains an Internet Connection Sharing (ICS) group only if there are multiple connections on the computer. If the computer includes a dial-up connection and a local area network (LAN) connection, the ICS settings appear on the property sheet for the dial-up connection.*

Click Settings to open the Windows Firewall dialog box (Figure 12-8). The options on the General tab include the following:

- **On**   Choose this option to turn on Windows Firewall. By default, Windows Firewall is enabled for all connections, including both dialup and LAN.

- **Don't allow exceptions**   Choose this option to ignore the exceptions listed on the Exceptions tab (explained shortly). Generally, you use this option when you are working from a public network and want to provide full protection for your computer.

- **Off**   Choose this option to turn off Windows Firewall.

The following sections explain the other properties you can configure for Windows Firewall and how to use different settings on different connections.

Managing Exception Lists and Rule Scope

As we hinted at in the previous section, you can create a list of exceptions for Windows Firewall. Exceptions allow Windows Firewall to allow incoming traffic for specific ports to support specific services that use those ports. For example, if you want to allow others to

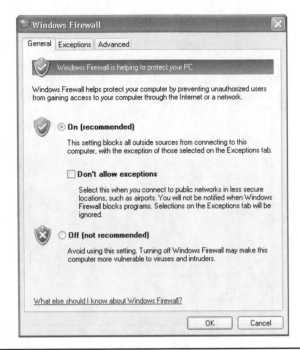

FIGURE 12-8   Use the Windows Firewall General tab to enable or disable the firewall.

help you with Remote Assistance, you need to allow Remote Assistance traffic through Windows Firewall. Otherwise, Windows Firewall will block the traffic.

To configure exceptions, open the properties for Windows Firewall and click the Exceptions tab (Figure 12-9). By default, the Programs and Services list on the Exceptions tab includes four services:

- **File and Printer Sharing**   This service enables your computer to share its folders and printers with other users. It should not be enabled on your Internet connection but can be enabled on your LAN connection. In our discussion of scope (in this section), we show you how to enable a service for the LAN but not the Internet.

- **Remote Assistance**   This service enables others to connect to your computer to provide remote assistance.

- **Remote Desktop**   This service enables you or others to connect to and control your computer from a remote location. For example, you could use Remote Desktop to access your home computer when you are at the office, or vice versa.

- **UPnP Framework**.   Universal Plug and Play (UPnP) provides a mechanism by which systems can discover Plug and Play devices on the Network. In most cases, you should not allow incoming UPnP traffic from the Internet because it poses a security risk.

FIGURE 12-9 Use the Exceptions tab to allow incoming traffic for specific ports and services

By default, all of these four services are excluded, which means Windows Firewall will not accept traffic on their respective ports. If you need to allow traffic from one of these sources, you can select the check box to allow the traffic.

TIP Windows Firewall will add most instant messaging (IM) clients to the exceptions list automatically to enable them to function.

If you decide to allow one of these default services or add your own, you should check and configure the *scope* for the service. The scope settings enable Windows Firewall to allow incoming traffic from certain locations but block it from others. For example, let's assume you want to enable Remote Desktop for your computer so you can connect to it from another computer on the local network, but you don't want anyone to be able to get to it from the Internet. Here's how to configure the scope accordingly:

1. Open the properties for Windows Firewall and click the Exceptions tab.
2. Select Remote Desktop to enable it, then click Edit to open the Edit a Service dialog box. Then, click Change Scope to open the Change Scope dialog box (Figure 12-10).

Choose one of the following options:

- **Any computer (including those on the Internet)** This option allows incoming traffic from any source, whether local or from the Internet.

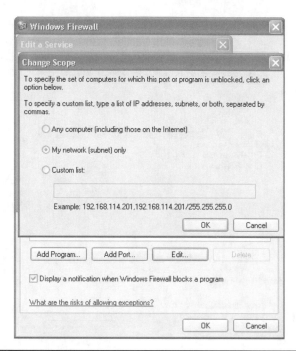

FIGURE 12-10   Use the Change Scope dialog box to control the allowed source(s) for incoming traffic.

- **My network (subnet) only**   Choose this option to allow incoming traffic for the specified service only from IP addresses in the same subnet as your computer. In effect, this allows traffic only from computers on your local network.

- **Custom list**   Choose this option to specify a list of individual addresses and/or subnets that should be allowed in for the specified port(s).

In some cases, you might want to allow a selection of addresses or subnets, and the Custom List option is the solution. For example, assume you want to enable Remote Desktop for your local network but also want to be able to connect to your computer from home over a broadband Internet connection. In this case, you would use the Custom List option, specify your subnet (or individual addresses on your network), and also specify the public Internet protocol (IP) address of your home Internet connection. To specify a subnet, enter the IP address followed by the subnet mask, such as 192.168.0.1/255.255.255.0. Add multiple addresses or subnets to the list separated by commas.

TIP   *If you're not sure what your public IP address is at home, navigate to http://www.boyce.us and check the status bar for your public IP address.*

Enabling Services and Ports in the Exceptions List

At some point you are likely to want to open certain ports for your computer. For example, you might want to play an online game or host your own Web Services. Unless you open the ports for those services, the traffic won't reach your computer.

You can add programs as well as ports. When you add a program, you direct Windows Firewall to allow incoming traffic to the specified application. When you add a port, you direct Windows Firewall to allow incoming traffic on that port, regardless of the destination.

Follow these steps to add a program:

1. Open the properties for Windows Firewall and click the Exceptions tab.

2. Click Add Program to open the Add A Program dialog box (Figure 12-11).

3. Browse for and select the application's executable file.

4. If you need to change scope for the application, click Change Scope and configure scope as described in the previous section. The default scope is to allow traffic from any source.

5. Click OK; then click OK to close the firewall properties.

Follow these steps to add a port:

1. Open the properties for Windows Firewall and click the Exceptions tab.

FIGURE 12-11   Choose a program from the Add A Program dialog box.

2. Click Add Port to open the Add A Port dialog box (Figure 12-12).

3. In the Name field, type a descriptive name for the service that will use the port, such as FTP (for the FTP service).

4. In the Port Number field, type the port number used by the service.

TIP *For a complete list of port assignments, see http://www.iana.org/assignments/port-numbers.*

5. Choose either Transmission Control Protocol (TCP) or User Datagram Protocol (UDP) depending on which protocol will be used.

6. Set the scope for the port/service if necessary; then click OK to add the port to the Exceptions list.

Enabling Common Services and Port Mapping

If a server on your network or your own computer will be hosting common services such as HTTP, FTP, or others, you must configure Windows Firewall to allow incoming traffic. If the service is running on a different computer on the network and your computer is serving as a gateway, then you must also configure port forwarding to enable the incoming traffic to be forwarded to the appropriate computer.

To enable services, follow these steps:

1. Open the properties for Windows Firewall, click the Advanced tab, select the interface, and click Settings.

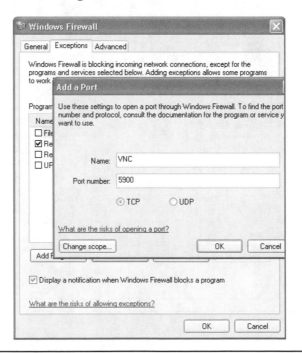

FIGURE 12-12 Specify a service name and port number.

2. In the Advanced Settings dialog box (Figure 12-13), select an existing service. Windows Firewall automatically opens the Service Settings dialog box (Figure 12-14).

3. Windows Firewall automatically adds the name of the local computer in the Name or IP address field. If the service is hosted by a different computer on the network, enter the IP address of the other computer.

4. Click OK to close the dialog box; then click OK to close the Advanced Settings dialog box.

If the service you want to host isn't listed in the Services tab, you can certainly add it. Just click Add to open the Service Settings dialog box and enter the information for the service:

- **Description of service**   You can enter anything here, but it's a good idea to use the service name (such as FTP, Diablo, pcAnywhere, VNC, and so on).

- **Name or IP address**   Enter the host name or IP address of the computer on the local network that hosts the service.

- **External Port number for this service**   Specify the port to which remote computers will send the traffic for this service.

- **Internal Port number for this service**   Specify the port on the local server to which the traffic will be forwarded.

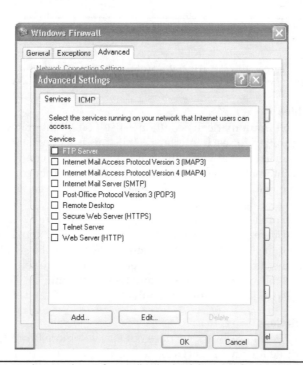

FIGURE 12-13   Enable services and port forwarding in the Advanced Settings dialog box.

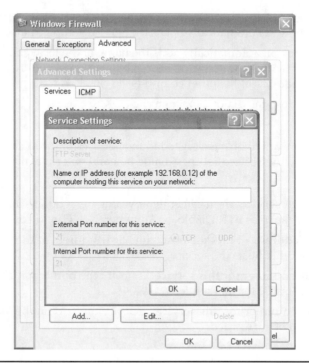

FIGURE 12-14 Use the Service Settings dialog box to specify the target computer for the service.

- **TCP/UDP** Choose the appropriate protocol according to the requirements of the service.

Using Multiple Profiles

Windows Firewall in SP2 automatically configures itself on all interfaces and, by default, uses the same configuration for each interface. While this is a good starting point from a security standpoint, it's likely that you will want to use different configurations for your local connection and Internet connection (assuming there are other computers on the local network). For example, you might want to be able to play online games across your local network, but not allow traffic from the Internet.

The Advanced tab of the Windows Firewall properties (Figure 12-13) is the place to go to configure settings differently for each interface. The list in the Network Connection Settings area lists all of the interfaces. You can turn off Windows Firewall for a particular interface by clearing the check box beside the interface. To change settings for a specific interface, first click on the interface in the list and then click Settings. The settings you configure will apply to the selected interface only.

RPC Interface Restrictions

Internet Connection Firewall prior to SP2 does not allow Remote Procedure Call (RPC) traffic, which is required for several services such as file and print sharing, remote administration, and others. Windows Firewall with SP2 treats RPC differently. An RPC server application can request that Windows Firewall open the necessary ports as long as the application is running in the Local System, Network Service, or Local Service security contexts. In addition, you can configure the RPC application on the exceptions list to enable it to accept incoming traffic on dynamic ports.

TIP *To learn about RPC interface restrictions and how an SP2 system handles incoming RPC, see the "RPC Interface Restriction" section in Chapter 4.*

Configuring Windows Firewall with Group Policy

Windows Firewall can be configured through a broad range of group policy settings, giving administrators the capability to control and manage firewall settings automatically across the network. Windows Firewall group policies control the firewall through computer policy, rather than user policy.

To configure Windows Firewall group policy at the local level, open the Group Policy Editor (gpedit.msc) and navigate to the Computer Configuration\Administrative Templates\Network\Network Connections\Windows Firewall branch. This branch contains two containers: Domain Profile and Standard Profile. The policies in these two containers control Windows Firewall in domain and nondomain environments, respectively. The policies are the same from one container to the other, but apply in different networking configurations.

TIP *To learn about a specific Windows Firewall group policy setting, choose the Extended task-pane view, click on the policy setting, and view the description in the left half of the Details pane.*

Managing the Firewall with Netsh (SP2)

Windows XP SP2 adds some additional commands to the firewall context of the Netsh command-line utility to help you manage Windows Firewall from a console prompt. The complete list of commands for the firewall context includes the following (new SP2 commands are indicated):

- **add (SP2)**   Use this command to add programs or ports to the exceptions list and configure the scope for the added program or port.

- **delete (SP2)**   Use this command to remove programs or ports from the exceptions list.

- **dump**   Dump the current configuration to a script.

- **reset (SP2)**   Reset the firewall configuration to the default settings.

- **set**   Use this command to configure a variety of firewall settings, including allow programs and ports, Internet Control Message Protocol (ICMP) configuration, logging, multicast broadcast, notification, operation mode, ports, and services.

- **show**   Show the current configuration of specified firewall configuration items.

Generally, it's much easier to use the graphical interface or group policy to configure Windows Firewall than it is to perform the same tasks with Netsh. However, Netsh is useful when you need to incorporate firewall management into scripts. It provides full configuration capability for this purpose.

TIP *You can issue commands with Netsh from a console prompt, or issue the Netsh command by itself to enter the Netsh interactive command prompt. Use the former approach for scripting and the latter for issuing commands dynamically.*

For help using Netsh, including all commands and parameters, enter **Netsh** at a console prompt to enter interactive mode. Then, type **firewall** to enter firewall management mode, and type **?** for a list of commands. Type a command followed by **?** to view help for that specific command.

Other Firewall Applications

Windows Firewall is a significant improvement over Internet Connection Firewall. Network administrators, in particular, should appreciate the changes, specifically the capability to configure and manage the firewall through group policy.

Windows Firewall certainly isn't the only software-based firewall for Windows XP. There are other solutions that offer additional capabilities. One of the most popular is ZoneAlarm (http://www.zonelabs.com). Zone Labs offers several products with different features to serve a range of needs. The basic ZoneAlarm firewall, for example, adds the capability to quarantine suspicious e-mail attachments; ZoneAlarm with Antivirus adds virus detection and scrubbing; ZoneAlarm Pro adds several other privacy and security features; and ZoneAlarm Security Suite adds content blocking, IM encryption, and several additional security features.

Another software-based firewall to consider is Tiny Firewall, from Tiny Software (http://www.tinysoftware.com). This product provides extended firewall features, intrusion detection and prevention, application security, and file system protection. It integrates virus and worm protection and support for multiple profiles.

When should you turn to a firewall solution other than Windows Firewall? If you only want or need basic firewall protection, Windows Firewall is a good solution. When it's configured properly, it does a good job of protecting your computer from Internet worms and other network-borne threats. If you are looking for additional capability such as antivirus integration, e-mail scanning, extended reporting, or other features, then a third-party firewall is the solution.

Benefits of a Network Firewall

Another approach to take when protecting your network and computer systems is placing a firewall at the perimeter of your network. This type of configuration provides protection at the gateway before traffic enters your network and can be used instead of or in conjunction with Windows Firewall or other workstation-based protection methods.

A perimeter firewall offers a handful of advantages over workstation-based solutions and is a good choice whether you are connecting a small home network to the Internet or connecting a large business network. First, a perimeter firewall blocks attacks before they reach your network, not only improving security but also possibly reducing traffic on your network. A perimeter firewall also provides a centralized point of administration, simplifying management more and more as the number of computers on the network increases. A perimeter firewall that supports content filtering also provides the means to monitor and block web site access by everyone on the network based on a range of criteria.

You'll find both hardware- and software-based solutions for perimeter protection, and both are good approaches. A hardware solution provides simplicity and a software solution offers flexibility: you can often run other services on the firewall computer. For example, you might run a gateway antivirus scrubber on the same server.

Following are some popular perimeter firewall vendors and solutions to consider:

- **Microsoft Internet and Security Acceleration (ISA) Server**   A full-featured firewall running on Windows Server: http://www.microsoft.com/isaserver.

- **Symantec Enterprise Firewall**   Offers a range of perimeter security solutions in hardware and software: http://enterprisesecurity.symantec.com/content/productlink.cfm.

- **SonicWALL**   Provides a range of firewall and VPN solutions: http://www.sonicwall.com.

- **Check Point**.   One of the most widely-used perimeter firewall: http://www.checkpoint.com.

There are also several choices for the small office/home office market. SonicWALL offers products targeted at small networks, as does D-Link (http://www.dlink.com), Linksys (http://www.linksys.com), and several others.

TIP   *For many home networks, a firewall that provides Network Address Translation (NAT) and port blocking is adequate. See Chapter 16 for detailed discussion of network setup and configuration.*

Using and Controlling the Security Center

The Security Center (Figure 12-15) is a new addition in SP2. It provides a centralized location where you can view Windows Firewall, Automatic Updates, and antivirus protection status.

The Security Center does not give you the means to actually control these security-related options, but, instead, simply shows you whether or not Windows Firewall is turned on, whether you have an antivirus solution installed on the computer, and whether the Automatic Updates feature is turned on. For that reason, the Security Center is really not terribly useful. However, it does offer a warning when these three items are not configured on the computer, no doubt a move by Microsoft to get more personal Windows XP users to implement these security features.

One thing you can control from the Security Center is whether Windows XP notifies you about these security features. To turn off notification for one or more items, open the Security Center and click the link Change the way Security Center alerts me. Security Center displays an Alert Settings dialog box (Figure 12-16) that enables you to turn off notification for each of the three features.

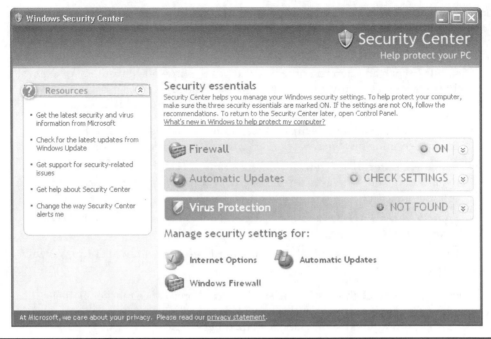

FIGURE 12-15 The Security Center provides centralized security management.

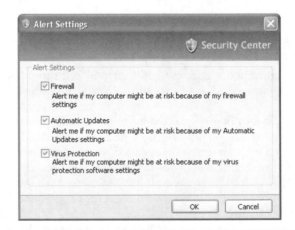

FIGURE 12-16 You can enable or disable security notifications.

System Management Tools

I n this chapter you'll find the answers to the following questions:

- Can you explain what all the programs are in the Administrative Tools folder?
- How do I manage settings for my computer?
- When I try to configure my computer, Windows XP tells me I don't have the necessary privileges. What do I do?
- Tell me about the event logs and how I can use them.
- How do I manage disks in Windows XP?
- Is it possible to change the drive letter of a hard disk or CD/DVD drive?
- What programs are available in Windows XP to manage hardware?
- Can I combine different administrative tools into a custom management tool?
- I'd like to simplify the way a management console looks. Is that possible?
- Are there any changes in Service Pack 2 (SP2) that affect the management tools in Windows XP?

Windows XP includes several management tools to help you configure and manage the system. Understanding how these tools work and knowing their capabilities will help you not only manage your own computer, but also manage others across the network. This chapter offers tips on using the preconfigured management tools included with Windows XP.

The modular nature of the Microsoft Management Console (MMC) also makes it possible for you to create your own custom management consoles with collections of tools that suit the way you work. You can combine different snap-ins and create custom taskpads to simplify common tasks. This chapter explains how to customize MMC consoles both ways.

Finally, SP2 introduces some changes that affect system management, particularly across the network. This chapter explains how to accommodate these changes.

Overview of Preconfigured Management Tools

Windows XP includes several management tools, some of which are MMC console snap-ins and some of which are standalone tools. This section explores the most commonly used management tools.

Computer Management

The Computer Management console (Figure 13-1) integrates several management and configuration tools. These tools are almost identical between Home Edition and Professional, with the exception of the Local Users and Groups branch, which is not included in Home Edition. To open the Computer Management console, right-click My Computer and choose Manage or Computer Management from the Administrative Tools folder.

The Computer Management console includes these snap-ins:

- **Event Viewer**   The Event Viewer enables you to view events recorded by Windows XP. There are three event logs: Application, Security, and System. The Application event log stores events related to applications, the Security log stores security-related events, and the System log stores events that are global to the system. Use Event Viewer to troubleshoot problems with the system and applications, or to identify security breaches or problems with user authentication and resource sharing.

- **Shared Folders**   Shared Folders enables you to view and manage shared folders. Subbranches under Shared Folders give you access to shares, connected sessions, and open files. Use Shared Folders to manage shared network folders and their use.

- **Local Users and Groups**   Local Users And Groups enables you to create and manage local user accounts and groups. The User Accounts applet in the Control Panel provides access to accounts in Home Edition.

- **Performance Logs and Alerts**   Performance Logs And Alerts enables you to configure performance counters and alerts. You can also access Performance Logs And Alerts through the Performance applet in the Administrative Tools folder.

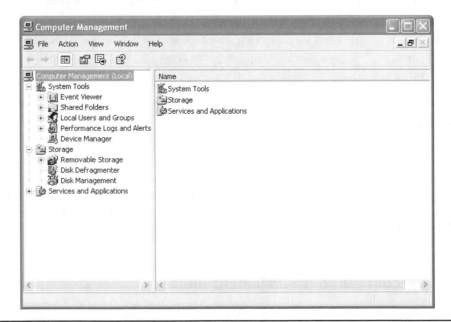

FIGURE 13-1   The Computer Management console integrates several management tools.

- **Device Manager**   Device Manager is the place to go to check for hardware problems and update drivers, and view hardware information.

- **Removable Storage**   Removable Storage enables you to manage removable storage libraries, such as a tape autochanger. It is most applicable to server environments, so very few Windows XP users have need for removable storage on their systems. For that reason, Removable Storage is not covered in this chapter.

- **Disk Defragmenter**   The Disk Defragmenter snap-in enables you to analyze a hard disk for fragmentation and to defragment the disk. Defragmenting a disk moves as much data as possible into a contiguous space on the disk to decrease file access time and improve performance.

- **Disk Management**   The Disk Management snap-in provides the means to view disk properties, create partitions and volumes, format volumes, and manage disks in other ways.

- **Services**   Use the Services snap-in to view and manage service properties. For example, you can configure the service startup type, service authentication, recovery, and other options through the Services snap-in. See the "Managing Services" section in Chapter 5 for details on managing services with the Services snap-in.

- **WMI Control**   Windows Management Instrumentation (WMI) is Microsoft's implementation of Web Based Enterprise Management (WBEM), an Industry initiative to provide management of systems, networks, users, and applications across multiple vendor environments. WMI provides a framework to manage computers across the network. Use the WMI Control snap-in to manage the local computer or a remote computer.

- **Indexing Service**   The Indexing Service indexes files on the computer to facilitate document searches. The Indexing Service can index Hypertext Markup Language (HTML), text, Microsoft Office, Internet mail and news (with Internet Information Server, known as IIS, installed), and any other document type for which the Indexing Service has a document filter. As with Removable Storage, indexing is more useful on a server.

Some of the management tools in the Computer Management console are covered in other chapters. The following rest of this chapter offers tips on using the remaining management tools.

TIP   *Most of the snap-ins in the Computer Management console are also available from the Administrative Tools folder. In addition, you can add each of the snap-ins to your own custom MMC console, as explained later in the section, "Creating Your Own Management Console."*

Running Computer Management in an Administrator Context

As we've mentioned in other chapters, it's a bad idea to use an account with administrator privileges as your regular working account. However, it's also often inconvenient to log off and log on as an administrator just to tweak a setting in Device Manager or make other changes that are restricted from regular user accounts. Fortunately, you can easily start the Computer Management console in an administrator context, which gives you full administrative privileges and you don't have to log off of your regular account.

To run Computer Management with the Administrator account, click Start | Run and issue the following command:

```
RUNAS /user:administrator "mmc.exe compmgmt.msc"
```

Windows XP opens a console window and prompts you for the password for the Administrator account. Type the password and press ENTER, and the Computer Management console opens.

TIP You can create a shortcut on the desktop or in the Quick Launch folder to the RUNAS command to quickly launch any application with a different user context.

Tips for Using Event Viewer

The "Working with Events and the Event Viewer" section, in Chapter 5 explained how to work with the Event Viewer to troubleshoot problems and get more information about events. This section explains some of the more advanced tasks you can perform with the Event Viewer.

Viewing Events on Another Computer

The Event Viewer, like many other Windows XP administrative tools, enables you to manage remote computers as well as your own. To connect to a remote computer and view its events, open the Event Viewer and choose Action | Connect to Another Computer to open the Select Computer dialog box (Figure 13-2). If you know the name of the computer, enter it in the Another Computer field. Otherwise, click Browse to browse the network for the computer. After you click OK, the event logs for the target computer appear in the Event Viewer.

Saving and Clearing the Event Logs

If the event logs were allowed to continue adding new events indefinitely, the disk where the logs are stored would eventually fill up. So, the event logs are configured for a maximum default log size of 512KB. When the event log reaches that size, Event Viewer starts overwriting events that are older than seven days. You can configure the logs for a different capacity and behavior. To do so, right-click a log in the Event Viewer and choose Properties to open its property sheet (Figure 13-3). Use the properties on the General tab to specify the location of

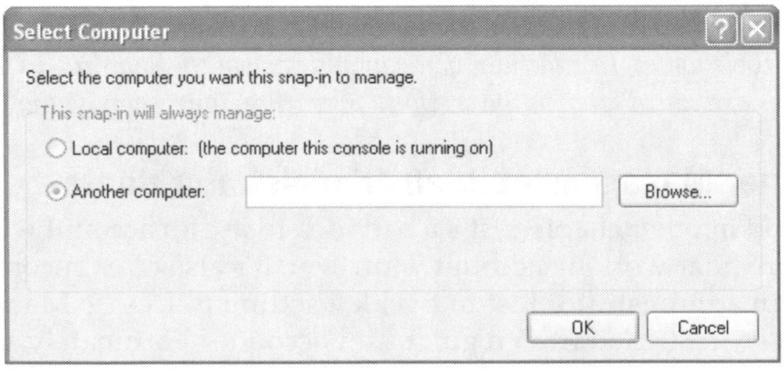

FIGURE 13-2   Specify the name of the computer or browse the network for it.

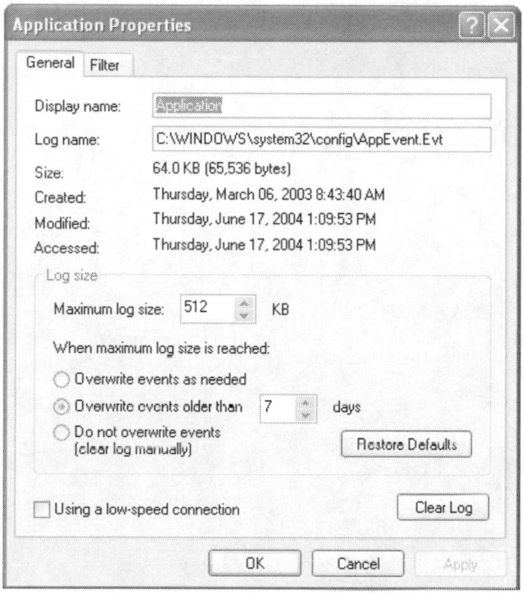

FIGURE 13-3 You can configure the log size and overwrite behavior.

the event log, its maximum size, and what action Windows XP should take when the log reaches the maximum size.

You can also clear a log as needed. For example, maybe you are troubleshooting a specific problem and want to start with a clean log file. Whatever your reason for clearing the log, it's easy to do. However, you should also save the existing log contents in case you need to refer back to them. To accomplish both in one operation, right-click the log in Event Viewer and choose Clear All Events. Click Yes when Event Viewer prompts you to save the log, then enter a log file name and click Save.

Filtering Event Logs

Be default, Event Viewer shows all events in a selected log. When you are troubleshooting a problem, it's often useful to filter the log to show only specific events. For example, you might be interested in all events with a given event ID.

Follow these steps to filter the log:

1. Select a log and choose View | Filter to open the Filter tab of the log's property sheet (Figure 13-4).

2. Configure the options that define which events you want to view, then click OK.

3. When you want to restore the view to show all events, choose View | All Records.

TIP *You can organize the view of the event log based on each of the columns in the log. Just click on a column heading to organize the events based on the selected column.*

FIGURE 13-4   You can filter the event logs to show specific types of events.

Opening a Log File

As the "Saving and Clearing the Event Logs" section earlier in this chapter explained, you can save an event log to disk. If needed, you can later open the log file to view its contents. To open a log file, open Event Viewer and choose Action | Open Log File. Browse for and select the previously saved file and click Open.

Tips for Managing Disks

The Disk Management console, which is available in Computer Management as well as a standalone console, lets you manage disks, partitions, and volumes. By default you can manage the local computer's disks from Disk Management. If you want to manage disks on another computer, follow these steps:

1. Click Start | Run, and enter **MMC** in the Run dialog box.

2. After the MMC opens, choose File | Add/Remove Snap-in.

3. In the Add/Remove Snap-in dialog box, click Add.

4. Choose the Disk Management snap-in from the list (Figure 13-5) and click Add.

5. Next, you have the option of choosing the local computer or specifying a remote computer. Click the option The Following Computer and either enter the computer name or click Browse to browse the network for it. Then, click Finish.

6. Click Close in the Add Standalone Snap-in dialog box; then click OK in the Add/Remove Snap-in dialog box.

The following sections offer tips on managing disk with Disk Management.

FIGURE 13-5   Choose the Disk Management snap-in.

Advanced Volume Types

Windows XP supports two types of disks: basic and dynamic. Basic disks are the same type of disks supported by previous versions of Windows and Disk Operating System (DOS). Basic disks can contain up to four partitions, either four primary partitions or one primary partition and three extended partitions. A primary partition can contain a single volume; extended partitions can contain multiple logical volumes.

Dynamic disks use a different structure and are not limited to four partitions like basic disks. Windows XP supports three types of volumes on a dynamic disk:

- **Simple**   This is essentially the same as a volume on a basic disk. Simple volumes cannot be extended.

- **Spanned**   A spanned volume uses unallocated space from two or more disks to create a single logical volume. You can increase the volume size by extending it with additional unallocated space.

- **Striped**   A striped volume writes data across multiple disks in the stripe set to increase disk performance.

You can create each of these three types of volumes—simple, spanned, and striped—on a Windows XP dynamic disk. For details on creating these volume types, see the Help content for Disk Management.

TIP   *Although Windows XP doesn't enable you to create mirrored or RAID 5 array volumes on a Windows XP computer, you can use the Disk Management console on a Windows XP computer to manage mirrored disks and RAID 5 arrays on other computers running Windows 2000 Server or Windows Server 2003.*

Fault Tolerance and Redundancy

Neither spanned nor striped volumes offer any fault tolerance or redundancy. If a volume in a spanned or striped set fails, the entire volume is lost. So, if you choose to use either type of volume, make sure you implement a backup strategy that backs up the logical volume associated with the set.

If you're looking for an option that provides fault tolerance, Redundant Array of Independent Disks (RAID) 5 is a solution. A RAID 5 array provides data striping across multiple disks for performance enhancement and also stripes parity data that enables the volume to continue to be used even if one of the disks in the array fails. You can then swap out the failed disk and rebuild the array without losing any data. Windows XP doesn't support the creation of RAID 5 arrays in software through Disk Management. If you need this type of data redundancy on a Windows XP computer, you need to implement a hardware-based RAID solution, such as those offered by Adaptec (http://www.adaptec.com) and other manufacturers.

Should you use spanned or striped volumes, and if so, when are they a good idea? Spanned volumes are a good idea when you have multiple physical disks that you would like to combine into a single, large logical volume. Striped volumes can improve disk performance, although probably not to a degree that will be noticeable to the average user. Again, however, make sure you implement a backup and recovery scheme that enables you to recover your data if one of the volumes in a set fails.

Mounted volumes are an alternative to a spanned volume, as the next section, "Using Mounted Volumes," explains.

Using Mounted Volumes

Windows XP offers the capability to mount a volume into an empty NT File System (NTFS) folder. The contents of the mounted volume then appear as if they reside in the NTFS folder. For example, assume you create an empty folder on drive C called data. You add a second hard disk to the system and mount it under C:\data. You (and your applications) can now use the new drive as if it were a part of drive C.

Mounted volumes can be useful in a handful of situations. For example, they provide a means to increase the apparent capacity of a disk without replacing the disk, mounted volumes also enable an entire volume to be treated as a subfolder of a disk. And they enable you to apply quotas differently on a single volume, something that is not possible without a mounted volume. This is because quotas apply to an entire volume. However, quota assignments for the mounted volume can be different from the volume under which it is mounted because they are still separate volumes.

It isn't difficult to mount a volume. Here's how to do it:

1. Create an empty folder on an NTFS volume.

2. Add the new disk to the system, partition it, and create a volume.

3. Open the Disk Management console, right-click the volume, and choose Change Drive Letter and Paths to open the Change Drive Letter and Paths dialog box (Figure 13-6).

A DFS Alternative—Sort Of

Windows Server supports a feature called Distributed File System (DFS), which enables administrators to create a homogenous file system from disparate shares and volumes. For example, an administrator might combine shared folders from several different servers on the network into a DFS root. Users who browse to the DFS root see a single file system and can access it as such, even thought the underlying shares reside on different computers. DFS, therefore, simplifies file access for users.

You can use mounted volumes as a sort of alternative to DFS. Although you can't mount remote shares, you can mount several local volumes under a single NTFS folder, and then share that folder. Users who connect to the folder see a single file structure, making it easier for them to access the folders and files. For example, if you use Windows XP Professional for your small office file server, mounted volumes can help you add more disk space to your server without affecting the way users access folders and files.

4. Click Add to open the Add Drive Letter or Path dialog box (Figure 13-7).

5. Choose the option Mount in the following empty NTFS folder, then click Browse and browse for the folder (or simply type its path in the text box).

6. Click OK twice.

To see the results of mounting the volume, open My Computer and open the drive where the volume is mounted. Open the folder where you mounted the drive, and you should see any folders and files that exist on that volume.

TIP *A mounted volume retains its existing drive letter assignment unless you specify otherwise. So, you can access the volume through its drive letter or through the mount point.*

Changing Drive Letters

Occasionally you might need to change a drive letter assignment for a drive. For example, perhaps you want to add another hard disk to a computer and want it to be drive D, but

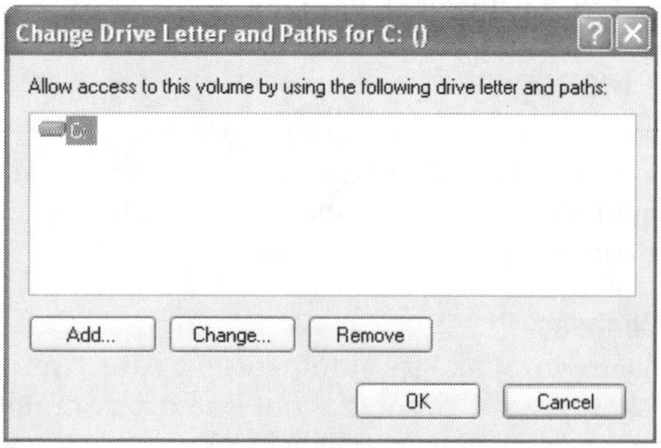

FIGURE 13-6   The Change Drive Letter and Paths dialog box lists the current assignments.

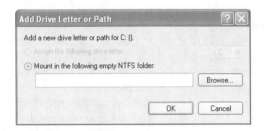

FIGURE 13-7 Use the Add Drive Letter or Path dialog box to mount a volume.

you already have a CD-ROM drive as drive D. So, you change the CD-ROM to drive E, making D available for the new hard disk.

WARNING *Before you assign a different drive letter to a CD-ROM drive, consider the possible unintended affects. Already installed applications might expect the CD-ROM drive to have a specific drive letter. This is particularly true of games that need to read from the CD during play. You can often fix this problem by changing the drive letter setting for the application in the registry or in the game's INI file. There is no consistent method, so you'll have to do a little research or contact the game publisher to find out how to change the drive assignment within the game.*

Here's how to change drive letters:

1. Open the Disk Management console, right-click the volume, and click Change Drive Letter and Paths.

2. Select the existing drive letter and click Change to open the Change Drive Letter or Path dialog box (similar to Figure 13-7).

3. Choose a new drive letter from the drop-down list and click OK; then click OK to close the remaining dialog box.

NOTE *You can't assign more than one drive letter to a disk.*

Tips for Using Device Manager

Device Manager is the place to go to troubleshoot hardware, update drivers, disable or enable devices, and view information about a system's hardware. You can manage the local computer's hardware from Device Manager, and also use it to view read-only information about hardware on other computers.

Scanning for Hardware Changes

Windows XP notes some hardware changes automatically. Attach a Universal Serial Bus (USB) device, for example, and Windows XP knows about it and accommodates the new device. Sometimes, however, you might need to initiate a hardware scan yourself. For example, assume you have an external modem that is turned off when you start the computer. Some of the applications that use the modem might not work properly because the modem wasn't detected at startup. Rather than reboot the computer, just direct Windows to scan for hardware changes. Open Device Manager, click the computer in the right pane, and choose Action | Scan for Hardware Changes.

Changing Views

You might not have realized it, but Device Manager offers more than one way to view hardware information. The default view (Figure 13-8) displays devices by type. Device Manager also offers the capability to view devices by connection, resources by type, and resources by connection. For the general user, the Devices by Type view is the most useful. When you need to identify resource assignment, however, the Resources by Type view lets you view interrupt request line (IRQ), input/output (I/O), direct memory access (DMA), and memory address.

To change view, just choose View, followed by the view you want to use.

TIP *Choose View | Show Hidden Devices to display the Non-Plug and Play Drivers and Storage Volumes branches in Device Manager.*

Connecting to Another Computer

Device Manager, like many Windows XP management tools, enables you to work with remote computers as well as the local computer. Although you can't make any device

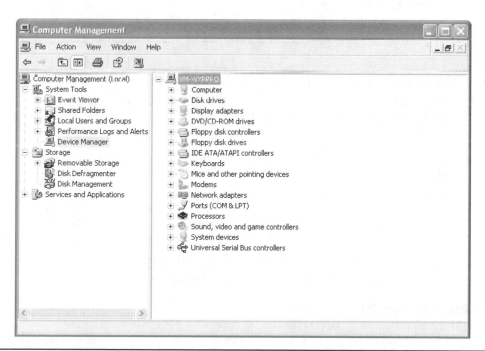

FIGURE 13-8   The default Device Manager view is the most useful for most situations.

changes to a remote computer, you can use Device Manager to view hardware and driver properties:

1. Open Computer Management, right-click Computer Management in the left pane, and choose Connect to Another Computer.

2. In the Select Computer dialog box, enter the name of the computer, and click OK.

3. Expand the System Tools branch and click the Device Manager. Device Manager displays a message that it is running in read-only mode because you are connected to a remote computer.

Creating Your Own Management Console

Most of the Windows XP management tools are MMC snap-ins. MMC provides a common framework for management applications, and also makes it possible to combine snap-ins to create your own custom management console. For example, if you are managing a Windows XP computer you use as a server, you might create a console that includes the Disk Defragmenter, Disk Management, Shared Folders, and Local Users and Groups snap-ins.

In addition to combining snap-ins to create a custom console, you can also customize consoles by creating taskpads, which help simplify working with consoles and performing common tasks. The following sections explain these customization topics.

Creating a Custom Console

Creating a custom console that contains your own selection of management tools is really very easy. It's mainly a matter of adding a selection of snap-ins to a console and then saving the console. Here's how to create the console:

1. Choose Start | Run, and enter **MMC** in the Run dialog box.

2. When the MMC opens, choose File | Add/Remove Snap-in to open the Add/Remove Snap-in dialog box (Figure 13-9).

3. Click Add to display the Add Standalone Snap-in dialog box (Figure 13-10).

4. Choose a snap-in from the list in the Add Standalone Snap-in dialog box, then click Add.

5. Many of the snap-ins prompt for additional information. For example, the Computer Management console prompts you to choose the local computer or specify a remote computer (Figure 13-11). This additional information varies by snap-in. Enter the requested information and click Finish.

6. Click Close to close the Add Standalone Snap-in dialog box.

7. Click OK to close the Add/Remove Snap-in dialog box.

Organizing a Custom Console

The Folder snap-in gives you the capability to organize your custom management console by providing containers for other snap-ins. For example, you might create a Disk Tools folder and put the Disk Defragmenter and Disk Management consoles in it.

The Add/Remove Snap-in dialog box isn't very clear on how to build a folder structure,

FIGURE 13-9   Use the Add/Remove Snap-in dialog box to add snap-ins to a console.

FIGURE 13-10   Choose a snap-in from the list.

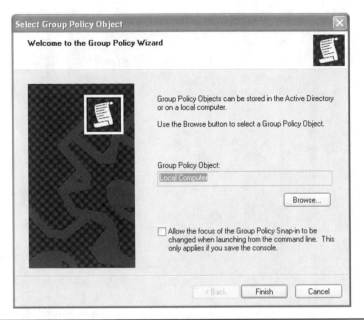

FIGURE 13-11   Many snap-ins prompt for additional information.

but it's easy once you know how to do it. The example sets up a console containing three folders and adds snap-ins to each one:

1. Run the MMC and choose File | Add/Remove Snap-in.
2. Click Add, select Folder, and click Add three times, then click Close.
3. Click OK to close the Add/Remove Snap-in dialog box.
4. Right-click the top folder and choose Rename, then give it the name Disk Tools.
5. Right-click the second middle folder and choose Rename, then give it the name System Tools.
6. Name the third folder Security Tools.
7. Choose File | Add/Remove Snap-in and choose Disk Tools from the Snap-ins Added To drop-down list.
8. Click Add and add the Disk Defragmenter and Disk Management snap-ins, then click Close.
9. Choose System Tools from the Snap-ins Added To drop-down list and add the Device Manager and Event Viewer snap-ins to it.
10. Select Security Tools from the drop-down list, click Add, and add the Group Policy and Local Users and Groups snap-ins to the Security Tools folder. Figure 13-12 shows the resulting console.

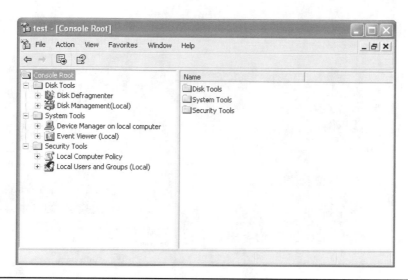

FIGURE 13-12   This custom console uses three folders to organize the snap-ins.

Including Web Resources in a Console

Another snap-in worth mentioning is the Link to Web Address snap-in, which lets you add web resources to a console. For example, you might add the URLs for remotely managed servers to a console, or you might add the URL to your web-based e-mail account so you can monitor your e-mail while you are managing systems. When you click the link in the console, the associated web page appears in the right pane. Figure 13-13 shows a Hotmail link in a custom console.

There isn't any magic about adding URL links to a console. Add the Link to Web Address snap-in to a console. When you do, the Link to Web Address Wizard prompts you for the URL and a name for the link.

Setting MMC Modes

In the examples in the previous few sections, you've been able to add or remove snap-ins from a custom console because the console was opened in *author mode*. This mode provides full capability to manage the console. In some situations, however, you might want to control the actions that users will have within a console. For example, perhaps you don't want them to be able to add or remove snap-ins.

You control what users can do within a management console by setting its console mode. If you don't already have the console open in author mode, include the /A switch when you run MMC and open the console. Click Start | Run, and enter **MMC** *console.msc* **/A** in the Run dialog box, where *console.msc* is the name of a console you have already saved. Then, click File | Options to open the Options dialog box (Figure 13-14).

The Console mode drop-down list offers four options, and each displays a description when you select it that explains its purpose. Choose the desired mode and click OK, then save the console. The mode you selected will apply the next time the console is opened.

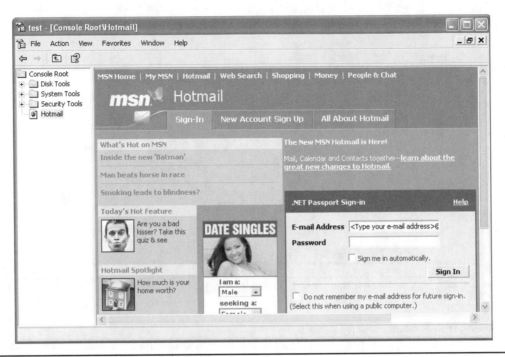

FIGURE 13-13 This console includes a link to Hotmail.

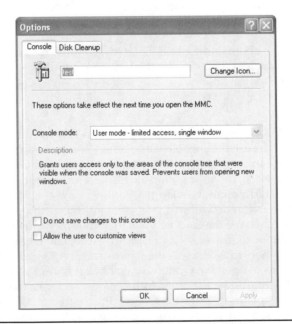

FIGURE 13-14 Configure the MMC user mode in the Options dialog box.

TIP *You can open a console in the MMC in author mode by using the /A switch. Just run MMC from the Run command in the Start menu; then choose File | Open and open the console.*

Creating and Using Taskpads

In the MMC, taskpads provide a simplified view of a console branch and also provide quick access to common tasks. Figure 13-15 shows a taskpad for the Event Viewer that includes icons for several common tasks.

Creating a taskpad comprises two main steps. First you create the taskpad view, and then you populate the taskpad with actions. The MMC provides a wizard to help you through the process:

1. Open the MMC and open the console for which you want to create taskpad views. This example assumes you are creating a taskpad for Event Viewer.

2. Right-click the object where you want to create the taskpad (Event Viewer, for example), choose New Taskpad View, and click Next when the wizard starts.

3. In the New Taskpad View Wizard (Figure 13-16), choose a style for the details pane and click Next.

4. In the Taskpad Target page, specify whether the taskpad will apply to the selected item only or to all similar tree items.

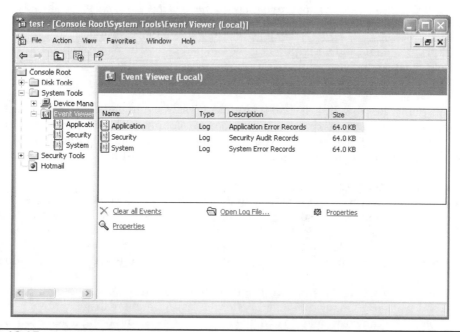

FIGURE 13-15 A taskpad view provides quick access to common commands.

Figure 13-16   You can choose one of three styles for the details pane.

Tip *It probably isn't crystal clear to you what purpose the Taskpad Target page options serve. Here's an example: Assume you have added two Event Viewer snap-ins to a console, one for the local computer and another for a remote server. You create a taskpad for the local Event Viewer and specify that it should apply to the selected item only. This means the taskpad is available when you work with the local Event Viewer snap-in but not when you work with the one for the remote server. If you choose the option to have the taskpad apply to items that are the same as the selected item, the taskpad will be available for both Event Viewer snap-ins.*

1. Specify a name and description for the taskpad view. The name appears at the top of the taskpad view and the description appears under the name.

2. Click Next, then click Finish.

At this point, the New Task Wizard (Figure 13-17) starts automatically. This wizard helps you add tasks to the taskpad. You can add menu commands, shell commands, or a link to a view in the Favorites tab. If you choose the Menu Command option, MMC displays the Shortcut Menu Command page shown in Figure 13-18.

Combine commands from different sources

The commands you choose do not have to be from the branch where you are creating the taskpad. For example, assume you're creating a taskpad for the Event Viewer snap-in but you also have the Device Manager snap-in in the console. You could add the Rescan Disks command from the Device Manager to the Event Viewer taskpad. The only requirement is that the snap-in that will be the source for the command be added to the console.

The capability to add commands from multiple snap-ins makes it possible to create a taskpad that serves many different functions across different management tools. It also means you can create a taskpad at the root of a console and bring together the most common commands from all of the snap-ins into that root taskpad.

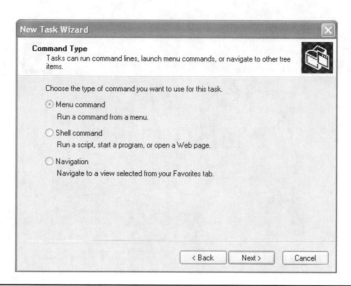

FIGURE 13-17   Use the New Task Wizard to add tasks to the taskpad.

Through the wizard, you specify the menu command, a task name and description, and an icon (Figure 13-19). If the icons supplied with MMC don't suit your needs, you can choose the Custom Icon option, click Browse, and choose an icon in an EXE, DLL, or icon (ICO) file.

If you choose the Shell Script option from the Command Type page, MMC displays the Enter Commands and Parameters page (Figure 13-20). Here you enter the program name and path, any additional startup parameters, the startup folder, and the window state. You

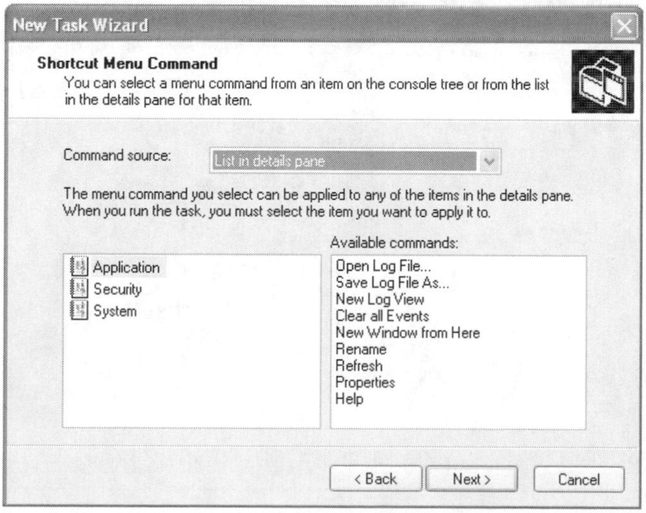

FIGURE 13-18   Choose the Menu Command option to add menu commands as tasks.

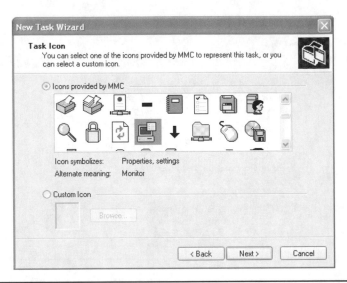

FIGURE 13-19   Choose an icon to associate with the task.

can start executables, Windows Script Host (WSH) scripts, or even open applications by document association. To open a Web resource such as a web page, specify the URL in the Command field.

Finally, if you choose the Navigation option from the Command Type page, the wizard prompts you to choose a view from your Favorites. To make the view available in the list, you must first add the view to the Favorites folder. Select the view, then choose Favorites | Add to Favorites.

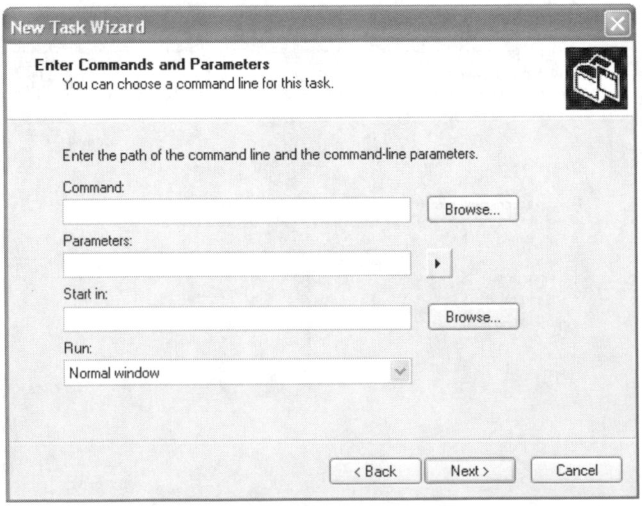

FIGURE 13-20   Use the Enter Commands and Parameters page to specify a program, script, document, or URL.

Management Changes for SP2

The introduction of an on-by-default firewall in Windows XP SP2 can cause certain management tools to fail that might have worked fine before installing SP2. Many of the client administration tools such as Computer Management, Group Policy, Local Users and Groups, Disk Management, Resultant Set of Policy, and several others will generate various errors when you try to manage a remote computer that has Windows Firewall enabled in its default configuration. The error varies depending on the management tool being used.

These administrative tools require that port 445 be open on the remote computer for incoming traffic but by default, Windows Firewall blocks port 445. You can resolve this problem by opening port 445 on the remote computer. There are a handful of ways to accomplish that. First, you can go to the remote computer and open the port through the properties for Windows Firewall.

TIP *If you don't have physical access to the remote computer but it is configured to allow Remote Desktop Connection or Remote Assistance connections, you can use either of these two methods to connect to the remote computer and configure Windows Firewall to allow incoming traffic on port 445.*

You can also use Netsh to configure the firewall. However, this method requires that you are either physically located at the remote computer or that you can open a telnet session to it. The capability to open a telnet session requires that the remote computer is running the Telnet server and the firewall is configured to allow telnet traffic. If you do have console access to the remote computer, use this command to open port 445:

netsh firewall set portopening TCP 445 ENABLE

Finally, you can open the port on the remote computer by modifying group policy as appropriate, and then refreshing group policy on the remote computer.

PART

Working with Applications

Internet Explorer Tips and Tricks

I n this chapter you'll find the answers to the following questions:

- How do I clear out my history and other information in Internet Explorer?
- Does Internet Explorer keep any of my personal data, and if so, how do I protect it?
- What are cookies? How do I see what cookies are on my computer?
- Can I delete cookies?
- Is there a way to control how Internet Explorer accepts or uses cookies?
- What are IE security zones?
- Is there anything in IE that will block specific types of Web sites?
- How do I block those annoying pop-up windows?
- Can I make IE remember information for forms and Web addresses so I don't have to type as much?
- What does Service Pack 2 include to improve security in Windows XP?

Considering the recent spate of Microsoft Internet Explorer–related security issues, security is a must-have if you use this browser. This chapter covers basic issues such as these:

This chapter focuses on Internet Explorer and how to customize it to work best on your computer or in your organization. Windows XP SP2 adds a number of new features to IE, including enhanced security features, a pop-up killer, and a tool to help you manage IE add-ons. In addition, you can set IE to display the new Information Bar when a pop-up is captured.

Much has been written about Internet Explorer (IE) since its release almost ten years ago. If you are just now beginning to use an Internet browser, feel free to consult another book on how to use the browser, and then come back here to learn how to really customize it.

Your IE Browsing History Revealed

The IE History folder contains information about all the sites you've visited recently. You can set up IE to keep shortcuts to these sites for up to 999 days. Because of the amount of disk space consumed by the history shortcuts, however, it's recommended that you limit the number of days to a couple of weeks or even ten days.

To see your history shortcuts, click the History button on the Standard Buttons toolbar. This displays the History pane on the left side of the IE window, as shown in Figure 14-1.

To set how display the listings, use the following options from the View drop-down list (from the History pane):

- **By Date**   Organizes history shortcuts by the date you visited the site.

- **By Site**   Organizes history shortcuts alphanumerically by the name of the site.

- **By Most Visited**   Organizes history shortcuts with the most visited links at the top and least visited at the bottom.

- **By Order Visited Today**   Organizes history shortcuts by the order in which you've visited them today.

By clicking one of the shortcuts in the History pane, you can return to that Web page or Internet resource. To close the History pane, click the History toolbar button again, or click the Close button (X) on the top right of the History pane.

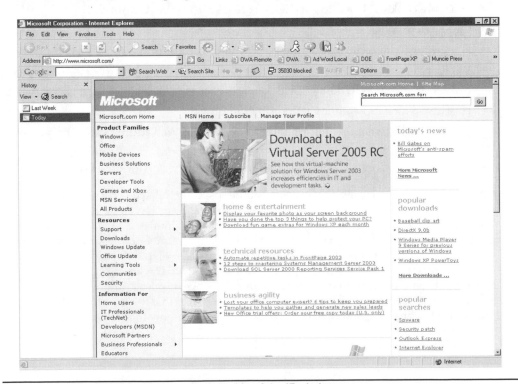

FIGURE 14-1   The History pane is on the left side of the IE window.

Purging IE's Cached Data and History

Over time your history folder and cached web pages (those pages and files that are downloaded to your computer as you navigate the Web) will begin to clutter up your hard drive. To alleviate the strain this might put on your hard disk, periodically purge the IE cache and history folders.

Clearing the History

Clearing items from the History folder can be done automatically after a specified number of days, or done manually at any time. To set up the number of days between purgings, or to clear the History folder manually, perform the following steps:

1. Open Internet Explorer.

2. Choose the Tools menu, and click Internet Options. This displays the Internet Options dialog box (see Figure 14-2).

3. In the Days To Keep Pages In History, set the value to the number of days to hold history data. If you want IE to empty the History folder after each time you close IE, set the value to 0.

4. To delete the History folder contents now, click Clear History and click Yes.

5. Click OK.

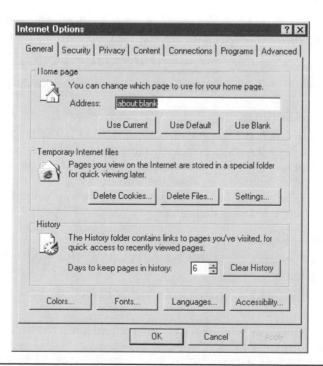

FIGURE 14-2   The Internet Options dialog box has options for configuring the History folder.

Purging Temporary Files

Whenever you visit a Web site, files are automatically downloaded to your computer. This is known as *cached* data. These files are what make up the Web pages and anything else the Web page author wants you to download. For example, if you visit the Microsoft site, you'll download a number of files just to view its home page, including HTML files, picture files, style sheets, active content, and more.

IE stores cached data so that you can quickly return to a Web page without re-downloading the file each time. Settings in IE determine how often stored pages are updated—from every visit to the page to never. Some sites update pages and data every day (or several times an hour, as news sites do), while others update only sporadically. You don't need to download the same page over and over if that page hasn't changed since your last visit. IE can simply pull up the cached files and display them.

During the course of a few hours of heavy Web site activity, you can download thousands of files to your hard drive. Over time, these downloads accumulate in the Temporary Internet Files folder (found in the Documents and Settings*username*\\Local Settings folder) until they are deleted. One way they are deleted is by deleting them manually.

To purge your system of temporary Internet files, follow these steps:

1. Open Internet Explorer.

2. Choose the Tools menu, and click Internet Options. This displays the Internet Options dialog box.

3. Click Delete Files.

4. To remove all offline data (sites you have made available offline using Internet Explorer's synchronization feature), select the Delete All Offline Content option.

5. Click OK.

You also can have IE manage the temporary files, as explained in the next section.

Controlling Cache Settings

Another way to control cached Internet data is to set the Internet cache setting to delete items automatically after a threshold is met. This threshold can be set so that older files are deleted to make room for newer files. For instance, you can set IE to use only 100MB of hard disk space for temporary Internet files. Once this threshold is met, IE automatically removes the oldest files in the cache until there is enough room for newer files to be stored.

To set the cache settings, follow these steps:

1. Open Internet Explorer.

2. Choose the Tools menu, and click Internet Options. This displays the Internet Options dialog box.

3. Click the Settings button on the General tab to display the Settings dialog box (see Figure 14-3).

4. Under the Temporary Internet files folder section, move the slider to the amount of disk space you want IE to use for temporary Internet files, or type a value in the box to the left of MB. For systems with large hard drives (40–60GB) you can set this value pretty high, such as 100MB or even more. For those with limited disk space, reduce the value to 50MB or such.

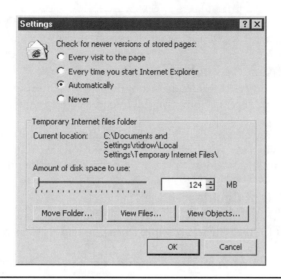

FIGURE 14-3   Modify your cached files settings on this dialog box.

5. Click OK.

The Real Story About Cookies

Internet cookies are small files created by Web site authors that store information about your browser and preferences. These preferences can be customized settings you've set up for the Web site you're visiting (such as a customized home page). Cookies reside on your computer and relay information to a Web site when you visit that site. Each Web site you visit that has cookies (not all sites use them) will place a cookie on your system.

Although cookie files are not large (usually less than 5KB in size), they can start cluttering up your hard drive. Consider deleting cookies after a period of time. If you do this, however, your customized settings will be lost and the next time you visit that site you will need to reestablish those settings. For most sites this is a matter of simply logging in with a username and password. Others, however, may require you to set up personalized settings again, such as reentering start page settings, an e-mail address, and the like.

To see what a cookie looks like, open the Cookies folder in the Documents and Settings\ *username*\ folder. Double-click a text file to view its contents in Notepad or WordPad. An example from the *Washington Times* Web site is as follows:

```
TheWashingtonTimes
165.138.171.129.125301077109951137
www.washtimes.com/
1024
2502183296
30353999
1338417776
29619744
*
```

NOTE *To find out more about cookies, visit the Cookies: What They Are, Why You Are in Charge web page at http://www.microsoft.com/info/cookies.htm.*

First-Party and Third-Party Cookies

First-party cookies are cookies downloaded from the site you are visiting at the time. For instance, when you visit MSNBC.Com, you download a cookie named username@msnbc .msn.txt.

Third-party cookies are cookies that originate from sites other than the one you're currently visiting. For example, let's say you visit MSNBC.Com. Along with the first-party cookie, a third-party cookie from an advertiser (let's say weather.com) is downloaded as well.

Session and Persistent Cookies

A *session cookie* is one that is downloaded to your computer and stays there only as long as you're on the Internet for that current session. Once you end the session, the cookie is deleted.

A *persistent cookie*, on the other hand, is one that remains on your hard drive until it expires or forever (or until you remove it).

Controlling Cookie Use

You can control what type of cookies can be downloaded to your system. For sake of security, you can even disable cookies altogether on your computer. However, many sites that offer cookies *require* them for viewing their sites. It's kind of a "pay-to-play" scheme: you download a cookie so that they can track your activities and you can view the content on the site.

To set how IE handles cookies, follow these steps:

1. Choose Tools and then Internet Options.
2. Click the Privacy tab and then click Advanced (see Figure 14-4).
3. Select Override Automatic Cookie Handling.
4. Under the First-Party Cookies and Third-Party Cookies headings, set IE to one of the following:
   - **Accept**   Allows all cookies to download to your computer.
   - **Block**   Blocks all cookies to your computer.
   - **Prompt**   Displays a prompt each time IE encounters a cookie to download. You must click Yes to allow the cookie to download.
5. To allow session cookies, select Always Allow Session Cookies.
6. Click OK.
7. Click OK again.

Viewing and Deleting Cookies

To look at the cookies stored on your computer, open the Documents and Settings*username*\\ and the Documents and Settings*username*\\Temporary Internet Files folders. You also can

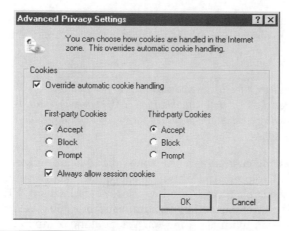

FIGURE 14-4   Use the Advanced Privacy Settings to customize how IE handles cookies.

click the Settings button on the General tab of the Internet Options dialog box and then click View Files.

To delete cookies, follow these steps:

1. Choose Tools and then Internet Options.

2. On the General tab, click Delete Cookies.

3. Click OK.

Working with IE Security Zones

Internet Explorer uses Security Zones to let you customize how Web content is treated in different "zones." IE can be configured so that all Internet and local intranet sites are allowed to be viewed. You also can restrict specific sites that IE is not allowed to view. Finally, you can specify trusted sites that IE can access. By default, IE lets you access all Web sites, at least those that are public or those you have to use a username/password for.

IE with SP2 prevents the security context for any link on a page from being higher than the overall security context of the root URL. This feature also blocks JavaScript navigation where the security context is absent. SP2 also imposes additional security restrictions on the local machine zone to help mitigate exploits that attempt to elevate privileges and gain access to the local file system and other resources.

Security Zones Explained

IE zones are divided into the following:

- Internet
- Local intranet
- Trusted sites
- Restricted sites

SP2 imposes additional security restrictions on the local machine zone to help mitigate exploits that attempt to elevate privileges and gain access to the local file system and other resources.

NOTE *Binary behaviors are a feature introduced in Internet Explorer 5.x that enable site developers to build functions for the Web that can modify HTML tags and resulting behavior, but without exposing the underlying code on the page as a script. By default, IE blocks binary behaviors in the Restricted Sites zone.*

Windows also lets you customize a fifth zone called My Computer, but you must use the Microsoft Internet Explorer Administration Kit (IEAK), which you can find out more about at http://www.microsoft.com/windows/ieak/default.mspx. . This kit provides tools and utilities that can be implemented by an administrator in an enterprise environment. You can use IEAK to set individual settings on a standalone computer.

Customizing Zone Settings

To customize the way IE handles security zones, follow these steps:

1. Choose the Tools menu and then click Internet Options.

2. Click the Security tab, as shown Figure 14-5.

3. Click the Local intranet icon.

4. Click Sites to display the Local Intranet dialog box (see Figure 14-6).

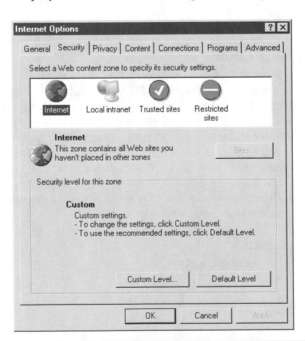

FIGURE 14-5   The Security tab lets you set up security settings for each zone.

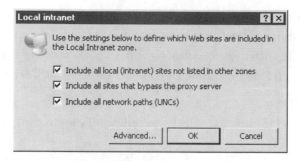

FIGURE 14-6   Define the type of Web site to include in your intranet settings.

5. Select from the following options:
   - Include all local (intranet) sites not listed in other zones
   - Include all sites that bypass the proxy server
   - Include all network paths (UNCs)

6. Click Advanced to display the Local Intranet dialog box, as shown in Figure 14-7.

7. Add a site you want to specify as an intranet zone and click Add.

8. Click OK when finished adding sites to the Local intranet zone.

9. Click OK.

10. Select the Trusted sites icon and click Sites.

11. Fill out the Trusted Sites dialog box, which is similar to the dialog box shown in Figure 14-7.

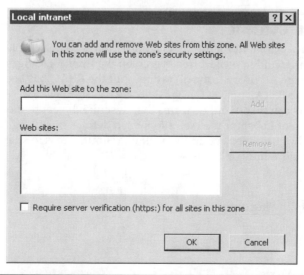

FIGURE 14-7   Use this dialog box to specify intranet sites to included in this security zone.

12. Click OK when finished adding sites to the Trusted Sites zone.

13. Select the Restricted Sites icon and click Sites.

14. Fill out the Restricted Sites dialog box with the sites you want to bar IE access to.

15. Click OK when finished adding sites to the Restricted sites zone.

16. Click Apply.

The Internet zone is set up automatically by including all sites that are not specified by the other zones.

NOTE *You can set up security levels for each zone by selecting the zone icon and then clicking the Custom Level button. On the Security Settings dialog box, configure the settings you desire. For example, to have IE prompt you each time it encounters as ActiveX control, select Prompt under the Download Signed ActiveX Controls and Download Unsigned ActiveX Controls sections. Click OK to return to the Security tab.*

Protecting Against Specific Threats

Let's say you know there is a Web page you don't want your users to access because of security threats. The best way to limit access to that site is to set it up in the Restricted sites zone.

NOTE *Businesses and organizations usually depend on layers of protection to help thwart potential online security risks. The fist line of defense usually is a strong proxy server that masks IP addresses of individual computers in the organization. This way, outside computers cannot "see" computers sitting behind the proxy. Another layer of defense is to employ filtering software that allows system administrators to block access to specific sites, categories of sites (such as Webmail), or Internet technologies (chat, FTP, etc.).*

Blocking Unwanted Content

IE uses ICRA (Internet Content Rating Association) ratings to help protect children from inappropriate material and to protect free speech on the Internet. Originally, IE used RSAC (Recreational Software Advisory Council) ratings, but the RSAC has been disbanded and incorporated into the ICRA.

Web site authors can fill out online forms that describe the content of their Web site. ICRA creates a Content Label for the Web site, which defines the rating categories of the site. Parents and other users can set up IE to allow or limit access to sites that they deem inappropriate for their family or business.

Site Ratings

Ratings fall in the following topics:

- Language
- Nudity
- Sex
- Violence

You can specify the degree to which you want to filter on each of the preceding topics. For instance, if you want to allow users full access to any site that offers all degrees of violence, set the level to 4, Wanton and gratuitous violence. However, if you want to limit the amount of violence a viewer can access, set it to Level 1, Fighting. Levels of violence above this settings (such as Killing, Killing with blood and gore, and Wanton and gratuitous violence) will not be accessible.

Using Content Advisor

IE use the Content Advisor to let you set the levels of ratings for each category. To use the Content Advisor, follow these steps:

1. Open Internet Explorer, choose Tools, and then choose Internet Options.
2. Click the Content tab.
3. Click Enable to display the Content Advisor dialog box, as shown in Figure 14-8.
4. Select a category (such as Language).
5. Move the slider to set the setting for what IE is allowed to display for the chosen category.
6. Click Apply.
7. Modify each category as needed. If you modify one category and leave the others as is, you will block all content for those other categories. Be sure to move the slider for each one to suit your particular needs. For instance, you may want to

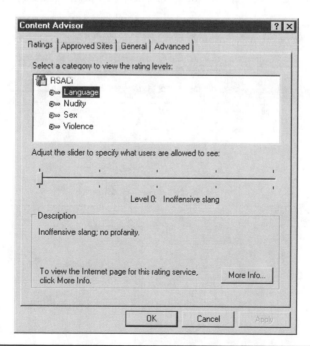

FIGURE 14-8 To enable Content Advisor, use this dialog box.

leave Nudity set to its highest setting (slider all the way to the left), but adjust the Violence a little to allow news reports and other similar content.

8. Click OK.

9. On the Create Supervisor Password dialog box, type a password and then confirm it. This password-protects your changes so that the user (such as an employee or family member) cannot change your settings.

10. Type a hint for the password to help you remember the password. You can actually enter the password here, but it's not recommended for obvious reasons.

11. Click OK and then OK again.

12. Click OK to close the Internet Options dialog box.

As the user navigates and hits a page that is not allowed due to the Content Ratings, the Content Advisor dialog box appears, warning the page cannot be shown. If a page is not rated, the default setting is to not display it at all but to show a warning dialog box like the one shown in Figure 14-9. To proceed, select a viewing option (from Always Allow The Page Or Web Site To Be Displayed To Allow Viewing Only This Time) and type the Content Advisor password.

Other Content Filter Options

Unfortunately not all Web sites subscribe to the ICRA ratings service. For this reason, you should not put all your content-filtering trust into Content Advisor. Because IE displays the Content Advisor dialog box each time for a nonrated Web page, you may spend all your time

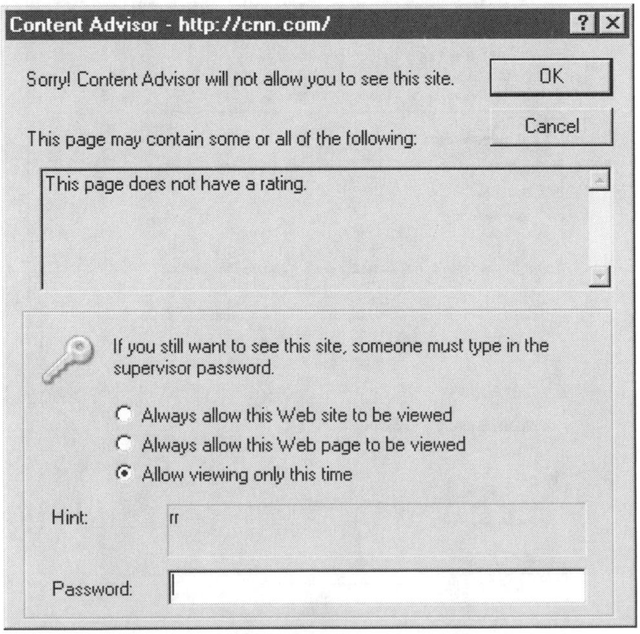

FIGURE 14-9   This dialog box warns the user that the Web page is not rated.

typing a password into IE for each page a user needs to view. This can be time-consuming and, quite frankly, a waste of time.

The other option is to let users view all Web sites that are not rated. To enable this option, open the Content Advisor dialog box, click the General tab, and select User Can See Sites That Have No Rating. This doesn't make a lot of sense either, since most sites don't have a rating and users will be able to view the content anyway. What's the purpose of enabling Content Advisor in the first place?

If you have a short list of sites you approve (this works well for users who don't need a lot of freedom to surf around the net), click the Approved Sites tab, enter the URL for the approved site, and click Always.

NOTE   *The majority of Web sites on the Internet do not use the ICRA ratings, so you may want to employ different solutions to filtering Web content. Choose the Advanced tab of the Content Advisor to specify different rating systems. Click the Find Rating Systems and Rating Systems buttons on the General tab for more information on these rating systems. Another option is to use third-party filtering products. Two such filtering products are Cyber Sitter (http://www. cybersitter.com) and 8e6Home (http://www.8e6technologies.com). Some products reside on local machines, while others can be managed from a centralized network server.*

Blocking Pop-ups (SP2)

Pop-ups are those annoying pages or small windows that display on your screen without your telling them to. Usually they just "pop" on your screen, hence their name. They usually appear a second or two after you've connected to a site that includes pop-ups, and they usually contain an advertisement.

Sometimes you may not even know you have a pop-up onscreen until you close out IE and find the window hiding in the background. Other times the pop-up may not have the standard Windows controls, including a Close button. To get rid of these kinds, you must use the Task Manager (press CTRL-ALT-DELETE and click Task Manager) to kill the process showing the pop-up.

New with Windows XP SP2 is the built-in Pop-up Blocker. This feature will block most incoming pop-ups from displaying on your screen. IE always blocks pop-ups that are larger than or outside of the viewable desktop. IE with SP2 imposes restrictions on the capability to open windows outside of the viewable area of the desktop. These changes help protect against malicious sites that attempt to hide site content from the user. In addition, the status bar is always enabled for all windows.

To enable and modify the Pop-Up Blocker, follow these steps:

1. Choose Tools and then Internet Options.
2. Click the Privacy tab.
3. Select Block Pop-ups as shown in Figure 14-10.
4. Click Settings to show the Pop-up Blocker dialog box (see Figure 14-11).
5. Modify the following properties:
   - **Allowed sites**   Type a Web site address and click Add for those sites that include pop-ups that you want to allow.

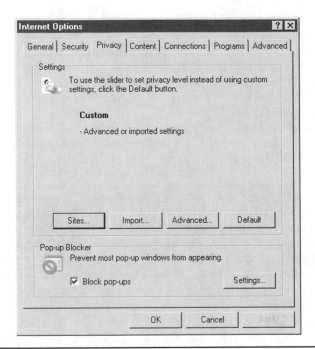

FIGURE 14-10   Enable the new Pop-up Blocker on the Privacy tab.

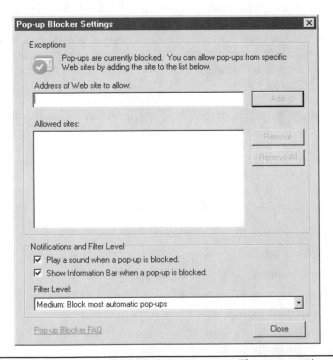

FIGURE 14-11   Use the Pop-up Blocker Settings dialog box to modify pop-up settings.

- **Play a sound**   When IE blocks a pop-up, a sound event plays to notify you.
- **Show Information Bar**   Shows the new Information Bar on the IE toolbars.
- **Filter Level**   Enables you to set the blocking constraints, from High (blocks all pop-ups) to Medium (blocks most pop-ups) to Low (allows pop-ups from secure sites).

6. Click Close.

7. Click OK.

NOTE *Other pop-up blockers are available on the Web. One outstanding one is the Google Popup Blocker, available from http://toolbar.google.com.*

The Information Bar is visible between the toolbars and the Web page area of the browser. One purpose of the Information Bar is to display information related to security, pop-up blocking, and similar warning and status information. Another purpose is provide information and links to help you install or update controls for displaying active or rich content on certain Web pages. For example, if a page requires a specific add-on (Adobe Reader, for instance) to display content and your system does not have the application installed, the Information Bar displays a message that you need the add-on and that you can click to download and install the add-on now.

The Information Bar hides again when you navigate away from the page that generated the error or warning.

PART III

Working with AutoComplete

Tired of entering the same personal information for Web forms? Try AutoComplete, which tells IE to store information you've entered on forms and other entries and use them again in the future for similar entries.

Using AutoComplete

To use AutoComplete, follow these steps:

1. Choose Tools, and then Internet Options.

2. Click the Content tab.

3. Click AutoComplete to display the AutoComplete Settings dialog box (Figure 14-12).

4. Select the options for what kind of content you want IE to save, such as Web addresses, Forms, and user names and passwords.

5. If you want IE to prompt you each time you enter a username and password, select Prompt Me To Save Passwords.

6. Click OK twice.

NOTE *AutoComplete stores personal information that you may not want to be made public. For this reason, computers that others will use, such as in a shared office space, library, school, or other public place, should not have AutoComplete enabled.*

FIGURE 14-12   The AutoComplete Settings dialog box.

Viewing and Managing AutoComplete Entries

You can create a personal profile that can be used on a Web site when it requests information. These profiles are created inside the Address Book using the Microsoft Profile Assistant on the Content tab.

To create a profile, follow these steps:

1. Choose Tools, and then Internet Options.

2. Click the Content tab.

3. Click My Profile to display the Address Book – Choose Profile dialog box.

4. Click OK and fill out the Properties dialog box with your personal information (see Figure 14-13).

5. Click OK.

6. Click My Profile to see your profile data, as shown in Figure 14-14.

7. Click OK and then OK again.

To clear all forms data and passwords currently saved in IE, open the AutoComplete Settings dialog box (see the preceding section) and click Clear Forms and Clear Passwords. You may want to do this at a later date if your personal data changes (such as your e-mail address) or if you don't want IE to store you passwords anymore. This does not, however, delete your Profile information you set up using the Microsoft Profile Assistant.

Managing Advanced Settings

The Advanced tab of the Internet Options dialog box includes a number of settings. Figure 14-15 shows the Advanced tab.

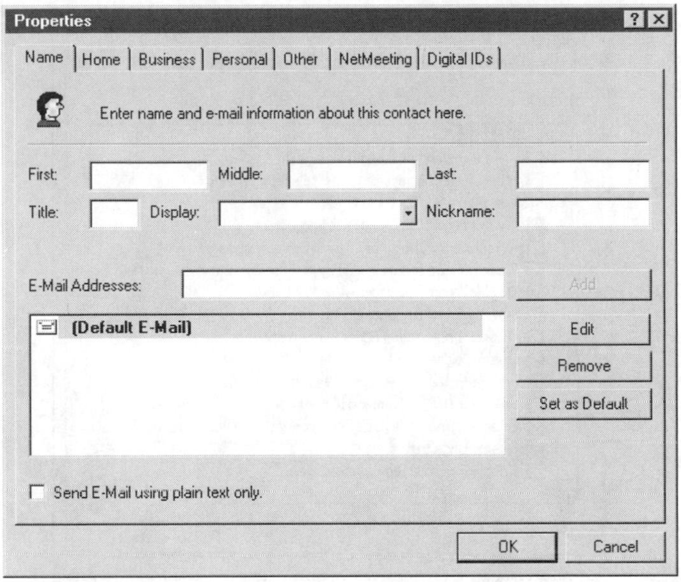

FIGURE 14-13   You can be as detailed as you want to be about your personal data when creating a profile.

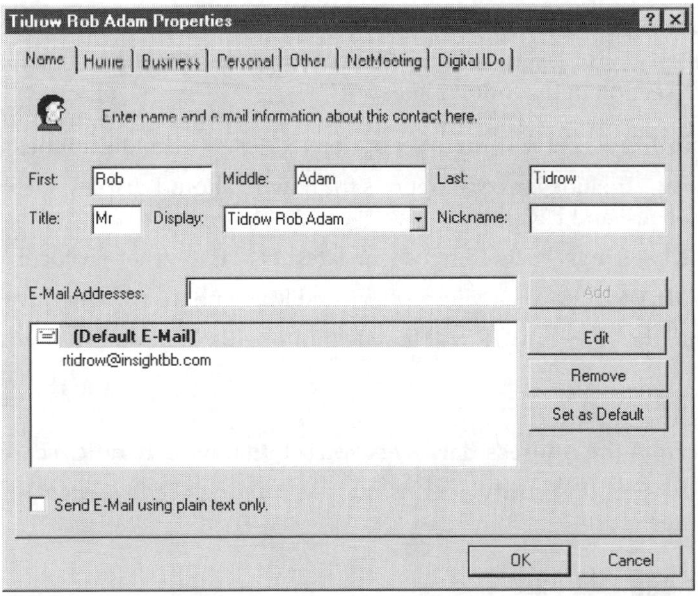

FIGURE 14-14   An example of a profile

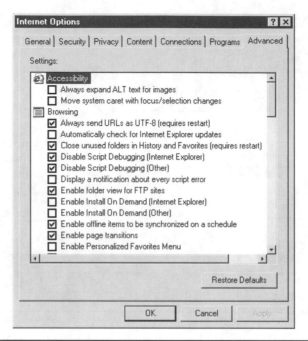

FIGURE 14-15   The IE Advanced tab

Advanced Settings Explained

The Advanced tab includes subheadings that have options relating to that heading. You can read about each section in the following list:

- **Accessibility**   Enables you to set options for users with disabilities
- **Browsing**   Includes several options for how IE should display Web pages, links, offline pages, and URLs
- **HTTP 1.1 settings**   Sets IE to use the latest HTTP Internet protocol (1.1)
- **Microsoft VM**   Enables Microsoft Virtual Machine for running Java applets
- **Multimedia**   Sets how IE will handle multimedia data, such as audio, video, and graphic files
- **Printing**   Sets IE printing options
- **Search from the Address Bar**   Lets you set up how IE handles search queries
- **Security**   Sets IE security options, such as running active content and server certificates

Setting Advanced Options

To set Advanced options, click the Advanced tab and select or deselect each item. Some options, such as the Search From The Address Bar option, have radio options. Several options are available in these cases, but only one can be chosen at a time.

Using a Java Virtual Machine

Internet Explorer includes a feature that lets you control how IE runs Java applets. Java applets are designed to run on multiple operating systems (multiple Windows versions, Apple Macintosh, UNIX, etc.). IE can run these applets in a Java console and/or using a Java virtual machine.

What Is a Java VM?

A Java virtual machine (VM) is software that enables IE to run Java applets inside the Web browser. Because of legal problems between Microsoft and Sun, the company that created Java, Microsoft is limited in how it can handle Java applets. To make sure you can run Java applets inside IE, you need a copy of the Java Virtual Machine.

Obtaining and Installing a Java VM

To obtain the Microsoft Java Virtual Machine, you cannot go to Microsoft. You must obtain it from a different source. One such source is the Java Virtual Machine Download Links page at http://java-virtual-machine.net/download.html.

To install the VM, download and run the install program as instructed by the Web site or readme attached to the VM you download. After you install the VM, you will need to shut down and restart Windows for the VM to work properly.

NOTE *The Microsoft JM is scheduled to be supported until December 31, 2007, at which time Microsoft will no longer support the JM.*

Managing Add-Ons (SP2)

Windows XP SP2 includes a new feature that lets you manage Internet Explorer Add-ons. Add-ons are programs that can be used to extend the capabilities of Internet Explorer. Two common add-ons are the Macromedia Shockwave and Macromedia Flash programs. Without these add-ons, you could not view many of the Flash and Shockwave animations that are included on various Web sites around the world. One such animation can be found at http://kids.msn.com.

Here are some other common add-ons:

- Adobe Reader
- Google Toolbar
- Shockwave ActiveX Control
- Windows Media Player
- Windows Messenger

To use the Add-On Manager, follow these steps:

1. In IE, choose Tools and then choose Internet Options.
2. Click the Programs tab and then click Manage Add-Ons.

3. On the Manage Add-ons dialog box (see Figure 14-16), select the type of add-ons you want to view from the Show list. You can view all add-ons that IE has used, or just show the ones currently loaded by IE.

4. To change the status of an add-on, select the add-on name and then click Enable to have it run, or Disable to shut it down.

5. For ActiveX add-ons, you can update them by selecting the control in the list and clicking Update ActiveX.

6. When finished with the Add-On Manager, click OK and OK again.

IE also attempts to detect crashes caused by add-ons and displays that information if possible, giving you the chance to block the add-on. SP2 adds a handful of group policies to enable administrators to configure these settings. These group policies are included in the Administrator Approved Controls policies. Learn how to change policies the next section.

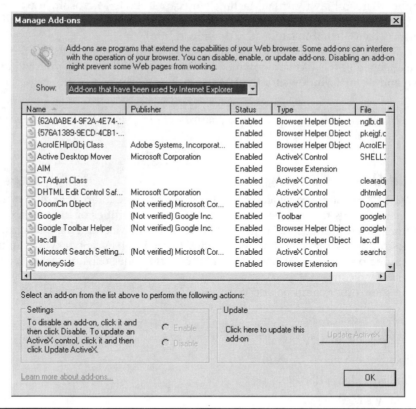

FIGURE 14-16 The Manage Add-Ons dialog box

Controlling Internet Explorer with Group Policy

With Windows XP's Group Policy, you can "get under the hood" of XP to control many Internet Explorer Registry settings not otherwise available via Control Panel and the Tools | Internet Options menu command. You use the Group Policy Editor to change policy settings.

With the Group Policy Editor, Windows XP lets you change the following areas of IE:

- Browser settings
- Connection settings
- Default browser Internet addresses, including home page, favorites, and link addresses
- Channels
- Security settings
- Program associations

NOTE *Changing Group Policies is something that only experienced users should attempt. You can lock yourself out of Windows entirely if you make the wrong modification to a setting. If you are unsure of how the Group Policy Editor works, read more about it at http://support.windows.com/default.aspx?scid=kb:en-us;314953.*

Using Group Policy Editor

To start the Group Policy Editor, follow these steps:

1. Click Start and then click the Run command.
2. Type **gpedit.msc** and press ENTER. The Group Policy Editor displays (see Figure 14-17).

The Group Policy Editor includes two panes. The left pane shows the Console Tree. In the Console Tree you can select the Policy and Configuration options available on your computer. For instance, policy changes for Internet Explorer can be found in the User Configuration section under the Windows Settings folder.

The right pane shows the individual Group Policy Objects you can modify for a setting. For instance, you can disable the option that lets you change the default home page using the Disable Changing Home Page settings.

Setting IE Policy Settings

Windows XP lets you set Group Policy settings for two different types of users. The first type of user is anyone who logs onto the computer. These settings, known as the Computer Configuration policies, affect the entire computer, regardless of who is currently logged in (you, an administrator, etc.). The second type of user is for the currently logged-in user. Anytime this user logs in, Windows applies the User Configuration policies to that user. For a computer with multiple users, such as for a shared work environment, this is handy if you want to restrict some IE features for some users, but not for other users.

To set IE global computer settings, follow these steps:

1. Start the Group Policy Editor.

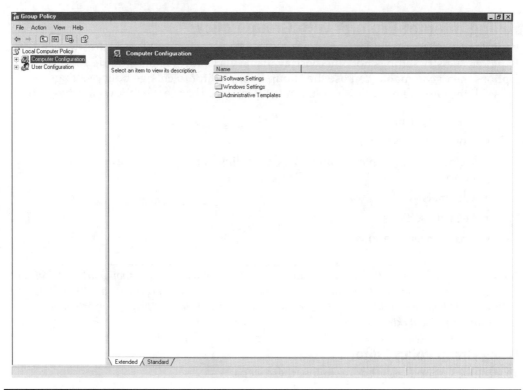

Figure 14-17   The Group Policy Editor lets you manage several "hidden" Internet Explorer options.

2. In the left pane, click to expand the Computer Configuration policy folder.

3. Click the Administrative Templates folder.

4. Click the Windows Components folder.

5. Click the Internet Explorer folder. This displays IE items in the right pane (see Figure 14-18).

6. Double-click an item to modify, such as Disable Automatic Install of Internet Explorer components. A property sheet for this item appears (see Figure 14-19).

7. Click Enabled to enable the item. Sometimes additional settings display that you can modify.

8. Set any other settings for the object, if available.

9. Click OK.

10. Continue until all machine-level objects are set as desired.

NOTE   *To learn more about a particular Group Policy Object, click the Explain tab on the object's property sheet. The Explain tab gives a description of the object and its settings.*

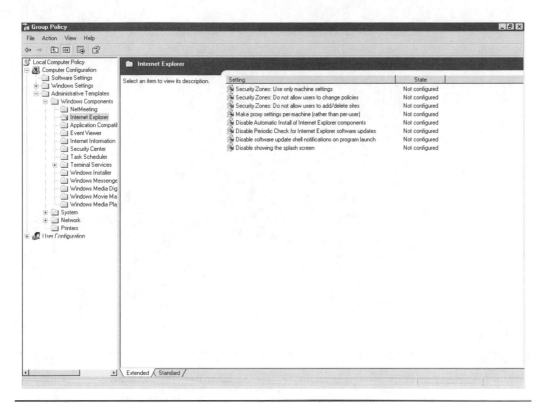

FIGURE 14-18   Display the Computer Configuration IE items in the right pane.

To set IE user-level settings, follow these steps:

1. Start Group Policy Editor.
2. In the left pane, click to expand the User Configuration policy folder.
3. Click the Administrative Templates folder.
4. Click the Internet Explorer folder. This displays IE items in the right pane. Note that there are many more options available here than under Computer Configuration.
5. Double-click an item and modify its setting(s) as desired.
6. Continue until you finish setting the IE objects as desired.

The following are the main subfolders of Group Policy Objects available under the Internet Explorer folder. Each of these subfolders includes specific objects you can modify for the current user:

- **Internet Control Panel**   Includes settings for displaying the tabs on the Internet Options property sheet (such as when you choose Tools | Internet Options in IE)
- **Offline Pages**   Includes settings for how IE saves and stores offline pages (previously known as synchronized pages)

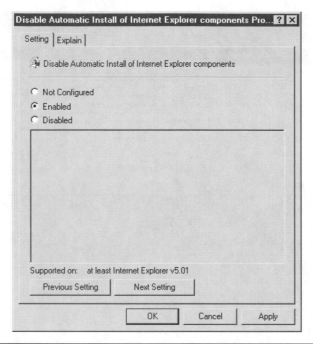

FIGURE 14-19 A property sheet for modifying a Group Policy object.

- **Browser menus** Includes settings for displaying or not hiding menus on the IE menu bar; also includes options for displaying or hiding some specific menu commands.

- **Toolbars** Includes setting for toolbar buttons on the main IE browser window

- **Persistence Behavior** Includes settings for limiting the amount of storage that IE zones use

- **Administrator Approved Controls** Includes settings for controls and IE add-ons

- **Security Features** Includes a number of IE security settings

TIP *See http://www.boyce.us/gp for a searchable database of group policy settings.*

Security Enhancements to IE in SP2

SP2 incorporates many changes and enhancements for Internet Explorer to improve browsing and add security. Some of these changes have been discussed in the preceding sections. The following are some other things SP2 adds to IE security:

- **Internet Explorer BindToObject Mitigation** SP2 applies the ActiveX security model to all cases where URL binding is used to create an instance of an object and initialize it. This change helps mitigate several IE exploits.

- **Internet Explorer Feature Control Security Zone Settings**   SP2 adds a handful of additional settings to Internet Explorer to help prevent certain exploits. These include MIME sniffing, which enables IE to detect file types by bit signature rather than file extension; changes to prevent privilege elevation; and restriction of script-initiated pop-up windows. These settings can be configured on a zone-by-zone basis as well as through group policy.

- **Internet Explorer MIME Handling Enforcement**   SP2 adds features to IE that help prevent MIME-related exploits. For example, IE now performs additional checks before it will open a served file and will not elevate the privileges of the file if the MIME type's registered application is unable to load the file. IE also now can employ MIME sniffing for this purpose.

- **Internet Explorer Object Caching**   IE with SP2 no longer allows a page to access objects cached from another site. This change helps prevent exposure of user data to malicious sites.

- **Internet Explorer Untrusted Publishers Mitigations**   IE with SP2 now offers users the capability to block all signed content from specific publishers. This feature blocks the content without repeated prompts and also blocks installation of code without valid signatures.

PART III

Outlook Express Tips and Tricks

In this chapter you'll find the answers to the following questions:

- How can I create rules in Outlook Express (OE) to handle messages automatically?
- Does OE offer any features to block spam?
- How can I be sure a message that I sent was received or read?
- I'd like to add a signature line to every message I send. How do I do that?
- Will OE block viruses?
- What should I do to prevent my computer from being infected by a virus?
- I don't want to lose my old messages. How do I back them up?

OE is a free e-mail and newsgroup application provided by Microsoft. It is included as part of Windows XP and has a few new features as part of Windows XP SP2. This chapter discusses the new security features of OE in XP SP2. It also discusses the basics of using OE to handle and manage your e-mail messages.

NOTE *Although OE is an excellent tool for basic e-mail and even newsgroup uses, OE does not offer other communication tools, such as calendaring, meeting management, and integration with Microsoft Exchange Server or Windows SharePoint Services. For these features you will need Microsoft Outlook 2003. To learn more about Outlook 2003 read* How To Do Everything with Microsoft Office Outlook 2003, *by Bill Mann (Osborne/McGraw-Hill, 2003).*

What's New with OE in Windows XP SP2

You probably won't notice too much of a difference with OE after you install SP2 (Figure 15-1). The main difference is in the way OE automatically protects users from possible virus attacks via file attachments and images that display in e-mail messages. To help reduce spam, OE includes a new feature that blocks external Hypertext Markup Language (HTML) content until you explicitly download it. Some spammers include links to remote content in messages so that when you view the message, that content is downloaded from the server and your e-mail address is verified as valid. Blocking the external content prevents those spammers

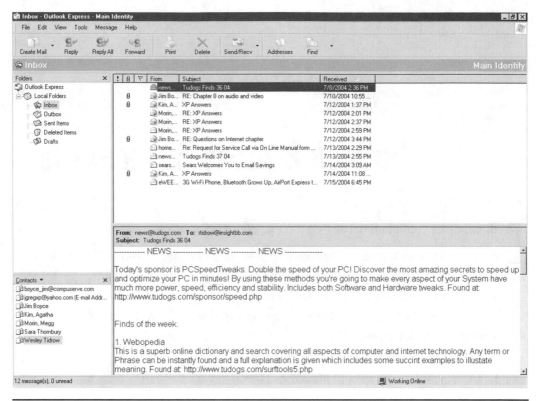

FIGURE 15-1   OE looks pretty much the same as it did prior to XP SP2, but it offers some new security features you'll like.

from validating your e-mail address. You can configure OE to allow external content downloads, if you prefer.

In an effort to help OE users ward off virus attacks, Windows XP SP2 includes a lock-down mode. With this feature, OE will not automatically execute e-mail file attachments, including those attachments that are EXE and COM files. Several mass-mailing viruses have been spread through e-mail attachments when messages are sent to multiple users by automatically culling users' Address Books. These viruses include Sobig.F, Nimda, Klez, Bugbear, and Aliz.

Prior to SP2's fixes, when OE received a message with an attachment, it automatically executed it; or if the message was written as HTML format, it displayed pictures and other objects n the message window. The problem with this is that if the file was not welcomed by the user, which is the case with most viruses, the file would run anyway on the user's computer. On computers that were not protected with real-time antivirus checkers (such as Symantec AntiVirus), it would be too late to stop the virus from causing harm to the computer.

With the lock-down mode, SP2 also prevents OE from automatically showing linked pictures in the message window. Messages containing linked pictures provide one way for e-mail spammers to find out if a recipient is a live account or an inactive account. When a message with a linked picture is opened in OE, a script runs that makes a connection (usually in the background without the user's knowledge) to a web site. This site records the user's information, such as an Internet Protocol (IP) address and e-mail address.

SP2's changes allow the user to read the message first and then, if the user deems the message is from a safe source (a coworker or family member, for instance), click a button to view the entire message or attachment.

Even if you determine that a message with a file attached is from a friendly sender, the file can still contain a virus that has automatically been sent to you from that sender. Always use antivirus software to protect your computer from files infected by viruses or worms. OE includes an Attachment Execution Service Application Programming Interface (API) that supports attachment checking for OE as well as external applications. So, applications that need to check an attachment in your OE mail store can call the AES API rather than incorporate code within the application itself to accomplish the same task. The AES API is, therefore, targeted at developers rather than end users. To learn more about this API, go to http://www.microsoft.com/technet/prodtechnol/winxppro/maintain/sp2email.mspx.

Run in Plain Text Mode

When displaying OE messages in text mode, scripts and graphics are not enabled. This greatly reduces possible virus attacks, but there are some limitations to your messages, including the following:

- Text size cannot be changed
- Fonts cannot be changed
- Graphics are not embedded in message
- Right-context menus are not available
- Hyperlinks are not clickable
- Messages cannot be text searched
- Margins in the preview pane are not available

TIP *Blocking external content can also reduce online time. When you are viewing a message offline with OE in SP2, it will not try to connect to the Internet to retrieve the HTML content.*

If your copy of OE is set to display messages in HTML format, you can change it to a plain text format using the following steps:

1. Open Outlook Express.
2. Choose the Tools menu and click Options.
3. Select the Read tab (Figure 15-2).
4. Select Read all messages in plain text.
5. Click OK.

All your messages are now shown in plain text format, like the one shown in Figure 15-3. This message was sent as an HTML formatted message and contains hyperlinks, different sized fonts, colored fonts, and embedded graphics. However in plain text view none of

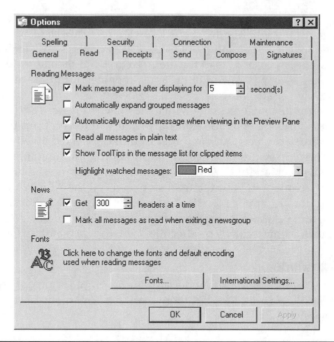

FIGURE 15-2 Set OE to show mail in plain text format.

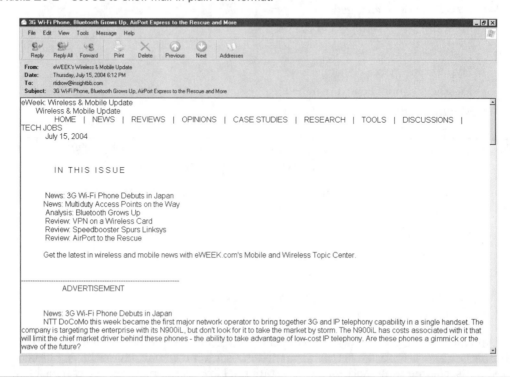

FIGURE 15-3 Originally an HTML formatted message, this message is now displayed in plain text format.

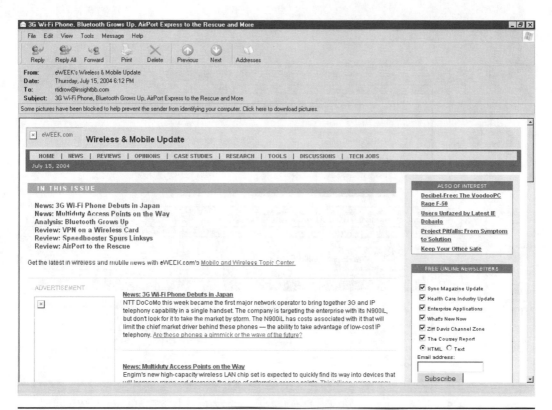

FIGURE 15-4   The same message shown in HTML format.

these features are shown. Figure 15-4 shows what the original message looks like.

To turn on HTML for the current message, press the ALT-V-H keyboard combination. Or choose the new SP2 menu command: Choose View | Message in HTML.

One thing you may notice in the HTML version, however, is that OE leaves a blank for the graphics to appear. This is a new feature in SP2. OE does not automatically download remote graphics so that recipients are not required to connect to the sender's web site to "grab" the image. Spammers will no longer be able to track users using this method.

To display the graphics in a message, do the following:

1. Open a message or click it to display it in the preview pane.

2. Click the Information Bar at the top of the message window (Figure 15-5) to download the graphics.

Plain text format is also handy for composing messages to recipients when you're not sure if they have a rich-text or HTML-compatible e-mail reader. In these cases, plain text is your best bet because it eliminates any rich text (such as formatted text or images) that may

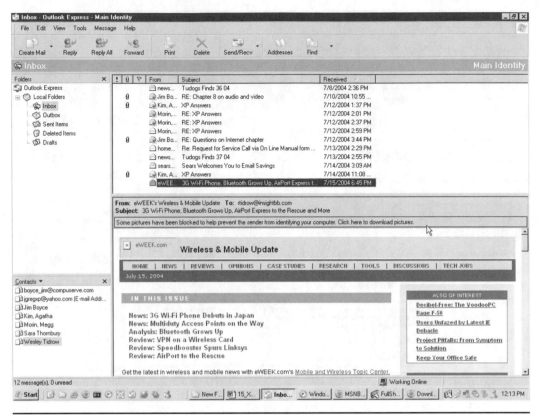

FIGURE 15-5   The Information Bar reports that some pictures have been blocked.

get into the message that your recipient cannot read. Also, plain text messages are smaller in size than rich text messages.

To set up OE to compose messages in plain text format, do the following:

1. Open OE.

2. Choose Tools | Options.

3. Click the Send tab (Figure 15-6).

4. Select Plain Text under the Mail Sending Format section.

5. Click the Plain Text Settings button to display the Plain Text Settings dialog box (Figure 15-7).

6. Modify the text settings as necessary, such as Multipurpose Internet Mail Extension (MIME), text wrapping, and indention settings.

7. Click OK.

8. Click OK again.

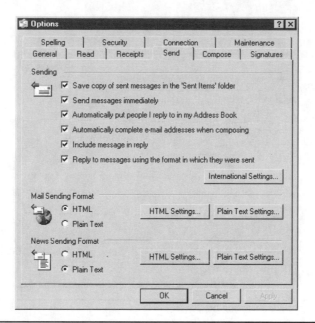

Figure 15-6   The Send tab.

Using OE for E-Mail

OE is one of the easiest applications to use for reading, composing, and managing e-mail messages. The OE window is set up with four distinct panes:

- **Folder list**   The top left pane is the folder list, which includes your e-mail folders. The Inbox, Outbox, Sent Items, Deleted Items, and Drafts folders are the default folders here. You can add more folders by choosing File | New | Folder and filling out the Create Folder dialog box (Figure 15-8). Click OK to create your folder.

- **Address Book pane**   The bottom left pane is the address book pane. This pane lists the contacts saved in your Address Book (choose Tools | Address Book to display

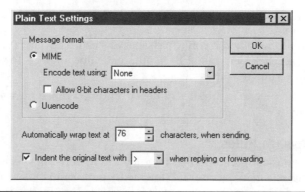

Figure 15-7   The Plain Text Settings dialog box.

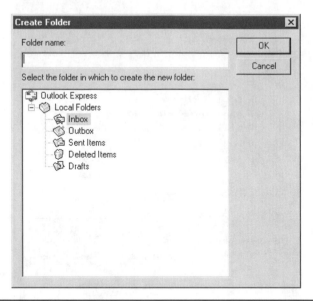

FIGURE **15-8**   The Create Folder dialog box.

your address book). You can create a new message to a contact by double-clicking the contact's name in this pane.

- **Message pane**   The top right pane displays all messages stored in the currently selected folder. For example, when you download new messages, they appear in the Inbox folder by default. Click that folder in the folder list pane to display all your Inbox messages in the message pane. To read a message, click a message to display it in the preview pane (see next bullet point) or double-click a message to display it in its own window.

- **Preview pane**   The bottom right pane is the preview pane. In here you can see the contents of any message you click on in the message pane. Only one message can display in the preview pane at once. To open more than one message simultaneously, however, you can double-click the messages in the message pane.

To download new messages to OE, do the following:

1. Open OE. If the Send and receive messages at startup option is selected (select Tools | Options, then click General tab), OE automatically connects to your mail server and downloads any new messages.

2. Click Send/Receive to manually connect to and download messages from your e-mail server.

Working with Message Rules

A message rule lets you set up criteria that instructs OE to perform specific actions on your messages. Rules help you manage your OE folders by performing tasks on messages as they arrive, when you read them, or when you start OE. This helps you keep track of messages, delete ones you don't want, and organize your messages for future reference.

To get an idea of a simple rule you can enforce, think of all the e-mail you get that is from people that work in the same department (or same business). Let's say you work in the sales department and many messages you receive are from marketing folks. All these messages can be automatically saved to a folder called "Marketing" based on the sender of the message. Or if your company uses subject lines to specify a product line that the message is discussing, you can set up a rule that automatically stores messages in folders based on product lines. This way all your similar messages are stored together.

To set up a rule, do the following:

1. Start OE.

2. Choose Tools | Message Rules, and then Mail. The New Mail Rule dialog box appears (Figure 15-9). (If you already have a rule created, the Message Rules dialog box appears, as shown in Figure 15-10, instead.) Click the New button to create a new rule from the New Mail Rule dialog box.

3. In the 1. Select the Conditions for your rule box, select a condition for the rule, such as Where the From line contains people.

4. In the 2. Select the Actions for your rule box, select an action for the rule, such as Move it to the specified folder.

5. In the 3. Rule Description (click on an underlined value to edit it) box, see the description of the rule. Underlined values need to be edited for specific data. For our example shown in Figure 15-11, you need to click the *contains people* and *specified* values. You then can specify the e-mail addresses you want OE to apply the rule to (Figure 15-12) and where you want the message moved to (Figure 15-13).

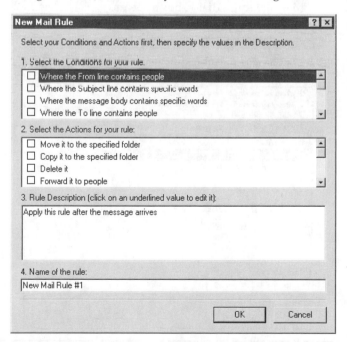

FIGURE 15-9   The New Mail Rule dialog box

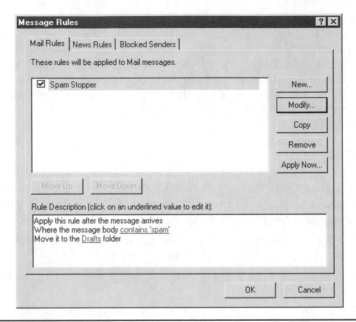

FIGURE 15-10 The Message Rules dialog box

6. In the 4. Name of the rule box, type a name for the rule.

7. Click OK. The Message Rules dialog box appears.

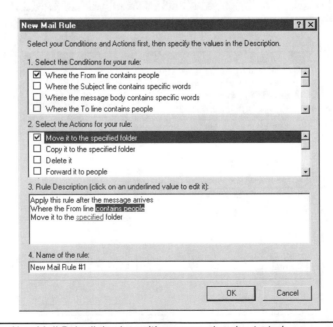

FIGURE 15-11 The New Mail Rule dialog box with an example rule started

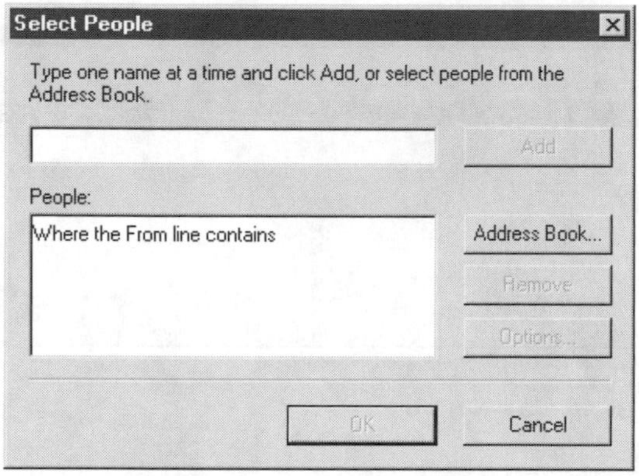

Figure showing the Select People dialog box:

Select People
Type one name at a time and click Add, or select people from the Address Book.

[   ]   Add

People:
Where the From line contains   Address Book...
                                 Remove
                                 Options...

                    OK   Cancel

FIGURE 15-12   The Select People dialog box

To tell OE to run the rule right now, click the Apply Now button. Select the rules to apply from the Apply Mail Rules Now dialog box (Figure 15-14) and then click the Apply Now button. OE applies the rules and when it's finished, displays a message stating that the rule(s) have been applied. Click OK and Close to return to the Message Rules dialog box.

Blocking Spam and External HTML Content (SP2)

Spam is unsolicited e-mail you receive. Some people get hundreds or even thousands of spam messages a day. Others may get only a few spam messages a day. Regardless of the number you get, you probably don't like them and probably want to block these types of messages. OE includes some features that help you do this.

One line of attack is the plain text feature we discussed earlier in the chapter. With that feature you can block future spam by not allowing external graphics to download to your

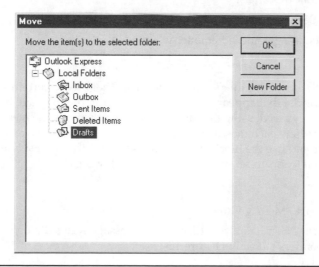

FIGURE 15-13   The Move dialog box

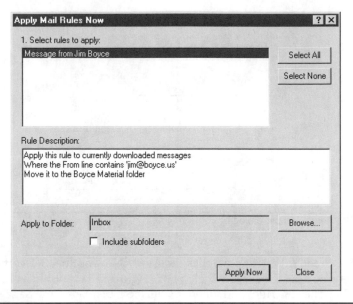

FIGURE 15-14   Select a rule to apply and click Apply Now.

messages automatically and, thereby, allowing the spammer to see that someone actually opened his message. If he determines that a "live" body is seeing his messages, the spammer can turn around and start sending additional messages to this address. To set up this feature, do the following:

1. Start OE.
2. Choose Tools | Options.
3. Select the Security tab (Figure 15-15).
4. Select Block images and other external contents.
5. Click OK.

Another way to block spammers is to create a rule that blocks certain words (such as sexually explicit words) that appear in the subject line or in the message body. Simply delete these messages as they arrive using the rule, or have the rule move the message to a separate folder so you can review each message in the future.

Finally, you should use the Blocked Senders List to specify those senders you don't want to receive mail from. To set up this list, do the following:

1. Start OE.
2. Choose Tools | Message Rules.
3. Select Blocked Senders List to display the Message Rules dialog box with the Blocked Senders tab active Figure 15-16).
4. Click the Add button.

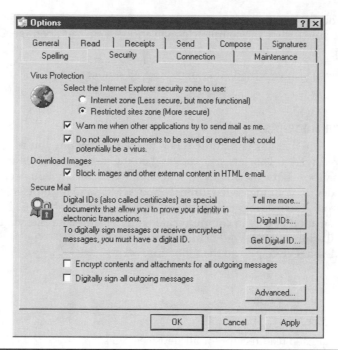

FIGURE 15-15   Use the Security tab to block external content.

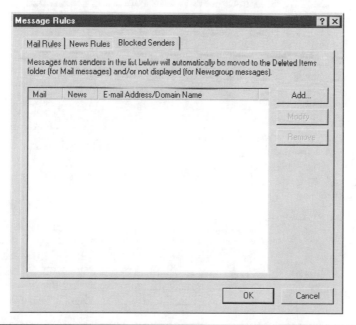

FIGURE 15-16   Set up and manage blocked senders here.

5. In the Add Sender dialog box, type the e-mail address of the sender you want to block. Be sure to type the complete e-mail address, such as spammer@spam.com.

6. Click OK.

7. Repeat until you've added all known blocked senders here.

8. Click OK.

Using Message Receipts

OE includes a feature that lets you know when the person whom you're sending the message to has received it. This lets you know when the message arrives and is opened in the recipient's mailbox. If the message you sent is time critical, say you need the recipient to read and responded to your message within 24 hours, Message Receipts lets you know if she has gotten around to reading the message within the time allotted. If she has not done so, you can choose another way to communicate with her (for example, via telephone, fax, alternative e-mail address, etc.).

To turn on Message Receipts, do the following:

1. Start OE.

2. Choose Tools | Options.

3. Click the Receipts tab (Figure 15-17).

4. Select Request a read receipt for all sent messages.

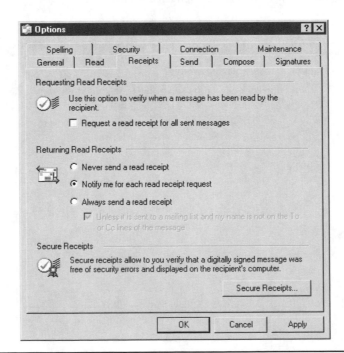

FIGURE 15-17   The Receipts tab

5. To set up requests for secure receipts—those that are digitally signed—click the Secure Receipts button and click the Request a secure receipt for all digitally signed messages. Click OK.

6. Click OK to close the Options dialog box.

If you want to control how OE returns the receipts you've requested, select the Notify me for each read receipt request option on the Receipts tab (Figure 15-17). This will prompt OE to ask you if you want it to send a receipt back to the sender requesting it. For some messages, such as those that are from potential spammers, you probably don't want receipts to be sent back to the sender.

Using Message Signatures

A message signature is a block of text or file that is added to your outgoing messages, including new messages and ones that you respond to or forward on. Using a signature is a good way to include boilerplate information to your messages, such as your name, address, phone numbers, and e-mail addresses. Some users also like to include pithy statements or a company slogan as their signatures.

Many organizations include boilerplate legal-type signatures to all outgoing e-mail. These signatures may include statements to the effect that the enclosed comments are not those of the company but of the individual sender, or statements about how the message has been checked for viruses.

To set up your own signature, do the following:

1. Open OE.

2. Choose Tools | Options.

3. Click the Signatures tab (Figure 15-18).

4. Set the Signature settings options as desired. For instance, if you want your signature to appear on all messages, including replies and forwards, deselect the Don't add signatures to Replies and Forwards.

5. Click the New button and then type your signature text in the empty text box at the bottom of the tab.

6. If you want to use an HTML or saved TXT file as your signature, click the File button and then click Browse. Select the file you want to use and click Open. OE uses this file as your signature. For any file you use as a signature, you'll want to keep it small so recipients do not have to download large files each time you send them a message.

7. Click Apply when finished.

8. Click OK to save your settings.

Protecting Against Viruses

The best way to guard against a virus is to run an antivirus program. There are several good products on the market in this category including the following:

- Symantec AntiVirus (previously Norton AntiVirus): http://www.symantec.com

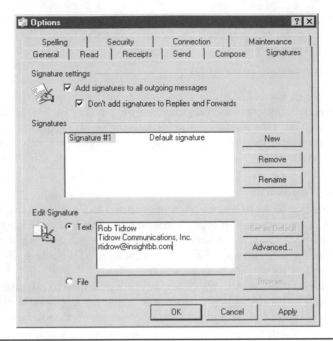

FIGURE 15-18 The Signatures tab.

- McAfee antivirus products: http://www.mcafee.com
- Trend antivirus products: http://www.trendmicro.com

You should purchase one that allows you to run real-time virus protection. This is when the antivirus software always runs so that any changes to a file or any files added to your file system are checked immediately. If a file is a found to be infected by a virus, the antivirus software can clean the file, quarantine it, or delete it before the virus has a chance to damage your system.

After you install an antivirus tool, you should keep it updated. This entails downloading new files from the antivirus software manufacturer daily or weekly to catch new viruses that have been released. If you don't update your antivirus software regularly, new viruses or new variations of old viruses can damage your system.

Figure 15-19 shows an example of an antivirus tool (Symantec) that is scanning a hard drive for viruses. When a virus is found, the tool performs an action on it that you have prescribed. The best way to rid your system of a virus is simply to delete the file. This way you cannot accidentally re-release the virus on your computer if you accidentally quarantine the file and then remove it from quarantine.

Backing Up and Restoring Your Mail Store

Before you lose any of those important messages stored in OE, back up your mail store. To do this, use the following steps:

1. Start OE.

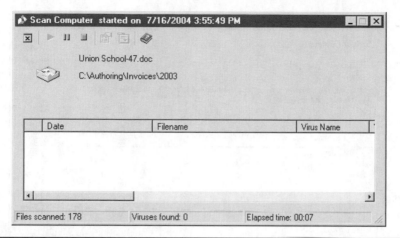

FIGURE 15-19 Symantec AntiVirus scanning for viruses

2. Choose the File menu and click Folder.

3. Choose Compact. OE compacts your messages (removes any empty spaces not needed for the messages) and backs up your messages to your OE Store Folder. The path to the Store Folder can be found by choosing Tools | Options and clicking the Maintenance tab. Click the Store Folders button to see the path.

To restore the Store Folder, do the following:

1. Start OE.

2. Choose File and then Import.

3. Choose Messages.

4. From the Select Program screen, select Microsoft OE 6.

5. Click Next.

6. Select Import mail from an OE6 store directory.

7. Click OK.

8. Click Browse and specify the Store Folder in which the backed up mail store is stored.

9. Click Next.

10. Select the message folders you want to import (Figure 15-20) and click Next.

11. Click Next and then click Finish.

Backing Up the Store Folders Manually

Another approach to backing up your Outlook data is to simply back up the file system folders that contain your OE messages. You can then simply copy them to a backup folder, another local drive, a network drive, or even burn them to a CD.

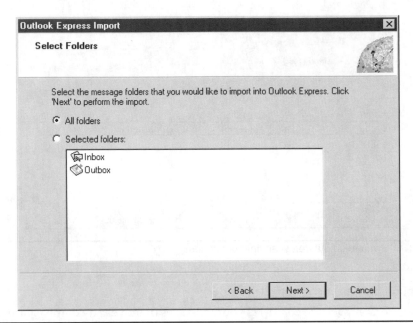

FIGURE 15-20   You can select to import all folders or individual folders.

To locate your folder store, open OE and choose Tools | Options. Click the Maintenance tab and then click the Store Folder button. Note the folder location in the Store Location dialog box (Figure 15-21), then click OK. Back up the entire contents of the folder to your desired backup location.

TIP   *The folder path to your information store is fairly long. Click in the folder path, press* HOME, *press* SHIFT-END *to select the entire string, then press* CTRL-C *to copy it to the Clipboard. Then, open My Computer, click in the Address field, delete any path already there, and press* CTRL-V. *Click Go or press* ENTER *to open the OE information store folder.*

Notice that in the Store Location dialog box you have the option of changing the store location. This is handy when you need to move your OE folders to a different location to gain more storage space or you want to place the store in a location that is more visible to you, such as My Documents.

FIGURE 15-21   Use the Store Location dialog box to view the location of the mail store and optionally change that location.

Networking, Communications, and Remote Access

Networking Windows XP

I n this chapter you'll find the answers to the following questions:

- Which is better for a small network: wired or wireless?
- I want to set up my own network. What kind of equipment and cables do I need?
- I'd really like a wireless network at home. What do I need and how to I set it up?
- Can anyone get into my wireless network? How do I make it secure?
- What do I need to install a fast Internet connection?
- Can I use a wireless and a wired network together?
- What do I use to connect my computers together?

I've been designing and managing networks for several years, including some for Internet Service Providers (ISPs), so I speak from experience when we say that networking isn't very difficult to accomplish. For someone without any networking background, however, it can be very daunting. Really, it's like any procedure—once you understand the basics and some terminology, the rest starts to fall into place.

In this chapter I explain how to set up, manage, and troubleshoot networks in a variety of situations. You will also learn how to configure and manage secure resource sharing on the network and deal with specific network applications such as Windows Messenger, Media Player, and others.

> **NOTE** *Networking is a broad topic that could easily fill several books. We'll focus on some very specific processes in this chapter to help you address common networking issues, such as integrating a wireless network with a wired network.*

Setting Up a Small Network

Whether you need to connect together two computers or a hundred, the process is much the same. You choose the type of network that best suits your needs, install the infrastructure to support it, then connect the computers to the network and begin setting up file and printer sharing and other network resources. The first step, regardless of how many computers you need to connect to the network, is to choose a network type and topology.

Wired Versus Wireless

Two main options exist for creating small local area network (LAN) today: wired and wireless. Wired networks offer a few advantages:

- **Speed**   A wired network can achieve speeds up to 1 gigabit (1Gbps) over standard Cat5 cable. By contrast, the fastest wireless networks run at about 108 megabits, or about 1/10th the speed of a 1Gbps network.

- **Simplicity**   Wired networks are generally very easy to configure, if you don't take into account the effort involved in running the cables.

- **Distance**   The standards for a typical 10/100Mbps Ethernet network specify 90-meter spans from a hub to a node (computer).

- **Security**   Unless someone has physical access to your network, he is unlikely to be able to steal bandwidth or sniff your network for passwords or other sensitive data.

Wireless is a good choice, as well, and offers its own advantages over wired solutions:

- **Portability**   Nothing beats being able to move from room to room or office to office with your notebook, personal digital assistant (PDA), or other wireless device while retaining network connectivity.

- **No cables to run**   In new construction sites, running network cables is easy. However, it isn't as easy to run cable in existing buildings.

Which one should you choose? The answer depends on several factors. First, consider speed. If you don't perform large file transfers across the LAN or expect to do streaming media across the LAN, a 10/100Mbps wired network or any of the wireless solutions will be fine. If you want to ramp up your network speed to get better Internet performance, keep in mind that your Internet connection is going to be slower than your LAN regardless of the type of network you install. The fastest connection most home and small business users will have is a 256Kbps Digital Subscriber Line (DSL) connection. Even with a full-band DSL account, your Internet connection's performance will still be considerably less than a 10Mbps wired network.

Some networking experts feel that wireless networks are far less secure than wired networks, but in our opinion, it boils down to whether you have adequately secured your wireless network. Properly implemented, a wireless network can provide sufficient security for home business users alike.

TIP *See the "Wireless Security" section later in this chapter for more details on securing a wireless network.*

The final main consideration is how comfortable you are in working with network devices and configuring the network. Wired LANs are typically a bit easier to set up than wireless ones, but today's wireless access points make it relatively easy to get things going.

Here's a summary of the points to consider when choosing between wired and wireless LANs:

- **Speed**   If you need the most speed possible because you will be transferring large amounts of data (100MB or more), choose a wired LAN. If you just share documents and printers and want the advantage of portability, go wireless.

- **Cutting the cables**   Running cables can be time-consuming. Wireless eliminates that effort altogether and gives you the freedom to put your computers wherever you like. Go wireless if you don't want the hassle of running cables and want to be able to move your computers around. Just make sure you adequately secure your network.

- **Distance**   If you think wireless is the solution for you, make sure you'll have sufficient signal strength everywhere a computer needs to be. For example, even in a wood frame house, you might have difficulty getting a strong enough signal from a second floor if your access point is in the basement. Moving the access point to a central location could solve the problem. Check with the wireless manufacturer to determine signal range. Keep in mind that speed decrease as range increases.

- **Security**   If you need to eliminate the possibility that someone could sniff your network, choose wired over wireless.

TIP   There are networking solutions that use your electrical wiring to serve as the connection media between devices to eliminate the need to run additional cabling. These solutions can be useful where wireless networks are impractical and you don't want to run additional cable. Check with your computer retailer to learn what options are available.

Cabling Standards and Codes

If you choose a wired LAN, make sure to consider cabling standards and building codes in your area as you plan the network. For example, most codes dictate that you use plenum-rated cable—which has a different fire rating than nonrated cable—if you will be running cable in airspaces such as those above a suspended ceiling or below a raised floor. Also keep in mind the 90-meter limit for cable runs between a hub or switch and the device (computer, printer, etc.). If you need to go further than 90 meters, install a switch at the remote location and make further runs from there.

TIP   Choose Category 5e or 6 cabling so you can support 1Gbps devices in the future, even if you will be using a 10/100 network now.

How you terminate the cables is also important. Table 16-1 shows the T568B standard pin-outs for Ethernet cables. Table 16-2 shows the pin-outs for a crossover cable (often required to connect networking devices such as a DSL modem and a router). To locate pin 1 on the RJ45 cable connector (which is similar to a phone connector but has eight contacts), hold the connector facing you with the locking tab facing down. Pin 1 is at the right (Figure 16-1). Likewise, looking at an RJ45 receptacle, pin 1 is at the left.

PART IV

RJ45 Pin #	Wire Color
1	White/Orange
2	Orange
3	White/Green
4	Blue
5	White/Blue
6	Green
7	White/Brown
8	Brown

TABLE 16-1   T568B Straight-Through Cable Pin-Outs

RJ45 Pin # End 1	Wire Color	RJ45 Pin # End 2	
1	White/Orange	1	White/Green
2	Orange	2	Green
3	White/Green	3	White/Orange
4	Blue	4	Blue
5	White/Blue	5	White/Blue
6	Green	6	Orange
7	White/Brown	7	White/Brown
8	Brown	8	Brown

TABLE 16-2   T568A Cross-Over Cable Pin-Outs

Where is pin #1?

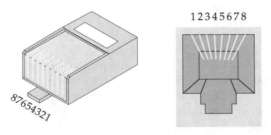

FIGURE 16-1   RJ45 connector and receptacle pin-outs

If at all possible, don't try to crimp your own connections. For short cables to connect your computer to the network jack, buy premanufactured patch cables. Use punch-down connections for long cable runs from a switch (or integrated router/switch) to receptacles. You can purchase a punch-down tool, receptacles, and patch panels at most computer retailers and at many home improvement stores. The patch panel contains multiple jacks with punch-down connections on the back. The cables connect to the back of the panel and premanufactured patch cables connect the individual receptacles on the switch or router to the patch panel. The receptacles at the wall where the computer plug in should also have punch-down connections in back, with a patch cable connecting the computer or printer to the receptacle. That way, you don't have to crimp any connectors at all.

TIP *Why not crimp connections? They are a royal pain to make. Even after you become proficient at it, you'll spend at least a couple of minutes on each connection, stripping the wire, inserting the individual wires in the connector, and crimping it. You'll be able to punch down ten connections in the time it takes you to crimp one cable end. What's more, some percentage of your crimped connections will have to be redone because a wire didn't make contact.*

Choosing Your Network Hardware

There are several items you'll need to purchase for a wired LAN, with fewer required for most wireless networks. First, you'll need network interface cards (NICs) for each computer. Lesser known brands are often less expensive, but will generally work well in most situations. We recommend choosing NICs from major vendors because driver upgrades will be readily available if you need them in the future. Regardless of the manufacturer you ultimately choose, you should standardize. Use the same type of NIC in each computer where possible to simplify configuration and support.

NOTE *Many computers purchased in the last few years have integrated network adapters built onto the motherboard. Check the back of your computers for network connections before you run out to the store to buy NICs.*

If you will be buying wireless adapters for your computers, standardization is just as important to ensure compatibility and simplify configuration and management. If you install wireless adapters inside your desktop computers, keep in mind that the antenna will be at the back of the computer. If the computer is located where range could be a problem, you might need to attach an add-on antenna that will sit on the desk. Not all wireless adapters support these add-on antennas, so check with the vendor beforehand. If you choose Universal Serial Bus (USB) wireless adapters, you'll be able to locate the adapter on the desktop and position for optimum range.

Next, consider the hubs or switches you will need, if any, for your network. Hubs and switches serve as a distribution point between (usually) a router and multiple computers. Figure 16-2 shows a typical, small LAN.

Hubs broadcast traffic to all ports. Switches send traffic to specific ports based on the learned address of the computer. For that reason, switches reduce network packet collisions (two computers transmitting simultaneously), which reduces performance. Given switches are nearly as inexpensive as hubs, choose a switch rather than a hub.

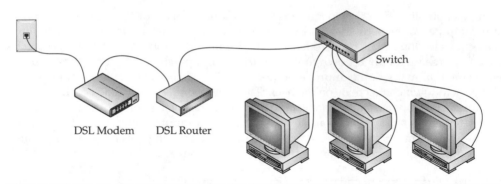

FIGURE 16-2.   This small LAN includes a DSL modem, DSL router, and switch.

NOTE *Most routers designed for small office/home office (SOHO) networks include built-in switches, so you might not have to buy a separate switch unless you need to accommodate more computers than the number of ports available in the built-in switch.*

Finally, consider your broadband connection, if any, when choosing hardware. We recommend you install a hardware firewall at the perimeter of the network. Many of today's SOHO routers include a rudimentary firewall. If you need advanced firewall capabilities, purchase a dedicated firewall appliance.

Running Cables

Running network cables is simply manual labor. There is nothing magical or overly difficult about it. However, we can offer some advice to make the job easier and ensure better performance:

- **Fishing**   Buy a good fish tape from a home improvement store or electrical supply house. You'll use this to fish wires through existing walls. A fish tape is nothing more than a narrow steel band that's coiled with a bent end for connecting to the cable. Use duct tape or electrical tape to connect the cable to the fish tape when pulling the cable.

- **Service loop**   Make the cable a little longer than necessary to allow for repositioning or recrimping. Loop the extra cable and secure it with a cable tie or simply push it back into the wall.

- **Avoid light fixtures and electrical cabling**   Where possible, run network cables several feet away from fluorescent fixtures. If you need to cross electrical cables, do so at a 90-degree angle. Don't run electrical cables and network cables together in the same raceway unless it's unavoidable. Avoid running cables near motors (refrigerators, freezers, compressors, etc.) where possible.

- **Don't untwist pairs**   Only untwist the bare minimum (half an inch or so) needed to make connections.

- **Pull a backup string**   Where you think you might need to run additional cables in the future, pull a length of heavy contractor's string along with the first cable. You can later use the string to pull additional cables, if needed. Pull another string with the next set for future use. If you didn't run a string but need to pull another cable, you can always run an extra cable and use the existing cable to pull the new ones, replacing it with a new one.

- **Be neat**   Run and organize cables neatly and use cable ties to secure the cables for a neat installation. Buy an inexpensive labeler and label each cable for identification.

Setting Up the Network

A methodical approach is the best when setting up a network. If you are installing a broadband connection, install the router, switch, and other devices, and configure them as directed by your service provider. Then, install the network adapters in each computer, install the drivers, connect the cables, and check for link lights on the NICs. When all computers show a link light, you're ready to start testing.

TIP   *No link light? Make sure you have connected both ends of the cable. If you have crimped your own connections, check the connections and if needed, remake the connection.*

NOTE   *See the, "Installing a Broadband Internet Connection" section later in this chapter for tips on choosing and configuring broadband equipment.*

Testing

After your network is set up and configured, you're ready to start testing connections. We're going to assume that you're using TCP/IP because it's now the most common networking protocol. Follow these steps to test connectivity and basic network function:

1. If you have a broadband connection to the Internet, open a web browser and see if you can browse the Internet. If so, the network is working fine for this computer. Check the next one in the same fashion.

2. If you can't browse the Internet, open a command console and type the command **ipconfig /all**. The ipconfig command displays information about your network interfaces. Verify that you have an address in the correct subnet and that the default gateway is properly specified (the gateway is not needed if you don't have an Internet connection). If a computer has an address in the 169.254.0.1 through 169.254.255.254 address range, the computer is configured for dynamic addressing but is not able to contact your Dynamic Host Configuration Protocol (DHCP) server. If there is no DHCP server and you don't have an Internet connection, this subnet will work fine for local networking as long as all other computers are on the same subnet.

3. Trying pinging your local computer with the command **ping localhost**. If you don't get replies, the network configuration of the computer is incorrect.

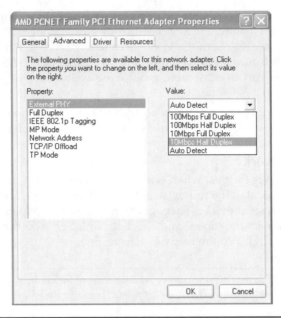

FIGURE 16-3   If you have problems, configure each computer for an explicit speed and mode, rather than using AutoDetect.

4. If pinging localhost works, ping another computer on the network with **ping <address>**, where <address> is the IP address of the other computer. Example: **ping 192.168.1.10**

5. Trying pinging your gateway address if you have a broadband connection. This is the address of your router (or Cable/DSL modem).

If you can ping localhost but nothing else from a computer, it's likely that you have a cable problem. Also verify that you are using the same speed for all computers. For example, configure all computers to use 100Mbps Full Duplex. To configure this setting, open the Network Connections folder from the Control Panel, right-click the network interface, and choose Properties. Click Configure under the network adapter; then click the Advanced tab (Figure 16-3).

Setting Up a Wireless LAN

Wireless networks require a different approach to setup and configuration. This section provides tips on installing, configuring, and securing a wireless network.

Wireless LANs Explained

A wireless LAN essentially replaces cables with radio waves. Just like a cordless phone uses radio frequency to send voice from your handset to the base unit, wireless LANs use radio frequency to send data between wireless network devices.

Small wireless LANs generally come in two flavors: infrastructure or peer-to-peer. In an infrastructure network, a wireless access point serves as a point of connection for the wireless computers and other wireless devices. Often, the access point also connects to a broadband Internet connection or a wired network, but this isn't a requirement to use an access point. In a peer-to-peer wireless network (also called an ad-hoc network), each of the wireless devices communicates with the others and there is no access point.

Windows XP supports infrastructure and ad-hoc wireless networks. It supports three modes for choosing the network (Figure 16-4):

- **Any available network (access point preferred)**   Windows XP will use any available wireless network but will connect to an access point if available.

- **Access point (infrastructure) networks only**   Windows XP will only connect through an access point, even if ad-hoc networks are available.

- **Computer-to-computer (ad-hoc) networks only**.   Windows XP will only connect to ad-hoc networks and will not connect to an access point, even if one is available.

NOTE *See the "Configuring Wireless Connections" section to learn more about configuring Windows XP wireless options.*

Wireless Security

Windows XP supports a couple of features to help you secure your wireless network. First, Windows XP supports Wireless Equivalent Privacy, or WEP, which is a security protocol defined in the 802.11b wireless networking standard. WEP encrypts traffic between wireless nodes to add security and reduce the risk of interception and tampering. To use WEP with Windows XP, you must provide a network key that is used to encrypt the traffic. You can enter the key manually in the wireless device configuration or allow Windows XP to use a key already present in the device.

In addition, Windows XP supports authentication for wireless access. When authentication is enabled, the local wireless client and the remote server (such as an access point) authenticate one another and generate a per-session key to encrypt data. Using WEP and authentication can significantly improve security for your wireless network to prevent unauthorized users from stealing your bandwidth or accessing your data.

TIP *You must enable WEP to enable authentication.*

FIGURE 16-4   You can choose the mode Windows XP will use for connecting to wireless networks.

Choosing Your Hardware

If you don't already have wireless hardware, there are only a few bits of advice you need to make a good choice. They are:

- **Zero Configuration Wireless service**   Make sure the devices you buy support the Windows XP Zero Configuration Wireless service. This feature enables wireless devices to identify and connect to networks automatically.

- **Standardize**   Although it's not a necessity, using devices from a single manufacturer can simplify configuration and management and helps ensure compatibility.

- **Form factor**   The PC Card form factor is the best choice for notebooks that do not already have built-in wireless support. You can use PC Card (formerly PCMCIA) cards in desktop computers as well, but the computer must have a PC Card adapter to accept the card. A better alternative is an external USB adapter, which you can place on the desktop for better range and performance.

Configuring Wireless Connections

The first step in setting up your wireless network is to configure the access point (assuming an infrastructure network). Then, you configure the client devices.

Configuring an Access Point

Typically, you configure an access point with a Web browser, but some manufacturers provide a configuration program that searches the network for access points and provides an interface for configuring them. You'll have to consult the access point's documentation to learn the specific steps for accessing the management interface and setting up the device. Figure 16-5 shows a typical configuration interface for an access point. However, there are some common items you will need to consider when configuring the access point:

- **Wireless access network (WAN) address and type**   You must configure the WAN address type for a wireless access point that serves as a gateway to the Internet or to a wired network. Typical types include Dynamic Host Configuration Protocol (DHCP), Point-to-Point Protocol over Ethernet (PPPoE), Static, and Point-to-Point Tunneling Protocol (PPTP). DHCP pulls the address from a DHCP server on the WAN side of the network. PPPoE requires a user name and password to connect to the remote network. Static simply assigns a fixed address and subnet mask to the device. PPTP requires an IP address, subnet mask, user name, and password for the connection. If you are setting up a wireless access point in your existing wired network, use DHCP if your wired network includes a DHCP server (such as a router that assigns addresses with DHCP), or assign a static IP address to the access point. The address must be an unused address from the wired network's subnet and one not allocated by DHCP on the wired LAN.

- **LAN IP address/subnet mask**   These are the IP address and subnet mask assigned to the wireless side of the access point. Many manufacturers use either 192.168.0.1 or 192.168.1.1 as the default LAN IP address and 255.255.255.0 as the subnet mask, and there is generally no reason to change these values. However, you can use any nonroutable subnet.

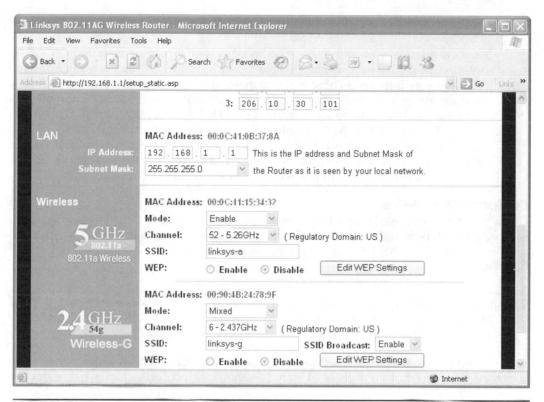

FIGURE 16-5 This is the configuration interface for a Linksys Dual-Band Wireless A+G access point.

- **Service Set Identifier (SSID)** This is the SSID for the access point and uniquely identifies it to wireless devices. The SSIS is in effect the wireless network name. All devices that need to connect to the access point must provide the SSID.

- **SSID broadcast** Access points can broadcast their SSIDs to enable wireless devices to automatically detect the access point. While turning off SSID broadcasts can add a little security to your wireless network, it isn't a foolproof means for preventing unauthorized access. However, it is a first step.

- **WEP** Decide whether you will enable WEP on the access point. If so, you will need to provide an encryption level and a passphrase used to generate the encryption key. Each wireless device that needs to connect to the access point will need to have the encryption key, as well.

- **DHCP** Decide whether your access point will allocate addresses to wireless devices with DHCP. If not, you will need to assign static addresses to each wireless device. Using DHCP is the simplest way to assign addresses.

- **Authentication mode** You must choose between Open System and Shared Key authentication modes for the access point. Choose Open System if wireless client devices do not use authentication. Choose Shared Key if you want to improve security. See the "Configuring the Wireless Client" section, later in this chapter, for details on configuring a shared key.

- **Remote management**   Most access points allow remote management through a Web interface. Enabling remote management can be useful when you are away from your network but need to open a port to make other configuration changes to access resources in your network. If you enable remote management, specify a port other than that used by common services such as HTTP. For example, you might choose a port in the range 8081 to 8087. See http://www.iana.org/assignments/port-numbers for a list of well-known port numbers to identify an available port. Also, make sure you change the default user name and password for the access point and use an account name and password that will be difficult to guess.

Configuring Client Devices

If you purchase wireless adapters that are compatible with Windows XP, configuration is relatively easy. If not, you'll have to use the configuration software that comes with your wireless devices. This chapter assumes you are using Windows XP to configure the wireless devices.

TIP   *To use third-party software to configure your wireless device, right-click the wireless connection in the Network Connections folder and choose Properties. Click the Wireless Networks tab and clear the checkbox Use Windows to configure my wireless network settings.*

To configure the wireless connection, open the Network Connections folder, right-click the connection, and choose Properties. Figure 16-6 shows the properties for a wireless device.

FIGURE 16-6   This is the property sheet for an ORiNOCO USB wireless client.

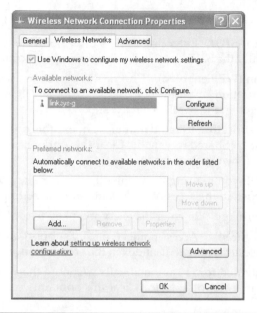

FIGURE 16-7   Use the Wireless Networks tab to choose a wireless network.

Next, click the Wireless Networks tab (Figure 16-7). If your access point is configured to broadcast its SSID, the SSID should show up in the Available Networks list. Click on the SSID and click Configure to open the Wireless Network Properties dialog box shown in Figure 16-8.

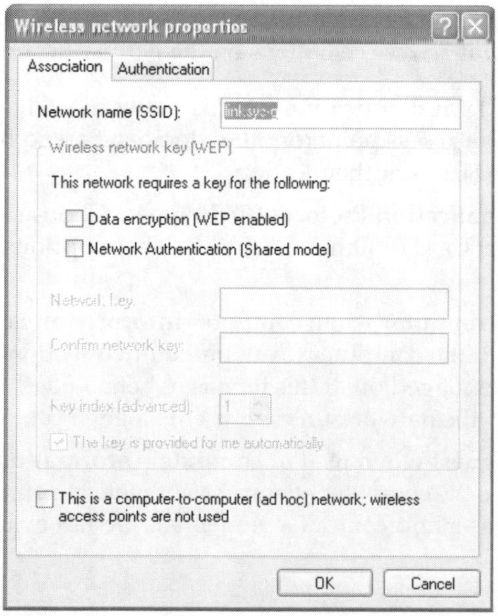

FIGURE 16-8   Configure the wireless connection from the Wireless network properties dialog box.

The following list explains the options on the Wireless network properties dialog box:

- **Network name (SSID)**   Enter the wireless LAN's SSID here. If you're using an access point, enter the SSID specified in the access point configuration.

- **Data encryption (WEP enabled)**   Choose this option to use WEP. You must either specify the encryption key yourself in the Network key field or use an encryption key already stored in the wireless device.

- **Network Authentication (Shared mode)**   Choose this option if you've configured the access point for Shared Key mode. Clear this option if you've configured the access point for Open System mode.

- **Network key**   If you're using WEP, enter the network key here. This must be the same key specified in the access point's configuration settings.

- **Confirm network key**   Re-enter the encryption key to confirm it.

- **Key index (advanced).**   Access points typically support more than one key. Specify which key to use according to its index in the access point configuration.

- **This key is provided for me automatically**   Choose this option if the key is already stored in the wireless access device. Clear this option if you will be entering the key yourself.

- **This is a computer-to-computer (ad hoc) network; wireless access points are not used**   Choose this option if you are configuring an ad hoc wireless network without an access point. All devices in the network must be assigned the same SSID.

Configuring Authentication

If you enable WEP for the wireless LAN, you can also configure authentication properties if required by the WLAN. To do so, choose the Data encryption (WEP-enabled) option on the Association tab, and then click the Authentication tab (Figure 16-9).

The following list summarizes the options on the Authentication tab:

- **Enable IEEE 802.1x authentication for this network**   Choose this option to enable authentication. The access point (or other devices if an ad hoc network) must be configured to use 802.1x authentication.

- **Extensible Authentication Protocol (EAP) type**   Choose between Protected EAP (PEAP) and Smart Card or Other Certificate. These options are explained later in this section.

- **Authenticate as computer when computer information is available**   Choose this option if you want the computer to attempt authentication on the network even when a user is not logged on. If this item is not enabled, the computer will not be able to connect to the network unless a user is logged on.

- **Authenticate as guest when user or computer information is unavailable**   Choose this option to have the computer attempt to authenticate on the wireless LAN (WLAN) as a guest when user and computer credentials are not available.

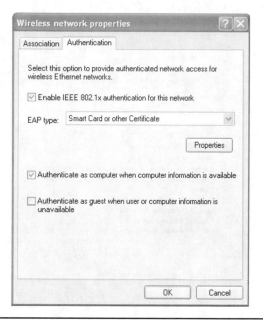

Figure 16-9   Use the Authentication tab if your wireless network will use 802.1x authentication.

To choose and configure an authentication type, choose Smart Card or Other Certificate or Protected EAP (PEAP) from the EAP type drop-down list. Then, click Properties to configure properties for the selected type. Figure 16-10 shows the Smart Card or Other Certificate Properties dialog box. Figure 16-11 shows the Protected EAP Properties dialog box.

Following is a summary of the available options in both dialog boxes:

- **When connecting**   Use the options in this group to choose between a smart card and a certificate on your local computer as the source for authentication credentials that are passed to the remote device.

- **Validate server certificate**   Choose this option to have Windows XP verify that the certificate presented by the remote server is valid and has not expired.

- **Connect to these servers**   Use this option to restrict connections to servers in a specific domain. For example, enter your domain here if you have a Certification Authority (CA) server running in your network and want to restrict wireless clients to validating certificates only within your network.

- **Trusted Root Certification Authorities**   Choose the trusted root CAs that you want Windows XP to check for certificate validity.

- **View Certificate**   Select a certificate and click this button to view the certificate's properties.

PART IV

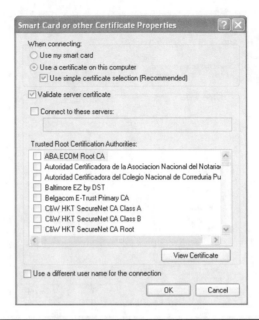

FIGURE 16-10   Use the Smart Card or Other Certificate Properties dialog box to configure a smart card or other certificate-based authentication.

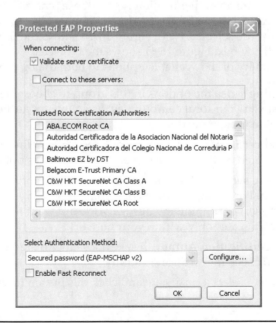

FIGURE 16-11   Use Protected EAP Properties dialog box to configure PEAP.

- **Use a different name for the connection**   Choose this option if the user credentials in the smart card or certificate are different from your credentials in the remote domain in which you are logging on.

- **Select Authentication Method**.   If you're using PEAP, select the authentication method required by the remote device.

- **Enable Fast Reconnect**   Fast Reconnect enables roaming users to maintain network connectivity when traveling between different wireless access points on the same network. Each wireless access point must be configured as a client of the same RADIUS server, and both the wireless client and the RADIUS server must have fast reconnect enabled.

Testing

The steps for testing a wireless LAN are essentially the same as those for testing a wired LAN, which are covered earlier in this chapter in the section, "Testing." If you can't get a computer to see the WLAN, verify that you have the correct SSID, WEP settings, and other settings to
match the access point (infrastructure) or other computers (ad hoc). Also, verify that you have good signal strength. Double-click the wireless connection in the Network Connections folder to view its status, including its signal strength (Figure 16-12).

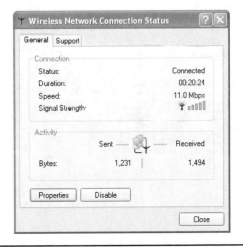

FIGURE 6-12   A WLAN's status dialog box indicates signal strength.

Understanding Wireless Provisioning Services and Other Wireless Changes in SP2

Chapter 5 introduced Wireless Provisioning Services (WPS). WPS combined new features in Windows Server 2003 Service Pack 1 with new features in Windows XP SP2 to simplify the client's connection to wireless hotspots. When a client comes in the range of a WPS network, Windows XP connects to the hotspot as a guest. However, the gateway blocks the client from getting on the Internet because he is not yet authenticated.

Next, the client downloads provisioning information from the server using XML, and signup files are transferred to the client. At this point, the Wireless Internet Service Provider (WISP) wizard runs to determine how the user will be given access. WISP supports one-time pay-per-use and various subscription models that can be integrated into the wizard. For example, you might purchase a one-time connection at a coffee shop and receive an access code (Figure 16-13), which you enter in the wizard to gain access to the Internet through the coffee shop's hotspot.

After the access method is determined and approved, the provisioning server submits a request to the Active Directory for user credentials, which are provided to the client. Windows XP then uses these credentials to sign on to the network. Now that the client is authenticated, the gateway gives him access to the network (typically, the Internet) as shown in Figure 16-14.

FIGURE 6-13   In this wizard example, the client enters a code for prepaid access.

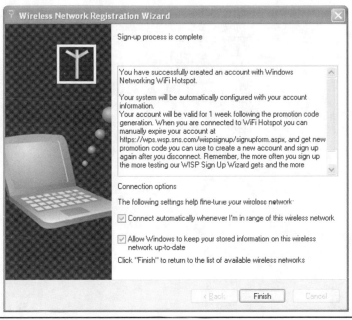

FIGURE 6-14   The wizard has completed and the client now has wireless Internet access.

Wireless Priority Service (WPS) is integrated into Windows XP's wireless client settings. Figure 16-15 shows the new Wireless Network Connection Folder, which replaces the Available Networks section on the Wireless Networks tab of the connection's properties (Figure 16-16). The Wireless Network Connection folder lists available wireless networks and enables you to select a network and connect to it. Links in the left pane provide access to wireless Help topics, additional wireless settings, and the Wireless Network Setup Wizard (explained in the next section, "Using the Wireless Network Setup Wizard (SP2)").

Windows XP SP2 also adds a new tab to the wireless network's properties. Figure 16-17 shows the Connection tab, which enables you to specify that your computer will connect to the network automatically whenever it is in range.

The changes in wireless networking in SP2 apply to private wireless networks such as your home network, as well as public hotspots such as those at the mall, coffee shop, and similar locations. There are not separate interfaces for each one, which offers the advantage of simplifying wireless access for users.

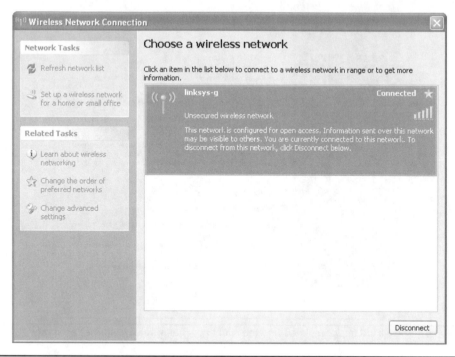

FIGURE 6-15 Use the new Wireless Network Connection folder in SP2 to view wireless networks.

FIGURE 16-16 In SP2, the Wireless Networks tab changes slightly.

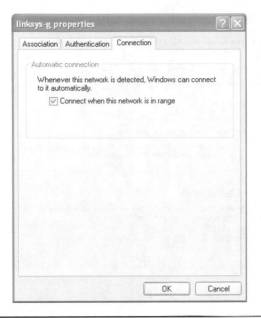

FIGURE 16-17   Use the Connection tab to specify that Windows XP should connect to the wireless network whenever it is in range.

Using the Wireless Network Setup Wizard (SP2)

Another new feature in Windows XP SP2 for wireless networking is the Wireless Network Setup Wizard (Figure 16-18). To start the wizard, double-click the wireless connection icon in the tray and click View Wireless Networks on the General tab of the connection properties, and then click the link Set up a wireless network for a home or small office. Or, open My Network Places from the Start menu and click the same link in the Network Tasks pane.

This wizard is designed to simplify setup and configuration of a wireless network by prompting you for common settings and storing those settings on a removable device for transfer to other computers on the network (Figure 16-19).

TIP   *Although the wizard asks for a USB flash drive, you can also use a floppy drive to transfer settings. Windows XP doesn't support autoplay for floppy drives as it does for USB flash drives, however, so you'll have to start the wizard manually.*

The final page of the wizard gives you the opportunity to print the settings you've configured for the network so you can transfer them to computers without flash or floppy drives. The final page also displays the computers that you have configured for the network and gives you an option to remove the configuration data from the flash drive. If you will need to configure additional devices in the future, you can leave the data on the drive. However, you should store the flash drive (or floppy disk) in a safe location because it contains security settings and other information that would enable someone to easily connect to your wireless network. If you do delete the information from the drive, run the wizard again and choose the option Add new computers or devices to the <name> network, where <name> is the network's SSID (Figure 16-20).

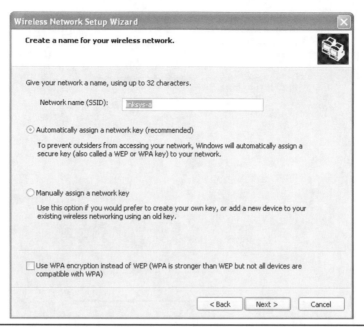

FIGURE 16-18 The Wireless Network Setup Wizard prompts for the SSID and other wireless network properties.

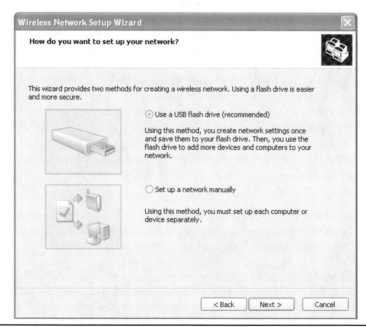

FIGURE 16-19 The wizard copies the settings to a USB or floppy disk for transfer to other computers and devices.

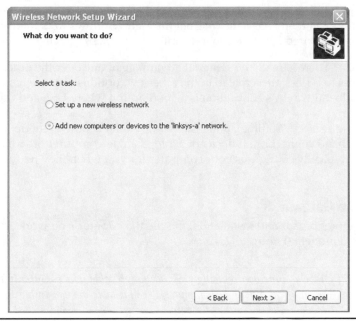

FIGURE 16-20   You can run the wizard again to re-create the transfer data.

Installing a Broadband Internet Connection

Broadband Internet access provides always-on, high-speed Internet access, generally as much as five to ten times as fast as a fast dial-up connection. Although broadband Internet connections have been available for some time, there are still a lot of dial-up users who have yet to make the switch. This section offers a quick overview of broadband options and explains how to configure a small Windows XP network for broadband.

Broadband Connection Options

Commonly available broadband connections fall into three categories:

- **Digital Subscriber Line (DSL)**   DSL piggybacks an Internet connection on your phone line. The phone company (or you) installs a DSL modem that connects to your phone line. A filter is required to connect the phone to the line, and the filter is built into the modem. You can also get small filters for other phone jacks on the same line. Other computers can access the Internet through a wired or wireless LAN if you install a router on the network.

- **Cable**   Cable broadband piggybacks Internet access on your cable TV line. The cable company installs a cable modem that splits the Internet and cable TV signals. Other computers can access the Internet connection through a wired or wireless LAN if you install a router on the network. Some ISPs offer network setup and configuration services, also.

- **Wireless**   In some areas, high-speed wireless Internet access is available. Typically, the provider installs an external antenna outside your building, and the antenna runs to a wireless network transceiver installed in one of your computers. Other computers can then access the Internet through Windows XP's Internet Connection Sharing on a wired LAN (or separate, internal wireless LAN).

Which is best? There is really no clear cut advantage of one over the other, although we consider wireless to be less attractive than the other two options because it's less secure. Even so, a broadband wireless connection is a good option where DSL and cable access are not yet available.

The following section, "Setting Up the Gateway," explains how to set up a small network to share a broadband connection. It does not explore single-computer broadband scenarios because the ISP typically configures your computer for you when they perform the modem installation.

Setting Up the Gateway

In a single-computer broadband installation, the client computer's network adapter connects to the broadband modem (Figure 16-21).

Note   *In this section we assume you're using DSL, although cable uses essentially the same configuration—the only real difference is the presence of a cable modem rather than a DSL modem. Past the modem, the network is the same.*

When you want to add more computers to the network to share the connection, you'll need to add a router. The sits between the broadband modem and the rest of the network and routes traffic between them. Some broadband modems include a built-in router; others require the addition of an external router. Figure 16-22 illustrates a typical wired LAN sharing a broadband connection. The router serves as the *gateway* for the network to the Internet.

Every device on the Internet must have a unique IP address. In most cases, your ISP will assign a single IP address to your broadband connection. Some ISPs provide a static address, while others use dynamic addressing. If your ISP has assigned a static address, you must configure the router's external (WAN) address to use that address, along with the subnet mask the ISP has given you. If the ISP uses dynamic addressing, you must configure your router's WAN address to use the same method of dynamic addressing required by your ISP.

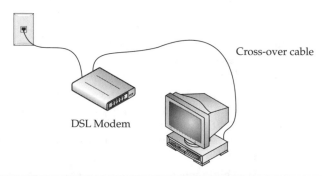

Cross-over cable

DSL Modem

Figure 16-21   This is a typical single-computer broadband configuration.

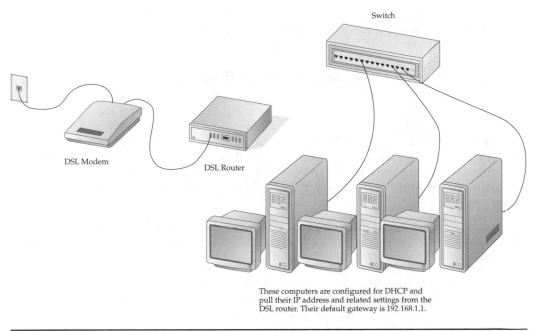

These computers are configured for DHCP and
pull their IP address and related settings from the
DSL router. Their default gateway is 192.168.1.1.

FIGURE 16-22   This small wired LAN shares a broadband connection.

NOTE   *Often, static addressing is used for business customers and dynamic addresses are used
for home users. However, many ISPs offer static IP addresses as an option for home users.*

TIP   *Your router will have a default LAN address, probably in the 192.168.0.0/24 or 192.168.1.0/24 subnet.
This subnet uses a subnet mask of 255.255.255.0. Check the router documentation to determine the
default address and subnet mask for your router and specific steps for configuring its settings.*

TIP   *The WAN address assigned to your router might not be a public, routable address. As Figure
16-23 illustrates, the ISP could be using a private, nonroutable subnet for all of its broadband
users. However, your router will still have a public IP address assigned to it upstream, whether
it's static or dynamic.*

Now that the router is configured, it's time to connect the computers to the router. Most
small network broadband routers include a built-in switch, typically with five ports—one
WAN connection for the broadband modem and four LAN connections for computers.

TIP   *If your router includes a four-port switch but you need to connect more than four computers
on your LAN, you can chain another switch to the router. When two switches are connected, the
connecting port for one of the devices must be set to uplink mode. Check the switch to see if it
supports automatic link detection to switch one of its ports to uplink mode or includes a button
or switch that sets one of the ports in uplink mode. If neither device supports uplink, use a cross-
over cable between the router and the additional switch. An alternative is to purchase a switch
with enough ports to accommodate all of the computers on the LAN.*

Now, connecting your computers to the Internet is as easy as connecting their LAN adapters to the switch. The following section, "Configuring Your Computer and Network for Broadband Access," explains how to configure the computers' network settings.

Configuring Your Computer and Network for Broadband Access

When the computers are connected to the switch, your network is almost ready to go. You just need to assign network settings to your computers. If the router is configured to support dynamic addressing through DHCP, the computers will take their addresses automatically because Windows XP's default configuration is to use DHCP for address assignment. Make sure each computer is configured for DHCP, boot the computer, and you should be surfing away. If you can't surf the Internet, make sure you have assigned the gateway address in the router's settings. The gateway address should be the LAN address of the router.

NOTE *In this section we assume your computers contain Ethernet NICs. See the section, "Using Wireless and Wired Networks Together," later in this chapter, for wireless options.*

If you choose to disable dynamic addressing in the router, you must assign a unique static IP address to each computer on the LAN. Specify an IP address and corresponding subnet mask in the same subnet as the router's LAN address.

TIP *The main scenario to use static addressing for client computers is when the computer will host a Web Service (such as a Web server) or you are running a networked game that requires port-mapping at the router. Otherwise, dynamic addressing is much easier to set up and manage. Keep in mind that you can mix static and dynamic addressing on the LAN. When you configure the router's DHCP settings, leave a range of addresses unassigned, making them available for static addressing for devices as needed.*

One final step you should take is to protect your network with a firewall. Most broadband routers include a rudimentary built-in firewall. You can supplement these firewalls with a separate hardware firewall (Figure 16-23) and/or use Windows Firewall at each computer. See the "Using a Firewall" section in Chapter 12 for details.

TIP *If you have more than one firewall in place on the network and are having problems getting certain traffic through to the network, keep in mind that the firewalls don't coordinate with one another in any way. You might have opened a port in the external firewall but have forgotten to open the port in the router's built-in firewall or in Windows Firewall.*

Using Wireless and Wired Networks Together

My home network combines a wireless LAN and a wired LAN, all sharing a single DSL Internet connection. Figure 16-24 illustrates my network.

Combining a wireless and wired LAN certainly has its advantages. I enjoy the benefit of speed for large file transfers on the wired computers and the convenience of wireless access for my notebooks and other wireless devices.

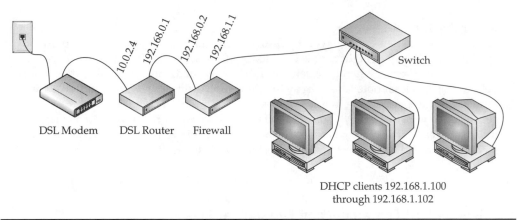

FIGURE 16-23   Here, a hardware firewall is used to protect the network.

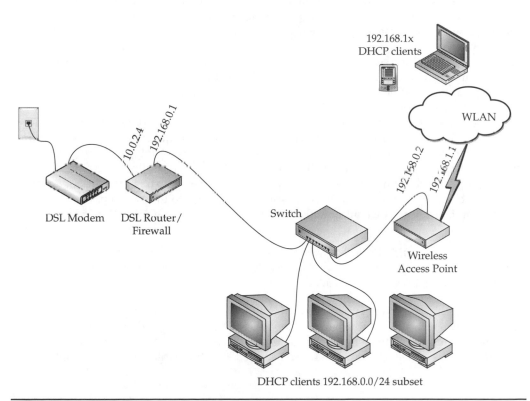

FIGURE 16-24   This network combines wireless and wired segments that share a broadband connection.

> **Fooling My Firewall**
> I also get around one limitation of my firewall by installing a wireless access point on my LAN. I've licensed eight connections for the firewall, and it blocks computers from accessing the Internet when the license number is reached. However, all of the devices behind the wireless router are seen by the firewall as a single IP address because the wireless router performs network Address Translation (NAT). The wireless router and seven computers on the LAN max out the firewall license, but we can add as many other devices to the wireless segment as needed. The wireless router includes a built-in switch, so I could connect several hundred computers to it, if needed. I suspect I won't do that, however.

Configuring Port Forwarding and Firewall Settings Between Wired and Wireless Segments

If your wireless segment will contain computers that will host Web services or you want to play network games on wireless computers, you must configure the access point's router to perform port forwarding. If you simply want to be able to share files easily between the wired and wireless segments, you must open some ports in the access point to allow that traffic through.

In the case of a Web service or game, map the required incoming port to the IP address of the computer on the wireless segment that will host the service or game (Figure 16-25 shows an example). When traffic comes in destined for a target port, the router forwards the traffic to the IP address specified in the port map.

If your access point supports it, you can also use *port triggering* to dynamically open ports in the access point's firewall. With port triggering, outbound traffic on a specific port or range of ports *triggers* the access point to open certain ports for inbound traffic, allowing that traffic to flow to the originating client computer. When you configure port triggering, you specify the outbound and inbound ports, which do not have to be the same. For example, outbound traffic on ports 5900–5910 could trigger the access point to open ports 5800–5810. It's all a matter of how you configure the trigger settings (Figure 16-26).

NOTE *The access point holds the triggered ports open for a specific period of time and then closes them again. Check your access point's documentation or vendor support to determine the hold-open period and whether you can adjust it.*

One problem you might run into is the inability to perform two-way file and printer sharing between the wired and wireless segments. The services will likely work from the wireless segment to the wired segment, but not vice versa because the access point's firewall will block the traffic coming from the wired segment. Unless you can disable the

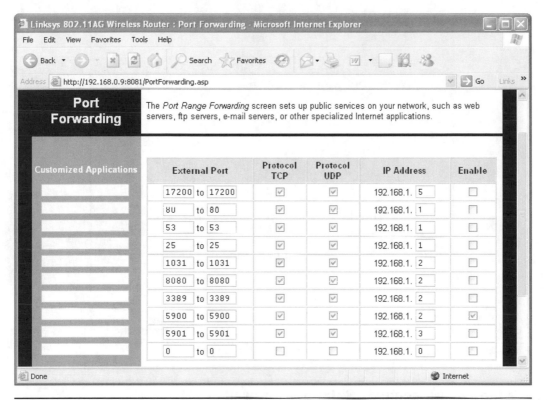

FIGURE 16-25   Use port forwarding to statically map an incoming port to an IP address behind the access point.

access point's firewall, there is little you can do to make file and printer sharing work from the wired segment to the wireless segment. Check with the vendor to determine if you can disable the access point's firewall and how to do so if you need to enable file and printer sharing into the wireless segment.

TIP *If you only need to access a single computer on the wireless LAN for file and printer sharing, see if your access point provides a demilitarized zone (DMZ) feature. With DMZ enabled, the access point will allow all traffic through to a specific IP address. Or, your access point might include a DMZ port to which you can connect the computer you need to access from the wired segment.*

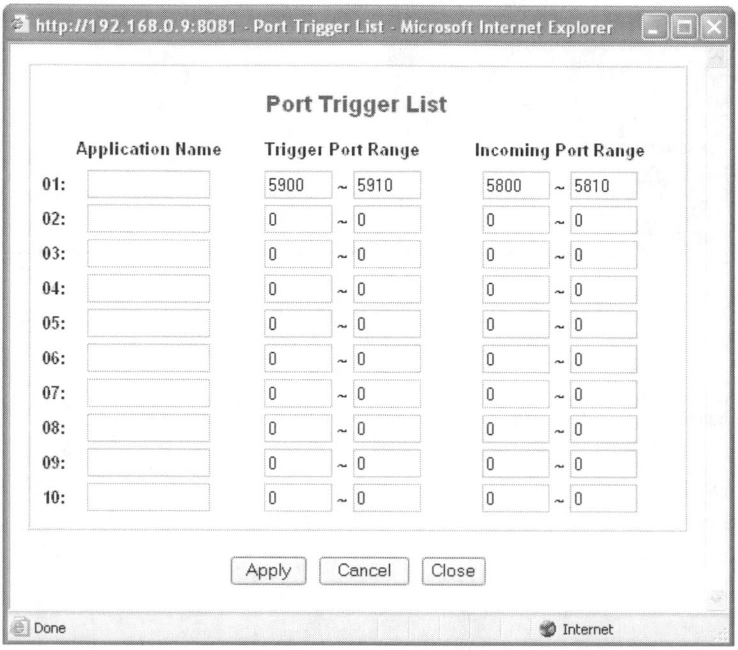

FIGURE 16-26   You can use port triggering to dynamically open ports.

Using Windows Messenger Behind a Firewall

Some applications have special requirements or raise certain issues for networking. This next section, "Windows Messenger and MSN Messenger," explores some of the more common network-related applications and services.

Windows Messenger and MSN Messenger

Windows Messenger ships with Windows XP and provides chat, desktop conferencing, application sharing, messaging to mobile devices, and the capability to transfer files between computers. MSN Messenger offers much the same set of features, but is targeted at the consumer market. MSN Messenger adds the capability to play games with other MSN Messenger users, create your own emoticons, keep a log of past instant messaging (IM) sessions, make Internet-based phone calls, and a handful of other features. The "Messenger and Firewalls" section address common problems with Messenger that relate to networking and security.

Messenger and Firewalls

Like almost all network applications, Messenger uses specific ports for certain tasks. If you are running Messenger behind a firewall, you need to consider how the firewall is configured if you want to use all of Messenger's features.

When you run Windows Messenger for the first time and sign in using your .NET Passport, Windows XP with SP2 automatically adds Windows Messenger to the Exceptions list in Windows Firewall, enabling the application to get past the firewall. However, if you have an upstream firewall, you also need to open certain ports in the firewall to support Windows Messenger. Table 16-3 lists port requirements for Windows Messenger.

TIP   *If you remove Windows Messenger from the Exceptions list, you will have to restore it to the list manually or through group policy in order for Windows Messenger to work with Windows Firewall.*

Feature	Port(s)	Notes
File transfer	6891–6900	Used sequentially starting at 6891; number of ports open limits the number of file transfer sessions
Voice-to-phone	UDP 2001–2120, 6801, 6901	See Microsoft Knowledgebase Article 324214
Voice computer-to-computer	TCP/UDP 6901	See Microsoft Knowledgebase Article 324214
Messaging	TCP 1863	See Microsoft Knowledgebase Article 324214

TABLE 16-3   Windows Messenger Port Assignments

If your firewall is not UPnP-compatible, Windows Messenger will not work properly for audio and video streams. To make audio visual (AV) work with these non-UPnP firewalls, you must open ports 5004 through 65535, which is a major security risk. Check with your firewall vendor to determine if it can be upgraded to UPnP compatibility.

TIP   *See http://www.microsoft.com/technet/prodtechnol/winxppro/deploy/nwlfw.mspx for more information on Windows Messenger and firewall configuration.*

Disabling Messenger

Although it is certainly a useful application, not everyone has a need for Windows Messenger. In fact, many companies prefer to disable it to prevent users from spending time chatting with others or potentially exposing the network and internal data to outsiders through its application sharing and file transfer features.

To prevent Windows Messenger from running on Windows XP Professional systems with group policy, enable the policy Computer Configuration\Administrative Templates\Windows Components\Windows Messenger\Do not allow Windows Messenger to run. For either Windows XP Home Edition or Professional, you can use a registry change to disable Windows Messenger. Open Registry Editor, create the DWORD value HKEY_LOCAL_MACHINE\ Software\Policies\Microsoft\Messenger\Client\PreventRun, and set its value to 1.

TIP   *This registry change works for Windows Messenger 4.5 or later.*

Using Windows XP Remote Access Options

In this chapter you'll find the answers to the following questions:

- How does remote access networking differ from local area networking?
- What are the most popular methods of connecting to a network from a remote location?
- Are there differences in remote access functionality between the Windows XP Home and Professional editions?
- What are the advantages of a virtual private networking (VPN) connection over a dial-up connection?
- How do I create and configure a dialup connection in Windows XP?
- How can I allow others to dial into my Windows XP computer and access its resources?
- What VPN protocols does Windows XP support and what are the differences between them?
- How do I create and configure a VPN connection from my XP computer to my company's network?
- Can I use a smart card or token to authenticate to my company's VPN server?
- Is the data I send over a VPN connection encrypted by default?
- Can I set up my Windows XP computer to accept incoming VPN connections?
- How do I use the Remote Assistance feature to ask a more experienced user for help?
- How do I provide help to a less experienced user via Remote Assistance?
- How does the Remote Desktop feature in Windows XP Professional differ from Remote Assistance?
- How do I enable or disable Remote Desktop?
- What's the difference between Remote Desktop and Windows Terminal Services?

- How do I control which users can connect to my computer using Remote Desktop?
- How can I use Windows 9x, NT, and 2000 computers to connect to my Windows XP computer via Remote Desktop?
- What third-party programs can I use to provide the same functionality as Remote Desktop for Windows 9x, NT, and 2000 computers?
- What are some of the common troubleshooting issues that involve Remote Assistance and Remote Desktop, and how can I resolve them?

The earliest Windows operating systems (through Windows 3.1) were designed for standalone systems. At that time, the need for computers to communicate with one another was less obvious and most PCs were not networked. Then local area networks (LANs) became common, and in the 90s, the availability of low-cost Internet access for businesses and individuals changed computing forever. Each subsequent version of Windows reflected these changes. Windows for Workgroups 3.11 added limited local networking support, and Windows 95 introduced the first easily configured dial-up networking and Transmission Control Protocol/Internet Protocol (TCP/IP) stack. Windows 2000 included advanced networking features such as IP Security (IPSec) and Layer Two Tunneling Protocol (L2TP). Today, connectivity is the name of the game, and Windows XP is even more network-friendly than its recent predecessors, with full support and a user-friendly configuration for both local and remote access networking.

Whereas local area networking involves connecting computers in close physical proximity (such as within a building or a campus), remote access networking involves connecting one computer to another that is geographically distant. This was traditionally accomplished over regular analog phone lines, special integrated services digital network (ISDN) (digital) phone lines, or dedicated leased lines (T-carriers) provided by the telephone company. Remote networking can also be done over cable TV (CATV) cable or even via the electric company's power lines.

A remote access connection can be made directly, by dialing into (or having a dedicated line run to) a server whose resources you want to access, or you can connect over a public network (the Internet) to which both the client and the distant server are connected.

In this chapter, we look at the remote access options offered by the various "flavors" of Windows XP. Specifically, we show you how to use the following technologies to connect your XP system to remote computers or allow remote computers to connect to your XP computer:

- Dial-up networking
- Virtual private networking (VPN)
- Remote Assistance
- Remote Desktop

When it comes to remote access networking, all "flavors" of Windows XP are not created equal. Remote Desktop server functionality is supported by XP Pro and its supersets (Tablet PC Edition and Media Center Edition), but not by XP Home Edition. Home Edition can, however, be used as a Remote Desktop client. Both Home Edition and the Pro variants support Remote Assistance, VPN, and dial-up networking. In a nutshell, XP Pro is designed with business and power users in mind. With XP Pro and its supersets, you can enjoy full domain membership functionality and advanced remote connectivity, whereas XP Home is limited to more common consumer-level functionality.

The first step in using XP's remote access features is to get your computer "talking" to another computer at another location. There are two ways to do this: via a dial-up connection or through a virtual private network link that takes advantage of your Internet connection.

NOTE *A VPN connection requires that both the VPN client and the VPN server be connected to the Internet. The Internet connection can be through a dial-up account, digital subscriber line (DSL), cable, the local area network's (LAN's) T-1 connection, or through new technologies (currently in testing stages) such as power line Internet access.*

After you connect your computer to the remote system, it's time for the fun part. You can use technologies such as Remote Assistance and Remote Desktop to obtain technical help, remotely manage and control the desktop of the other computer, or run applications from a terminal server.

First, let's start with the basics: how to use Windows XP's dial-up networking features to access a remote server or allow remote systems to access your computer.

NOTE *When you establish a remote access connection to another computer or network, it's like being connected over a wired network except that the connection speed is usually slower. This means when you connect to your company network via dial-up or VPN, you can endanger the entire network if you don't take security measures such as having a personal firewall installed and updating your anti-virus definitions regularly.*

Using Windows XP Dial-up Networking

The original—and still the most common—way to access a remote computer is by using a modem connected to an analog telephone line (sometimes called Plain Old Telephone Service, or POTS) to dial up a similarly modem-equipped computer that's configured to be a dialup server. The modem gets its name from the fact that it *mo*dulates and *dem*odulates the signals so that digital data from a computer can travel across the analog line and then be converted back to a digital format for the computer at the other end of the "conversation."

As with all forms of networking, there are two components to a connection: the client and the server. (Even in a so-called *peer-to-peer* network, during any given communications session one peer—the one accessing the other computer's resources—acts as a client, and the computer allowing its resources to be accessed acts as the server.)

Windows XP computers can be configured to participate in dial-up networking in either of these two ways: as a dial-up client or as a dial-up server.

Using Windows XP as a Dial-up Client

Dial-up connections require the use of a link layer protocol by which the two modem-equipped computers establish communications. This is generally the Point-to-Point Protocol (PPP), although it is also possible to use the older, slower and less functional Serial Line Internet Protocol (SLIP).

Back in the "olden days" of computing, installing a modem and configuring a computer to dial into an ISP or a remote access server on the company LAN could be a daunting task that required installing PPP software called Trumpet Winsock and configuring it via an initialization (INI) file. With Windows XP, it's a painless procedure that uses a wizard to walk you through the steps.

Creating a Dial-up Connection

Here's how to create a new dial-up connection from your XP computer to a remote access server at another location:

1. In Control Panel (Classic View), double-click the Network Connections applet (or alternatively, double-click My Network Places on the desktop or Start menu and select View network connections under Network Tasks in the left pane).

NOTE *In all of the step-by-step instructions in this chapter, we assume you have Control Panel set to display in Classic View. To switch from the default Windows XP Category View, click Switch to Classic View in the top left pane when you open Control Panel.*

2. Under Network Tasks, click Create a new connection. This will invoke the New Connection Wizard. Click Next on the first page of the wizard.

3. On the Network Connection Type page (Figure 17-1), select the type of dial-up connection you want to make. Select Connect to the Internet if you want to dial into an ISP. Select Connect to the network at my workplace if you want to dial directly into a remote access server on a company LAN, at a friend's house or (using your portable XP computer, for example) your own dial-up server at home. Click Next.

4. If you select to connect to the Internet, on the next page you'll be given the option to choose from a list of ISPs, set up the connection manually, or use a CD provided by your ISP. If you select to connect to the network at your workplace, you'll be given the options to create a dial-up or a VPN connection. For this example, we'll assume that you are connecting to a dial-up server on your company LAN, and that you've chosen to create a dial-up connection rather than a VPN. Click Next.

5. The next page of the wizard asks you to type a name for the connection (for example, the name of the company's dial-up server or simply the company's name—as shown in Figure 17-2). Do so, and click Next.

6. On the next page, you're asked to enter the telephone number of the dial-up server. You might need to preface the number with a 1 and/or the area code. Enter the number and click Next.

7. The next page of the wizard asks you to select whether the connection will be available for the use of anyone who logs onto the computer, or only for the account that is logged on as you are creating the connection. Make your selection and click Next.

8. The final page of the wizard completes the process and allows you to add a shortcut to the connection on your desktop by checking a checkbox. Clicking Finish creates the connection and saves it in the Network Connections folder.

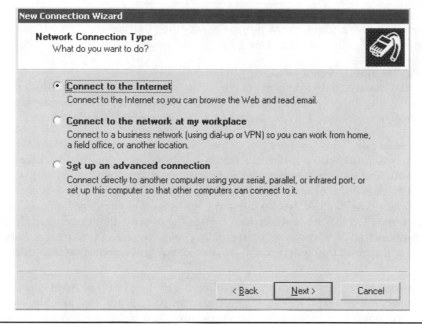

FIGURE 17-1   You can make a dial-up connection to an ISP or to any remote access server.

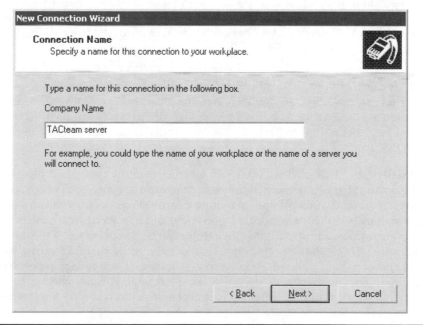

FIGURE 17-2   Enter a name to identify the dial-up connection.

NOTE *You must have a modem installed in your computer to use a dial-up connection. To install a modem, attach the hardware and then go to Control Panel | Phone and Modem Options to set up your dialing location and install the drivers for the modem.*

Configuring the Dial-up Connection

After you have created a dial-up connection, you can set configuration options by right clicking the connection icon in the Network Connections folder or on your desktop and selecting Properties. Then configure the connection's properties as follows:

- **General tab** This is where you can select and configure the modem to use for the connection (including setting the maximum speed, and enabling hardware flow control and modem error control and/or modem compression), enable or disable the modem speaker, and select to show a terminal window if the server you are dialing (usually a UNIX based server) requires you to enter credentials via the terminal). On this tab, you can also change the phone number or enter alternate numbers to dial, and choose to use dialing rules. By default, an icon is displayed in the notification tray when you're connected, but you can disable this functionality here.

- **Options tab** Here you can set the following dialing options: display progress while connecting; prompt for name, password, certificate, etc.; include Windows logon domain, and prompt for phone number. You can also select the number of times Windows will attempt to redial if a connection isn't made, the amount of time between redial attempts (in seconds or minutes), and whether you want the connection to hang up after a specified amount of idle time (from 1 minute to 24 hours). You can also select to automatically redial if the line is dropped. Should you be using an X.25 network, you can configure X.25 properties by clicking the X.25 button on this tab.

NOTE *X.25 is a networking technology whereby users dial into a Packet Assembler/Disassembler (PAD) or use special X.25 cards installed in their computers to bypass the regular telephone network and use the X.25 network. You'll need to know the name of the X.25 network you'll be using and the X.121 address for the server you want to dial. Your X.25 network provider can give you this information.*

- **Security tab** This is where you select whether to allow unsecured passwords (the default) for validating your identity, to require a secured password, or to use a smart card. If you choose to require a secured password, you can select to automatically use your Windows logon name and password. You can also require data encryption and specify that the connection be disconnected if the data is not encrypted. Using the Settings button, you can configure custom security settings and choose which authentication protocol(s) to use. If you're logging onto a server that requires you to enter credentials via the terminal, you can select to have a terminal window pop up when you connect and you can specify a script to run to complete the logon process.

- **Networking tab** On this tab, you can specify the type of dial-up server you're calling. The default is a PPP server (Windows 95/98/NT4/2000 or 2003). The other choice is a UNIX server using SLIP. Here you can also specify networking services and protocols used by the connection. By default, Microsoft file and printer sharing is turned off, while the Client for Microsoft Networks, TCP/IP, and the quality of service (QoS) packet scheduler are enabled. By clicking the Install button, you can install additional clients, services, and protocols. For example, if you are dialing into a server that uses the IPX/SPX networking protocols, you can install Microsoft's version of Internetwork Packet Exchange/Sequenced Packet Exchange (IPX/SPX), called NWLink. This is also where you can configure the TCP/IP properties for the connection. By default, the computer will attempt to use the Dynamic Host Configuration Protocol (DHCP) to obtain an IP address automatically on the network to which it connects. However, you can set it to use a manually entered address, and you can specify the addresses of Domain Name System (DNS) and Windows Internet Name Service (WINS) name resolution servers to use (for WINS settings, click the Advanced button).

- **Advanced tab**   The Advanced tab allows you to enable the Internet Connection Firewall (ICF) on the connection and to set up Internet Connection Sharing (ICS) so that other computers on your local network can go through your computer to share the connection.

NOTE ICF is the rudimentary "personal firewall" built into Windows XP. A personal firewall is designed to protect a single computer rather than an entire network as a perimeter or "edge" firewall does. It provides basic protection from Internet attacks as a "stateful" firewall that monitors outbound connections and allows inbound connections back through the firewall only if there is a matching outbound connection showing the communication originated with your computer. ICF does not provide more sophisticated firewall features such as application layer filtering (examining the actual content of data to determine if it should be allowed in). For more information about ICF, see Chapter 12, "Windows XP Security."

Using the Dial-up Connection

To connect your computer to the remote access server, double click the icon for the connection in the Control Panel | Network Connections folder or on your desktop. Your modem will dial and complete the "handshake" with the modem connected to the server. You may be prompted to enter a username and password (Figure 17-3).

You can select to save the credential information for your account only, or for anyone using the computer. In this case, the username and password will be entered for you subsequently. The password will not appear in the password box, however. Instead a message will appear saying "To change the saved password, click here."

If you need to change the connection properties (for example, if the server's phone number changes), you can do so by clicking the Properties button at the bottom of the connection dialog box.

Using Windows XP as a Dial-Up Server

Your Windows XP computer can act as a dial-up server, accepting incoming calls from another computer. This can be handy if you want a friend to be able to dial directly into and download files from your machine, or if you want to access your home computer from work or when you're on the road. Again, you need a modem installed and connected to a phone

FIGURE 17-3   Enter a username and password for connecting to the dial-up server.

line. Unlike Windows server operating systems, XP can only accept one incoming dial-up connection at a time.

To set up your dial-up server, you start with the same Network Connection Wizard that you used to configure a dial-up client connection:

1. Click Start | Control Panel | Network Connections to open the Network Connections folder.

2. In the left pane of the Network Connections folder, under Network Tasks, click Create a new connection. This starts the Wizard. On the first page, click Next.

3. On the Network Connection Type page, select Set up an advanced connection. Click Next.

4. On the Advanced Connections Options page, select Accept incoming connections (Figure 17-4). Click Next.

5. On the next page, select the device(s) you want the computer to use to accept incoming connections. Typically, this will be your modem. You can click the Properties button to configure call and data connection preferences and to bring up a terminal window before or after dialing. Click OK in the properties dialog box, then click Next.

6. The next page asks if you want to allow incoming VPN connections. We will discuss setting up your computer as a VPN server in a later section. If you are configuring a dial-up server, select Do not allow virtual private connections. Click Next.

7. On the User Permissions page, you will see a list of user accounts configured on the computer. Check the boxes next to the names of those to whom you want to give

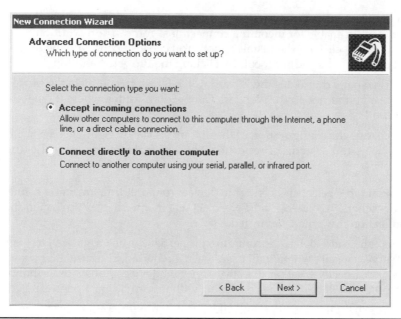

FIGURE 17-4   To set up a dial-up server, select the Accept incoming connections option.

permission to dial into the computer (Figure 17-5). You can configure properties for a user account by clicking the Properties button. After selecting the accounts, click Next.

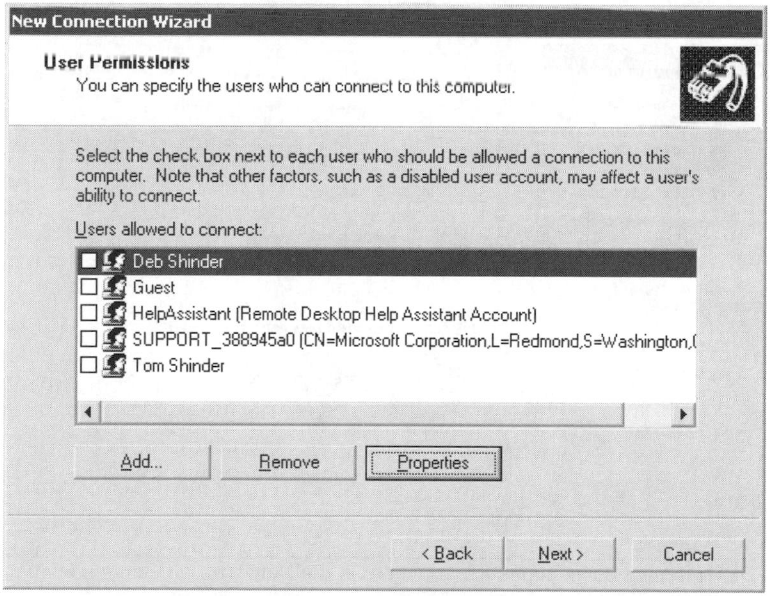

FIGURE 17-5   Select the user accounts of those who will be allowed to dial into the computer.

8. On the Networking Software page, select the networking services and protocols you want to enable for incoming connections. You can add additional services and protocols by clicking the Install button. You can also configure the properties of the installed services and protocols by clicking the Properties button. Click Next.

9. The final page completes the Wizard. Click Finish to complete the process and save the new connection in the Network Connections folder, where it will be displayed (Figure 17-6).

You can change the configuration of the dial-up server by right-clicking the Incoming Connections icon and selecting Properties. You can make changes by clicking the following tabs:

- **General tab**   Select and configure devices for accepting incoming connections. Allow others to connect via VPN. Select whether to display an icon in the notification tray when connected.

- **Users tab**   Add, delete, or configure properties for users allowed to dial into the XP server. Specify whether all users will be required to secure their passwords and data. Specify whether directly connected devices (for example, handheld computers) will be allowed to connect without providing a password.

- **Networking tab**   Install, uninstall, and configure the properties of the networking services and protocols to be used for the connection.

FIGURE 17-6   The Incoming Connections icon appears in the Network Connections folder.

Troubleshooting Dial-Up Remote Access

Creating, configuring, and using dial-up connections in Windows XP is pretty straightforward, but sometimes problems arise. Following are a few common dial-up dilemmas and what to do about them.

Preventing Disconnections Caused by Call Waiting Service

If a call comes in on the line your modem is using for a dial-up connection, you may get disconnected. You can prevent this by disabling call waiting. Here's how:

1. In Control Panel (Classic View), click Phone and Modem Options.

2. On the General tab, select My Location in the Locations list and click the Edit button.

3. Click to check the checkbox labeled To disable call waiting, dial:.

4. Click the arrow on the drop-down box to the right and select the code used by your telephone company (Figure 17-7). (Consult your telephone directory or call the phone company if you don't know which choice to select.)

5. Click the OK button to exit each open dialog box.

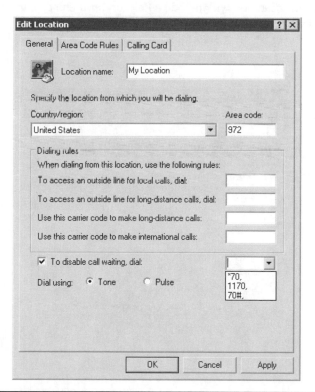

FIGURE 17-7 To disable call waiting, you need to know the code your phone company uses.

Sharing your Computer's Resources as a Dial-up Server

In Windows XP, the server service is called File and Printer Sharing for Microsoft Networks. This service must be installed and enabled in order for dial-up clients to access the resources on your computer. If clients are able to connect but cannot access any resources, check the Networking tab in the Incoming Connections properties to ensure that File and Printer Sharing for Microsoft Networks is checked (Figure 17-8).

Logging Onto Windows Domains

If the server onto which you want to log on with your dial-up connection requires you to enter a logon domain, you will need to perform the following steps before attempting to log on:

1. Double click the connection icon in the Network Connections folder or on your desktop.
2. In the connection dialog box, click the Properties button.
3. Click the Options tab.
4. Check the box labeled Include Windows logon domain   (Figure 17-9).
5. Click OK.
6. Now the connection box will include a field under the username and password fields where you can enter the Windows domain.

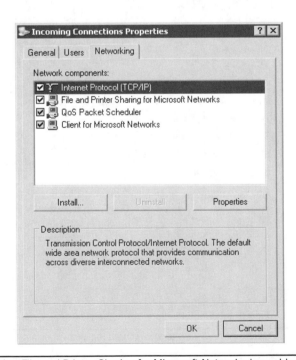

FIGURE 17-8   Ensure that File and Printer Sharing for Microsoft Networks is enabled for your dial-up server.

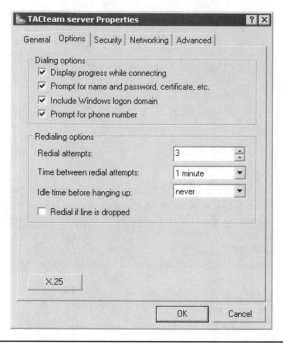

FIGURE 17-9   You can set up the connection to allow the entry of a Windows domain name.

Using Windows XP for VPN

Instead of dialing directly into a server on your company's network, you might be able to connect to the company LAN using a VPN. This will work only if these three things are in place:

- Your computer has a connection to the Internet.
- Your company network has a connection to the Internet.
- There is a server on your company network that is set up as a VPN server.

If you're not within the same calling area as your company's remote access server, connecting via dial-up can cost a lot in long distance charges. By using a VPN, you can dial a local Internet Service Provider (ISP) or use your DSL or cable Internet connection instead of making an expensive long distance call.

Understanding VPN

If your home computer is connected to the Internet and the server you want to access at your workplace is also connected to the Internet, you can use the Internet to establish a connection to that server. This connection is called a *virtual* network. However, the Internet is a public network and you don't want your communications with the company server to be intercepted by others, so you need a means to make your virtual network *private*. VPN technology uses "tunneling" protocols to establish the connection and encryption protocols to ensure the privacy of the communications. Thus, you can communicate over a *virtual private network.*

Configuring a VPN Connection

Windows XP includes two built-in VPN client programs:

- Point-to-Point Tunneling Protocol (PPTP), which uses the Microsoft Point-to-Point Encryption protocol (MPPE) for encryption
- Layer Two Tunneling Protocol (L2TP), which uses the Internet Protocol Security protocol (IPSec) for encryption

The type of VPN you use depends on which type is supported by the VPN server to which you want to connect. L2TP is considered more secure. By default, your XP computer will be configured to automatically determine the VPN type supported by the server.

Configuring a VPN Connection

The New Connection Wizard is used to set up a VPN connection:

1. Open the Network Connections applet in Control Panel and click Create a new connection in the left top pane.
2. Click Next on the first page of the New Connection Wizard.
3. On the next page, select Connect to the network at my workplace. Click Next.
4. On the Network Connection page, select Virtual Private Network connection. Click Next.
5. On the Connection Name page, enter a name in the text field for the VPN server to which you want to connect. Click Next.
6. On the Public Network page, select whether Windows should dial into your ISP before making the VPN connection. If you use a dial-up connection to the Internet, select Automatically dial this connection and choose the ISP dial-up connection from the drop-down list (Figure 17-10). If you have DSL, cable Internet, T-1 through a LAN or another "always-on" connection to the Internet, select Do not dial the initial connection.
7. On the VPN Server Selection page, you must enter the computer name or IP address of the VPN server. Ask your company network administrator for this information.
8. The final page completes the process. You can choose to add a desktop shortcut to the VPN connection by checking the checkbox. Click Finish to save the connection in the Network Connections folder (Figure 17-11).

NOTE *You can create multiple VPN connections to connect to different VPN servers.*

Configuring your VPN Connection

To make configuration changes to your VPN connection, right-click its icon in the Network Connections folder and select Properties. Each tab includes options that you can set.

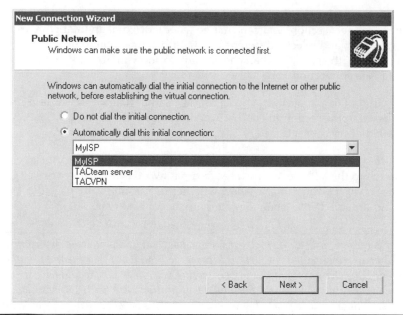

FIGURE 17-10   Tell Windows to dial your ISP before establishing the VPN connection.

FIGURE 17-11   VPN Connections are displayed under the Virtual Private Network section in the Network Connections folder.

General Tab In the top text box, you can change the name or IP address of the VPN server.

In the First connect section, you can change whether to dial an ISP before establishing the VPN connection, and select a different ISP dial-up connection to use.

At the bottom of the page, you can check a box to show an icon in the notification tray when your VPN is connection.

Options Tab Under Dialing options, you can set the same dialing options and redialing options discussed in the section titled "Using Windows XP as a Dial-Up Client," the section on configuring dial-up connections.

Security Tab If you select to use the typical (default) security options, you can choose to identify yourself to the VPN server by a secured password or by using a Smart Card or token such as SecureID. You can also select whether to automatically use your Windows credentials and domain name when logging onto the VPN server.

NOTE *Smart cards are credit-card sized devices that hold a digital certificate that confirms your identity. If your computer has a smart card reader, you can use a smart card for authentication. This decreases the chance of someone impersonating you, since they would have to have physical possession of the card and know the Personal Identification Number (PIN) associated with the smart card in order to log on using your account. This is called two-factor authentication. Smart card authentication support is built into the XP operating system. Another two-factor authentication method is the use of secure tokens; these are proprietary hardware key generators offered by a number of vendors.*

By default, the data you send will be encrypted. If the server does not support encryption, your computer will disconnect. You can uncheck this box to communicate with a server that does not support encryption, although it is not recommended.

If you select Advanced (custom settings), you can configure encryption requirements more granularly from among four options on the Advanced Security Settings subpage:

- **No encryption allowed** Your computer will disconnect if the server requires encryption.

- **Optional encryption** Your computer will use encryption if the server supports it, but if the server does not, the computer will still connect and communicate without encryption.

- **Require encryption** If the server doesn't support encryption, your computer will disconnect.

- **Maximum strength encryption** If the server does not support strong encryption, your computer will disconnect.

You can also choose which authentication protocols to allow and whether to automatically use your Windows logon name, password, and domain for Microsoft authentication protocols (for example, MS-CHAP or MS-CHAP v2).

Back on the Security page, the IPSec Settings button allows you to use a preshared key (a string of characters that functions somewhat like a password) for IPSec if you are unable to use a more secure authentication method such as digital certificates.

Networking Tab   This is where you can set the VPN type (PPTP or L2TP). Select from the top drop-down box (Figure 17-12). The default setting is Automatic, whereby the computer detects the VPN type supported by the server.

You can also install, uninstall, and configure the properties of networking services and protocols such as TCP/IP, IPX/SPX, File and Printer Sharing and the Client for Microsoft Networks, as discussed in the section titled *Using Windows XP as a Dial-Up Client.*

Advanced Tab   As with dial-up connections, the Advanced tab allows you to protect the connection with the built in firewall (called Internet Connection Firewall or ICF in computers without Service Pack 2 installed, and referred to as the Windows Firewall in Service Pack 2 computers) and/or set up Internet Connection Sharing so others on your local network can share the VPN connection.

Using the VPN Connection

Double-click the VPN connection icon in the Network Connections folder to bring up a dialog box like the one used for dial-up connections. Click the Connect button and you will see a progress box as the computer connects to the server and authenticates. The Status column will display "Connected" and the VPN icon will appear in the notification tray. Double clicking it will display the Status box.

In the Status box, the General tab will show the duration of the connection and number of bytes sent and received. The Details tab gives you information about the server and client and the protocols being used for the connection (Figure 17-13).

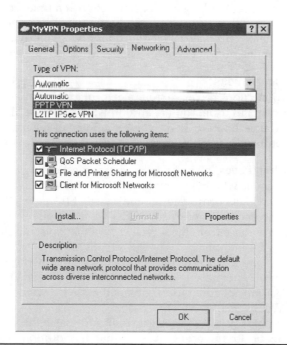

FIGURE 17-12   You can select the VPN type (PPTP or L2TP) or use the Automatic setting.

FIGURE 17-13 The VPN Status box provides information about the connection.

Making your Windows XP Computer a VPN Server

Your Windows XP computer can function as a VPN server. Unlike Windows server operating systems, it can accept only one VPN connection at a time. To configure your computer as a VPN server, follow the same steps discussed in the section on setting up a dial-up server, but on the Wizard page labeled Incoming Virtual Private Network (VPN) Connection, select the option button that says Allow virtual private connections.

Troubleshooting VPN Connections

Problems with VPN connections can arise from many different sources (for example, client configuration, server configuration, routers and firewalls in between, or the Internet connection itself), so troubleshooting can be complex. Some of the most common problems include connectivity, authentication, and firewall issues.

Troubleshooting Connectivity Issues   The first step in troubleshooting a VPN connection that doesn't work is to determine whether you have TCP/IP connectivity between the VPN client and server. Use the PING command to send a packet from the client machine to the server's IP address. If a response is returned, TCP/IP connectivity is intact.

If you cannot get a response from the server, ensure that both the client and server have working connections to the Internet.

If your VPN client is on a local network behind a device that performs Network Address Translation (NAT), you may not be able to establish an L2TP/IPSec VPN connection. This is because IPSec and NAT are not compatible, unless the NAT device supports a newer technology called NAT Traversal (NAT-T).

If you entered the VPN server's name (instead of IP address) in the VPN client configuration setup, you might be unable to connect because of a name resolution problem. Try entering the IP address instead to determine if this is the case.

You can't establish a VPN connection unless the server and client are both configured to use at least one common networking protocol (for example, TCP/IP or IPX/SPX). Check the connection's properties to ensure that the client is using the same protocol(s) as the server.

Remember that Windows XP can only accept one incoming connection. If the XP VPN server already has a VPN connection active, you won't be able to establish another.

Troubleshooting Authentication Issues   *Authentication* is the process of identifying a user or computer to determine whether he/she/it is authorized to connect. First, the client and server must both support the same authentication protocol(s). This is different from the networking protocols discussed in the previous section. If the progress box shows your computer connecting to the VPN server, but the server disconnects during the "Authenticating" stage, you have an authentication problem.

By default, XP VPN connections allow the use of the Microsoft Challenge-Handshake Authentication Protocol (MS-CHAP), both the original version and version 2. If the VPN server doesn't support MS-CHAP, you may have to enable a different authentication protocol such as the Password Authentication Protocol (PAP) or Shiva PAP (SPAP). Use the Advanced Security Settings, accessible from the Security tab of the VPN connection's Properties box, to enable and disable authentication protocols.

Next, the data encryption requirements must be compatible. If the client is set to require encryption and the server does not support it, or if the client does not allow encryption and the server requires it, the VPN will be disconnected. Change this setting on the Advanced Security Settings page.

Finally, the credentials the client provides to the server must be valid. Your user account must be granted permission to establish a VPN connection with the server and the username, password, Windows domain (if applicable), and/or digital certificate (if applicable) must be valid.

Troubleshooting Firewall Issues   Another common problem that prevents VPN connections is a firewall between the client and server. If you're using ICF, Windows automatically configures ICF so VPN communications can pass through when you set up the VPN connection. However, if you're using third-party personal firewall software or a hardware firewall (such as one built into your cable, DSL router, or modem), you may need to configure the firewall to allow the VPN messages to go through.

PPTP requires that TCP port 1723 be open on the firewall. L2TP requires that UDP port 1701 be open, and you'll also need to open UDP port 500 for Internet Key Exchange (IKE) traffic that is used by IPSec.

Using Windows XP Remote Assistance

A feature that's brand new in Windows XP is *Remote Assistance,* which extends the Help and Support functionality by giving novices a way to get personal assistance from more experienced users, or helpers, without requiring that the helpers physically visit the desks of the users requesting help.

The novice sends an invitation to the helper. The invitation requests assistance from the helper. After the helper accepts the invitation, the helper can view the novice user's desktop and even control it remotely, across the local network or across the Internet. The helper can open dialog boxes, make configuration changes, and run applications on the novice's computer, and the novice can watch what the helper is doing on the screen. During the help session, the two can discuss the problem via text chat, audio, or video conferencing.

Getting help begins with a user clicking a link in the XP Help and Support Center interface (Figure 17-14).

The convenience of Remote Assistance, like any other remote access technology, comes with a tradeoff in terms of security. Enabling Remote Assistance does present security issues, which we discuss in more detail at the end of this section.

Understanding the Remote Assistance Technology

Remote Assistance is built on the same terminal services technology as Windows XP's Remote Desktop, which we'll discuss in the next section, "Enabling or Disabling Remote Assistance." Unlike the Remote Desktop service, Remote Assistance is included in both XP Home and Professional editions, as well as all the Pro variants such as Tablet PC and Media Center PC. Remote Assistance is also included in Windows Server 2003. Both computers (that of the novice and that of the helper) must be running Windows XP or Windows Server 2003. Remote Assistance doesn't work with earlier versions of Windows.

NOTE *To use Remote Assistance in Windows XP Home Edition, the user must log on with an account with Administrator privileges.*

Remote Assistance uses a special local user account called HelpAssistant. It is disabled by default, but when you request assistance, it is automatically enabled. This is the account the helper uses to log onto the novice's computer.

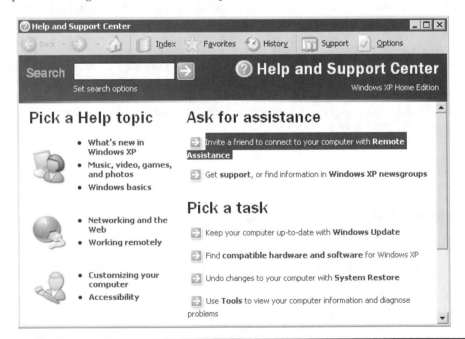

FIGURE 17-14 To ask for Remote Assistance, click the link in the Help and Support Center.

Enabling or Disabling Remote Assistance

Remote Assistance is enabled by default, but it can be disabled or configured through the Control Panel | System applet. Click the Remote tab and check or uncheck the box (Figure 17-15).

NOTE *On a Windows XP Home edition computer, Remote Assistance is the only option that appears on the Remote tab. The Remote tab on an XP Pro computer also includes a section for enabling, disabling, and configuring the Remote Desktop service.*

Setting Remote Assistance Preferences

You can allow Remote Assistance without allowing the helper to control your desktop. This can be set on a global or per-connection basis. To prevent helpers from ever controlling the desktop, click the Advanced button on the Remote tab and uncheck Allow this computer to be controlled remotely (Figure 17-16).

You can also set a maximum time that assistance invitations remain valid. The default is 30 days, but you can set a time ranging from one minute to 99 days.

Requesting Help with Remote Assistance

To request assistance, open the Help and Support Center from the Start menu and click Invite a friend to connect to your computer with Remote Assistance at the top of the right

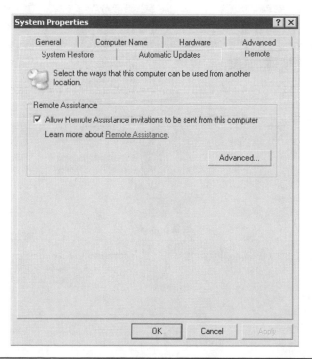

FIGURE 17-15   The Remote tab in System Properties allows you to enable or disable Remote Assistance.

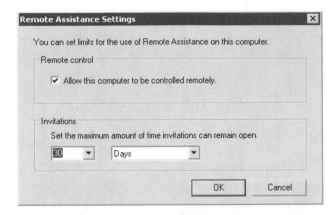

FIGURE 17-16 You can prevent those providing assistance from remotely controlling the computer.

column. Then, on the next page, click Invite someone to help you in the right column. This opens the Remote Assistance invitation screen shown (Figure 17-17).

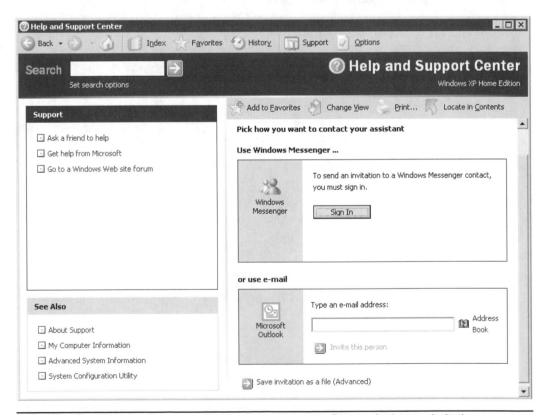

FIGURE 17-17 Select the method by which you want to send a Remote Assistance invitation.

There are three ways to invite a helper to provide Remote Assistance:

- Sign onto Windows Messenger and use instant messaging (IM) to contact the helper
- Send an e-mail invitation to the helper
- Save the invitation as a file and place it on a network share, a removable disk, or other location where the helper can access it

Requesting Help via Windows Messenger

You can use Windows Messenger to request assistance, either from within the Help and Support Center interface or from within the Messenger interface.

Requesting Assistance via Messenger from the Help and Support Center Interface   First, click the Sign in button to sign into Windows Messenger. If you don't already have a .NET passport associated with the user account, the .NET Passport Wizard will appear and walk you through the steps to add one. A Hotmail account will be created for you if you don't already have an e-mail address.

NOTE *You might also be prompted to install an updated version of Messenger before signing in. If you do so, you will be required to restart the computer.*

The people listed in your contacts list will appear in the Windows Messenger box in Help and Support (Figure 17-18). If the person is online, double click to send an IM requesting assistance. If the person is not online and you click the name, you will be asked if you want to send an e-mail invitation.

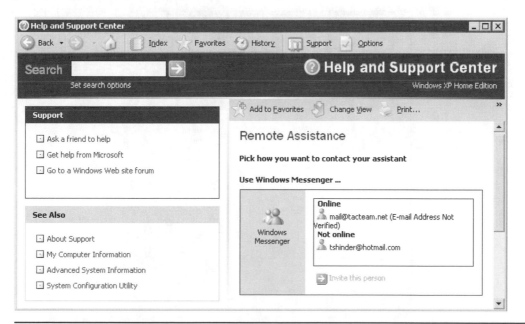

FIGURE 17-18   Your Messenger contacts will appear in two lists, showing which are online.

FIGURE 17-19   You will be informed when your invitation has been sent.

When you double-click the name of a contact, the Remote Assistance Web Page Dialog box will be displayed, informing you that the invitation has been sent (Figure 17-19). You can click the Cancel button to retract the invitation.

The person you've invited will receive a Messenger message asking if the person wants to accept your invitation to start using Remote Assistance (Figure 17-20). The helper can accept or decline by clicking the appropriate link or using keyboard shortcuts (ALT-T to accept; ALT-D to decline).

When the helper accepts your invitation, the Web Page Dialog box will notify you and ask if you want to let this person view your screen and chat with you. Click Yes to initiate the Remote Assistance session.

The Remote Assistance screen (Figure 17-21) will be displayed on both your and the helper's monitors. You can type text messages into the Message Entry area to communicate

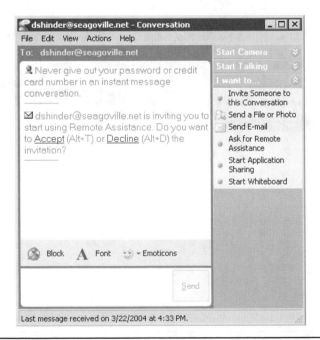

FIGURE 17-20   The helper to whom the invitation is sent receives notification via Messenger.

with one another. The entire conversation can be viewed in the Chat History area. You can also carry on an audio or video conference if both computers have the proper hardware equipment to do so.

On the right side of the screen, a column of buttons lets you perform the following actions:

- **Stop Control**   You can also do this by pressing ESC.
- **Send a file**
- **Start talking**   You will both need microphones and sound cards to have an audio conversation.
- **Configure settings**   You can select the audio quality according to the speed of your Internet connection, and use the Audio Tuning Wizard to verify that your microphone, speakers, and camera are working properly.
- **Disconnect**
- **Help**   Get help with using Remote Assistance

By default, the helper can view your desktop but cannot control it. To take control, the helper clicks the Take Control icon at the top of his or her Remote Assistance window (Figure 17-22).

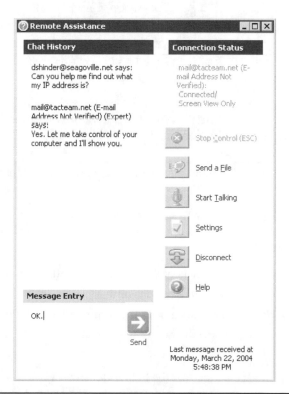

FIGURE 17-21   The Remote Assistance screen allows you to chat and control the session.

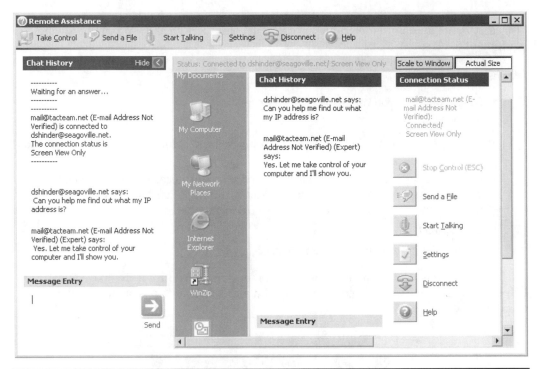

FIGURE 17-22 To take control, the helper clicks the Take Control icon at the top left side of the window.

A message box will appear on your screen, asking if you want to allow the helper to share control of your computer. Click Yes to do so. Either of you can end the control session by pressing ESC or any key combination that includes the ESC key.

***

NOTE *When a helper is remotely controlling your computer, you and the helper should not try to use the mouse at the same time.*

***

Requesting Help via Messenger from the Windows Messenger Interface   Instead of requesting assistance through the Help and Support Center, you can do it directly from the Windows Messenger interface:

1. Start Windows Messenger. Lists of your online and offline contacts are displayed.

2. Right click the name of a contact who is online.

3. Select Ask for Remote Assistance from the context menu (Figure 17-23).

4. An invitation will be sent to the helper to start using Remote Assistance.

Requesting Help via E-mail

If you don't use Windows Messenger (or the helper doesn't, or isn't online when you want to request assistance), you can use the e-mail option to send the invitation. You must have

FIGURE 17-23   You can request assistance directly within the Messenger interface.

an e-mail client (Outlook, Outlook Express, etc.) configured on your computer to use this option.

In the Remote Assistance pane of the Help and Support Center, type the e-mail address in the address field. You can click the Address Book icon to look up the address. If your address book is stored on an Exchange server, you'll be asked to enter your username, password, and domain for your mailbox.

After entering the e-mail address, click the Invite this person icon.

On the next page, you will be asked to enter a personal message to be included in the e-mail, describing the problem with which you need assistance and instructions on how to contact you (Figure 17-24).

On the next page, you can set a time duration for the invitation to remain open. This reduces the chance that someone else will intercept the invitation and use it to gain access to your computer. The default is 1 hour, but you can set a time ranging from 1 minute to 99 days.

For more security, you can specify a password that the helper will have to enter when connecting to your computer via Remote Assistance. You should communicate this password to the helper in a secure way (over the phone or via a separate encrypted e-mail message).

The screen for setting these security options is shown in Figure 17-25.

After you enter and confirm the password, click the Send Invitation button at the bottom of the screen.

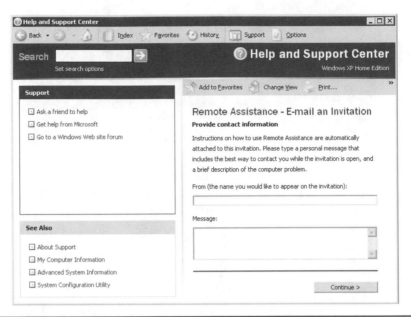

FIGURE 17-24   You can e-mail an invitation that includes a personal message.

NOTE *If you are using Microsoft Outlook as your e-mail client, you may receive a message that a program is trying to access e-mail addresses you have stored in Outlook or send e-mail on your behalf. Click Yes to allow Remote Assistance to do so.*

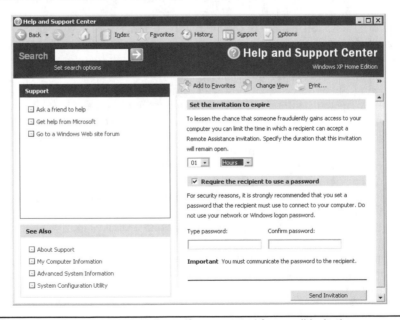

FIGURE 17-25   You can set a time limit and specify a password for e-mail invitations.

Saving a Request for Help to a File

Yet another way to request assistance is to save the invitation as a file and make it available to the helper via a network share or e-mail attachment. On the Remote Assistance page in the Help and Support Center, click Save invitation as a file (Advanced) at the bottom.

The next page asks you to type the name you want to appear on the invitation in the From field, and set a time duration for the invitation to remain valid. After entering this information, click the Continue button. The next page allows you to set a password, as we discussed in the subsection titled "Requesting Help via E-mail". After you enter the password, click the Save Invitation button.

You will be prompted to save the file as an MsRcIncident file with the extension .msrcincident. The default name is RAInvitation and the default location is the My Documents folder. You will be notified of the full path to which the file was saved (Figure 17-26).

Viewing the Status of Invitations

You can keep track of the status of the assistance invitations you've sent. On the Remote Assistance page in the Help and Support Center, click View invitation status. A number will appear in parenthesis beside this link, showing the number of invitations you have open.

You can view or change an invitation by clicking its option button in the Sent to column (Figure 17-27), then clicking one of the following buttons:

- **Details**   View information about the invitation, including when it was sent or saved, when it expires, and whether it is password protected.

- **Expire**   Immediately expire the invitation so that it cannot be used to connect to your computer.

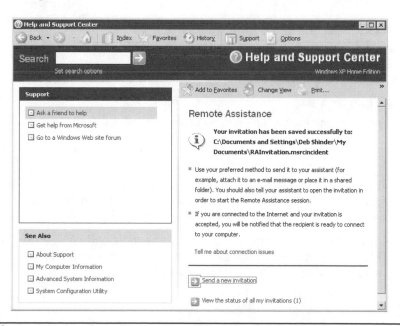

FIGURE 17-26   By default, an invitation saved as a file is stored in the My Documents folder.

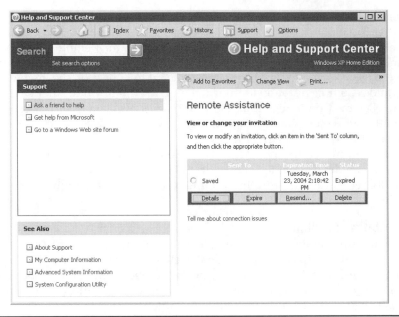

FIGURE 17-27 You can view or modify an invitation you've sent or saved.

- **Resend** Send the invitation again.
- **Delete** Remove the invitation from the list.

Providing Assistance Through Remote Assistance

Providing assistance to another user is a simple process. After you accept the invitation, you can view the novice's screen and, if the novice gives permission, take control of the remote computer to fix the problem.

Accepting the Invitation

The process for accepting the invitation depends on how it was sent:

- If you are invited via Windows Messenger, click the Accept hyperlink in the message or use the ALT-T keyboard shortcut.
- If you are invited via e-mail, double-click the attached MsRcIncident file and click the Yes button to connect to the novice's computer. If the invitation is password protected, you will be asked to enter the password (Figure 17-28).

If you are invited via a saved file, navigate to the MsRcIncident file on the network share or other location and double click to open it. Click the Yes button (after entering the password, if required) to connect to the novice's computer.

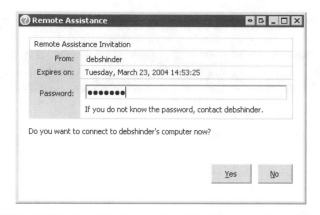

Figure 17-28   An e-mail invitation includes an attached MsRcIncident file by which you can connect to the novice's computer.

Initiating a Remote Assistance Session

The remote assistance session is generally initiated when the novice user sends an invitation. It is also possible for the helper to initiate the session by sending an offer to assist, but this is generally done only in a corporate environment, because both computers must be members of the same Windows domain.

In addition, the novice's computer must be configured to receive Remote Assistance offers. By default, XP computers cannot receive offers. The local group policy must be edited to allow a machine to accept offers.

Note   *Because XP Home computers cannot join Windows domains and do not support Group Policy, only XP Pro computers can receive offers of assistance.*

To offer assistance, the helper must have administrative privileges and must know the computer name or IP address of the computer that he or she wants to assist.

When all these criteria are met, the helper can send the offer of assistance by opening the following URL in Internet Explorer:
hcp://CN=Microsoft Corporation,L=Redmond,S=Washington,C=US/Remote Assistance/Escalation/unsolicited/unsolicitedrcui.htm.

This opens the Offer Remote Assistance page in Help and Support Center (Figure 17-29).

After entering the computer name or IP address and clicking Start Remote Assistance, a dialog box will display on the novice's screen stating that the "Network administrator <name> would like to view your screen, chat with you in real time, and work on your computer." The novice must select Yes to allow you to connect.

Remotely Controlling the Desktop

The novice user has ultimate control over the Remote Assistance session and can determine whether the helper will be able to only view the desktop or remotely control it as well. In view-only mode, the helper can see all actions performed by the novice and can instruct the novice what to do via text chat or audio/video communications.

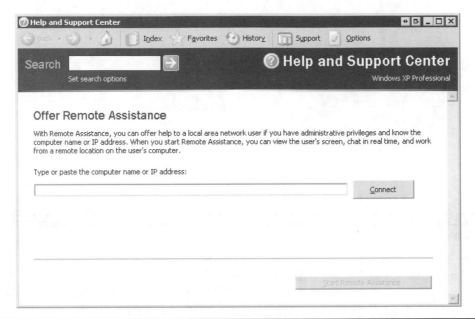

FIGURE 17-29 A helper can offer assistance to computers configured to receive such offers.

NOTE *To use a voice connection, click the Start Talking button in the right column of the Remote Assistance window. Both computers must be equipped with full duplex sound cards, speakers, and microphones. Voice works best over a high speed (500Mbps or above) network connection.*

To request to take control of the novice's computer, the helper can click Take Control at the top of the Remote Assistance window at any time during the session. A dialog box will then be displayed on the novice's computer, asking for permission to take control. The novice must click Yes in order for the helper to remotely control the computer.

When the helper takes control, both helper and novice can perform tasks (control the cursor, enter text, etc.) on the novice's computer. The novice can terminate remote control or the entire Remote Assistance session at any time.

Remote Assistance Security Issues

Remote Assistance can present a security risk because it opens a pathway for someone else to access your computer across the LAN or Internet. To minimize the risk, you should set a short time duration for invitations to remain open, password protect invitations, and convey the password through a secure means.

The Remote Assistance technology includes security features to prevent exploitation. Invitations are encrypted using public key cryptography. Additionally, even though the novice has sent an invitation, the helper cannot connect until the novice explicitly grants permission.

Companies that deal with very sensitive data on the network and have high security requirements may disable the Remote Assistance feature. This can be done on XP Professional machines using Group Policy (see Chapter 12 for more information).

Troubleshooting Remote Assistance

As we've mentioned, network policies can prevent Remote Assistance from being used. Additionally, if your computer is on a network, you might not be able to use Remote Assistance because of the firewall. Like Windows Terminal Services, Remote Assistance uses the Remote Desktop Protocol (RDP), which by default uses TCP port 3398. If that port is blocked by the firewall configuration, Remote Assistance won't work. Policy and firewall issues should be taken up with the network administrator.

The ICF personal firewall on Windows XP can also cause problems if the computer has more than one network interface card (NIC). In this case, the novice can send an invitation but the helper cannot connect in response. This occurs because, although Windows opens port 3398 when you initiate Remote Assistance, it opens it only on the NIC that is at the top of the binding order.

NAT and ICS can interfere with establishing Remote Assistance connections sent via e-mail. In this case, you should use Windows Messenger to request assistance.

Most Remote Assistance problems are caused by the misconfiguration of either the novice's or helper's computer.

If the helper is able to connect to the Remote Assistance session but is unable to take control of the desktop, the novice's computer might be configured (in Control Panel | System | Remote tab | Advanced button) not to allow the computer to be controlled remotely. In this case, the helper will receive a message that says "Remote Control of this computer is not allowed."

To send invitations via Windows Messenger, you must have a valid Passport account. To send invitations via e-mail, you must use Outlook or Outlook Express or a third-party e-mail client that uses simple MAPI (SMAPI). If you use an e-mail client that doesn't support SMAPI, you can save the invitation as a file and then manually attach it to an e-mail message to send.

Using Windows XP Remote Desktop

XP's Remote Desktop feature allows you to connect to your XP computer from another computer and control its desktop. You can run applications, access files, and do anything you could do if you were physically sitting in front of the machine. It differs from Remote Assistance in that with Remote Assistance two people can share control of the machine: the person sitting at the machine and the remote helper. With Remote Desktop, the local desktop is locked and only the remote user can control it.

Remote Desktop is great if you need to work on a Word document, for example, and don't have Word installed on your portable computer. You can connect to an XP machine on the network that does have Word installed and work on the document from the portable computer.

Understanding the Remote Desktop Technology

The technology used for Remote Desktop was originally introduced by Citrix and then adopted by Microsoft for Windows terminal services. A terminal server allows other computers to connect to it and run desktop sessions remotely. Until XP, only Windows server operating systems could function as terminal servers. Now XP Pro can act as a "mini" terminal server, allowing only one concurrent session. XP Home does not include Remote Desktop server functionality.

Remote desktop, like the full-fledged terminal services included with Windows server products, uses RDP for communications between the remote client and the Remote Desktop server.

NOTE *The "one concurrent session" limitation can be overcome with third-party software. Cinemar (http://www.cinemaronline.com) makes a product that allows up to 21 clients to log onto an XP Remote Desktop machine simultaneously.*

The Remote Desktop client machine (the computer from which you remotely connect to your XP Pro desktop) can be running XP Home or Pro, Windows 2000, Windows NT, or Windows 9x/Me. Remote Desktop client software must be installed on non-XP/2003 computers.

NOTE *Some distributions of Linux, such as Fedora, come with a Windows terminal services client called rdesktop that can be used to connect to an XP Remote Desktop server. There is even a remote desktop client available for Apple's Macintosh OS X.*

The client computer does *not* have to meet the system requirements for running Windows XP because XP and its applications run entirely on the Remote Desktop server computer; only the graphical elements and commands you perform are transferred over the network.

Configuring the XP Remote Desktop Server

There are two simple steps involved in setting up your XP Pro computer to be a Remote Desktop server:

1. Enable Remote Desktop services.
2. Select remote users who will be permitted to use Remote Desktop.

Enabling or Disabling XP Remote Desktop Server

By default, Remote Desktop services are not enabled on your XP Pro computer. To enable it, open the System applet from Control Panel and click the Remote tab.

Check the box under Remote Desktop that is labeled Allow users to connect remotely to this computer (Figure 17-30).

Selecting Remote Users

By default, administrators can connect via Remote Desktop. This includes both the default Administrator account and all members of the administrators group.

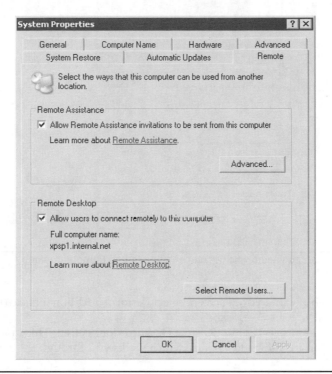

FIGURE 17-30   Enable Remote Desktop via the Remote tab in System Properties.

To add other user accounts, on the Control Panel | System | Remote tab, click the Select Remote Users button. In the Remote Users dialog box (Figure 17-31), click the Add button.

In the Select Users dialog box, enter the user names to which you want to give Remote Desktop access, and click OK. The names will appear in the Remote Desktop Users list. Click OK again to exit the dialog box.

Using the Remote Desktop Client

The Remote Desktop Connection client software is built into both Windows XP Pro and Home computers. The client software is included on the XP Pro installation CD-ROM and can be installed on all other Windows 32-bit operating systems (9x/Me, NT, and 2000). Windows Server 2003 also comes with the Remote Desktop Connection (RDC) client preinstalled.

The RDC client can be used to connect to Windows NT, 2000, and Server 2003 terminal servers as well as XP Pro Remote Desktop servers. You can have multiple instances of the RDC client running simultaneously, with windows to control several different Remote Desktop or terminal servers.

Installing the RDC Client on non-XP Computers

To install the RDC Client on non-XP Computers, insert your XP Pro installation CD into the CD-ROM drive on the client computer on which you want to install the RDC client software.

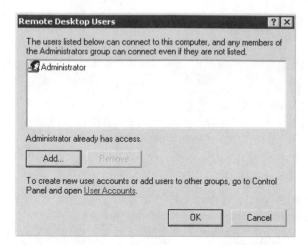

FIGURE 17-31   You can add users who will be permitted to use Remote Desktop

At the "What do you want to do?" screen, select Perform additional tasks (Do *not* select Install Windows XP).

On the next screen, select Set up Remote Desktop Connection. This invokes the Remote Desktop Connection InstallShield Wizard, which walks you through the steps of installing the RDC client.

Connecting to an XP Remote Desktop Server or Windows Terminal Server

To use the RDC client software to connect to an XP Pro Remote Desktop server or a Windows terminal server, click Start | Programs (or All Programs) | Accessories | Communications and select Remote Desktop Connection from the menu.

NOTE   *If you use the RDC client often, you might want to make a shortcut on your desktop or taskbar by right-dragging the RDC icon from the Start menu.*

The Remote Desktop Connection dialog box is shown in Figure 17-32. From the drop-down box, select the name or IP address of the Remote Desktop server or terminal server to which you want to connect. Servers to which you have previously connected will appear here. If the server doesn't appear here, type its name or IP address in the field, and click the Connect button.

The desktop of the Remote Desktop server or terminal server will appear in a window. The size of the window depends on the resolution settings, which we'll discuss in the "Setting RDC Options" section. The standard Windows logon dialog box appears on the remote desktop. Enter credentials for a user account that has permission to access the Remote Desktop or terminal services, and click OK.

You may be notified that a user account is currently logged onto the computer, and if you continue, it will be logged off. Click Yes to continue. The remote computer's full desktop appears, including any applications that are open. You can use the computer as if you were sitting at it locally.

FIGURE 17-32   Enter or select the name of the server to which you want to connect.

NOTE   You might see a Remote Desktop Connection Security Warning that notifies you that some of your local devices will be made available to the remote computer, and that this may be potentially unsafe. You can select not to have this prompt appear again. You can also prevent local devices from being made available to the remote machine by configuring local resource options, as discussed in the "Setting RDC Options" section.

Setting RDC Options

There are a number of options you can set to configure how the RDC client behaves. To configure options, click the Options button on the connection dialog box. This displays five tabs: General, Display, Local Resources, Programs, and Experience.

Setting General Options   On the General tab (Figure 17-33), you can set logon and connection options. Under Logon settings, you can select or type in a Remote Desktop or terminal server and enter a username, password, and domain to be used to log onto it. You can also check a box to save the password. This prevents you from having to enter your credentials each time you connect to the server.

You can also save the current settings, or open a connection that you have previously saved, by clicking Save as or Open under Connection settings.

Setting Display Options   On the Display tab (Figure 17-34), you can select the desktop resolution. This determines the size of the Remote Desktop window, and can be adjusted from 640x480 to full screen. The higher the resolution, the larger the window will be. If you select full screen, you will be able to close or minimize the window with a connection bar that appears at the top of the screen by default. You can uncheck the box at the bottom of the Display tab to prevent the connection bar from displaying.

You can also set color depth for the Remote Desktop window on this tab, from 256 colors to true color (24-bit). However, the remote computer must support the color depth you select or a lower color depth will be used.

NOTE   If you are connecting to the Remote Desktop server over a slow modem connection, you can improve performance by selecting a smaller screen resolution and lower color depth.

Setting Local Resource Options   On the Local Resources tab (Figure 17-35), you can select to bring the sound from the remote computer to the client computer. Of course, the client computer must have a sound card installed. You can also choose to leave the sound at the remote computer, or select not to play the sounds at either computer.

FIGURE 17-33   You can configure logon and connection settings on the General tab.

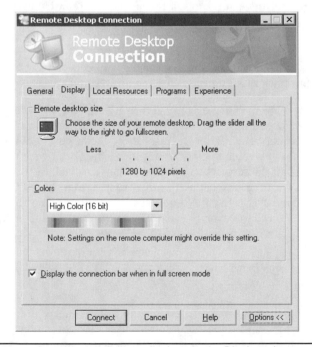

FIGURE 17-34   You can configure desktop size and colors on the Display tab.

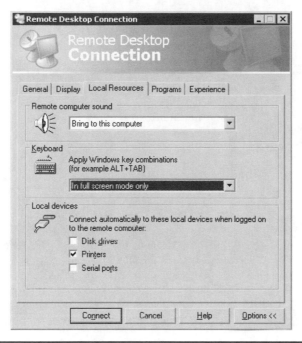

FIGURE 17-35   You can configure sound, keyboard, and local device options on the Local Resources tab.

Under Keyboard, you can select whether Windows key combinations should be applied on the local computer, on the remote computer, or only when the remote desktop window is in full screen mode. In other words, if you hit a key combination such as ALT-TAB, this setting determines whether the Switch Tasks box will appear on your local machine for the programs running there or in the remote desktop window for the programs running on the remote computer.

Under Local devices, you can choose which of your local devices (disk drives, printers, and/or serial ports) will be automatically accessible to the remote computer when you log on. For example, if you make your local disk drives available, when you open Windows Explorer on the Remote Desktop server, you will see the drives for both the remote system and your local system.

Setting Program Options   On the Programs tab (Figure 17-36), you can instruct Windows to start a specified program on the remote computer when you connect to it. You'll need to enter the path and file name where the program executable is stored. You can also specify a folder in which the program should start.

Setting Experience Options   The Experience tab (Figure 17-37) allows you to configure settings that will affect performance. Depending on the connection speed you select, different check boxes will be automatically selected:

• If you select Modem (28.8 Kbps), only bitmap caching will be enabled.

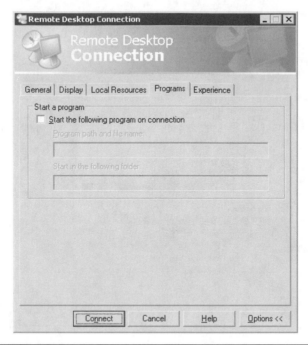

FIGURE 17-36   You can configure programs to run when you connect on the Programs tab.

- If you select Modem (56 Kbps), bitmap caching and themes will be enabled.
- If you select Broadband (128 Kbps to 1.5 Mbps), bitmap caching, themes, menu and window animation, and show contents of window while dragging will be enabled.
- If you select LAN (10 Mbps or higher), all boxes, including the desktop background, will be selected.

Choose the speed at which you will connect to the particular Remote Desktop or terminal server. You can enable more options for a server to which you connect over the local Ethernet network than for one to which you connect over the Internet (especially over a modem connection) without adversely affecting desktop performance.

Troubleshooting Remote Desktop

If you receive a "server not found" message when you attempt to connect, you might have mistyped the name of the Remote Desktop or terminal server, or this message might be due to a name resolution problem. Attempt to connect via an IP address instead.

If you are unable to log on, ensure that your user account has been given permission to log on via Remote Desktop, in the System Properties' Remote tab, Select Users dialog box. This adds you to the Remote Desktop Users group on the remote computer. Only members of this group and the administrators group can log on via Remote Desktop.

If you don't see the Start button and taskbar on the remote desktop, you might need to scroll down because the resolution you've selected doesn't allow the entire desktop to be

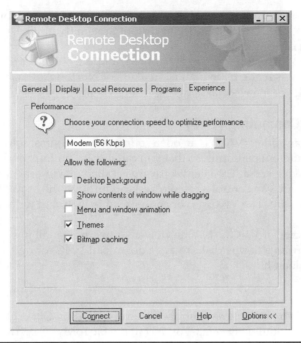

FIGURE 17-37   You can configure performance settings on the Experience tab.

displayed. You can change the resolution in the RDC client options (Display tab) or run the session in full screen mode.

Some programs will not run via Remote Desktop. For example, you can connect to a Windows XP Media Center Edition PC using the RDC client (if it has been configured in System properties to allow remote desktop connections), but you cannot run the Media Center application remotely.

Using Third-Party Remote Access Options

There are several third-party programs that offer similar functionality to Remote Desktop/Remote Assistance. Some of the most popular include:

- pcAnywhere
- Virtual Network Computing (VNC)
- GoToMyPC

pcAnywhere

pcAnywhere is one of the oldest and still most popular remote control programs. The current version is 11.0. It can be used to manage servers remotely, in the same way as Remote Desktop, or for troubleshooting and helpdesk functionality, also in the same way as Remote

Assistance. It supports the quick transfer of multiple files, and allows you to connect over a LAN using IPX/SPX or Network Basic Input Output System (NetBIOS). (TCP/IP is, of course, required to connect over the Internet.)

A minimum of 35MB of disk space is required, and the cost for a single user license is $199. pcAnywhere is made by Symantec (makers of Norton Anti-Virus). For more information, see http://www.symantec.com/pcanywhere/Consumer/index.html.

Virtual Network Computing (VNC)

Virtual Network Computing (VNC) is an open source remote control solution from RealVNC that works across different platforms, so that you can display a Linux desktop on a Windows client computer, or vice versa. The client software is called a "viewer." VNC also supports a Java viewer so that you can control a remote desktop through the browser, without having to install client software. The VNC server component is included with many popular versions of Linux.

Another advantage of VNC is that the viewer software is small in size (about 150KB) and you can run it from a floppy disk. You can download VNC for no cost at http://www.realvnc.com/download.html.

GoToMyPC

GoToMyPC is a web-based remote control service operated by Citrix Online that works with most popular operating systems. You install the GoToMyPC software on the host (server) computer and register it on the GoToMyPC web site. Then, to connect to it from any other computer over the Internet, log in at the web site with your user account, click Connect, and you'll be able to view and control the desktop of the computer on which you installed the software.

The software is small in size (1.4MB) and runs as a service. When it receives a connection request, you are prompted for an access code before you can connect. A chat function is included for helpdesk functionality. An Internet connection is required. (You cannot connect directly over a LAN.)

The service costs $19.95 per month or $179.40 per year for one host PC. Volume plans are also available. For more information, see http://www.gotomypc.com.

Hacking Windows XP

In this chapter you'll find the answers to the following questions:

- Is it possible to back up or recover Windows XP passwords?
- I want to make my password hard to guess. What are some guidelines?
- I can't remember the Administrator password for my computer. Can I change it?
- What programs are available to help me recover lost passwords?
- My computer won't boot. Are there any special programs that will let me boot the computer to access files or fix the computer?
- I'm interested in seeing what information is stored on my computer. Are there any tools that will show me that information?
- Is it possible to see what traffic is coming and going through my network?
- I've lost my CD key and need to reinstall Windows XP. How do I recover the key?
- Is it possible to change the CD key in an existing Windows XP installation?

If you've turned to this chapter in hopes of learning how to be a hacker, you'll have to look elsewhere. However, there are several issues that can crop up when using any computer system, and being able to work around the operating system can save the day.

In this chapter I explore some of the most common problems you might face and how to use built-in capabilities or third-party tools to work around those problems. For example, there are a couple of techniques you can use either to recover a lost administrator password or to essentially clear out the password and start fresh. These techniques can help you regain full access to the system. This chapter also covers other topics that will help you work around problems with the operating system and troubleshoot network problems.

This chapter isn't intended for network administrators, most of whom have an even bigger arsenal of weapons to lay siege to any computer problem. Nor is this chapter targeted at users who work in a large enterprise—doing some of the things in this chapter could well get you fired! Instead, this chapter is geared toward individual users and people who need to manage computers for others in a small network.

TIP *Don't go surfing the Internet looking for hacking or cracking sites. Invariably, you will run into one that will infect your system or pull a nasty trick like disabling Internet Explorer. If you disregard my advice, make sure you have several restore points available from which to restore your system.*

Backing Up and Recovering Windows XP Passwords

If you never connect your computer to the Internet and no one else ever has physical access to it, passwords can be an annoyance. But the minute those two situations reverse, having a password is your first line of defense in securing your data and system. Having a *good* password is even more important.

For example, for best security your password should not include personal information, any part of your user name, or easily guessed words. What's more, the password should include a mix of letters, numbers, and special characters to make it impossible to guess and not susceptible to a brute-force password attack in which an automated system repeatedly attempts to crack the password.

Here are some tips for creating a good password:

- **Use a mix of characters and case** Use letters, numbers, and special characters such as ! and #. Example: MyPass2W0rd!9

- **Don't use any real words** Many brute-force applications rely on the fact that many people use words they can remember as their passwords. Example: pe845jd#65!

- **Use a mnemonic to help you remember the password** Remember Every Good Boy Does Fine for the lines on the treble cleft in music class? Come up with your own mnemonic and throw in some special characters. Example: Joe eats 2 bananas with 7 grapes, or je2bw7g!

Why am I explaining how to create a good password in a section about backing up and restoring passwords? If you take my advice, your passwords will be much harder to remember, particularly if you don't use them often. For example, you might need the administrator password for your computer only once or twice a month to install some new software. Even if you use a mnemonic, there's a chance you'll forget the password. So, you should back up your passwords so that you can recover them if needed.

You could tape a sheet of paper with your passwords on it under your desk, but Windows XP offers a more technically advanced method—a password reset disk. This method requires that you have previously created a password backup disk.

Creating a Password Reset Diskette for a Workgroup Computer

Here's how to create the backup disk for a computer in a workgroup (not a domain member):

1. Open the Users Accounts applet from the Control Panel (Figure 18-1).

2. If you logged on with an account that is a member of the Administrators group, click the account for which you want to create a password recovery disk. If you are logged on with a limited account, your account is selected automatically.

3. In the Related Tasks area of the left pane, click Prevent A Forgotten Password to start the Forgotten Password Wizard.

4. Click Next, insert a blank, formatted disk in drive A, and click Next.

5. When prompted (Figure 18-2), enter the current account password and click Next.

6. Click Next when the wizard indicates it has created the disk, then click Finish.

7. Label the diskette with the account name and store the diskette in a safe place.

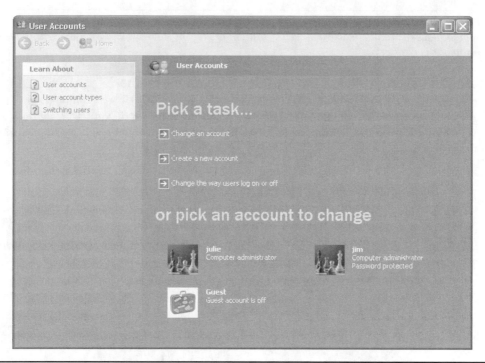

FIGURE 18-1   The Users Accounts applet lets you create a password recovery diskette.

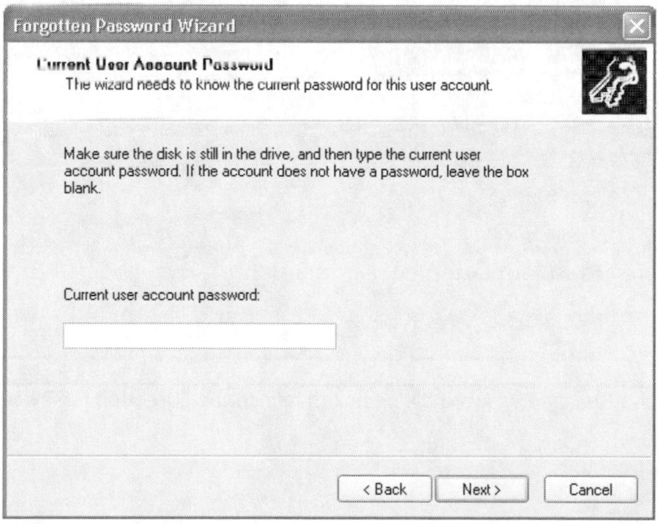

FIGURE 18-2   Enter the password for the account.

NOTE *The password recovery disk can be used only on the computer where it was created. You should place the recovery disk in a secure location to prevent someone else from using it to break into your computer.*

Creating a Password Reset Diskette for a Domain Member

The process for creating a password reset diskette for a computer that is a member of a domain is a bit different. Note that you can use the password reset diskette to reset the password for a local user account only. A domain administrator must reset the password for a domain account.

Follow these steps to create a password reset diskette for a domain member computer:

1. Log on to the computer with your user account.

2. Press CTRL-ALT-DEL to open the Windows Security dialog box, then click Change Password to open the Change Password dialog box.

3. From the Log On To drop-down list, choose the local computer. The Backup button should now appear on the dialog box (Figure 18-3).

4. Complete the wizard as described in the previous section.

FIGURE 18-3 Use the Change Password dialog box to launch the Forgotten Password Wizard.

Using the Password Reset Diskette

If the time comes that you discover you've forgotten the password, you can use the diskette to create a new password for the account. Here's how:

NOTE *Windows XP offers the options to reset the password only if you have previously created a password recovery diskette for the specified user account.*

---

1. Boot the system and at the Welcome screen, click the account you want to use; then click the green arrow button beside it and click the Use Your Password Reset Disk in the message balloon that pops up (Figure 18-4). If your computer is configured to display the Logon dialog box rather than the Welcome screen, enter the user name but leave the password blank, and then click OK. Windows displays the Logon Failed dialog box (Figure 18-5). Click Reset to start the wizard.

2. After the wizard starts, click Next, insert the password recovery diskette for this account in drive A, and click Next.

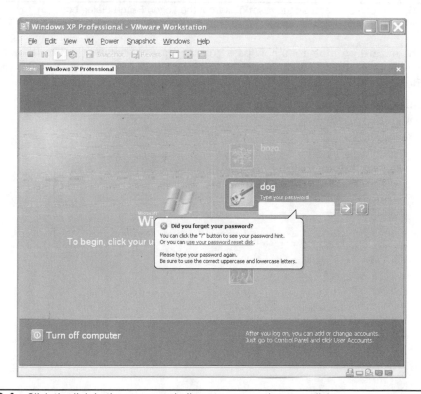

FIGURE 18-4   Click the link in the message balloon to access the reset disk.

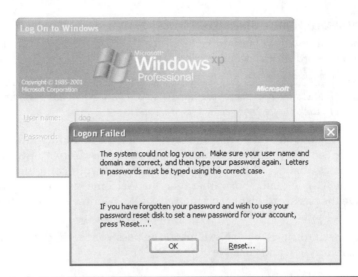

FIGURE 18-5   You can also access the reset disk from the Logon Failed dialog box

3. The wizard prompts for a new password and password hint (Figure 18-6). Enter the new password and hint and click Next. Click Finish after the password is reset by the wizard.

4. Enter the new password in the Welcome screen or Logon dialog box and log on as you normally would.

FIGURE 18-6   Enter the new password when prompted.

Recovering from a Lost Administrator Password

If you have the password for any account on the computer with administrator privileges, you can reset the password for any other account through the Local Users and Groups console or Users Accounts applet in the Control Panel. If you lose the Administrator account password, however, you won't be able to reset any password except your own. You also won't be able to reconfigure the system or perform other system-wide tasks.

There are a couple of methods you can use if you need to recover a lost Administrator password. The method you use depends on the computer's configuration. Here is a summary of the methods, requirements, and consequences:

- **Delete the SAM registry hive file** This method deletes all accounts and blanks the Administrator account password. Although accounts are deleted, user profiles and their corresponding documents are not lost. However, you might have to reassociate the profile directory with the user account after re creating the account. This method also requires access to the file system so that you can delete the SAM file.

- **Use a third-party recovery tool** There are a handful of recovery tools available for recovering passwords and failed systems. One I like is ERD Commander, from http://www.winternals.com.

Delete the SAM Registry Hive File

This method is a bit drastic because it deletes all accounts on the system. However, applications and other settings are unaffected, and user profile folders and documents are retained. After you create new local accounts, you can reassociate the new accounts with their old profiles. Before you take this approach, however, check the next section for a list of third-party alternatives that don't delete the SAM and therefore don't delete the accounts from the system.

TIP *The SAM file is the portion of the registry that stores user accounts.*

If you choose to go the route of deleting the SAM, you'll need to gain access to the %systemroot%\System32\Config folder, which is where the registry hive files are located. Using one of the methods described in the preceding section, navigate to the %systemroot%\System32\Config folder and rename the SAM file:

```
C:\Windows\System32\Config>rename sam sam.old
```

Then, reboot the system. The Administrator account will now have a blank password.

Useful Third-Party Password Recovery Tools

Lots of tools are available for various recovery tasks, including resetting the Administrator account password. The following list summarizes some of these tools and indicates whether they are freeware, shareware, or commercial software:

- **Winternals ERD Commander** This is one of my favorite recovery tools. It boots even unbootable systems from a CD and gives you the capability to reset the Administrator password, recover lost files, recover Windows XP restore points, and perform many other tasks. http://www.winternals.com. Commercial software.

Changing Profile Location

If the computer contained user accounts before you deleted the SAM file, you'll need to recreate the accounts. If the accounts do take on the old user profile location, you can reassociate the old profile folder with the new account. Open the Registry Editor and expand the branch HKEY_LOCAL_MACHINE\ Software\ Microsoft\ Windows NT\ CurrentVersion\ ProfileList. This branch includes settings that specify the location of the profiles directory as well as the location of the All Users and Default User profiles. You can change the settings to change the location, if needed.

Under the ProfileList key you'll find additional keys that define each user's profile. You can click the key to view and change the profile settings. For example, change the ProfileImagePath setting if you need to point Windows 2000 to a different profile for the selected user.

- **Offline NT Password and Registry Editor**   This tool, developed by Petter Nordahl-Hagen, includes a bootable CD image and the capability to reset the Administrator password for the local computer without deleting any accounts. http://home.eunet.no/<126>pnordahl/ntpasswd. Freeware.

- **EBCD**   This is a bootable CD developed by Mikhail Kupchik that enables you to boot XP (and other) systems and perform a variety of tasks, including resetting any account password without knowing the old password. http://ebcd.pcministry .com. Freeware.

- **Austrumi**   Another bootable Linux-based CD, this tool fits on a business-size CD, which means you can carry it in your wallet! It enables you to reset the Administrator password and perform other recovery tasks. http://sourceforge.net/projects/ austrumi.Freeware.

- **Windows XP / 2000 / NT Key**   This bootable CD enables you to reset passwords on 2003, XP, 2000, and NT systems. http://www.lostpassword.com/windows-xp-2000-nt.htm. Commercial software.

- **NTAccess**   This tool can be used from a set of boot diskettes or bootable CD to reset the Administrator password. The tool also displays the current name of the Administrator account if it has been renamed. http://www.mirider.com/ntaccess. html. Commercial software.

Recovering Other Passwords and Booting Dead Systems

Account passwords are not the only passwords you'll find on a Windows XP computer, nor are they the only ones you're likely to forget. These include passwords for Outlook Express, FTP sites in Internet Explorer or other FTP applications, passwords for Web sites, and others. Windows and applications generally display these passwords as asterisks. There are several utilities that essentially "peek behind" the asterisks to show you the real password, but one of the most popular is iOpus Password Recovery XP. This inexpensive tool reveals the password hidden behind asterisks in dialog boxes and works for Windows and any application that stores the password in the displayed dialog box (including Internet Explorer, CuteFTP, and many others). See http://www.iopus.com/password_recovery.htm for details. There are lots of tools available that enable you to boot dead Windows XP systems, recover files, reset passwords, and perform other recovery tasks. One of the more popular solutions is Knoppix, a bootable Linux CD that gives you an amazing array of tools to manage files, sniff the network, recover files, and perform other tasks. You'll find information about Knoppix and a download at http://www.knoppix.com. See the section "Sniffing the Network with Knoppix and EtherApe" later in this chapter for more details.

Sniffing the Network

There is a lot of information floating across your network. The capability to monitor network traffic can be a real lifesaver sometimes, whether you're trying to determine if a computer on your network is spitting out excessive packets or you want to know what sites your computer is trying to access on the Internet on its own (a sure sign of adware infection).

Using the Network Monitor

The Windows XP CD includes a Support\Tools folder that contains several useful tools for Windows XP. One of these is Netcap.exe, a client-side capture tool that enables you to capture network packets for viewing with Network Monitor. However, Network Monitor is not included with Windows XP. Instead, you need to turn to Windows 2000 Server or Windows Server 2003 for Network Monitor. You can, however, capture the data with Netcap .exe and view it on the server.

NOTE *I won't go into detail about Netcap.exe here because you need Windows 2000 Server or Windows Server 2003 (or SMS) with the GUI-based Network Monitor application to view the captured packets. Instead, I include this section so that you'll know that a capture driver for Network Monitor is available with Windows XP.*

You can install the support tools by running Setup.exe from the \Support\Tools folder, but if Netcap.exe is all you want, just copy it from the cabinet file to your system. Insert the Windows XP CD, open a command console, use CD to change to the \Support\Tools folder on the CD, and then issue the following command, replacing <dest> with the path to the folder where you want to store Netcap.exe:

```
D:\Support\Tools>expand support.cab -f:netcap.exe <dest>
```

The first time you run Netcap.exe, it installs itself on all network interfaces automatically. Rather than explore the command syntax or parameters for Netcap here, however, I'll point you instead to the online help. Just use the command **netcap /?** at a console prompt to view syntax and parameters.

Sniffing the Network with Ethereal

If you're interested in a Windows-based sniffer application, consider Ethereal (Figure 18-7), available for Linux and Windows at http://www.ethereal.com. Ethereal is a free application, and the 32-bit Windows version runs on Windows 98 or later.

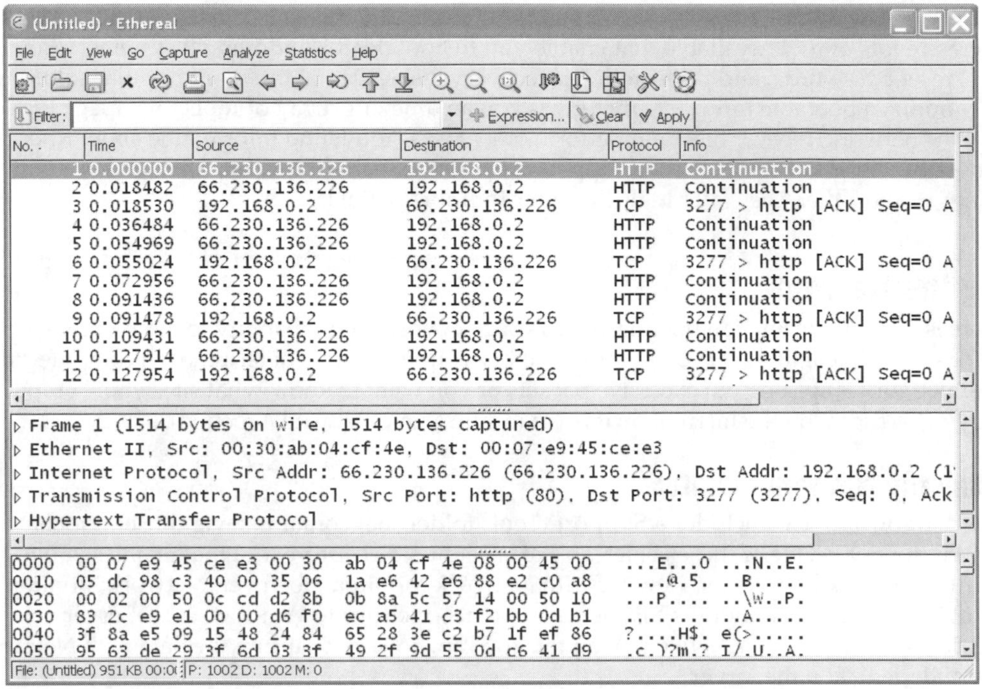

FIGURE 18-7 Ethereal is a freeware sniffer available for Windows and Linux.

In its default configuration, Ethereal will capture all packets. You can configure capture filters to capture specific types of packets. For example, suppose you are trying to diagnose a problem with a particular host and want to capture everything except port 80. To configure port filters, choose Capture | Capture Filters to open the Capture Filter dialog box (Figure 18-8). Click New, click the newly created filter in the list, and enter a filter name and filter string in the Filter Name and Filter String fields. The following filter string would cause Ethereal to capture all traffic for 192.138.0.2 except TCP port 80:

    host 192.168.0.2 and not tcp port 80

To begin using the filter, click Save and then click Close. Choose Capture | Start to open the Capture Options dialog box (Figure 18-9). Click Capture Filter, choose the filter you just created, and click OK to start the capture.

After you've captured what you feel are enough packets, click Stop. The packets appear in the main Ethereal window, as shown previously in Figure 18-7. You can create a display filter to display only certain information. To create a display filter, choose Analyze | Display Filters to show the Display Filter dialog box (Figure 18-10). Click New, click the newly added filter, and enter a name and filter string for it. You can click Expression to build a

FIGURE 18-8   Create filters with the Capture Filter dialog box.

filter expression with the Filter Expression dialog box (Figure 18-11). If the filter is correct, the Filter String field in the Display Filter dialog box will appear in green. If the string is incorrect, the field displays red. When you have the filter string you need, click Apply to apply it and then click Close.

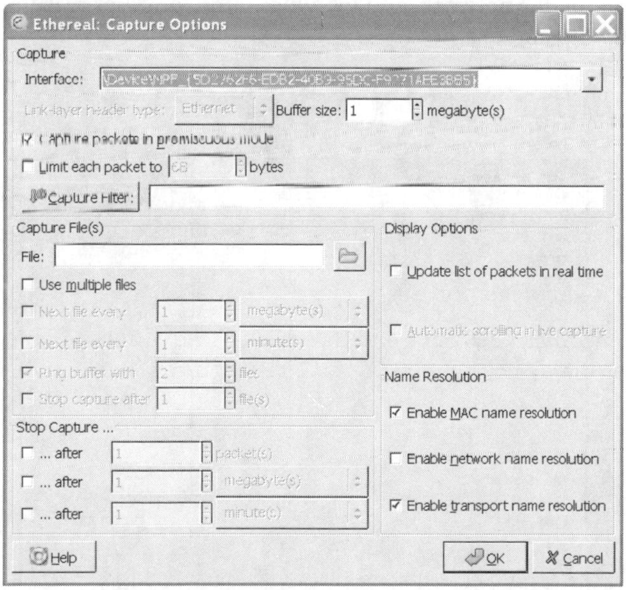

FIGURE 18-9   Use the Capture Options dialog box to set options for capturing packets.

FIGURE 18-10   Use the Display Filters dialog box to create a filter for displaying captured packets.

Sniffing the Network with Knoppix and EtherApe

Another useful tool is EtherApe, which is included in the Knoppix distribution. Unlike
Ethereal, EtherApe provides a graphical view of network traffic (Figure 18-12). EtherApe
can be very useful for identifying at a glance what external sites are being hit, seeing where
traffic is coming from on the network, and viewing traffic for other reasons. The main benefit
is that it is easy to set up and use.

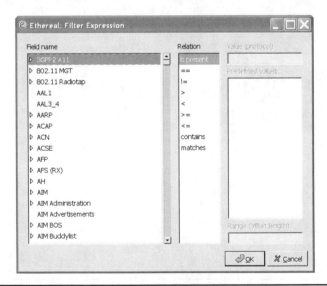

FIGURE 18-11   Create a filter expression with the Filter Expression dialog box.

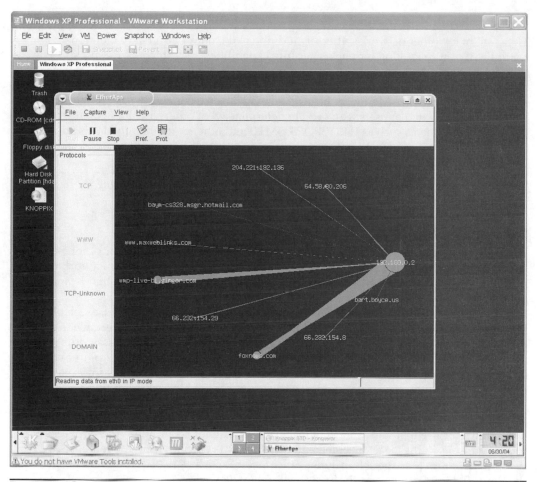

Figure 18-12   Use EtherApe to view network traffic in graphical format.

Tip *You'll find EtherApe in the Network Utilities menu.*

EtherApe does not capture or display packets per se, although it does keep a running count of packets by protocol. Its primary use is to view the interaction between systems on the network and outside of the network. EtherApe displays different protocols using different colors to help you identify at a glance what protocol is running between two systems.

EtherApe supports Token Ring, FDDI, and Ethernet, and it can display data in either IP or TCP modes. To choose a mode, choose Capture | Mode and then either IP or TCP, depending on how you want to view traffic on the network. Choose File | Preferences to open the EtherApe:Preferences dialog box, where you specify a variety of options that control the way EtherApe works and looks.

Other Network Sniffing Tools

There are many other network sniffers in addition to the ones I've already mentioned. For example, if you're looking for packet capture capabilities and Ethereal doesn't suit you, check out EtherDetect, from http://www.etherdetect.com. The program offers some great features for filtering the capture as well as the display. If you're looking for something a little sneakier, check out Give Me Too, at http://www.spyarsenal.com/network-sniffer. Give Me Too is mainly targeted at users who need to determine what others are doing on the network for common protocols such as HTTP, POP3, SMTP, and others. Another good candidate is Softperfect Network Protocol Analyzer, available from http://www.softperfect.com.

TIP *To find other sniffer applications, run a search at your favorite search site using the keyphrase "network sniffer software."*

Sniffing for Passwords

I include this section not because I think you should sniff the network for other users' passwords, but because I occasionally find it necessary to sniff the network to recover passwords for e-mail accounts, services, Internet sites, and so on that I can't obtain using other methods.

One of the most useful tools of this kind in my opinion is Cain and Abel, available from http://www.oxid.it/cain.html. Without doing any sniffing, the program can pull an amazing amount of information out of your system, from e-mail passwords to accounts, passwords, and other information you have entered in Internet Explorer with AutoComplete. Figure 18-13 shows the program with the Protected Storage information extracted. The actual sites, users' names, and passwords are blurred for privacy.

Cain and Abel is actually two sets of applications. Cain provides the GUI and related features, including sniffing, password cracking, SID scanning, and much more. Abel is a Windows service that you can install locally or on a remote computer. Abel provides a remote console on the target machine and can dump user hashes from the remote SAM (Security Account Manager). It includes other features such as the LSA Secrets dumper, the Route Table Manager, and the TCP/UDP Table Viewer.

Cain and Abel is a fairly complex application, and detailing all of its inner workings is beyond the scope of this chapter. Many users will find Cain and Abel useful simply for pulling information from your existing password and Internet Explorer caches on a computer. To do so, run Cain, click the Protected Storage tab, and then click the plus sign icon on the toolbar to dump the information.

Recovering and Changing Your CD Key

When you install Windows XP, you must enter a CD key, which either is listed on a label on the back of your CD case or appears on your Certificate of Authenticity. Windows Product Activation (WPA) uses the CD key and your hardware's signature to create a unique installation identifier that is used to activate the product. Sometimes it can be necessary to recover the CD key from an existing Windows XP installation or even change the key assigned to the computer. This section explains how to accomplish both tasks.

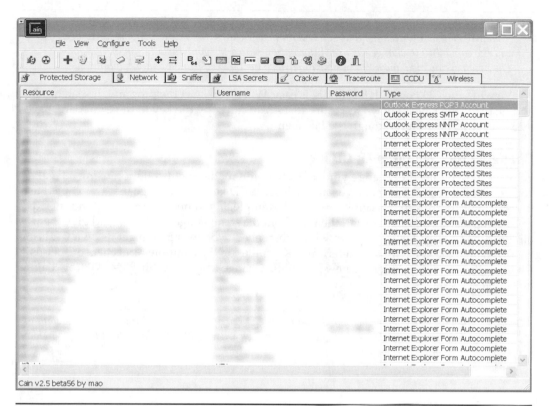

FIGURE 18-13   Cain and Abel, without doing any sniffing, can display an amazing amount of information from your own computer.

TIP   Windows XP obtained under an open license does not require activation.

Recovering Your CD Key

Just the other day, I realized I had lost the case for one of my Windows XP CDs. In some previous Windows versions, you could recover the CD key easily enough because it was stored as plain text in the registry. Windows XP doesn't store the CD key in that way, however. There began a quest to find a way to retrieve the CD key from my Windows XP installation. Assuming (correctly) that Microsoft's tech support staff would not be able to tell me how to extract the information from my registry, I searched the Internet for a magical tool that would grab the key for me. I found it at http://www.magicaljellybean.com.

Keyfinder is a simple application that not only extracts your CD key from Windows 9*x*, Windows Me, Windows NT 4, Windows 2000, Windows XP, and Windows Server 2003. You can also use Keyfinder to change the CD key on all of these platforms except NT, 2000, and 2003.

Tip *Keyfinder also can recover the CD key for Office 97 and Office XP. The release version (it is currently beta as I write this) will add several new features, including support for Office 2003 and the capability to change the user information stored for your installation of Windows XP. The new version also makes it possible to retrieve the CD key from a remote computer.*

Viewing the CD key with Keyfinder is easy. When you start the program, it searches for and displays the key as shown in Figure 18-14. You can copy the key to the Clipboard, save it to a text file, or print it through the File menu.

Changing Your Windows XP CD Key

Why would you need to change your CD key if you made the installation using a legal copy of Windows XP? The main reason is to insert a CD key for an image that was copied to several computers from the same source. For example, if you need to roll out Windows XP to 25 computers, you might install them all from the same image, which would give them all the same CD key. Each computer would then need to be tweaked to get its own CD key.

To change the key with Keyfinder, open Keyfinder on the computer and choose Options | Change Windows Key. Enter the new key in the Change Microsoft Windows XP Key dialog box and click Change.

Tip *Microsoft offers its own method for changing the CD key on an existing Windows XP installation. See http://support.microsoft.com/default.aspx?scid=kb;en-us;Q328874 to learn how to use Windows Product Activation to change the key.*

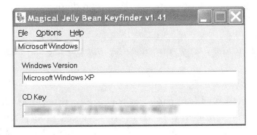

Figure 18-14   Keyfinder will extract the CD key from your local Windows XP installation.

Index

INTERNATIONAL CONTACT INFORMATION

AUSTRALIA
McGraw-Hill Book Company
Australia Pty. Ltd.
TEL +61-2-9900-1800
FAX +61-2-9878-8881
http://www.mcgraw-hill.com.au
books-it_sydney@mcgraw-hill.com

CANADA
McGraw-Hill Ryerson Ltd.
TEL +905-430-5000
FAX +905-430-5020
http://www.mcgraw-hill.ca

**GREECE, MIDDLE EAST, & AFRICA
(Excluding South Africa)**
McGraw-Hill Hellas
TEL +30-210-6560-990
TEL +30-210-6560-993
TEL +30-210-6560-994
FAX +30-210-6545-525

MEXICO (Also serving Latin America)
McGraw-Hill Interamericana Editores
S.A. de C.V.
TEL +525-1500-5108
FAX +525-117-1589
http://www.mcgraw-hill.com.mx
carlos_ruiz@mcgraw-hill.com

SINGAPORE (Serving Asia)
McGraw-Hill Book Company
TEL +65-6863-1580
FAX +65-6862-3354
http://www.mcgraw-hill.com.sg
mghasia@mcgraw-hill.com

SOUTH AFRICA
McGraw-Hill South Africa
TEL +27-11-622-7512
FAX +27-11-622-9045
robyn_swanepoel@mcgraw-hill.com

SPAIN
McGraw-Hill/
Interamericana de España, S.A.U.
TEL +34-91-180-3000
FAX +34-91-372-8513
http://www.mcgraw-hill.es
professional@mcgraw-hill.es

**UNITED KINGDOM, NORTHERN,
EASTERN, & CENTRAL EUROPE**
McGraw-Hill Education Europe
TEL +44-1-628-502500
FAX +44-1-628-770224
http://www.mcgraw-hill.co.uk
emea_queries@mcgraw-hill.com

ALL OTHER INQUIRIES Contact:
McGraw-Hill/Osborne
TEL +1-510-420-7700
FAX +1-510-420-7703
http://www.osborne.com
omg_international@mcgraw-hill.com

Sound Off!

Visit us at **www.osborne.com/bookregistration** and let us know what you thought of this book. While you're online you'll have the opportunity to register for newsletters and special offers from McGraw-Hill/Osborne.

We want to hear from you!

Sneak Peek

Visit us today at **www.betabooks.com** and see what's coming from McGraw-Hill/Osborne tomorrow!

Based on the successful software paradigm, Bet@Books™ allows computing professionals to view partial and sometimes complete text versions of selected titles online. Bet@Books™ viewing is free, invites comments and feedback, and allows you to "test drive" books in progress on the subjects that interest you the most.

OSBORNE DELIVERS RESULTS!

OSBORNE
www.osborne.com